ETHICAL LEADERSHIP IN INTERNATIONAL ORGANIZATIONS

This book offers an innovative interdisciplinary approach that elucidates the importance of virtue ethics to help better understand the role of leadership in international organizations. The authors use a combination of theoretical and conceptual narratives, as well as case studies to highlight both the advantages and weaknesses that the angle of virtue ethics offers. This is a particularly important step in times of uncertainty or crisis when the demand for leadership becomes more urgent yet more daunting. In this sense, this volume oscillates between critique and hope, since it provides a plausible, rather than a purely abstract, approach to the conceptualization and concretization of ethical leadership.

Guilherme Vasconcelos Vilaça is Profesor Asociado at Instituto Tecnológico Autónomo de México (ITAM), Law School. He has a global and interdisciplinary research profile and has held previous appointments in Australia, China, Colombia, Finland, and Italy. His research focuses on law, ethics, and humanities as modes of social ordering and meaning-making.

Maria Varaki is Lecturer in International Law at King's College London, War Studies Department. She is a scholar of International Law and has held previous research and teaching positions in Helsinki, Jerusalem, Melbourne, Istanbul, Copenhagen, and Ireland. Her research focuses on the interaction of law, ethics, and judgment.

ASIL STUDIES IN INTERNATIONAL LEGAL THEORY

Series Editors

Mark Agrast, ASIL
Mortimer Sellers, University of Baltimore

Editorial Board

Samantha Besson, Université de Fribourg
Allen Buchanan, Duke University
David Kennedy, Harvard University
Jan Klabbers, University of Helsinki
David Luban, Georgetown University
Larry May, Vanderbilt University
Mary Ellen O'Connell, University of Notre Dame
Onuma Yasuaki, Meiji University
Helen Stacy, Stanford University
John Tasioulas, University College London
Fernando Tesón, Florida State University

The purpose of the ASIL Studies in International Legal Theory series is to clarify and improve the theoretical foundations of international law. Too often the progressive development and implementation of international law has foundered on confusion about first principles. This series raises the level of public and scholarly discussion about the structure and purposes of the world legal order and how best to achieve global justice through law. This series grows out of the International Legal Theory project of the American Society of International Law. The ASIL Studies in International Legal Theory series deepens this conversation by publishing scholarly monographs and edited volumes of essays considering subjects in international legal theory.

Books in the series

Ethical Leadership in International Organizations: Concepts, Narratives, Judgment, and Assessment
Edited by Guilherme Vasconcelos Vilaça and Maria Varaki

International Law as Behavior
Edited by Harlan Grant Cohen and Timothy Meyer

Space and Fates of International Law: Between Leibniz and Hobbes
Ekaterina Yahyaoui Krivenko

Why Punish Perpetrators of Mass Atrocities?: Purposes of Punishment in International Criminal Law
Edited by Florian Jeßberger and Julia Geneuss

The Challenge of Inter-legality
Edited by Jan Klabbers and Gianluigi Palombella

The Nature of International Law
Miodrag A. Jovanović

Reexamining Customary International Law
Edited by Brian D. Lepard

Theoretical Boundaries of Armed Conflict and Human Rights
Edited by Jens David Ohlin

Human Rights in Emergencies
Edited by Evan J. Criddle

The Theory of Self-Determination
Edited by Fernando R. Tesón

Negotiating State and Non-State Law: Global and Local Legal Pluralism
Edited by Michael A. Helfand

Jus Post Bellum and Transitional Justice
Edited by Larry May and Elizabeth Edenberg

Normative Pluralism and International Law: Exploring Global Governance
Edited by Jan Klabbers and Touko Piipaerinen

The Future of International Law: Global Government Joel P. Trachtman

Morality, Jus Post Bellum, and International Law
Edited by Larry May and Andrew T. Forcehimes

Global Justice and International Economic Law: Opportunities and Prospects
Edited by Chios Carmody, Frank J. Garcia, and John Linarelli

Parochialism, Cosmopolitanism, and the Foundations of International Law
Edited by Mortimer Sellers

The Role of Ethics in International Law
Edited by Donald Earl Childress III

The New Global Law
Rafael Domingo

Customary International Law: A New Theory with Practical Applications
Brian D. Lepard

International Criminal Law and Philosophy
Edited by Larry May and Zachary Hoskins

Whither the West?: Concepts on International Law in Europe and the United States
Edited by Chiara Giorgetti and Guglielmo Verdirame

Ethical Leadership in International Organizations

CONCEPTS, NARRATIVES, JUDGMENT, AND ASSESSMENT

Edited by

GUILHERME VASCONCELOS VILAÇA

Instituto Tecnológico Autónomo de México

MARIA VARAKI

King's College London

CAMBRIDGE
UNIVERSITY PRESS

University Printing House, Cambridge CB2 8BS, United Kingdom

One Liberty Plaza, 20th Floor, New York, NY 10006, USA

477 Williamstown Road, Port Melbourne, VIC 3207, Australia

314–321, 3rd Floor, Plot 3, Splendor Forum, Jasola District Centre, New Delhi – 110025, India

79 Anson Road, #06–04/06, Singapore 079906

Cambridge University Press is part of the University of Cambridge.

It furthers the University's mission by disseminating knowledge in the pursuit of education, learning, and research at the highest international levels of excellence.

www.cambridge.org
Information on this title: www.cambridge.org/9781108485869
DOI: 10.1017/9781108641715

© Cambridge University Press 2021

This publication is in copyright. Subject to statutory exception and to the provisions of relevant collective licensing agreements, no reproduction of any part may take place without the written permission of Cambridge University Press.

First published 2021

A catalogue record for this publication is available from the British Library.

Library of Congress Cataloging-in-Publication Data
NAMES: Varaki, Maria, editor. | Vilaca, Guilherme Vasconcelos, editor.
TITLE: Ethical leadership in international organizations : concepts, narratives, judgment, and assessment / edited by Maria Varaki, Guilherme Vasconcelos Vilaca.
DESCRIPTION: Cambridge ; New York, NY : Cambridge University Press, 2021. | Series: ASIL studies in international legal theory | Includes bibliographical references and index.
IDENTIFIERS: LCCN 2020039487 (print) | LCCN 2020039488 (ebook) | ISBN 9781108485869 (hardback) | ISBN 9781108725293 (paperback) | ISBN 9781108641715 (ebook)
SUBJECTS: LCSH: International agencies – Moral and ethical aspects. | Leadership – Moral and ethical aspects. | Management – Moral and ethical aspects.
CLASSIFICATION: LCC JZ4839 .E84 2021 (print) | LCC JZ4839 (ebook) | DDC 352.23/6211–dc23
LC record available at https://lccn.loc.gov/2020039487
LC ebook record available at https://lccn.loc.gov/2020039488

ISBN 978-1-108-48586-9 Hardback

Cambridge University Press has no responsibility for the persistence or accuracy of URLs for external or third-party internet websites referred to in this publication and does not guarantee that any content on such websites is, or will remain, accurate or appropriate.

We dedicate this book to Jan Klabbers, a truly generous and virtuous mentor.

Ethical Leadership in International Organizations: Concepts, Narratives, Judgment, and Assessment

Guilherme Vasconcelos Vilaça and Maria Varaki (editors)

Contents

List of Contributors	*page* xi
Acknowledgments	xii

INTRODUCTION

1 The Place of Ethical Leadership, Virtues, and Narrative in International Organizations
Guilherme Vasconcelos Vilaça — 1

PART I CONCEPTS — 49

2 Authority, Law, and Knowledge: Some Critical Remarks on 'Theories' of Practice and the Paradoxes of 'Virtue' Ethics
Friedrich Kratochwil — 51

3 Commitment to the Rule of Law: From a Political to an Organizational Ideal
Sanne Taekema — 83

4 Exemplarism, Virtue, and Ethical Leadership in International Organizations
Amalia Amaya — 101

PART II ETHICAL NARRATIVES AND ORGANIZATIONS — 129

5 Virtue in Algorithms? Law and Ethics in Algorithmic Governance
René Urueña — 131

x *Contents*

6   Ethics in International Sporting Institutions
    Lorenzo Casini   160

7   Modes of Acting Virtuously at the Universal Periodic Review
    Jane K. Cowan   176

    **PART III   JUDGMENT AND ASSESSMENT OF ETHICAL NARRATIVES
    AND LEADERSHIP**   203

8   Imaginary Leadership and Displacement: A Laboratory
    of Dilemmas?
    Maria Varaki   205

9   Revisiting *Rainbow Warrior*: Virtue and Understanding in
    International Arbitration
    Jan Klabbers   229

10 Virtue and Leadership in the World Health Organization
    Guilherme Vasconcelos Vilaça   249

    CONCLUSION

11 Ethical Leadership in Times of 'Crisis'
    Maria Varaki   290

Index   310

Contributors

Editors

GUILHERME VASCONCELOS VILAÇA, Profesor Asociado, Instituto Tecnológico Autónomo de México (ITAM)

MARIA VARAKI, Lecturer in International Law, King's College London

Contributors

AMALIA AMAYA, Research Fellow (Tenured), Universidad Nacional Autónoma de México (UNAM)

FRIEDRICH KRATOCHWIL, Emeritus Professor of International Relations, European University Institute

GUILHERME VASCONCELOS VILAÇA, Profesor Asociado, Instituto Tecnológico Autónomo de México (ITAM)

JAN KLABBERS, Professor of International Law, University of Helsinki

JANE COWAN, Professor of Social Anthropology, University of Sussex

LORENZO CASINI, Professor of Administrative Law, IMT School for Advanced Studies Lucca

MARIA VARAKI, Lecturer in International Law, King's College London

RENÉ URUEÑA, Associate Professor in International Law, Universidad de los Andes

SANNE TAEKEMA, Professor of Jurisprudence, Erasmus University of Rotterdam

Acknowledgments

This book was born of a conference organized in Helsinki in June 2018 dedicated to ethical leadership in international organizations. We would like to thank the speakers, participants, and audience of the conference for providing much food for thought and help in shaping this book. We are also grateful to the contributors to this volume for their willingness and commitment to engage with our comments.

Guilherme would like to thank his wife, Sara de Santis, for her unwavering support throughout the writing and editing of this book, which was finalized in challenging, epidemic times.

Maria would particularly like to thank both her parents for their love and invaluable lessons of decent resilience during the unprecedented pandemic lockdown of the final stage of this academic endeavor.

1

The Place of Ethical Leadership, Virtues, and Narrative in International Organizations

Guilherme Vasconcelos Vilaça[*]

Je ne suis pas de ceux qui disent que leurs actions ne leur ressemblent pas. Il faut bien qu'elles le fassent, puisqu'elles sont ma seule mesure, et le seul moyen de me dessiner dans la mémoire des hommes, ou dans la mienne propre; puisque c'est peut-être l'impossibilité de continuer à s'exprimer et à se modifier par l'action qui constitue la différence entre l'état de mort et celui de vivant. Mais il y a entre moi et ces actes dont je suis fait un hiatus indéfinissable.

Marguerite Yourcenar, *Mémoires d'Hadrien*

1.1 PREMISE OF THE BOOK

International organizations (IOs) were once expected to guarantee the 'salvation of mankind' but have increasingly come to be questioned.[1] On the one hand, waves of populism, nationalism, and isolationism threaten the stability of the international legal order and the capacity of IOs to address policy dilemmas.[2] On the other hand, these policy dilemmas keep piling up – for example, the influx of refugees, climate change, global health issues, cyber

---

[*] My most sincere thanks to Gonçalo Vilaça, William Kirkland, Michael Schultheiß, and Jan Klabbers for detailed comments and criticism that greatly improved the flow and quality of the argument. I also thank an anonymous referee for the suggestion (and challenge) to sketch the introduction of the book as a full-fledged chapter building a comprehensive narrative linking the complex and disparate available literatures as well as showing the need for an interdisciplinary approach to ethical leadership and virtue in international organizations. All errors remain mine.

[1] For an overview of the history of IOs from messianic hope to existential crisis, criticism, and calls for reform, see Alvarez, José E. (2006), 'International Organizations: Then and Now', *American Journal of International Law*, 100 (2), 324–47.

[2] For this link, see Copelovitch, Mark and Pevehouse, Jon C. W. (2019), 'International Organizations in a New Era of Populist Nationalism', *The Review of International Organizations*, 14 (2), 169–86.

wars, growing inequality, and widespread poverty. It appears that what is needed are more global cooperation and leadership, at a time when the mission and capacities of IOs may be at risk. Compounding the problem, the latter are also often accused of corruption, embezzlement, negative externalities, political capture, poor and immoral performance, and so on.[3]

IOs are necessary, but, so it seems, they cannot be trusted, or they may not always be desirable or produce positive results.[4] It is enough to think of Kofi Annan's son's involvement in the United Nations' 'Iraq oil-for-food plan' that called into question the quality of leadership and oversight applied by the programme; the different sexual misconduct accusations both in the field – that is, humanitarian interventions and peacekeeping operations – and in offices across the world; or corruption allegations in different missions, such as the one in Western Sahara. Appropriately, the United Nations was portrayed by an IO veteran and former United Nations Deputy Secretary-General, Britain's Mark Malloch-Brown, like this:

> The institution itself is labyrinthian, hard to penetrate and often apparently immune to tragedy, which it seems from the outside it could do more to stop. Publicly, it has an image of Gucci-shoed bureaucrats taking long lunches. The truth is that it is a Jekyll and Hyde institution: while there are people who work there who just want to get by, there are many others who have a personal sense of commitment to making a real difference. The two live in permanent tension with one another.[5]

This is a rather troubling criticism to IOs – often seen as a 'force for good' fulfilling functions necessary to ensure a good, peaceful, healthy and prosperous global order – since their autonomy and legitimacy were and are largely premised on pure, functional, apolitical, and expertise-based operations.[6]

---

[3]   Articulating a fresh empirical approach to legitimacy and legitimation of IOs, see Tallberg, Jonas and Zürn, Michael (2019), 'The Legitimacy and Legitimation of International Organizations: Introduction and Framework', *The Review of International Organizations*, 14 (4), 581–606.

[4]   For an early accusation that the literature on IOs largely ignored their negative effects, see Gallarotti, Giulio M. (1991), 'The Limits of International Organization: Systematic Failure in the Management of International Relations', *International Organization*, 45 (2), 83–220.

[5]   Malloch-Brown, Mark (2015), 'The UN Is an Under-Funded, Bureaucratic Labyrinth – and a Force for Good in the World', *Telegraph*, 26 June 2015 at www.telegraph.co.uk/news/worldnews/11699243/The-UN-is-an-under-funded-bureaucratic-labyrinth-and-a-force-for-good-in-the-world.html.

[6]   See Klabbers, Jan (2014), 'The Emergence of Functionalism in International Institutional Law: Colonial Inspirations', *The European Journal of International Law*, 25 (3), 645–75 at 646. For an analysis of the relationship between autonomy, functionalism and the difficulties to exercise control over IOs, see Klabbers, Jan (2011), 'Autonomy, Constitutionalism and Virtue in International Institutional Law', in Richard Collins and Nigel D. White (eds.), *International Organizations and the Idea of Autonomy: Institutional Independence in the International Legal Order* (Abingdon; New York: Routledge), 120–40.

Ethical Leadership, Virtues, and Narrative in International Organizations 3

Many different approaches have been advanced in order to control IOs, curb their excesses, evaluate their activities, discipline them in case of wrongdoing and instil the right set of incentives to ensure the fulfilment of their missions while respecting integrity and ethical values. The disciplines of international law, international relations, political science, economics, management and organization studies, sociology, and political theory have insisted on human rights, codes of ethics and conduct, legal responsibility, compliance, managerial and accountability frameworks. Yet these have not been able to do the trick.

Compliance[7] and managerial[8] logics are largely technocratic based on efficiency and effectiveness considerations often setting aside the pursuit of normative ideals beyond the mandates and rules of organizations. Recall that, conversely, ethical or moral reasoning is overwhelmingly conceptualized as *other*-regarding, this being the source of the challenge morality places upon us.[9] Discourses of accountability portraying it as a 'supervening force' and premised on 'better oversight through tougher regulation, combined with harsh penalties as a deterrent', have proved insufficient too.[10]

These *ex post* and *external discourses* crucially depend on monitoring, scorekeeping, sanctioning, and enforcement capacities (and the existence, quality and interplay of rules, norms and standards that have to be administered), which in turn are stretched beyond their powers in highly complex environments such as IOs.[11] Moreover, the specific organizational form and control apparatuses may create strong incentives against 'doing the right thing' or exercising independent virtuous judgment.[12]

---

7 Alford, Roger P. and Tierney, James Fallows (2012), 'Moral Reasoning in International Law', in Donald Earl Childress III (ed.), *The Role of Ethics in International Law* (New York: Cambridge University Press), 11–51, and Peters, Anne (2016), 'International Organizations and International Law', in Jacob Katz Cogan, Ian Hurd and Ian Johnstone (eds.), *The Oxford Handbook of International Organizations* (Oxford: Oxford University Press), 33–59.

8 Missoni, Eduardo and Alesani, Daniele (2013), *Management of International Institutions and NGOs: Frameworks, Practices and Challenges* (Abingdon; New York: Routledge).

9 Finlay, Stephen (2007), 'Too Much Morality', in Paul Bloomfield (ed.), *Morality and Self-Interest* (Oxford: Oxford University Press), 136–54.

10 See Weisband, Edward and Ebrahim, Alnoor (2007), 'Introduction: Forging Global Accountabilities', in Edward Weisband and Alnoor Ebrahim (eds.), *Global Accountabilities: Participation, Pluralism, And Public Ethics* (Cambridge; New York: Cambridge University Press), 1–24 at 1.

11 Making it a natural companion to principal–agent theory. See Gailmard, Sean (2014), 'Accountability and Principal–Agent Theory', in Mark Bovens, Robert E. Goodin, and Thomas Schillemans (eds.), *The Oxford Handbook of Public Accountability* (Oxford: Oxford University Press).

12 Kratochwil, Friedrich (2017), 'Practicing Law: Spoudaios, Professional, Expert, or "Macher"? Reflections on the Changing Nature of an Occupation', in Wouter Werner, Marieke de Hoon

Guilherme Vasconcelos Vilaça

Human rights standards need to be rendered concrete and actualized through human action, which frequently requires more rules and solving conflicts between the latter, making apportioning and exercising responsibility a difficult matter.[13] By the same token, deontological codes of conduct easily lend themselves to create a new set of broad principles and rules without clarifying which behaviours are actually prescribed or envisioned.[14] As with human rights, this does not mean they do not fulfil a symbolic and normative function – that is, creating an image of the 'professional' and establishing a vision of moral excellence[15] – only that little guidance is offered to agents, either trying to uphold standards or evaluating behaviour against them, as the standards need *someone* to apply them.

The premise underlying this volume is that the way to respond to the crisis of governance and rehabilitate IOs is to go beyond all these discourses and frameworks and focus on *ethical* leadership, *individual* and *organizational*, in IOs.

To be fair, a small group of scholars has abandoned the dominant focus on international norms, mandates and structures and recognized the autonomous impact of *individual* leadership and *personality features* of executive heads and staffs on the empowerment, growth, and performance of IOs.[16] The approach is

---

and Alexis Galán (eds.), *The Law of International Lawyers: Reading Martti Koskenniemi* (Cambridge: Cambridge University Press), 225–64.

[13] See Antaki, Mark (2004), 'The World(lessness) of Human Rights', *McGill Law Journal*, 49, 203–22 at 212.

[14] Getz, Kathleen A. (1990), 'International Codes of Conduct: An Analysis of Ethical Reasoning', *Journal of Business Ethics*, 9 (7), 567–77 and Cohen, Steven and Eimicke, William B. (1995), 'Ethics and the Public Administrator', *Ethics in American Public Service*, 537, 86–108 at 102.

[15] See Gilman, Stuart C. (2005), 'Ethics Codes and Codes of Conduct as Tools for Promoting an Ethical and Professional Public Service: Comparative Successes and Lessons' (Washington, DC: World Bank) at www.oecd.org/mena/governance/35521418.pdf.

[16] See Cox, Robert (1969), 'The Executive Head: An Essay on Leadership in International Organization', *International Organization*, 23 (2), 205–30, Schechter, Michael G. (1987), 'Leadership in International Organizations: Systemic, Organizational and Personality Factors', *Review of International Studies*, 13 (3), 197–220, Schroeder, Michael Bluman (2014), 'Executive Leadership in the Study of International Organization: A Framework for Analysis', *International Studies Review*, 16 (3), 339–61. For useful surveys, see Reinalda, Bob and Verbeek, Bertjan (2014), 'Leadership of International Organizations', in R. A. W. Rhodes and Paul 't Hart (eds.), *The Oxford Handbook of Political Leadership* (Oxford: Oxford University Press), and Masciulli, Joseph, Molchanov, Mikhail A. and Knight, W. Andy (2009), 'Political Leadership in Context', in Joseph Masciulli, Mikhail A. Molchanov and W. Andy Knight (eds.), *The Ashgate Research Companion to Political Leadership* (London: Routledge), 3–29. Focusing on the relationship between personality traits and behaviour of leaders, see Kille, Kent J. and Scully, Roger M. (2003), 'Executive Heads and the Role of Intergovernmental Organizations: Expansionist Leadership in the United Nations and the European Union', *Political Psychology*, 24 (1), 175–98.

Ethical Leadership, Virtues, and Narrative in International Organizations 5

often comparative, pitting bureaucracies or particular individuals, for example Boutros-Ghali, Kofi Annan, Robert McNamara, Dag Hammarskjöld, and Albert Thomas, with their personalities, values and biographical details against the contexts they faced in order to draw out potential lessons on the impact of leadership and leadership styles.[17] Selection procedures are also studied even though it is recognized that, given the principals' interest (Member States) in controlling IOs, the chosen leaders are typically those expected not to rock the boat. Durão Barroso for the European Commission and Kurt Waldheim for the United Nations easily fit the picture. Nevertheless, this does not mean that leaders themselves see their tenure in the same way. Boutros-Ghali, for instance, highlighted the independence, moral responsibility, and importance of his role even if it ought to be performed behind the scenes.[18]

Ultimately, however, this literature concentrates on effective and functional, *not ethical*, leadership, describing ways in which leaders, personality traits and different modes of leadership help to overcome environmental, political, legal, budgetary, and organizational constraints.[19] Effective leadership is then theorized as needed to enhance IOs' legitimacy and consequently create an 'epistemic-discursive' community in which IOs are transparent, rely on input from external constituencies and revise their own accountability standards.[20]

Against this background, the present book takes a further and original step by explicitly linking leadership and ethics.[21] If leadership matters, we submit that developing *ethical leadership* may prove essential to improve the way in

[17] The literature frequently conflates the causal contribution towards organizational outcomes of bureaucracies and individual leaders perhaps because of its sociology of organization pedigree. See Parker, Charles and Karlsson, Christer (2014), 'Leadership and International Cooperation', in R. A. W. Rhodes and Paul 't Hart (eds.), *The Oxford Handbook of Political Leadership* (Oxford: Oxford University Press). For a rigorous detailed comparative study of international (environmental) secretariats and departments, see Biermann, Frank and Siebenhüner, Bernd (eds.) (2009), *Managers of Global Change: The Influence of International Environmental Bureaucracies* (Cambridge; London: MIT Press).
[18] See Boutros-Ghali, Boutros (1996), 'Global Leadership after the Cold War', *Foreign Affairs*, 75 (2), 86–98.
[19] Hall, Nina and Woods, Ngaire (2018), 'Theorizing the Role of Executive Heads in International Organizations', *European Journal of International Relations*, 24 (4), 865–86. Even when it is acknowledged that there is the need for a leadership plan and vision and that moral authority 'comes with the office', accounts remain largely functional. See Schroeder, Michael Bluman (2014), 'Executive Leadership in the Study of International Organization: A Framework for Analysis', *International Studies Review*, 16 (3), 339–61 at 348ff.
[20] This is the normative framework built by Buchanan, Allen and Keohane, Robert O. (2006), 'The Legitimacy of Global Governance Institutions', *Ethics & International Affairs*, 20 (4), 405–37. See also Woods, Ngaire (2003), 'Holding Intergovernmental Institutions to Account', *Ethics & International Affairs*, 17 (1), 69–80.
[21] This is not a given in leadership studies. See Keohane, Nannerl O. (2010), *Thinking About Leadership* (Princeton; Oxford: Princeton University Press), Chapter 1.

which IOs exercise responsibility in caring for our common world. If ethics matters, we claim that we need to go beyond the usual ethical frameworks relied upon so far. Indeed, the phenomenon of ethical decision-making by international legal and policy experts and the quest for global justice has relied upon analytic normative ethics, typically deontologism and consequentialism. Instead, we propose that we ought to endorse *virtue ethics* to ground thicker and novel descriptions, judgments, and assessments of the ethical life and action of individuals in IOs.[22] We conceive the deployment of virtues as an indispensable step to stimulate and expand our moral imagination in creating new narratives regarding IOs' normative and functional worlds. Hence, this edited volume starts a so far unexplored interdisciplinary conversation and examination of ethics in IOs[23] taking as a stepping stone the language of *virtues*.[24]

Within this context, the quest for ethical leadership in IOs provides a platform for new normative, conceptual, and policy considerations. To what extent can the ethical standing and character of individuals and organizations provide an answer to IOs' current predicament? How does a focus on virtues expand our powers of description of classical moral scenarios and choices? And if it offers a credible response, then how can ethical leadership be conceptualized, what are its sources of inspiration, what kind of new standards does it generate and how can it be assessed? In this context, the various case studies that are examined by the contributors offer a revealing picture of the potentials and limits of an aretaic theory of ethics that focuses on human agency and the quest for virtuous judgment. Specifically, the book illustrates the potential of virtues to inform descriptive, explanatory, normative, evaluative and decision-making analyses, diversifying the ways in which

---

[22] For an early statement of this line of inquiry, see Klabbers, Jan (2011), 'Autonomy, Constitutionalism and Virtue in International Institutional Law', in Richard Collins and Nigel D. White (eds.), *International Organizations and the Idea of Autonomy: Institutional Independence in the International Legal Order* (Abingdon; New York: Routledge), 120–40 at 120, stressing the need to tap 'into the sense of responsibility of the individuals working for those bureaucracies'.

[23] For a rare work connecting the (different) ethical frameworks, biographies, and mandates of select United Nations Secretaries General, see Kent J. Kille (ed.) (2007), *The UN Secretary-General and Moral Authority: Ethics and Religion in International Leadership* (Washington, DC: Georgetown University Press).

[24] Early efforts to deploy the language of virtues to international law and international relations include Klabbers, Jan (2014), 'The Virtues of Expertise', in Monika Ambrus, et al. (eds.), *The Role of 'Experts' in International and European Decision-Making Processes: Advisors, Decision Makers or Irrelevant Actors?* (Cambridge: Cambridge University Press), 82–102, and Gaskarth, Jamie (2012), 'The Virtues in International Society', *European Journal of International Relations*, 18 (3), 431–53.

Ethical Leadership, Virtues, and Narrative in International Organizations 7

the virtues can play a role in shaping discourses on responsible or otherwise ethical leadership and reformulating the future of so-called global governance.[25]

Overall, we believe that a focus on ethical leadership and the vocabulary of virtues promotes an *ex ante, preventive and internal approach* to IOs and their leaders – an approach that emphasizes responsibility (the internal side of conduct) more than accountability (the external side of conduct)[26] – and acknowledges that ruling is always *ruling by persons* as laws, rules, principles, and values are not self-applicable. This largely forgotten point, but rich in consequences for ethical and legal thinking in organizations, is developed by Sanne Taekema in Chapter 3. She uses it to argue that, understood like this, the rule of law ideal ought to guide IOs but does not need to be pursued through law, opening the possibility for virtuous leaders to be the drivers of the process.

The recovery of the virtues' moral vocabulary also enables external *ex post* scrutiny of IOs' leaders' behaviour and organizational forms of life by the public sphere, though its main contribution is the internalization of the need for agents to exercise prudence and judgment, as a *performative*, not theoretical, activity, in the pursuit of IOs' missions and activities irrespectively of the existence of pre-existing, applicable and enforceable rules, economic incentives, and sanctions.

The book is also innovative in the *interdisciplinary approach* it adopts to the study of ethics in IOs. Indeed, contributions to the volume come from disciplines as disparate as anthropology, international law, political science, philosophy, ethics, and international relations. This is no mere fancy. As will be argued later in detail, interdisciplinarity and a multi-method approach are required by the sheer level of added complexity that the adoption of a virtues-based robust research programme on ethical leadership in IOs, as sketched in this chapter, imposes. Taken seriously, this shift makes it unfeasible to do (international) ethics solely at the ideal theory level in philosophy departments. Instead, ethical analysis, imagination, and criticism must be embedded in concrete factual, legal, and normative scenarios mobilizing a plethora of different academic disciplines. A useful metaphor of the paradigm shift at

---

[25] An attempt to conceptualize and examine the concept of responsible governance can be found in Klabbers, Jan, Varaki, Maria and Vilaça, Guilherme Vasconcelos (eds.) (2018), *Towards Responsible Global Governance* (Helsinki: Helsinki University Press). The potential of virtue ethics to capture the kind of 'reciprocal trust' needed to establish a postmodern public ethics is acknowledged, but not developed, in Weisband, Edward (2007), 'Conclusion: Prolegomena to a Postmodern Public Ethics: Images of Accountability in Global Frames', in Edward Weisband and Alnoor Ebrahim (eds.), *Global Accountabilities: Participation, Pluralism, and Public Ethics* (Cambridge; New York: Cambridge University Press), 307–39.

[26] On this difference, see Mulgan, Richard (2000), '"Accountability": An Ever-Expanding Concept?', *Public Administration*, 78 (3), 555–73 at 558.

8   Guilherme Vasconcelos Vilaça

stake here comes from Siqueiros, one of the great classical Mexican muralists, and his explanation for the methodological changes that moving from easel to muralist painting triggered – that is, the need for group work, spatial thinking and the fact that virtuous technique in easel painting did not translate into superior mural works.[27] Likewise, in this book, the reader should not expect to see this complexity reflected in each individual chapter. Rather, the book works holistically because only by going through the whole book can the complex task of doing justice to the problem of ethical leadership in IOs be fully grasped.

In the remainder of this chapter, I map two different narratives that are central to identifying and justifying (i) the manifold contributions of the book; (ii) the nature of the challenge it advances against established thinking; and, (iii) the power of virtue ethics to attract, agglutinate and deploy a number of disciplines and approaches that have so far remained disparate and yet can reshape the study of international ethics in IOs.

The first narrative focuses on ethics. It starts by mapping the use of deontologism and consequentialism in global ethics debates and showing how they legitimated highly abstract accounts of international responsibility (Sections 1.2 and 1.3). It then describes how concentrating on virtues radically changes the questions being asked (and the knowledge we need making pragmatism a surprising ally), highlights the role of persons and characters, can be fashioned to apply to organizations, puts into stark relief different salient features of moral scenarios, emphasizes judgment and moral imagination, fits some basic common moral intuitions, and allows us to engage in ethical analysis in much greater complexity and detail (Sections 1.4 and 1.5).

The second narrative traces a recent convergence towards virtue ethics in different fields such as leadership, psychology, organization and business studies, all emphasizing the importance of practical wisdom and ethical leadership (Section 1.7). This is important because these disciplines offer lessons and resources that impact research on ethical – virtuous – leadership in IOs, notably on the following questions: 'What is virtuous leadership in organizations?', 'How is it exercised?', and 'What is its impact?' Throughout these two narratives, I also forge an innovative account according to which, from a virtues perspective, there is a natural link between ethics and narrative given that ethical analysis (and criticism) requires considering concrete normative and factual materials from agents, organizations, environments, and situations. For this reason we need to mobilize resources from a plethora of disciplinary traditions that can

---

[27] Siqueiros, David Alfaro (1979), *Como Se Pinta Un Mural* (3rd ed.; Cuernavaca: Ediciones Taller Siqueiros), chapter 4.

Ethical Leadership, Virtues, and Narrative in International Organizations 9

provide us with such elements, for example, narrative studies, anthropology, biographical research and casuistry, not to mention those invoked previously that deal specifically with organizations (Section 1.6).

I close the chapter by tackling the challenge of thinking about ethical leadership and virtues in postmodern times (Section 1.8) and providing a chapter breakdown (Section 1.9).

1.2 AN OVERVIEW OF ETHICS IN INTERNATIONAL POLITICS

Focus on IOs, leadership, character, and virtues is not, and has not been, common when imagining the desirable design for the world. Indeed, and after the long-standing realist and neorealist emphasis on power and material interests, international ethics has developed robustly after the 1990s with the global justice literature discussing the idea of cosmopolitanism. The latter became a hot topic in international political and normative theory mostly following Charles Beitz's seminal work.[28]

In a nutshell, the mainstream version of cosmopolitanism postulates *universalism*. In its moral bent, it aims at pushing forward the idea that all human beings are owed the same in virtue of their sharing the same human nature and, thus, irrespectively of arbitrary distinctions triggered by concepts such as gender, culture, nationality or religion.[29] Debate then rages around identifying which rights do we all have and which duties do we owe towards our fellow human beings.[30] Issue areas include global inequality and poverty, open

---

[28] See Beitz, Charles (1979), *Political Theory and International Relations* (Princeton: Princeton University Press) and Kleingeld, Pauline and Brown, Eric (2019), 'Cosmopolitanism', in Edward N. Zalta (ed.), *Stanford Encyclopedia of Philosophy*, https://plato.stanford.edu/entries/cosmopolit anism/. The cosmopolitan tradition is traced back, quite simplistically, to Kant, Immanuel (1991), 'Toward Perpetual Peace: A Philosophical Sketch', in Pauline Kleingeld (ed.), *Toward Perpetual Peace and Other Writings on Politics, Peace, and History* (New Haven; London: Yale University Press), 67–109. A rather unique Chinese cosmopolitan statement is Kang, Youwei and Thompson, Laurence (2005), *Ta T'ung Shu: The One-World Philosophy of K'ang Yu-wei* (London; New York: Routledge). For a taxonomy of cosmopolitanism, see Lu, Catherine (2000), 'One and Many Faces of Cosmopolitanism', *The Journal of Political Philosophy*, 8 (2), 244–67. For a critical account, see Mignolo, Walter D. (2000), 'The Many Faces of Cosmo-polis: Border Thinking and Critical Cosmopolitanism', *Public Culture*, 12 (3), 721–48.

[29] The sparring partner here was communitarianism with its emphasis on human beings' historical, linguistic, political, and social rootedness. For a classical statement, see Walzer, Michael (1983), *Spheres of Justice: A Defense of Pluralism and Equality* (New York: Basic Books). The leading recent account is Miller, David (2007), *National Responsibility and Global Justice* (New York: Oxford University Press).

[30] See Charvet, John (1998), 'The Possibility of a Cosmopolitan Ethical Order Based on the Idea of Universal Human Rights', *Millennium – Journal of International Studies*, 27 (3), 523–42, and O'Neill, Onora (2005), 'The Dark Side of Human Rights', *International Affairs*, 81 (2), 427–39,

borders, climate change, just war, humanitarian intervention and fair trade, among others. Politically, cosmopolitanism imposes the need to transcend states and state-based institutions and move towards models of global or transnational governance. Discussions and proposals revolve around the duties, scale, and level of the institutional arrangements needed to uphold the common moral status of human beings. Other attempts searched for ways of legitimating and articulating global forms of politics and society.[31]

As Delanty argued,[32] however, many of these writings presuppose(d) a scission between the political and the social world given the fact that the latter is an arena of boundaries, cultures, political choices, and other taxonomies – the arena from which cosmopolitanism, the herald of universalism, wished to free human beings and thinking alike. Logically, the articulation of a universal moral or political view does violence to alternative visions leading to a critique of the mainstream cosmopolitan account. Critical cosmopolitanism, normative[33] and sociological,[34] eschews a single world and cosmopolitanism, focusing instead on discourse and its capacity to mediate encounters between different agents which produces forms of cosmopolitanism that are open to difference. This shift takes its cue from: (i) the historical realization that world-making projects were typical of empires combining;[35] (ii) the normative point that cosmopolitanism's universalism (and democracy) is Western and thus accepting it would amount to having a *part* of the world determining a universal blueprint for the *whole* world; and, (iii) the empirical point that there is no single humanity, since human experience and products are always embedded.

The critique's emphasis on the rootedness of human experience, projects, and values helped to highlight a few features of the global justice debates useful

for a critique. For the seminal critique of rights, understood abstractly and without reference to duties, as 'nonsense upon stilts', see Bentham, Jeremy (1843), 'Anarchical Fallacies: Being an Examination of the Declarations of Rights Issued during the French Revolution', in John Bowring (ed.), *The Works of Jeremy Bentham* (vol. II; Edinburgh: William Tait).

[31] Archibugi, Daniele (2012), 'Cosmopolitan Democracy: A Restatement', *Cambridge Journal of Education*, 42 (1), 9–20.

[32] Delanty, Gerard (2006), 'The Cosmopolitan Imagination: Critical Cosmopolitanism and Social Theory', *The British Journal of Sociology*, 57 (1), 25–47.

[33] Shapcott, Richard (2003), *Justice, Community and Dialogue in International Relations* (Cambridge; New York: Cambridge University Press).

[34] Delanty, Gerard (2006), 'The Cosmopolitan Imagination: Critical Cosmopolitanism and Social Theory', *The British Journal of Sociology*, 57 (1), 25–47.

[35] Mendieta, Eduardo (2009), 'From Imperial to Dialogical Cosmopolitanism', *Ethics & Global Politics*, 2 (3), 241–58. On how the epistemological and normative violence of empires makes us overlook the contributions made from the margins of the system, see Aydin, Cemil (2019), *Il Lungo Ottocento: Una Storia Politica Internazionale* (Torino: Einaudi). For a legal historical perspective, see Lorca, Arnulf Becker (2016), *Mestizo International Law: A Global Intellectual History 1842–1933* (Cambridge: Cambridge University Press).

Ethical Leadership, Virtues, and Narrative in International Organizations   11

for our analysis. First, such debates remained largely stuck within *ideal theory*,[36] in which the goal was to establish the abstract foundations of cosmopolitan rules and values, the basic structure of international society, and sometimes vague political arrangements irrespective of more practical aspects such as 'how to get from our present situation to the ideal state?', 'how to apply universal rules and values in specific situations and contexts?', and 'through which specific institutional arrangements?'

Undoubtedly, the purpose was to adopt the standpoint of the *legislator* coming up with and establishing the normative values we ought to pursue without telling us how, while equating the task of producing universal norms with the task of acting. Furthermore, there was little clear specific institutional normative thinking on how IOs (and other actors) should act from an ethical standpoint.[37] Hence, to give one example, the belief that states should open their borders to those in need because of the common human dignity shared by all human beings has triggered few accounts discussing and stipulating which agents should take up such duties, to what extent, and in virtue of which principles. Concretely, consider the muddled thinking impregnating the European Union Member States' reaction(s) to the recent refugee crisis. Theoretically, Kant famously prescribed to states the duty of hospitality, though not that of residence. 'But what does such duty entail?' That this is a question worth many answers is shown by Marco Polo's discussion of a custom of a faraway tribe according to which hospitality required that husbands should leave their houses and let the male guests take their places at home with their wives including bedding them.[38]

1.3 INTERNATIONAL ETHICS' RELIANCE ON DEONTOLOGISM AND UTILITARIANISM

It did not help that international normative ethics relied on deontological and consequentialist (typically utilitarian) ethical approaches.[39] Deontological

---

[36]   Robeyns, Ingrid (2008), 'Ideal Theory in Theory and Practice', *Social Theory and Practice*, 34 (3), 341–62.

[37]   Ratner, Steven (2013), 'Ethics and International Law: Integrating the Global Justice Project(s)', *International Theory*, 5 (1), 1–34.

[38]   Polo, Marco (2003), *The Travels of Marco Polo [The Venetian]* (New York: Liveright).

[39]   For a critique along the lines sketched in the main text emphasizing practical reasoning and eschewing ideal approaches to morality, see Kratochwil, Friedrich (2001), 'International Law as an Approach to International Ethics: A Plea for a Jurisprudential Diagnostics', in Jean-Marc Coicaud and Daniel Warner (eds.), *Ethics and International Affairs: Extent and Limits* (New York: United Nations University Press), 14–41.

approaches[40] emphasize rules that ought to be made universal and are pure, that is, their normativity does not depend on empirical factors whatsoever.[41] As such, the abstract and *impartial* morality of duty makes context, situation and agent-relative features irrelevant.[42] Furthermore, deontologism has a hard time addressing conflicts of rules or moral duties such as when one is bound to follow rules preventing armed intervention while at the same time doing it would be necessary to uphold human rights and avoid their breach. As Anscombe put it 'His [Kant's] rule about universalizable maxims is *useless without stipulations* as to what should count as a relevant description of an action with a view to constructing a maxim about it.'[43]

If deontologism proposes a recipe for a normative stalemate, consequentialism does not fare much better. Consequentialism focuses not on a priori duties and rules but determines the goodness of an action based on its consequences measured according to a common metric (e.g. utility for utilitarianism).[44] Here the brunt of ethical analysis lies in the quantification and calculation of costs and benefits but similarly context, situation and the features and life-projects of agents are taken as given or ignored[45] and calculation applies to a fixed set of streamlined facts. Consequentialism is limited by both calculation and conceptual problems (e.g. 'Which consequences should we attend to: potential or certain, present or future, if future which future ...?' and 'Why should we focus on a single principle such as utility maximization?') leading to wars of numbers and axiological monism. The latter impoverishes human existence by denying the plurality of goods held as important in human existence.[46] For

---

[40] For a useful overview, see Alexander, Larry and Moore, Michael (2016), 'Deontological Ethics', in Edward N. Zalta (ed.), *Stanford Encyclopedia of Philosophy* at https://plato.stanford.edu/entries/ethics-deontological/.

[41] Paradigmatically, Kant, Immanuel (1998), *Groundwork of the Metaphysics of Morals*, trans. Mary Gregor (Cambridge: Cambridge University Press) at 3.

[42] Reviewing character-based consequentialist and deontological formulations but arguing that they do not overcome these frameworks' limits, see Oakley, Justin and Cocking, Dean (2001), *Virtue Ethics and Professional Roles* (Cambridge: Cambridge University Press).

[43] Anscombe, G. E. M. (1958), 'Modern Moral Philosophy', *Philosophy*, 33 (124), 1–19 at 2, emphasis added.

[44] The canonical Western statement is Bentham, Jeremy (2000), *An Introduction to the Principles of Morals and Legislation* (Kitchener: Batoche). However, the Chinese text *Mozi* predated the Western formulation by much. See Johnston, Ian (2013), *The Book of Master Mo*, trans. Ian Johnston (London: Penguin Books) at 73ff.

[45] Recall the critique of Bernard Williams to utilitarianism: 'the reason why utilitarianism cannot understand integrity is that it cannot coherently describe the relations between a man's projects and his actions.' See Smart, J. J. C. and Williams, Bernard (1973), *Utilitarianism: For and Against* (Cambridge University Press) at 100.

[46] Emphatically, claiming this monism as false, Dancy, Jonathan (1983), 'Ethical Particularism and Morally Relevant Properties', *Mind*, XCII, 530–47 at 531.

Ethical Leadership, Virtues, and Narrative in International Organizations 13

instance, should we all follow Singer and believe that it is our moral duty to end luxury consumption patterns in order to eradicate poverty through direct contributions? Would this improve general welfare?[47] Likewise, was NATO's bombing of Yugoslavia justified from a utilitarian moral perspective, that is, did it increase total or average utility? Here, beyond the obvious difficulties behind making these sorts of calculations and the narrowness of deciding when to act prescribed by a single ethical principle and good, a central issue is that very few authors actually engage in such calculations. Therewith, consequentialist approaches deal in highly abstract moral scenarios and reify the ideal (or ideological) nature of their ethical claims.

The literature's ideal theory stance favoured, too, a neutralization of non-Western ethical theories such as Confucianism or Ubuntu. Removed from their social contexts, cleansed from their non-progressive assumptions, and abstracted from the practices that embed and articulate them, these approaches were successfully made global. However, this came with a steep price. According to Praeg, Ubuntu became a 'shorthand for being nice' or an 'Afro-chic artefact'.[48] Openness to the Oriental world (for Confucianism) is expected from progressive Western cosmopolitans, but for the narratives to blend smoothly, depoliticized versions of Confucianism and classical Chinese philosophy are in order.[49]

Be that as it may, as Nussbaum put it, it seems that the reductionist mistake of both deontologism and utilitarianism lies in their starting question and how the latter is dominated, a priori, by a narrow kind of moral narrative, theory, and procedure

> 'How should one live?' This choice of starting point is significant … The point is to state the opening question in a general and inclusive way, excluding at the start no major story about the good life for human beings.[50]

---

[47] Singer, Peter (1972), 'Famine, Affluence, and Morality', *Philosophy & Public Affairs*, 1 (3), 229–43. For a critique, see Kuper, Andrew (2002), 'More Than Charity: Cosmopolitan Alternatives to the "Singer Solution"', *Ethics and International Affairs*, 16 (1), 107–20.

[48] Praeg, Leonhard (2014), 'From ubuntu to Ubuntu: Four Historic a Prioris', in Leonhard Praeg and Siphokazi Magadla (eds.), *Ubuntu: Curating the Archive* (Pietermaritzburg: University of KwaZulu-Natal Press), 96–120 at 116. See also Keevy, Ilze (2014), 'Ubuntu Versus the Core Values of the South African Constitution', in Leonhard Praeg and Siphokazi Magadla (eds.), *Ubuntu: Curating the Archive* (Pietermaritzburg: University of KwaZulu-Natal Press), 54–95.

[49] For the Chinese version, see Dan, Yu (2010), *Confucius From the Heart: Ancient Wisdom for Today's World*, trans. Esther Tyldesley (London: Pan Books). For the Western counterpart, see Puett, Michael and Gross-Loh, Christine (2016), *The Path: A New Way to Think About Everything* (London: Viking).

[50] Nussbaum, Martha (1990), *Love's Knowledge: Essays on Philosophy and Literature* (New York: Oxford University Press) at 173.

Forgetting this lesson may be dangerous when deontological and consequentialist approaches cannot yield us a prescription on how to act. That is, when rules do not exist, when they conflict, or when the calculation of consequences is not possible, these ethical approaches may disarm ethical evaluation and analysis. Or they may clash with our moral intuitions, when they scream at us that something is out of place. The analysis that Jan Klabbers performs in Chapter 9 documents some of these concerns highlighting the explanatory role of the virtues in providing a better *understanding* of some legal decisions. Specifically, he analyses the *Rainbow Warrior* award to show that the arbitration panel reached a decision that seems to be *contra legem* but weirdly does not appear wrong. Yet, deontological and consequentialist frameworks cannot explain why.

Additionally, ethical literature operates typically by choosing *a single theory*, either deontologism or consequentialism, to the exclusion of all other ethical frameworks. Thus, it is not only that theoretical ethics applies unchanging and narrow principles to a given situation but also that such principles must come from a unique ethical tradition.[51] Presciently, Dewey has shown that this stance not only falsifies our moral experience but also removes moral conflict as such because

> ... uncertainty and conflict are inherent in morals; it is characteristic of any situation properly called moral that one is ignorant of the end and of good consequences, of the right and just approach, of the direction of virtuous conduct, and that one must search for them. The essence of the moral situation is an internal and intrinsic conflict; the necessity for judgment and for choice comes from the fact that one has to manage forces with no common denominator.[52]

But moral conflict persists, leading to paradoxical results, for example, rejecting abortion on the grounds that it violates the right to life may breach the same right. After all, making abortion illegal is associated with avoidable deaths by creating the conditions for abortion to be performed in suboptimal conditions. In its radical formulation, the critique of deontologism based on human rights leads to a denial of the possibility of morally justifiable radical political action in the name of rights, because the latter always

---

[51] Not to mention other non-theoretical resources such as our intuitions, self-evident truths, or our ordinary way of moral decision-making. See Kaspar, David (2015), 'How Do We Decide in Moral Situations', *Philosophy*, 90 (1), 59–81 at 63, 'By narrowing its action-guiding tools down to one, moral theories leave agents less practically equipped after committing to a moral theory than they were before.'

[52] Dewey, John (1981), 'Three Independent Factors in Morals', in J. A. Boydston (ed.), *The Later Works, 1925–1953* (vol. 5; Carbondale: Southern Illinois University Press), 315–20 at 316.

Ethical Leadership, Virtues, and Narrative in International Organizations 15

breaches existing rights.[53] On the other hand, a focus on consequences sees values as a priori available and thus may justify all kinds of conducts.

Partially, the problem lies in deontologism's and utilitarianism's abstraction from the motivations of the agents, their life-projects, and their characters as expressing dispositional traits that were built over time, and how they are deployed in each situation. In overlooking these features, deontologism and consequentialism leave us empty-handed, missing salient features of the way human beings make moral decisions. Since they do not tackle the complexities of real-life situations, a deductive approach to morality is all they can offer, that is, to prescribe a set of a priori principles[54] to a situation without allowing the latter to model the content and application of the former.[55]

In international relations and international law, pragmatism opposed this situation by recalling American classical and contemporary pragmatist lessons.[56] A favourite, John Dewey, had described the task of moral philosophy as follows:

> A moral philosophy which should frankly recognize the impossibility of reducing all the elements in moral situations to a single commensurable principle, which should recognize that each human being has to make the best adjustment he can among forces which are genuinely disparate, would throw light upon actual predicaments of conduct and help individuals in making a juster estimate of the force of each competing factor.[57]

In Chapter 2 of this book, Friedrich Kratochwil develops this thread of analysis by studying the impoverishment of our concept of practical wisdom, replaced by a theory of action in which agents neither choose the ends of their actions nor display a commitment towards them. As he puts it, this is the result of conceptualizing *action as production*.

---

[53] See Badiou, Alain (2013), *Logics of Worlds*, trans. Alberto Toscano (London; New York: Bloomsbury) speaking of 'democratic materialism'.

[54] The core of the 'ethical particularism' project led by Dancy denies the existence of principles *tout court*. See Dancy, Jonathan (1983), 'Ethical Particularism and Morally Relevant Properties', *Mind*, XCII, 530–47.

[55] For an early critique to what he called the 'tyranny of principles', see Toulmin, Stephen (1981), 'The Tyranny of Principles', *Hastings Center Report*, 11 (6), 31–39.

[56] See Kratochwil, Friedrich (2018), *Praxis: On Acting and Knowing* (Cambridge: Cambridge University Press), Cochran, Molly (2004), *Normative Theory in International Relations: A Pragmatic Approach* (Cambridge: Cambridge University Press), and Schieder, Siegrief (2000), 'Pragmatism as a Path Towards a Discursive and Open Theory of International Law', *European Journal of International Law*, 11 (3), 663–98.

[57] Dewey, John (1981), 'Three Independent Factors in Morals', in J. A. Boydston (ed.), *The Later Works, 1925–1953* (vol. 5; Carbondale: Southern Illinois University Press), 315–20 at 320.

16 *Guilherme Vasconcelos Vilaça*

If pragmatism contributed to free our thinking from speculative, positivist, and structuralist assumptions, it seems to have been less successful in escaping the methodological and epistemological debates, since the analysis ends typically like this: 'it is up to human beings themselves to construct *their own contingent and contestable ethics.*'[58] Stopping here, in these robes or Rorty's liberal ironist ones,[59] evokes Foucault's famous statement that we ought to build ourselves like works of art. A daunting task, especially given collective action problems and our disciplined societies. Either way, it was not only in morality that this erasure of creative *judgment* and improvisation took place.

> Both the legal and musical ideologies that developed during the Enlightenment sought the preservation and the glorification of an internally coherent and authoritative text at the expense of an earlier Aristotelian emphasis on character and judgment.[60]

In other words, in morality (and law and music) we have assumed a universal 'score' that can be reproduced 'error-free'[61] and thus neither context nor the performing agent is given a constitutive role in determining action, that is, performing or exercising judgment.[62] Nelson summarizes this model of moral reasoning as follows:

> On the juridical model, morality is a matter of solitary judges applying codified rules derived from comprehensive theories as criteria for assessing wrongdoing and making rational choices. This picture of morality represents it as a body of *knowledge*: the (solitary) moral philosopher's task is to construct, test, and refine covering laws that exhibit this knowledge, while the task of moral justification is carried out by the covering principles or procedures that make up the moral theory. The more one knows about the foundations of the theories, their content, their relative merits, and how they are to be applied to specific problems, the greater one's claim to ethical expertise. And like other forms of expertise, moral knowledge is neither easily acquired nor competently wielded by amateurs.[63]

---

[58] Morgan, Marcus (2014), 'The Poverty of (Moral) Philosophy: Towards an Empirical and Pragmatic Ethics', *European Journal of Social Theory*, 17 (2), 129–46, emphasis added.

[59] Cochran, Molly (1996), 'The Liberal Ironist, Ethics and International Relations Theory', *Millennium – Journal of International Studies*, 25 (1), 29–52.

[60] Manderson, Desmond (2010), 'Fission to Fusion: From Improvisation and Formalism in Law and Music', *Critical Studies in Improvisation/Études Critiques en Improvisation*, 6 (1), 1–9 at 5.

[61] *Ibid.*

[62] Distinguishing between abstract and concrete uses of context in moral reasoning, see Nelson, Hilde Lindemann (2004), 'Context: Backward, Sideways, and Forward', in Rita Charon and Martha Montello (eds.), *Stories Matter: The Role of Narrative in Medical Ethics* (New York; London: Routledge), 39–47.

[63] *Idem*, at 46, footnote omitted.

Ethical Leadership, Virtues, and Narrative in International Organizations 17

This model may at first glance seem more fit to address moral dilemmas, but this is because it oversimplifies moral analysis and human action as seen above. But two other consequences are worth exploring. First, this is a model that impoverishes our understanding of morality, by denying that the latter is not only a discrete, static and atomized activity but also a collective, continuous, and dynamic enterprise in fashioning normative narratives for forms of life such as organizations. Second, a conception of morality and moral judgment as a matter of knowledge as sketched above creates incentives for individuals and organizations *to outsource* the tasks of creating the normative worlds they wish to experience together and exercising constant responsibility towards the common world to someone else, that is, a class of experts that is far removed from the specific *living community*, further entrenching individual alienation from ethical responsibility.

Together, the juridical model of morality and the false conceptualization of the position we are in when we make moral choices drastically reduce our capacity to scrutinize dimensions of ethical behaviour, leaving many choices, ideals, and organizational cultures beyond moral evaluation. Instead, we need an ethical approach that can consider the real complexity of agents, situations, and judgment in actual ethical reasoning and life even if the results of such operation remain ever open to new facts, interpretations, and contestation.

Ultimately, we can surmise that the end-result of ethical analysis most of us, arguably, look for is the elucidation of the vision or an answer (that can take different forms) to a given moral scenario, *not coherence* between principles, theories, and their application. All this brings us closer to *persons* rather than just rules, principles, and consequences. Nussbaum describes the ethical task that accounts for the features identified above as *practical*

> ... in that it is conducted by people who are themselves involved in acting and choosing and who see the inquiry as having a bearing on their own practical ends. They do not inquire in a 'pure' or detached manner, asking what the truth about ethical value might be as if they were asking for a description of some separately existing Platonic reality. They are looking for something in human life, something, in fact, that they themselves are going to try bring about in their lives. What they are asking is not what is the good 'out there', but what can we best live by, and live together as social beings?[64]

---

[64] Nussbaum, Martha (1990), *Love's Knowledge: Essays on Philosophy and Literature* (New York: Oxford University Press) at 173.

1.4 VIRTUES AND COMPLEXITY IN ETHICAL ANALYSIS

In the section above I have shown some of the shortcomings of deontologism and consequentialism that help to explain the turn to the language of virtues and virtue ethics. This refers to a discourse that fell out of favour within moral philosophy until Anscombe's reminder and MacIntyre's re-articulation of the tradition.[65] Thus, a general characterization is perhaps in use.

> In ancient ethical theories, the entry point for ethical reflection is the agent's reflection *on her life as a whole,* and *the ordering of her priorities.* Although ancient moral philosophers do not neglect cases of ethical conflict as much as is often thought, *they do not regard ethical theory primarily as a mechanism for solving ethical conflict.* Rather, the assumption is that each of us has a vague and unarticulated idea of an overall or final goal in our life, and the task of ethical theory is to give each person a clear, articulated, and correct account of this overall goal and how to achieve it.[66]

The lineage of virtue ethics is often traced back to Aristotle whose thought is described generally below.[67] However, save for the centrality of *practical wisdom* of Aristotelian flavour,[68] no strong form of virtue ethics is prescribed throughout the chapter and the book. Virtue ethics is based on a practical, not theoretical, account of human action. If action becomes open-ended, geared towards a plurality of ends that need to be rendered concrete in specific circumstances and situations also taking into account the (moral) traits of the agent, then questions of judgment and practical wisdom become paramount since acting well can never be known in advance.

Virtues, such as courage or moderation, are stable 'excellent trait[s] of character'[69] making those that acquire them excellent and, in some renditions, exemplary or worthy of admiration. Virtues are important because they promote

---

[65] Anscombe, G. E. M. (1958), 'Modern Moral Philosophy', *Philosophy,* 33 (124), 1–19 and MacIntyre, Alasdair (2007), *After Virtue: A Study in Moral Theory* (3rd edn.; London: Duckworth).

[66] Annas, Julia (1995), 'Prudence and Morality in Ancient and Modern Ethics', *Ethics,* 105 (2), 241–57 at 241, emphasis added.

[67] For a useful overview of different schools of virtue ethics, see Hursthouse, Rosalind and Pettigrove, Glen (2016), 'Virtue Ethics', in Edward N. Zalta (ed.), *Stanford Encyclopedia of Philosophy* at https://plato.stanford.edu/entries/ethics-virtue/#Virt.

[68] See Swanton, Christine (2013), 'The Definition of Virtue Ethics', in Daniel C. Russell (ed.), *The Cambridge Companion to Virtue Ethics* (Cambridge: Cambridge University Press), 315–38 at 323. For a recent comprehensive articulation of a virtue ethics account based on phronesis, see Russell, Daniel C. (2009), *Practical Intelligence and the Virtues* (Oxford; New York: Oxford University Press).

[69] See Hursthouse, Rosalind and Pettigrove, Glen (2016), 'Virtue Ethics', in Edward N. Zalta (ed.), *Stanford Encyclopedia of Philosophy* at https://plato.stanford.edu/entries/ethics-virtue/

human flourishing, Aristotle's *telos* for human beings. But, for Aristotle, it is not enough to have understood intellectually what virtues require. The phronimos or practically wise person knows *when* to exercise the virtues (*kairos*) and this can only occur in concrete situations.

> So too anyone can get angry, or give and spend money – these are easy; *but doing them in relation to the right person, in the right amount, at the right time, with the right aim in view, and in the right way* – that is not something anyone can do, nor is it easy. This is why excellence in these things is rare, praiseworthy and noble.[70]

Then,

> For Aristotle, therefore, becoming phronimos requires an individual to (1) possess knowledge of what constitutes virtuous behavior, (2) possess knowledge of the means necessary to attain virtuous ends, and (3) act in a manner that allows one to attain these ends.[71]

In any case, as Annas' citation above reminds us, classical virtue ethics emphasizes a long-term construction and education of moral character in which orienting oneself towards a given goal – *eudaimonia* for Aristotle – is more important than looking for the right action in individual situations. Partially, this is because Aristotle's account of ethics assumes that one cannot know theoretically what the right answer is since *action*, not knowledge, is the province of ethics.[72] Partially, because practical wisdom does not have as object universal and ahistorical knowledge,[73] it has to be acquired through reflection and *experience* which in turn requires socialization within family, social, and political roles.

Notice that, while virtue ethics captures the crux of the argument against moral theory by highlighting the agent's position, life-projects, and context, in truth, it does not ask the same 'What should I do?' question, but rather 'How should I live?'

#Virt. Some strands of psychoanalysis claim that virtues cannot be understood in isolation, separated from the 'integral structure of character'. See Fromm, Erich (2016), *Ética y Psicoanálisis*, trans. Heriberto F. Morck (2nd ed.; Ciudad de México: Fondo de Cultura Económica) at 48.

70 Aristotle (2000), *Nicomachean Ethics*, trans. Roger Crisp (Cambridge: Cambridge University Press), 1109 a26–30, emphasis added.

71 Surprenant, Chris W. (2012), 'Politics and Practical Wisdom: Rethinking Aristotle's Account of Phronesis', *Topoi*, 31, 221–227 at 222.

72 The pragmatists universalized a relatable conception of knowledge as 'the output of a dynamic and experiential process of inquiry and discovery'. See Ralston, Shane (2011), 'Pragmatism in International Relations Theory and Research', *Eidos*, 14, 72–105 at 76–77.

73 Aristotle (2000), *Nicomachean Ethics*, trans. Roger Crisp (Cambridge: Cambridge University Press), 1141a1, emphasis added.

On the one hand, virtue ethics, as I interpret it, echoes the intuitionist W. D. Ross' perception that we cannot hope for a priori certainty when we act, since acting involves 'taking a moral risk'.[74] On the other hand, and relatedly, classic virtue ethics challenges the deontological and utilitarian ethical theories' thesis that a decision procedure is necessary to tell us right and wrong.[75] Thus, removing a false necessity in human life, that is, that normative ethical theory *had* a right answer to moral dilemmas and thus *could* guide action unproblematically.[76] Altogether, the combined effect of the virtues' focus on long-term character development, the impossibility of knowing a priori what is the right action as well as the contextual nature of action and moral judgment lead to a natural move of ethical theory away from the task of guiding decision making and identifying the right moral action,[77] and towards the task of illuminating and justifying our moral life and beliefs.[78]

More bothersome, however, is that the virtue ethics' challenge also clashes with our *common moral intuition* and desire to know 'what to do?' and 'how to act?' in given situations.[79] Without a decision procedure that we know can mechanically produce an answer, and faced with the complexity of ethical scenarios as built by virtue ethics, what are we left with and how can we go on? I believe that virtue ethics has to offer something in the form of an answer to this question and I will sketch this below. Here, it is enough to point out that ethical analysis and criticism true to the premises of virtue ethics must become

---

[74] Ross, David (2003), *The Right and the Good* (Oxford: Oxford University Press) at 30, emphasis added.

[75] See Kaspar, David (2015), 'How Do We Decide in Moral Situations', *Philosophy*, 90 (1), 59–81 at 61.

[76] This was the core of the 'anti-theory in ethics' movement that strongly opposed normative ethical theory. For a good overview of the debate, see Clarke, Stanley G. and Simpson, Evan (eds.) (1989), *Anti-Theory in Ethics and Moral Conservatism* (State University of New York Press). A more recent representative work of 'anti-theory in ethics' is Williams, Bernard (2006), *Ethics and the Limits of Philosophy* (London; New York: Routledge).

[77] On the circularity of virtue ethics when telling us what to do or how to live, recall Mackie, J. L. (1990), *Ethics: Inventing Right and Wrong* (Harmondsworth: Penguin) at 186.

[78] Zagzebski, Linda (2010), 'Exemplarist Virtue Theory', *Metaphilosophy*, 41 (1–2), 41–57 at 43. Insisting on ethics' need for directing practice, see Nussbaum, Martha C. (2000), 'Why Practice Needs Ethical Theory: Particularism, Principle, and Bad Behavior', in Steven J. Burton (ed.), *The Path of the Law and Its Influence: The Legacy of Oliver Wendell Holmes, Jr* (New York: Cambridge University Press), 50–86 at 57.

[79] Contemporary virtue ethicists have proposed different ways in which to articulate virtues and right action. See Zyl, Liezl Van (2013), 'Virtue Ethics and Right Action', in Daniel C. Russell (ed.), *The Cambridge Companion to Virtue Ethics* (New York: Cambridge University Press), 172–96, and Swanton, Christine (2001), 'A Virtue Ethical Account of Right Action', *Ethics*, 112, 32–52. For a critique emphasizing that such move leads to the loss of virtue ethics' distinctiveness, see Das, R. (2003), 'Virtue Ethics and Right Action', *Australasian Journal of Philosophy*, 81 (3), 324–39.

Ethical Leadership, Virtues, and Narrative in International Organizations 21

much more complex than usually acknowledged and performed. This complexity requires building *thick* ethical narratives that make the situation, agents, human goods, and choices involved morally *intelligible*.

Paradoxically, by dodging our intuition's nagging need for an answer to what to do, virtue ethics can help to make sense of otherwise morally absurd scenarios and decisions. Thus, in the movie *Sophie's Choice*, when the mother is asked to choose which child to send to death to avoid having both killed, virtue ethics' distance from the situation and focus on the long-term flourishing of the individual and the development of her character may assist us in understanding morally Sophie and her saying 'Take the little girl!'.[80] Ultimately, the rejection of the scientific approach to ethics by the so-called 'anti-theorists' leads to the recognition of the importance of character and prudential decision-making.

> Moral values and standards, after all, lack a substance of their own. There are no purely moral acts, *but only moral or immoral ways of working, buying and selling, engaging in friendships*, and so forth. Moral standards always qualify practices, habits, and kinds of conduct which are not at bottom 'moral,' but political, familial, and the like ... That moral standards exist which govern conduct in all these interdependent realms of life attests not necessarily to the existence of an independent moral realm, but to the *moral* point that *in all parts of life questions of character and conduct may arise and that the ideal of leading a good life as a whole can develop in consequence.*[81]

At stake, then, is a call for the exercise of judgment and imagination in fashioning one's life-projects grounded on a particular idea of the good and actualizing it in the concrete circumstances of life. Again, this does not do away with the need to account for actions and choices, but this assessment can no longer be done outside of someone's commitments, life-projects, and circumstances. This is crucial because it highlights features of ethical experience that had remained hidden. It also forces those assessing a given course of action to exercise moral imagination and engage in a genuine process of discovery of the normative narrative that wraps one's choices in given factual and normative situations. Notice that, from the pragmatist reconstruction of virtue ethics operated throughout this chapter, there is nothing against contemplating deontological and consequentialist ethical principles among the normative materials that the morally virtuous agent may consider. Doing

---

[80] *Sophie's Choice* (1982), Pakula, Alan J. (dir.).

[81] Noble, Cheryl N. (1979), 'Normative Ethical Theories', *The Monist*, 62 (4), 496–509 at 499, emphasis added. More recently, linking intuitionism and prudence, see Kaspar, David (2015), 'How Do We Decide in Moral Situations', *Philosophy*, 90 (1), 59–81.

otherwise would do violence to Dewey's proviso that *descriptively* we approach moral choices according to principles and maxims that come from different ethical traditions. And not allowing for deontological and consequentialist ideas to be considered would render virtue ethics liable to the same reductionist critique elaborated against the other ethical frameworks.

In other worlds, ethical life and judgment can no longer be conceptualized *as an encounter between strangers* about a moral order that lies outside of their existence. Rather, by historicizing the ethical experience and framing it as commitment towards a given life-project that has to be carried out in the social realm often within social roles, virtue ethics ultimately *socializes* ethics. The latter becomes not a disembodied succession of disparate actions (as a series of one-off sales contracts) but the fashioning (and living) of forms of collective life in which we may *dwell* assuredly and flourish.

Organizations, prime examples of collective formations to achieve a shared vision, become, from a virtues perspective, examples of the joint collective enterprise of ethical *narrative-making*; a common responsibility in defining and actualizing specific visions and forms of moral life. Hence, organizations can no longer be conceptualized solely as problem-solving entities; they are modes of existence – living communities – and contribute to give sense to our lives, justifying the *how* question highlighted throughout this section. Rather than concentrating all our energies on 'what to do?' and the *right* narrative, virtue ethics puts the emphasis on *acceptable* and *unacceptable* narratives, that is, the fact that it matters morally to us how we organize ourselves and experience life within collectives, the narrative we create to pursue their mission, and according to a vision that aims at human and organizational flourishing.

Against this background, it is easy to understand the constitutive function of ethics in organizations. For example, as Lorenzo Casini establishes in Chapter 6, the value of Olympism at the core of global sports' practice and institutions encapsulates a virtuous conception of sport that justifies (i) a series of behavioural expectations imposed on the relevant actors; and, (ii) existing rules and procedures necessary to uphold that conception.

This understanding of individuals and organizations as inhabiting normative worlds and narratives of their making[82] has deep methodological implications, articulated below, for ethical analysis forcing the latter to open up to

---

[82] Cover, Robert M. (1983), 'Nomos and Narrative', *Harvard Law Review*, 97 (4), 4–68.

Ethical Leadership, Virtues, and Narrative in International Organizations 23

other disciplines and approaches. In addition, it impacts, as pointed out above for the case of individuals, ethical criticism too.

> Here, the authority for a moral intuition rests on its embeddedness in a shared form of moral life, *while the basis for moral criticism lies in the tensions between, and the fissures within, the stories that circulate widely in the community* ... it is a view of morality in which the meaning of 'now' is indeterminate and must wait on the event.[83]

The virtues' emphasis on historicized forms of life and situations, not itemized rules or consequences, *draws a necessary connection between ethics and narrative*. While narratives were infantilized as 'fables, myths, legends, fit only for women and children'[84] because unprovable, it is now coming to be accepted more widely that there is no world beyond our descriptions or narratives.[85] The de-infantilization process also makes it clear that narratives are not necessarily good or progressive – a lesson that I explore below and that anyone wishing to deploy the language of virtues (and vices) should keep in mind.[86]

Importantly, the ethical narrative model, grounded on the idea that the objects of ethics are no longer discrete, atomistic, and ontologically independent but the product of a continuous commitment to live according to one's individual and organizational life-project, enables us to overcome the *situationist critique* against character-based ethical approaches. This critique advances two main claims: (i) character does not exist because human beings are ethically fragmented; and, (ii) character has no predictive power regarding future behaviour because what really determines human action is the situation in which they find themselves. In this chapter and the book, neither of these two strong views is maintained since there is no true opposition between person and situation. The argument made so far highlights that when one takes into account *real* agents, scenarios, organizations, and choices, (moral) character should not be seen as a binary property (either you have it or not) that is settled for good (either you have achieved it or not).

---

[83] Nelson, Hilde Lindemann (2004), 'Context: Backward, Sideways, And Forward', in Rita Charon and Martha Montello (eds.), *Stories Matter: The Role of Narrative in Medical Ethics* (New York; London: Routledge), 39–47 at 46, emphasis added.

[84] Lyotard, Jean François (1984), *The Postmodern Condition: A Report on Knowledge*, trans. Geoff Bennington and Brian Massumi (Manchester: Manchester University Press) at 27.

[85] Taking support from Nelson Goodman, see Winter, Steven L. (2014), 'Law, Culture and Humility', in Austin Sarat, Matthew Anderson and Cathrine O. Frank (eds.), *Law and the Humanities: An Introduction* (New York: Cambridge University Press), 98–121 at 119.

[86] For a rich account of vices based upon a wide array of literary sources, see Shklar, Judith N. (1984), *Ordinary Vices* (Cambridge; London: Belknap Press).

24   *Guilherme Vasconcelos Vilaça*

Thus, character cannot be expected to predict behaviour in a one-to-one relationship (though this does not mean that it has *no* predictive power whatsoever).[87]

1.5 VIRTUE ETHICS, PROFESSIONAL ROLES AND THE SELECTION PROBLEM

It goes without saying that only *individuals* and the ways they adopt to live together can give ethics a communal nature able to pierce and infuse values into collective entities of human and social life such as organizations, international and domestic alike. Whereas for some authors egalitarian grassroots forms of social life may be preferable, most organizations, and certainly IOs, are organized around hierarchical principles. This makes executive heads and leaders key in trickling down values and attitudes throughout the organization. This takes place, for example, through their commitment and example as well as through the selection of *hearts-minds* (心) that adhere to their and the organization's normative and practical ideals.

An organizational focus raises, however, a new question for ethics, that is, does the organizational context change the nature of the appropriate virtuous leader demanding different virtues and a distinctive exercise of the virtues? In virtue ethics theory, this aspect has been fully articulated as follows:

> Broadly speaking, what counts as acting well in the context of a professional role is in our view importantly determined by how well that role functions in serving the goals of the profession, and by how those goals are connected to with characteristic human activities. That is, good professional roles must be part of a good profession, and a good profession, on our virtue ethics approach, is one which involves a commitment to a key human good, a good which plays a crucial role in enabling us to live a humanly flourishing life.[88]

Let us explore this challenge through an example. In 1950, Wilmarth Lewis made a (self-flattering) speech listing the virtues and credentials expected from the candidates to succeed him to the presidency of Yale University (please bear the sexist tone of the description!).

---

[87] On the situationist critique, its relevance to virtue ethics and its overblown conclusions, see Sreenivasan, Gopal (2013), 'The Situationist Critique of Virtue Ethics', in Daniel C. Russell (ed.), *The Cambridge Companion to Virtue Ethics* (Cambridge: Cambridge University Press), 290–314, and Slingerland, Edward (2011), 'The Situationist Critique and Early Confucian Virtue Ethics', *Ethics*, 121 (2), 390–419.

[88] See Oakley, Justin and Cocking, Dean (2001), *Virtue Ethics and Professional Roles* (Cambridge: Cambridge University Press) at 74.

Ethical Leadership, Virtues, and Narrative in International Organizations 25

The Yale President must be a Yale man. He must be a person of character with religious convictions. He must be a scholar of international reputation with deep respect for science if he is a humanist and who loves the arts if he is a scientist. He must be a man of the present with knowledge of the past and a clear vision of the future. He must not be too far to the right, too far to the left, or a middle-of-the roader. Poised, clear-eyed, informed, he must be ready to give the ultimate word on every subject under the sun from how to handle the Russians to why undergraduates riot in the spring. As a speaker he must be profound with a wit that bubbles up and brims over in a cascade of brilliance; his writing must be lucid and cogent, his style both Augustan and contemporary. He must be young enough to have 'dynamic ideas', but old enough to be sensible about them; courageous but not foolhardy. He must be 'a great personality', by which is meant one who commands respect, who soothes the ruffled and charms the sentimental, an Olympian who is one of the boys without affectation or jocularity. He must have intimate knowledge of all the University's colleges, schools, departments, institutes, libraries, museums, and special projects, and know how to administer them efficiently and economically, delegating authority while keeping his finger on every pulse and in every pie. He must be a man with a heart who will share the private joys and sorrows of his faculty. Above all, he must be a leader, leading of course in the right direction, which is to money. Morning, noon, and night he must get money; money for salaries and money for buildings, money for scholarships, money for new projects that will prove he is dynamic. Since his job takes eighteen hours a day seven days a week eleven months a year, his health must be good – no colds, no ulcers, no slipped discs. Finally, his wife must be a combination of Queen Victoria, Florence Nightingale, and the Best-Dressed Woman of the Year. As I have been talking you have guessed who the leading candidate is, but there is a question about Him: *Is* God a Yale Man?[89]

Yale University is a historical symbol of classicism, humanism, and virtues in education. The message is fitting because, next to these traditional virtues, it highlights how leaders are expected to display excellence throughout a stunningly vast number of practical – normative, instrumental, and mundane – areas of intervention. Leaders are expected to be managers, administrators, visionaries, while displaying authority and grace as well as commanding an impressive body of theoretical-practical-institutional knowledge. Crucially, all this *in the pursuit of the human goods that the organization embodies and pursues.* This job description reveals the connection, theorized above in virtue ethics, between the goods that each organization

---

[89] In Kelley, Brooks Mather (1974), *Yale: A History* (New Haven; London: Yale University Press) at 425–426, emphasis in the original.

pursues and the demands they place upon certain roles within that organization. In other words, the virtues and character traits of a Yale University president would be shaped by the good *education*, a good that is necessary to human flourishing, and that shapes the ends of that profession and professional role. Virtues become, thus, role-, organization-, and profession-relative rather than being defined abstractly. What does this qualification add to the picture?

For example, an organization, such as a university or UNESCO, justified by its pursuit of education would not be able to make money a trump in moral dilemmas. Think of Saif al-Islam Gaddafi's donation to the London School of Economics or the United States' withdrawal from UNESCO – after having stopped paying the amounts due for years – for the latter's 'anti-Israel bias' and recognition of Palestine in different moments. While money is fundamental to educational institutions, as Lewis' speech confirms, it is not the good that informs the ends of these professional roles. Instead, its value is merely instrumental. Thus, according to this view, Member States were probably justified in letting go of around 22 per cent of the organization's funding as a consequence for not backing down from recognizing Palestine. Irina Bokova's reactions as the former head of UNESCO show the nature of the moral dilemma when one thinks outside of the organizational framework. First, she recognized that Palestine's membership was an important step towards *peace* in the region. Then, faced with UNESCO's worst funding crisis ever, she complained that it was unfair for the organization to be placed in the middle of political conflicts. Perhaps it would have been wiser to stick to the universality of education rather than the political effects of membership recognition.

Recognizing professional roles as being embedded in practices and organizational structures oriented towards specific goods adds complexity to virtue ethical accounts by opening the possibility of imposing special role-relative demands on leaders and bureaucrats. At the same time, and paying heed to the call against reductionism in ethics, I fear that following to the letter Oakley and Cocking's model would by definition lead us to predetermined outcomes in a way that fails to do justice to the full set of circumstances of agents, organizations, and particular situations. This is due to the paramount position assigned to a *single* unique human good in grounding the goodness of a given profession as well as the adoption of a single ethical framework. According to their formulation, the ends of the professional role always prevail over considerations typically excluded from the core of the professional practice at stake. As a result, ethical analysis operates *top-down* without recognizing the constitutive power that sometimes the features of the particular situation may command, justifying the exercise of virtues in a way that goes against the

Ethical Leadership, Virtues, and Narrative in International Organizations 27

ends of the practice. Hence, while their work expands the kinds of considerations we must include in our analyses, we should resist the temptation to give
them priority per se.

1.6 VIRTUE ETHICS, NARRATIVE AND INTERDISCIPLINARITY

As we have seen in the previous sections, embracing the different morally
salient dimensions in human action highlighted by virtue ethics justifies
establishing an intrinsic connection between virtues and narrative.
Accounting for character and virtues as well as the cultivation of organizations
and exercise of virtuous leadership in concrete situations, or considering
environmental factors necessitates thick and rich descriptions.[90]

Blatantly, to do justice to such a comprehensive programme, we need to go
beyond ethical and philosophical discourses and engage in an interdisciplinary analysis that acknowledges the historical, situated, axiological, personal,
institutional, and environmental materials. For that, we need to start from the
position in which individuals find themselves when they cultivate organizational leadership and make moral decisions.[91] Obviously, the final set of
specific disciplines and resources to be mobilized depends on the particular
research problem and goals to be pursued.

Given what was said so far, three traditions appear very handy: (i) casuistry,
a form of case-based moral reasoning and applied ethics;[92] (ii) anthropology,
which typically dedicates itself to examine micro-behaviours within local
contexts, is given a new role;[93] and, (iii) biographical research devoted to
study the lives of individuals.[94]

---

[90] The endorsement of prudential, narrative and case-based ethics has appeared first in recent
times in medical ethics. See Rita Charon and Martha Montello (eds.), *Stories Matter: The
Role of Narrative in Medical Ethics* (New York; London: Routledge).

[91] See Kaspar, David (2015), 'How Do We Decide in Moral Situations', *Philosophy*, 90 (1), 59–81
at 61.

[92] For a comprehensive manifesto, see Jonsen, Albert R. and Toulmin, Stephen (1990), *The
Abuse of Casuistry: A History of Moral Reasoning* (Berkeley; Los Angeles: University of
California Press), though Toulmin's *An Examination of the Place of Reason in Ethics* dating
back to the early fifties already anticipated these concerns. On the natural link between
casuistry and virtue ethics, see Palmero, María José Guerra (2013), 'Introducción: Casuística
y Razonamiento Moral', in Robert T. Hall and José Salvador Arellano (eds.), *La Casuística:
Una Metodología para la Ética Aplicada* (Ciudad de México: Editorial Fontamara), and
Anscombe, G. E. M. (1958), 'Modern Moral Philosophy', *Philosophy*, 33 (124), 1–19 at 10.

[93] See, for instance, Niezen, Ronald and Sapignoli, Maria (eds.) (2017), *Palaces of Hope: The
Anthropology of Global Organizations* (London: Cambridge University Press).

[94] For a primer, see Roberts, Brian (2002), *Biographical Research* (Buckingham; Philadelphia:
Open University Press). Caro, Robert A. (2020), *Working* (New York: Vintage Books) offers
a thrilling first-person account of what biography-writing entails and amounts to.

28 Guilherme Vasconcelos Vilaça

Casuistry throws us into the history of the case, making us compare it with known ones, describe, analyse, and weight concretely the different facts and values at stake as they are built from the circumstances of the situation and the features and position of the agent. What kind of circumstances? Those befitting the traditional questions of a journalistic piece, that is, 'Who? What? When? Why? How? And through which means?'[95] Remember that for casuistry, as for traditional common law, the conflict between norms and principles is not an end in itself. The conflict is not logical but practical. It is always the *case*, made of details, that requires a moral (or a legal) judgment.[96] This being the context for Holmes' famous dictum: 'the life of the law has not been logic: it has been experience.'

In respect of IOs, anthropology can open wide the rigid conceptual and descriptive picture lawyers and theorists work with, thus creating a richer and more complex starting picture that allows us to see *why character(s) matter*:

> ... ethnographers portray institutions by starting with the people who populate them, above all the ways they maneuver through structural obstacles and opportunities, and in the process reveal the tensions and contests behind formal appearances ... The institutions of global governance as depicted by anthropologists are social worlds with distinct characters, influenced by their connections with civil society, states, transnational corporations, and publics. They are also influenced by the visions and personalities of the people who work in them, situated in an ebb and flow that includes diplomats, consultants, activists, housekeepers, and security personnel. They are worlds apart, united by cosmopolitan ideals in their inspiration and commitment to diplomacy in their methods.[97]

Jane K. Cowan, in Chapter 7 of this book, picks one tack for anthropological ethics, examining collective actors as a whole. Following first-person observation, she examines the concrete styles of virtuous behaviour that member states adopt when performing the public review at the United Nations Universal Periodic Review. Her chapter showcases the potential of anthropological accounts to dispel theoretically biased narratives such as, for example, the one that assumes that virtuous leadership ought to be liberal.

---

[95] See Jonsen, Albert R. and Toulmin, Stephen (1990), *The Abuse of Casuistry: A History of Moral Reasoning* (Berkeley; Los Angeles: University of California Press) at 254.

[96] *Idem*, at 252ff.

[97] Niezen, Ronald and Sapignoli, Maria (2017), 'Introduction', in Ronald Niezen and Maria Sapignoli (eds.), *Palaces of Hope: The Anthropology of Global Organizations* (London: Cambridge University Press), 1–30 at 3. For rare examples of comprehensive biographical work on international figures by political and social scientists, see Fröhlich, Manuel (2010), *Political Ethics and the United Nations: Dag Hammarskjöld as Secretary-General* (New York: Routledge) and Kent J. Kille (ed.) (2007), *The UN Secretary-General and Moral Authority: Ethics and Religion in International Leadership* (Washington, DC: Georgetown University Press).

Ethical Leadership, Virtues, and Narrative in International Organizations 29

In a recent book rehearsing these themes and also conducting biographical research, Sinclair shows how, among other factors, the values and vision of some international leaders – such as Dag Hammarskjöld – regarding international order, human life, and their own role and mission of the organization at stake, proved fundamental to the development of IOs beyond their original mandates.[98] Cox's seminal study on leadership in IOs emphasized another important feature for leadership accomplishments: the institutional socialization and networks of leaders, stemming from previous appointments and their personal and career paths, both internationally and domestically.[99] It is easy to see that obtaining funding or expanding the reach of an IO will be received differently, if you are 'one of them'.

That character, class (broadly understood), and capital (probably) come together is no surprise at all. It suffices to think of the disparate worlds of international arbitration – and the genuine *noblesse de robe* that arose sharing 'impeccable social and moral credentials'[100] – and the contrasting life in a small Oaxacan town during the 1960s in which opening a bank account required a witness attesting to one's character, though not all witnesses would do; Zapotecs, the natives of that area – the Isthmus Zapotec – were ruled out.[101]

If ethical experience as all human experience is indissociable from narrative,[102] it is only logical that literary theory and narrative studies may help to conceptualize accounts of virtues and ethical leadership. Thus, in our narratives, we would gain from being attentive to present different standpoints as voices of distinctive individual characters (actors) that stand on their own

---

[98] Sinclair, Guy Fiti (2017), *To Reform the World: International Organizations and the Making of Modern States* (New York: Oxford University Press).

[99] Cox, Robert (1969), 'The Executive Head: An Essay on Leadership in International Organization', *International Organization*, 23 (2), 205–30.

[100] Dezalay, Yves and Garth, Bryant G. (1996), *Dealing in Virtue: International Commercial Arbitration and the Construction of a Transnational Legal Order* (Chicago: University of Chicago Press) at 193. Recall here Morgenthau, Hans (1948), 'The Twilight of International Morality', *Ethics*, 58 (2), 79–99, describing the decline of the international aristocratic society and the supranational scope of the virtues their members upheld.

[101] Chiñas, Beverly Newbold (1992), *La Zandunga: Of Fieldwork and Friendship in Southern Mexico* (Illinois: Waveland) at 11.

[102] Concurring, see Booth, Wayne C. (1998), 'Why Ethical Criticism Can Never Be Simple', *Style*, 32 (2), 351–64 at 353, emphasis added: 'no one who has thought about it for long can deny that we are at least partially constructed, in our most fundamental moral character, by the stories we have heard, or read, or viewed, or acted out in amateur theatricals: the stories we really have *listened* to.' Nussbaum has been the staunchest supporter of the intrinsic link between the humanities, literary theory and the (Aristotelian) ethical questions of character development and how to live well. She does not, however, engage in ethical analysis of complex moral scenarios. See, for example, Nussbaum, Martha (1990), *Love's Knowledge: Essays on Philosophy and Literature* (New York: Oxford University Press) *maxime* chapter 6.

released from their traditional hierarchies. This *polyphony*, Bakhtin's concept,[103] allows and draws readers into discussing and arguing with the different characters (rather than with the author), thus avoiding an immediate identification with a single narrative.[104] Since characters exceed authorial intention, they are never complete and final ('objects' in Bakhtin's language), and thus are always subject to further inquiry and examination. Each individual and her events and circumstances happen against and within a given environment and context being held together not in essentialist but *historical* terms.

Furthermore, narrative also prepares us for the uncertainty of life as things could always be different. This further helps the ethicist to acknowledge that, whatever the angle of analysis, her perspective will necessarily be non-totalizing and never definitive. A focus on virtues thus helps to stimulate and exercise our moral imagination. Lest we forget, imagination is always the first faculty to be eliminated in literary and cinematic dystopias. Perhaps because as affirmed in *La Antena*, a sublime Argentinian anti-utopia devoted to warning against the dangerous and totalitarian uses of mass media, 'La imaginación ha [siempre] salvado a los hombres'.[105]

1.7 ETHICAL LEADERSHIP: ORGANIZATIONS, PSYCHOLOGY, VIRTUES AND EXEMPLARITY

Concentrating on character and judgment allows us to recognize moral actions that are widely accepted from a descriptive point of view and escape deontological and utilitarian radars further linking virtues to other literatures. One example of such potential is virtue ethics' endorsement of 'positive defiance' to existing rules, principles, established thinking, or organizational cultures.[106]

This turn was also taken in organizational literature with the virtues being conceptualized as enabling behaviour that 'goes beyond what is

---

[103] A concept developed to characterize Dostoevsky's novels and defined as '[a] plurality of independent and unmerged voices and consciousnesses, a genuine polyphony of fully valid voices'. See Bakhtin, Mikhail M. (1984), *Problems of Dostoevsky's Poetics*, trans. Caryl Emerson (Minneapolis; London: University of Minnesota Press) at 6.

[104] Heinzelman, Susan Sage (2010), 'Imagining the Law: The Novel', in Austin Sarat, Matthew Anderson and Cathrine O. Frank (eds.), *Law and the Humanities: An Introduction* (New York: Cambridge University Press), 213–40 at 216.

[105] *La Antena* (2007), Sapir, Esteban (dir.).

[106] Manz, Charles C., et al. (2008), 'The Virtuous Organization: An Introduction', in Charles C. Manz, et al. (eds.), *The Virtuous Organization: Insights from Some of the World's Leading Management Thinkers* (London: World Scientific Publishing Company), 1–16 at 3. For the case of (postmodern) moral agency also advocating for the importance of daring to act positively beyond rules and systems, see Bauman, Zygmunt (1993), *Postmodern Ethics* (Malden; Oxford; Carlton: Blackwell Publishing).

expected'.[107] It should be added that this shift towards virtues in organizations is part of another turn towards *positive psychology* – away from a focus on treating individual suffering caused by pathologies and negative deviations – and its reception within organizational thinking. To be sure, the issue was not only the focus but also the *kind of therapy* deployed.

> *Psychology is not just the study of disease, weakness, and damage; it also is the study of strength and virtue.* Treatment is not just fixing what is wrong; it also is building what is right. Psychology is not just about illness or health; it also is about work, education, insight, love, growth, and play.[108]

> At the group level it [positive psychology] is about the civic virtues and the institutions that move individuals toward better citizenship: responsibility, nurturance, altruism, civility, moderation, tolerance, and work ethic.[109]

This is particularly important in international politics and IOs which are densely regulated contexts through member states' mandates, legal rules, codes of conducts, best practices, ethical frameworks, and the like. Emphasizing that ethics is about developing oneself, cannot be learned and applied deductively, and does not consist of a repetition of past lessons empowers the members of organizations to think of when they ought to act differently rather than doing what comes naturally in rule-based organizations: *complying*. As if members of organizations would work keeping in mind Weber's provocation, 'Will you simply and dully accept world and occupation?'

A fitting example is Maria Varaki's contribution, Chapter 11 of the book, discussing the exercise of ethical leadership in the context of the refugee crisis in Europe. According to Varaki, Angela Merkel's decision to open the German borders *against* the European Union Member States' procrastination and the world's silence constitutes a good example of exemplarity, practical wisdom, and moral imagination devising and acting on a decision that was at odds with the normative environment.

But virtues fit organizations in ordinary moments of their lives, not only in eventful extraordinary situations. Kim Cameron identifies five dimensions in which virtues improve organizational cultures:

---

[107] Cameron, Kim (2003), 'Organizational Virtuousness and Performance', in Kim S. Cameron, Jane E. Dutton and Robert Quinn (eds.), *Positive Organizational Scholarship* (San Francisco: Berrett-Koehler), 48–65.

[108] Seligman, Martin E. P. (2002), 'Positive Psychology, Positive Prevention, and Positive Therapy', in C. R. Snyder and Shane J. Lopez (eds.), *Handbook of Positive Psychology* (New York: Oxford University Press), 3–9 at 4, emphasis added.

[109] *Idem* at 3, references omitted.

'(1) Virtues foster a sense of meaning, well-being, and ennoblement in human beings.
(2) Virtues are experienced cognitively, emotionally, and behaviorally.
(3) Virtues foster harmony in relationships.
(4) Virtues are self-reinforcing and positively deviation amplifying.
(5) Virtues serve a buffering function and foster resilience.'[110]

The virtues discourse has also mushroomed within business ethics literature. As in the specialized literature on organizations, attention is paid to the contribution of virtues towards organizational growth, employee satisfaction, meeting stakeholders' values, and organizational learning.[111] In other words, relating virtues to the promotion of *intra*-organization goals, outcomes, values, and their outreach, thus risking the instrumentalization of the virtues in the process.

If we add to this the fact that there are situations in which rule-based normative approaches like morality or law do not work because there is no clear norm, there is a genuine normative conflict, calculation of expected costs and benefits is too messy, or responsibility is diluted within the organizational structure or impossible to establish,[112] then one sees better the potential of focusing on *prevention*; that is, of trying to instil a specific moral behaviour as good because contributing to moral and social organizational flourishing irrespective of sanctioning possibilities or clear-cut rules. This is the situation dealt with by René Urueña in Chapter 5 of this book. He shows that, due to technical limits and rooted social inequalities and discrimination, big data, and algorithmic governance require an *ex ante* regulatory approach subjecting the authors and users of algorithms to a code of virtues generated from within their community.

Virtues have also been associated with the distinctive problem of leadership. In an influential definition, organizational leadership is conceptualized as 'the ability of an individual to influence, motivate, and enable others to contribute toward the effectiveness and success of the organization . . .'[113] whereas a leader

---

[110] Quoted *in* Manz, Charles C., et al. (2008), 'The Virtuous Organization: An Introduction', in Charles C. Manz, et al. (eds.), *The Virtuous Organization: Insights from Some of the World's Leading Management Thinkers* (London: World Scientific Publishing Company), 1–16 at 3.

[111] Though the literature is clear on the lack of empirical research linking virtuousness to positive organizational performance. See for instance Cameron, Kim (2003), 'Organizational Virtuousness and Performance', in Kim S. Cameron, Jane E. Dutton, and Robert Quinn (eds.), *Positive Organizational Scholarship* (San Francisco: Berrett-Koehler), 48–65.

[112] This is the so-called 'many hands' problem. See Thompson, Dennis (1980), 'The Moral Responsibility of Public Officials: The Problem of Many Hands', *American Political Science Review*, 74, 905–16.

[113] House, R. J., et al. (1999), 'Cultural Influences on Leadership and Organizations: Project Globe', in M. J. Gesner and V. Arnold (eds.), *Advances in Global Leadership* (Stamford: JAI

Ethical Leadership, Virtues, and Narrative in International Organizations 33

in general appears as a 'group member whose influence on group attitudes, performance, or decision making greatly exceeds that of the average member of the group'.[114] In turn *virtuous leadership* is defined as

> *distinguishing right from wrong in one's leadership role*, taking steps to ensure justice and honesty, influencing and enabling others to pursue righteous and moral goals for themselves and their organizations and helping others to connect to a higher purpose.[115]

Consequently, 'How to select virtuous leaders?' and 'How to make sure they acted well?' became a paramount concern. Virtuous leadership is distinguished from (i) charismatic leadership since, as history teaches us, charismatic leaders may pursue horrific values;[116] and, (ii) visionary leadership which may tend to downgrade or misread environmental factors, constituencies' demands, and organizational interests in favour of the leader's personal vision.[117] In other words, the literature draws attention to the fact that, whereas we need some of the contempt for tradition and rules in leaders – to generate radical creative change – of the old Weberian 'charismatic authority',[118] we cannot let charismatic agents indulge freely in their own unruliness and exceptionality. The same train of thought led Weber, in later writings, to review his position attempting to strike a balance between released power (and passion) and carelessness.

> ... it is immensely moving when a *mature* man – no matter whether old or young in years – is aware of a responsibility for the consequences of his conduct and really feels such responsibility with heart and soul. He then acts by following an ethic of responsibility and somewhere he reaches the

---

Press), 171–233. I quote the document available at https://pdfs.semanticscholar.org/2609/cc a203b2e9ef8078d6fcb6e4dfdb78b4ee6e.pdf at 13.

[114] *In idem* at 13.

[115] Pearce, Craig L., Waldman, David A. and Csikszentmihalyi, Mihaly (2008), 'Virtuous Leadership: A Theoretical Model and Research Agenda', in Charles C. Manz, et al. (eds.), *The Virtuous Organization: Insights from Some of the World's Leading Management Thinkers* (London: World Scientific Publishing Company), 211–30 at 214, emphasis added.

[116] In leadership studies this led to the distinction between personalized and socialized charismatic leaders. See House, Robert J. and Howell, Jane M. (1992), 'Personality and Charismatic Leadership', *The Leadership Quarterly*, 3 (2), 81–108. Other accounts follow James MacGregor Burns' seminal work that reserves the concept 'transformational leadership' to joint action towards morally enlightened goals. For an explanation and critique of this usage, see Keohane, Nannerl O. (2010), *Thinking About Leadership* (Princeton; Oxford: Princeton University Press) at 41ff.

[117] Conger, Jay A. (1990), 'The Dark Side of Leadership', *Organizational Dynamics*, 19 (2), 44–55.

[118] For the impact of Weber's concept on organizational scholarship, see Conger, Jay A. (1993), 'Max Weber's Conceptualization of Charismatic Authority: Its Influence on Organizational Research', *Leadership Quarterly*, 4 (3/4), 277–88.

point where he says: 'Here I stand; I can do no other.' That is something genuinely human and moving. *And everyone of us who is not spiritually dead must realize the possibility of finding himself at some time in that position*. In so far as this is true, an ethic of ultimate ends and an ethic of responsibility are not absolute contrasts but rather supplements, which only in unison constitute a genuine man – a man who *can* have the 'calling for politics'.[119]

From the point of view of the pragmatic virtue ethics research programme I have built in this chapter, it should seem natural that appropriate ethical leadership in IOs cannot simply be theorized. Therefore, different contexts may require different types of leaders and leadership. This is a conclusion reached by Schechter, after studying the leadership style of past international leaders: Robert McNamara, A. W. Clausen, Amadou-Mahtar M'Bow and Frank Bradford Morse. He determined that periods of generous budgets and ideological hegemony demanded an activist leader, whereas periods of budget cuts and bipolarity asked for pragmatic leadership.[120] While this is a useful conclusion to bear in mind, we should always be attentive to the concrete fit between ethical leadership and context so as to avoid deducing pre-formed theoretical conclusions.

Another reason why leadership ought to be considered, according to these literatures, has to do with its impact on moral development and moral learning inside organizations. Virtuous leaders are often seen as exemplars to follow and imitate because we consider they are worthy of admiration (because embodying goodness), a thread of analysis that has gained traction lately even though it belongs to a long tradition of thought.[121] Virtuous leaders, exemplars or not, should then pay attention to communicating clearly their leadership values and how these infuse the procedures, practices, and mission of the organization.[122] In Chapter 4 of the book, Amalia Amaya illustrates the manifold roles of virtuous leadership in IOs, highlighting, however, a distinctive effect: exemplary leaders can claim authority and through the latter increase the legitimacy claim of IOs. Thus, it is only natural that Amaya

---

[119] Weber, Max (2013), 'Politics as Vocation', in H. H. Gerth and C. Wright Mills (eds.), *From Max Weber: Essays in Sociology* (New York: Routledge), 77–128 at 127, emphasis added.

[120] Schechter, Michael G. (1987), 'Leadership in International Organizations: Systemic, Organizational and Personality Factors', *Review of International Studies*, 13 (3), 197–220.

[121] See Zagzebski, Linda (2017), *Exemplarist Moral Theory* (New York: Oxford University Press), Wolf, Susan (1982), 'Moral Saints', *The Journal of Philosophy*, 79 (8), 419–39, and Goldman, Alvin I. (1993), 'Ethics and Cognitive Science', *Ethics*, 103 (2), 337–60 at 341.

[122] For a rare, even if limited, empirical survey of leadership models in IOs confirming this line of argument, see Thorn, I. Marlene (2012), 'Leadership in International Organizations: Global Leadership Competencies', *The Psychologist-Manager Journal*, 15 (3), 158–63.

Ethical Leadership, Virtues, and Narrative in International Organizations 35

also explores the importance of a moral, virtues-oriented, leadership education.[123]

Nevertheless, caution should be prescribed when pondering exemplars and exemplarity.[124] A distinction drawn by Max Scheler between leaders and exemplars shows why. For Scheler, leaders operate sociologically, here and now, they accept to lead, and they wish to shape the will of those they guide establishing outcomes and requesting actions. By the same token, followers are also fully aware of the fact that they are being guided. Conversely, exemplars or models work outside history and are not in a reciprocal relationship vis-à-vis their followers. As a matter of fact, in the same way they do not actively or deliberately lead, they do not have to know either that they are followed. In exemplarity, followers mimic out of love and devotion to a value.[125]

From this angle, it is easier to understand critiques to leadership portraying it as the ideological cover-up, 'a social hoax', for a return to atavistic modes of existence.

> ... a social myth symbolically represents a regressive wish to return to the symbiotic environment of the womb: to be absolved of consciousness, mindfulness, and responsibility for initiating responses to our environment to attain what we need and want.[126]

Because leadership postulates that causes of organizational behaviour and performance are explained properly by the enlightened and *magical* action of leaders, followers can renounce to face their own anxieties and fears of trying to exist and create actively in the context of uncertain complex societies. In short, leadership, and especially exemplarity defined as above, would justify and create *alienated passive* members of the organization. The consequences are twofold. First, this would lead to a discourse that does not promote fulfilled lives within organizations. Second, it would basically create an ethics of mimesis that obviously goes against the whole idea of applying practical wisdom and exercising judgment along all organizational levels. While this line of criticism may be less powerful in environments, like IOs, formed by

---

[123] After all, it seems that Darwin's hypothesis that virtuous habits would come to be fixed by inheritance did not materialize. See Darwin, Charles (1981), *The Descent of Man, and Selection in Relation to Sex* (New Jersey: Princeton University Press) at 104.

[124] I thank Adriana Alfaro for an eye-opening discussion in this regard.

[125] Scheler, Max (2018), *Modelos y Líderes*, trans. Sergio Sánchez-Migallón and Miguel Martí Sánchez (Salamanca: Ediciones Sígueme).

[126] Gemmill, Gary and Oakley, Judith (1992), 'Leadership: An Alienating Social Myth?', *Human Relations*, 45 (1), 113–29 at 8 in the electronic version consulted.

highly qualified and ambitious staffs, it is worth remembering that the promotion of ethical leadership should avoid the effects identified earlier.

Partially for different reasons to those invoked by the 'leadership as alienation' critique, mainstream international relations and political science also espouse deep scepticism against leadership accounts in IOs. These have been labelled as a cover-up for failed actions or self-justifying and self-praising exercises. Furthermore, since IOs are believed to be largely dominated by the environmental, geopolitical, and normative circumstances and the tight control exercised by Member States, through funding and selection rules, over leaders and organizations, individual leadership is often seen as irrelevant. Leaders are also portrayed as captives of internal constraints imposed by their mandates and staffs. Finally, leadership narratives are deemed to be unable to answer the counterfactual question of what would have happened under a different leadership.[127]

There is an interesting aspect to these criticisms. While widespread, the truth of the matter is that some individual leaders and staffs of IOs remained in history, deemed to have performed great feats, whereas others did not. For example, former United Nations Secretary-General Javier Perez de Cuellar is held by many international relations commentators as having failed to identify and capitalize on the opportunities open to the organization in a post-Cold War world. By the same token, irrespective of the methodological approaches and normative stances espoused, the literature is unanimous in the bashing of Hiroshi Nakajima's leadership style and outcomes while heading the World Health Organization. Conversely, Halfdan Mahler's period at the same organization is recalled with nostalgia and glory.

A possible explanation for such a contradiction may have to do with the criteria used to assess scholarship and other phenomena. If we are looking for true, systemic, and universal answers we cannot admit the relevance of our intuitions and pervasive assessments of leadership in IOs. Likewise, if we consider leadership from the standpoint of functional effectiveness and outcomes achieved, then we will not be able to appreciate other features of human experience that many find morally relevant. Even if the performance of institutions could be reproduced irrespective of the concrete leaders in place, this would not deny per se that it is morally important to many of us to see that outcomes are achieved virtuously, that is, displaying traits that we find

---

[127] For a summary of these critiques, see Hall, Nina and Woods, Ngaire (2018), 'Theorizing the Role of Executive Heads in International Organizations', *European Journal of International Relations*, 24 (4), 865–86 at 866.

admirable, or associated with individuals we appreciate and respect. This may help us to make sense of and accept orientations and decisions that we may disagree with, turning the narrative into an *acceptable* one. Again, the point is that the virtues sensitize us to the moral meaning of narratives, adding depth and complexity to the ways in which we make sense of the responsibility we all share taking care of the world. To put it differently, we are talking about *another kind of good* in moral life that is highlighted by virtue ethics, not just outcomes.

With the caveats above, if moral example, descriptively and normatively, can impact and guide human behaviour, we would be better off then promoting ethically robust leaders since their moral features and behaviours would trickle down to the whole organization, downgrading the need for rules and sanctions as setting the incentives for moral behaviour.

We have documented a disciplinary convergence towards the virtues and mapped the numerous themes and threads as well as the potential and opportunities for fresh thinking this turn embodies. However, the chapters of the book do not simply endorse virtues as a panacea and examine the pitfalls in which one is prone to fall. A crucial aspect in this regard is the idea that the virtues are not being proposed here by most authors in isolation, simply replacing the mainstream ethical frameworks. Rather, a recurring thread throughout the volume is the concern to make the virtues bear on existing approaches, intuitions, and frameworks.

1.8 DOING ETHICS IN POSTMODERN TIMES

Before moving on to describe in greater detail each chapter of the book, however, we need to consider some general difficulties associated with the deployment of the virtues. Whereas the multi-method approach highlighted the diversity of challenges ahead, it did not magically dissolve some basic issues that have been around virtue ethics since its revival. One fundamental question with giving voice to the virtues and its narrative-based structure relates to the worth and the comparability of the stories we build and tell.

Intuitively, it seems to be the case that it is one thing to accept the fallibilistic nature of our judgments and knowledge and another one to give in fully to standards of adequacy and correctness. The risk is that it will be the level of discursive power one has the key determinant in making one narrative sounder than the others. Something similar applies in contemporary art, when worldwide famous curators determine the criteria for what counts as *real* art without, however, explaining how and why such criteria and judgments are

38   *Guilherme Vasconcelos Vilaça*

warranted and should be seen as decisive.[128] Excellence, moral or artistic, seems to lie largely in the eye of the beholder as a native Mexican, in Bartolomé de las Casas' telling, reminds us:

> ... y que si quería creer aquello que le decía, que iría al cielo, donde había gloria y eterno descanso, y si no, que había de ir al infierno a padecer perpetuos tormentos y penas. Él, pensando un poco, preguntó al religioso si iban cristianos al cielo. El religioso le respondió que sí, pero que iban los que eran buenos. Dijo luego el cacique, sin más pensar, que no quería él ir allá, sino al infierno, por no estar donde estuviesen y por no ver tan cruel gente.[129]

And this should be taken seriously since *reading* narrative always entails the exercise of judgment given that neither context nor grammar provides unequivocal answers as de Man's take on the limits of using 'language about language' establishes.[130] His is a thesis on the *impossibility* of arriving at a single answer and thus of ending the analysis or reflection armed with a stable, definitive answer that puts to rest our doubts and immunizes us against having to reopen our beliefs and views. The resulting impossibility, especially after postmodernism, can trigger helplessness and anxiety over the worth of the whole enterprise of scrutinizing the ethical life of IOs and their people.

> There is a sense of 'hyper-reality' about accountability – a nagging conviction that the discourses of accountability are partially about civic virtue and learning, but that they also represent an elaborate façade, a series of images that obscure rather than enlighten. At times, the ironies of postmodernism seem to be unrelenting. The more the very 'presence' of accountability, the greater is the uncertainty, doubt, and skepticism over its capacity to remedy or ameliorate ... Postmodernism is grounded by suspicion. It is permeated by wariness towards modernism, with its ontological fixities, epistemological confidence, and conceptual certainties.[131]

---

[128] Bonami, Francesco (2017), *L'Arte Nel Cesso: Da Duchamp a Cattelan, Ascesa e Declino dell'Arte Contemporanea* (Milano: Mondadori).

[129] Casas, Fray Bartolomé de las (2011), *Brevísima Relación de la Destruición de las Indias* (Medellín: Editorial Universidad de Antioquia) at 37.

[130] Man, Paul de (2002), *The Resistance to Theory* (Minneapolis; London: University of Minnesota Press) at 15.

[131] Weisband, Edward (2007), 'Conclusion: Prolegomena to a Postmodern Public Ethics: Images of Accountability in Global Frames', in Edward Weisband and Alnoor Ebrahim (eds.), *Global Accountabilities: Participation, Pluralism, and Public Ethics* (Cambridge; New York: Cambridge University Press), 307–39 at 335. See also Lyotard, Jean François (1984), *The Postmodern Condition: A Report on Knowledge*, trans. Geoff Bennington and Brian Massumi (Manchester: Manchester University Press) at 83–84.

Ethical Leadership, Virtues, and Narrative in International Organizations 39

What can be said against such a sombre outlook? I believe part of the postmodern anxiety is self-inflicted and stems from a refusal to explore what lies beyond the abyss of the ethical, the sublimity of action, knowing the world escapes our control, in any tangible and concerted way.[132] The proviso of this book is that these are questions that cannot be addressed abstractly without considering the particulars of a given situation, the concrete legal ideas and materials, and the doings of alternative ethical frameworks. What is more, virtues have to be historicized (as does the human *telos*) and both their display and the results of their application require going deep into factual and normative scenarios. Otherwise, the deployment of virtue ethics will not overcome the 'application' and the 'essentialist' problems identified above plaguing deontological and consequentialist ethical theories. Then we are back to our opening question: How do different ethical narratives measure up? How do we adjudicate between different narratives? How can we avoid getting stuck in the following loop: 'You tell your story, I tell mine. So what?"[133]

This is the challenge taken by Guilherme Vasconcelos Vilaça in Chapter 10. Through a detailed comparison of the characters and actions of select former heads of the World Health Organization – Brock Chisholm, Hiroshi Nakajima, Marcolino Candau and Margaret Chang – the author shows how difficult it is to *evaluate* ethical leadership and judgment across narratives and characters due to the changing contexts in which virtues are applied as well as to the latter's cultural meaning and the need for considering alternative ethical frameworks. Yet, since there is no way out from narrating, the proposed solution is to overcome the ideal nature of most ethical work and produce the thickest descriptions possible of the salient features of the scenario under discussion.

Historicizing virtues amounts to giving flesh to Anscombe's challenge,[134] constructing, with every moral narrative, concrete understandings of virtues, and certain conceptions of human flourishing based on the agents, facts, and values of the situation at stake.[135] These are constructed in the sense that

---

[132] For a full-fledged argument, see Vilaça, Guilherme Vasconcelos (2020), 'Dominus Mundi: Political Sublime and the World Order', *Jurisprudence: An International Journal of Legal and Political Thought*, 11 (3), 493–501.

[133] Nelson, Hilde Lindemann (2004), 'Context: Backward, Sideways, And Forward', in Rita Charon and Martha Montello (eds.), *Stories Matter: The Role of Narrative in Medical Ethics* (New York; London: Routledge), 39–47 at 45.

[134] Anscombe, G. E. M. (1958), 'Modern Moral Philosophy', *Philosophy*, 33 (124), 1–19 at 15.

[135] Given the historicization of knowledge, anyone wishing to invoke Aristotle or Confucius as sources of moral authority is in trouble since such authority ought to be historicized too and thus loses its special power. This point is best made in Margolis, Joseph (1996), *Life without Principles: Reconciling Theory and Practice* (Cambridge; Oxford: Blackwell Publishers).

cannot be conceived abstractly and then imposed *qua* finished products onto the situation. Their power depends not on certainty but on their *persuasiveness*, and the latter is crucially dependent on the concrete construction of the ethical narrative we operate and the different rules of the art concerning the *savoirs* and languages employed.

While the postmodern challenge may leave us at first bewildered, in truth, as Perelman and Olbrechts-Tyteca had made evident, the rejection of a formalistic and logical model of reasoning generated the problem of *argumentation* and thus of persuasiveness. As they put it, there is no role for argumentation (and the *person* making arguments) when reasoning aims at certainty, validity, and logical truth. But accepting the need for argumentation does not mean falling in the hands of sophistry given the reservoir of traditional 'rational' argumentative techniques and ways of arranging discourse, which the authors examine.[136]

The virtues discourse hones moral imagination and sensibility, making us aware that moral responsibility is a never-ending task that we can ignore but not discard. For Booth, a leading proponent of the encounter between ethical criticism and literature, the purchase, despite predictable insuperable disagreement, is this:

> ... when undertaken seriously neither side is likely to feel fully victorious. Both sides will have learned something overlooked, either about the work itself or about the world of ethical values in which we all live. And both sides, whether in reading the work or in discussing it, are *undergoing the ethical growth* that serious encounters with such conflict can produce.[137]

The bottom line is perhaps the following. On the one hand, virtue ethics may serve as a language to draw a different picture of the moral situation, revealing and highlighting salient features that cannot be seen with other ethical conceptualizations. Its power would lie in its descriptive capacities and the appeal of the narrative so built. But we would always have to provide a contextual explanation as to why choosing this and not another (or in addition to other) ethical approach. On the other hand, we could use it to ground an emotional approach to the right action based on moral cultivation and its resonance on individual agents.

Ultimately, we are reminded that what really is unavailable to those wishing to exercise moral agency and responsibility is an easy way to discharge responsibility when engaging in ethical analysis, since we can rely neither on logic

---

[136] Perelman, Chaïm and Olbrechts-Tyteca, Lucie (2018), *Tratado de la Argumentación: La Nueva Retórica*, trans. Julia Sevilla Muñoz (4th ed.; Barcelona: GREDOS).

[137] Booth, Wayne C. (1998), 'Why Ethical Criticism Can Never Be Simple', *Style*, 32 (2), 351–64 at 361, emphasis added.

Ethical Leadership, Virtues, and Narrative in International Organizations   41

and abstraction nor on ungrounded claims. By the same token, emphasizing praxis and judgment as fundamentally creative activities only highlights the naked and painful position in which one finds oneself after discovering that following the rules of reasoning and arguing does not bring certainty and therefore closure. Instead, '[w]e savor it; we endure it; we suffer it'.[138]

1.9 CHAPTERS BREAKDOWN

The book is divided into three parts. Part I lays down preliminary conceptual work necessary to elucidate the way in which virtues and an ethics of individual responsibility can and do fare in highly complex organizational settings such as IOs. Parts II and III offer a collection of narratives showing the potential of the virtues to illuminate ethical leadership in a number of pressing issues under the purview of IOs. These cases also highlight the potential of virtues to sharpen our moral imagination in devising new or complementary responses to complex moral scenarios. Specifically, the chapters forming Part II articulate the regulatory, constitutive, and descriptive power of the virtues in sports, data, and human rights governance settings. Part III chapters instead focus on the explanation, judgment, and assessment of individual ethical leadership narratives regarding disparate events and actions, and covering the fields of migration, international arbitration, and global health.

Friedrich Kratochwil's chapter sets the scene by inquiring on the kind of concept of action needed to do justice to the complex task of conceiving acting well within organizations. He investigates the conceptual impoverishment of *'practical* choice' by noting how the latter was reduced to that of *'rational* choice'. The former involves judgment, choice of ends and is always historically contextualized; the latter is essentially theoretical, teleologically determined by the defined ideals, and concerned with being valid universally. In his view, in the 'rational choice' model there is no choice to be made since there is no room for discretion or judgment. Consequently, there is no room for individual responsibility either. Institutional and organizational settings define the parameters of agency often through roles that allow and disallow specific conducts. Kratochwil shows, however, that in such contexts there is no general view of responsibility from which one can derive what agents ought to

---

[138] Manderson, Desmond (2010), 'Judgment in Law and the Humanities', in Austin Sarat, Matthew Anderson and Cathrine O. Frank (eds.), *Law and the Humanities: An Introduction* (New York: Cambridge University Press), 496–516 at 507.

do. This is because social ordering is a never-ending creative *enacting* activity based on individual and collective political choices, social exchanges, and permanent reciprocal learning. It is not a prefabricated system we know in advance by fictionalizing 'situations' and believing in right, expertise-based, solutions.

It is worth treading again this conceptual path (taking the reader from the Book of Genesis to 'engineering and scientific management') because it underlies much of the discourse about action in the theory and practice of international affairs. Particularly important, is Kratochwil's list of differences between acting as making practical choices and acting as producing something and his ultimate rejection of the possibility of a theory of practice. On the other hand, even if Kratochwil wants to clear the path for a richer account of action linked to practical wisdom and recognizes that virtue ethics does tick the box with regard to some of the forgotten features of such a conception – choice of ends and commitments towards them – he defers a definitive judgment as to its desirability and superiority in accounting for action. Kratochwil's contribution removes the conceptual chains around a theory of action that forecloses the possibility to appreciate that virtue ethics may offer an adequate approach to the problem of how to act.

Sanne Taekema's contribution articulates a position according to which organizations should pursue the rule of law understood as an ideal, that is, the reduction of arbitrariness in the use of power. In her construction, virtuous and committed leadership to the ideal is key to the creation and maintenance of an organizational culture of legality that goes beyond nominalism and trickles down to the practices and commitments of all its members. Both moves are important for the purpose of enriching our conception of action within organizations (the space opened by Kratochwil) and introducing the virtues vocabulary concerning ethical leadership.

The shift operated by Taekema's view of the rule of law as a moral ideal has three important outcomes. First, it asserts that rules presuppose *individuals* to use and apply them and thus the rule of law is always rule of law by someone. Second, as an ideal concerned with arbitrariness in the exercise of power, the rule of law desacralizes law by allowing us to choose which normative techniques best pursue such *telos*. But third, since Taekema posits that the rule of law ideal ought to infuse organizational cultures, it cannot remain a theoretical abstraction. It must effectively shape and inform the organizational culture. All three passages recognize that law is not enough and may not be the best engine of organizational and normative change since the latter require and happen within much broader *human* practices and exchanges. It is leadership's responsibility to produce these changes within organizations.

But not any leadership will do, given that, for values to be successfully internalized within an organization (and not just as superficial commitments), leaders need to uphold and commit to them by example throughout time in order to shape the attitudes and practices of the remaining members. This aligns well with virtue ethics because the latter emphasises the acquisition of stable traits or dispositions that aim at human and organizational flourishing. In order to avoid a ritualistic pursuit of ideals, Taekema suggests that it is essential for leaders to steer organizations to become other-regarding, both hearing those affected by their decisions and being responsive to their claims; once again this is a process that requires the institutionalization of *commitments* over time.

In her chapter, **Amalia Amaya** develops a complex account of an exemplarist virtue approach to ethical leadership in IOs. Highlighting the advantages of virtue ethical accounts over competing ethical frameworks, Amaya recovers the old link between leadership and ethics proposing that leadership virtues are those dispositions that help IOs to fulfil their mission *properly*, that is, a reminder that the ends of the leadership role need not be judged by the ends of the organization. According to virtue ethics, good leaders should display moral, intellectual, and communicational virtues. The latter two sets are particularly important since intellectual virtues include practical wisdom which is necessary for all virtues and to make theoretical understanding bear on concrete cases, whereas communication virtues ensure that leaders can create robust and united organizations that are able to effectively engage their external constituencies and partners.

According to Amaya's account, virtuous leaders play a key role in IOs. Given their virtuous characters, they are exemplary, triggering admiration and the desire to emulate them in international civil servants, creating an important 'cascading effect', triggering moral learning within IOs. Importantly, she clarifies both that exemplars need not be fully virtuous and that negative exemplars can also be useful for moral organizational learning – a point often forgotten. Exemplary leaders fulfil other functions regarding ethical leadership in IOs, for example, providing normative ideals against which to assess characters and conducts or helping the task of theorizing ethical leadership by providing information about conceptual choices and questions to be asked from such a theory. Amaya also argues that virtuous leadership advances discussion on international authority. This is because, in her account, exemplary leaders command legitimate authority, and the latter improve the legitimacy of IOs. These arguments rely on re-establishing the connection between virtue, authority, and leadership, a link that had been lost with a purely expertise-based conception of authority. Altogether, she believes that there are very solid reasons to orient education and institutions towards the fostering of virtuous leadership in IOs, providing a number of ways in which this could be achieved.

René Urueña's chapter proposes that virtue ethics can be a powerful tool to add to existing approaches to curb the new ways in which power can be exercised after the big data and computing capacity revolutions. In fact, these are now becoming widely deployed and relied upon by IOs and NGOs in fields ranging from trade and finance to aid relief and sustainable development. He argues that the adopted accountability mechanisms, to wit human rights discourses and transparency discourses, are both *ex-post* and cannot penetrate the making of algorithmic governance. Human rights cannot easily bind soft legal normativity issued by non-state actors atomizing accountability. The transparency movement cannot eliminate inequalities that are already part of the world since 'deep learning' operates on top of existing data and all its existing inequalities without the need for an intentionally human-designed discriminatory algorithm.

Both processes are necessary for Urueña but incomplete, and incapable of expanding effective accountability over algorithm governance. Thus, he suggests a change of narrative: an *ex-ante 'from within' regulatory approach* based on the idea that virtues should be exercised by developers and users of algorithms. This requires rejecting the view that algorithms are autonomous and focusing instead on the human beings behind them to capture and tackle existing human-made unequal social power relations. Virtue ethics appears as congenial because it focuses on *human* beings (neither norms nor autonomous decision-making systems), their characters, and prudential action. The latter should be determined, according to Urueña, based on what the community of developers and users of algorithms retains as virtuous or 'good-sense ethics'. Deontologism meets the virtues since the latter sees norms as necessarily deployed by someone (as stressed by Taekema). Corollaries of this approach would strengthen human 'algorithm accountability': (i) professional ethics binding actors to values deemed important (e.g. non-discrimination or privacy); (ii) organizational compliance-based ethics that can provide incentives that lead to the emergence of virtuous performance of organizational tasks by its members; and, (iii) the imposition of fiduciary obligations onto online providers, given their de facto control over our data and privileged knowledge of their value, risks, and uses.

In his contribution, **Lorenzo Casini** discusses the role of ethics in regulating an autonomous global legal order such as the sports world. Notwithstanding the latter's private and non-governmental nature, Casini shows how sport is at the core necessarily ethical. This is because players have to accept beforehand the different rules of the games and ought to

Ethical Leadership, Virtues, and Narrative in International Organizations 45

observe them, preserving the level playing field they impose. In other words, it is the ethics underlying competitions that justifies rules to ensure *fairness* and a virtuous engagement, that is, prohibition or regulation of doping or sports technology. A constitutional function of ethics in sports institutions and realities can be discerned in the Olympic Charter stressing, in a way germane to virtue ethics, that Olympism is a philosophy of life, linking sport to the flourishing of mankind as well as to other noble ideals, necessary for human and social blooming, such as gender equality or social and environmental justice to name a few. Casini also lists the regulative function fulfilled by ethics in sports values and legislation infusing institutional procedures within, for example, the International Olympic Committee or FIFA through the workings of their ethics commissions. In this context, ethics protects first and foremost integrity in sport and its mammoth multi-level networked institutional structure by promoting the impartial selection of good leaders and host countries for major events, fighting the fixing of results in sports competitions, ensuring athletes' integrity and interests in decision-making involving wrongdoing by organizations and athletes, and so on. Casini's chapter aptly shows how ethics shapes our conception of sport and its constitutive rules and values, is the source of sports law's legitimacy and accountability, and the driver for change in this complex transnational legal order.

Jane K. Cowan understands the Universal Periodic Review (UPR), dedicated to human rights protection and compliance, as a sign of the United Nations' recent commitment to change and reinvigorated ethical leadership. The UPR appears, in Cowan's words, to aim to create 'virtuous sovereign subjects' engaged in 'a [public] ritual of state responsibilisation in relation to human rights' during the *public review*. It prompts states to act by engaging in a *peer-to-peer* relation with the state under review. The chapter highlights the pragmatic, state-centred nature of the UPR and its relative insulation from human rights experts as well as the fact that states behave differently, more diplomatically, than in other human rights bodies such as the Human Rights Council. But how do states act at the UPR and do they act virtuously?

Based on her anthropological work, she identifies three ways in which countries, likened to individuals with characters and features, can act virtuously within the UPR: 'liberal', 'subaltern' and 'parrhesiastic'. Cowan unmasks the liberal assumption that the liberal mode of virtuous state action is the only ethical one, showing that the other two are equally principled, shattering a necessary link between virtue and liberal values. Cowan's chapter skilfully illustrates how behaviours are deemed virtuous against the specific acts that have to be performed within the UPR mechanisms and the public review. The liberal model emphasizes setting an example through transparency, openness

46   *Guilherme Vasconcelos Vilaça*

to dialogue and active criticism, and responsiveness. Subaltern performance emphasizes solidarity, loyalty, and anticipating effects of criticism towards supporting states. Finally, Cowan documents parrhesiastic performance through the declarations produced by Iceland (reviewing Greece in 2016) that *exceed* the UPR, *naming* what everyone knew: the dramatic effects of the financial and economic crisis in Greece also had to do with creditors and the responsibility for refugees was a shared one. This gesture clearly goes beyond the UPR's *bilateral* focus – the practice of not blaming external parties and involving third countries – which, however, prevents analysis of the deep causes of human rights violations. Ultimately, the invaluable lesson is that the study of virtue in international settings requires factoring in the current power and institutional landscape so we can make sense of what virtue is, for whom, and why.

Jan Klabbers shares his own personal journey regarding what to do when one is puzzled by specific aspects of international judgments and awards. His focus rests with trying to understand (reflexively) how particular decisions can be understood, in this case discussing an arbitral award rather than IO decision-making (although arbitral tribunals are organizations too). He proposes that virtue ethics can offer new explanations when international legal methods and rival ethical theories cannot help us to 'go on'. The chapter revolves around the *Rainbow Warrior* award and Klabbers zooms in on the paradox of having a tribunal going against the treaty applicable to the specific case while producing a decision that, nonetheless, does not feel wrong.

The problem is how to justify it. Deontological ethicists would get stuck in the multiple rules applicable to the case and thus would need to find a master rule, for example, human rights, but one can always find another clashing human right leading to an endless loop. Consequentialism is plagued by problems too, according to Klabbers, since one can never fully define the range of consequences that must be included. Furthermore, can stable legal orders be established on the assumption that their rules can be overthrown whenever the benefits outweigh the costs? Klabbers breaks the circle by resorting to virtue ethics, employing it in a novel way. As he demonstrates, the panellists did not exhibit particular vices (e.g. partiality or rashness). They were judicious. Were they courageous? On the one hand, panellists produced an inventive decision. On the other hand, they seem to have protected the great power involved in the case, that is, France. Furthermore, institutional virtues connected to long-term trust, reputation, and fulfilment of their function hardly apply to fleeting international arbitration tribunals. Instead, Klabbers shows that *prudence* can help explain the decision, that is, *careful consideration* of the situation led the judges to reach this verdict in order to

Ethical Leadership, Virtues, and Narrative in International Organizations 47

pacify relations between France and New Zealand in the long run. Klabbers' contribution is thought-provoking because, while it accepts that prudence cannot tell us in advance what a virtuous decision would amount to, it highlights features of the decision unavailable to a positivist lawyer, a deontologist, or a consequentialist moral theorist.

In her chapter, **Maria Varaki** examines the refugee dilemma pitting the polarised nationalist and populist discourses representing the power of *raison d'état* to exclude against art installations and images, such as the famous one of Alan Kurdi, expressing the full plight of human condition in forced displacement. Varaki explores this dichotomy through states' attitudes and documents concerning the refugee crisis between 2015 and 2018, the years of the New York Declaration and the United Nations Global Compact on Migration (GCM). Despite its soft law nature, the United States, followed by other states including a number of EU Member States, decided not to ratify the GCM.

Varaki deploys the language of virtue ethics to formulate a two-pronged moral critique of this stance. First, the principles encapsulated in the GCM articulate a rich conception of the common good that aims at long-term flourishing and realistically acknowledge a set of important human values from state sovereignty to human rights and gender, giving children special consideration. Second, Angela Merkel's decision in 2015 not to close the German borders to around one million Syrian refugees was an exemplary action embodying practical wisdom, courage, and moral imagination. The strength of the juxtaposition of these two dimensions lies in the contrast between the fact that, while Merkel acted in line with the spirit of the negotiations and principles *collectively* established in the GCM, she was the *only* leader to resolutely act in accordance with them. Ultimately, virtue ethics helps us to distinguish between legislating and acting, showing that phronesis and moral imagination are needed for ethically inspired leaders to deliberate in concrete circumstances according to the common good. In doing so, it provides a vocabulary to transcend the situation and go beyond what is expected and set an example for future behaviour and the future effectiveness of normative guidelines such as the GCM.

Guilherme Vasconcelos Vilaça also deals with actual scenarios but scrutinizes the *evaluative*, not explanatory, potential of virtue ethics. He readily accepts that the vocabulary of virtues is often used and fulfils a function that was largely forgotten in social and political life. Yet, Vilaça questions the level of abstraction that underlies existing writings on virtue ethics, as if, magically, authors and readers always knew what it is to be virtuous or to act virtuously. Conversely, for the author, the question virtue ethicists should be addressing is 'What makes a given ethical narrative a good one?' and 'How can we know and judge a leader to be virtuous or to act virtuously?'

In order to do that, he argues, we need to engage with detailed biographical accounts, the choices of leaders, and the contexts in which they were made, and he examines the lives and actions of former leaders of the World Health Organization for that effect. But doing this exposes the frailties of a virtue ethics account of life since one comes quickly to the conclusion that it is hard to make evaluative judgments in complex situations. In fact, all too often the judgment we cast and the opinions we have about past leaders are made *with hindsight* and not based on a genuine analysis of characters, decisions, and contexts at that historical time. Furthermore, while we appreciate character features in leaders we deem exemplary, these cannot ensure per se that their decisions are morally good. As the chapter notes, while, for instance, Brock Chisholm's internationalism was key to the entrenchment of the World Health Organization, the same internationalist spirit has led to the expansion of Western epistemology and control over other nations. As in Klabbers' chapter, a role for the virtues' capacity to reveal ethically relevant aspects of situations and the performance of leaders is acknowledged. However, it is argued that proponents of virtue ethics must offer thicker descriptions of leadership and need to explain how the exercise of virtues within roles can be equated to skills' acquisition when excelling in sports or craftsmanship.

PART I

CONCEPTS

2

Authority, Law, and Knowledge

Some Critical Remarks on 'Theories' of Practice and the Paradoxes of 'Virtue' Ethics

Friedrich Kratochwil

2.1 INTRODUCTION

What do we owe to others when interacting with them and what should we know when asking this question? Those seemingly straightforward queries get quickly more complicated when we realize that many of our actions take place not only in institutional contexts – such as promising or contracting – but also in organizations when we are vested with 'authority'. In both cases special responsibilities are created, but in the latter case they can no longer be ascribed to us as 'persons' when we act as 'managers' of an organization, or as magistrates, holding public office.

This change from acting within an institution to one of making decisions for an organization has been analysed in different disciplines of social science, but the link to the analysis of practical choice in philosophy has been all but lost. The dominant 'rational action' model in which actors focus on strategies for realizing their 'given' ends has dramatically reduced the scope of the earlier approaches to *praxis*, such as Aristotle's 'Ethics', or Hume's conventionalist account.

Three reductions exhibited by the rational choice model will particularly occupy us below. First, in the case of individual choices the selection among *competing ends* is considered exogenous to the choice problematique (unless it can be translated into an end/means problem) since supposedly *de gustibus non est disputandum* – about 'tastes one cannot argue'. As later Bentham put it so nicely, 'if the quantity of pleasure be the same, pushpin is as good as poetry' as an 'end' since it is the amount of satisfaction to the chooser that counts. To that extent Mill's later distinction of higher and lower 'ends' attempted to correct this simplification, but did so at the price of incoherence of the 'theory' of choice.

Second, since acting in organizations abounds with unintended consequences, establishing priorities of competing 'ends' requires some form of ordering guided by some criteria derived from a 'model'. This could be a static 'system', or a 'product' – in which case either the logic of part/whole distinction established the fit, or – in a more dynamic version – the specified steps of the process derived from the logic of producing an object. In that case the steps had not only to fit 'functionally' but also to occur at a specific time.

Third, since social systems are hardly 'stable' or self-equilibrating, but entail transformative changes 'the purposes' of the system as a whole, which is not physically given but has to be 'reproduced' by the actions of the agents, cannot be as clearly specified aside from giving some bare-bone criteria.[1] Consequently, such a categorization is pretty loose and does not tell us what specific goals we have to prioritize at which moment, or why we should still maintain this existing system or 'exit' and create a new system with different ordering priorities.

Raising the latter type of questions explodes the model based on 'production' and also 'functionalist' criteria since in the case of transformative change the non-return to a previously stable equilibrium has to be explained. For that purpose, a frame becomes necessary to allow us to understand transformative change and the different order. This frame was in modernity supplied by 'history' which served as the universal horizon that united all particular 'stories' about the 'houses' of nobility, states, individual great deeds or events, familiar from traditional modes of reflection on the past. The distinction between traditional 'histories' – which had always been partial – and 'history' tout court used in the collective singular is striking. It construed 'mankind' as its subject,[2] as exemplified by Kant's construction[3] as the historical individual, whose march through time can now be represented as an 'encompassing development'. Despite its misleading nomenclature, this construct is not the result of a critical historiographical project. Instead, it is a thinly veiled secularization of the New Testamentarian account of the 'end of history' (telos) brought about by the 'cunning of nature' (List der Natur). That this 'end' is reached not by divine intervention and the dies irae of the final judgment is perhaps less important than the realization that its linearity allows us to assess actions – individual, collective, and organizational ones – as 'progressive' or as 'reactionary' episodes in the course of events.

---

[1] Hume as well as Bull point out that all social systems have to curtail the resort to force among the actors, establish the presumption that promises are kept and define rules for the acquisition and transfer of titles. See Hedley Bull, *The Anarchical Society* 3rd ed. (New York: Palgrave, 2002): Part I.

[2] See the seminal article by Reinhart Koselleck, 'Historia Magistra Vitae: The Dissolution of the Topos into the Perspective of a Modernized Historical Process', in Reinhard Koselleck (ed.), *Futures Past: On the Semantics of Historical Times* (Cambridge Mass: MIT Press, 1985): 21–38.

[3] See Immanuel Kant [1784], *Idea for a Universal History with a Cosmopolitan Purpose*, in Hans Reiss (ed.) *Kant: Political Writings* (Cambridge: Cambridge University Press, 1991): 41–53.

Authority, Law, and Knowledge

While I think these traditional ways of thinking about making practical choices have on the whole been a disservice to understanding 'action', a closer examination of their specific generative grammar is necessary. For one, it lets us unearth the semantic field within which the present discussions about the 'turn to practice',[4] about new actors and institutions in domestic, international and global politics,[5] about 'professional'[6] and individual responsibility,[7] about legal universalism and pluralism,[8] and about 'ideal theory' vs. case-based methods of inquiry[9] are carried out in law, the social sciences, and in philosophy.[10] In doing so, I do not want to prejudice the investigation by proposing a new 'theory', as is wont in the social sciences,[11] since that would nicely collapse again the distinction of *being* and *meaning*, by reducing the latter to an issue of 'truth' and subjecting *praxis* to 'theory'. I also do not want to interpret the newer developments of law as a 'cosmopolitan turn'[12] or even presume a *telos* of history, which haunts the discussions in legal[13] and

---

[4] For an excellent overview of the literature and philosophical issues raised by making practices the focus for social analysis, see Joseph Rouse, 'Practice Theory', in Dov M. Gabbay, Paul Thagard, John Woods (eds.) *Handbook of the Philosophy of Science*, Vol 15 (Amsterdam; Boston: Elsevier, 2007), available at http://lchc.ucsd.edu/MCA/Mail/xmcamail.2011_08.dir/p df9AaVC3H3k5.pdf, accessed last 5 February 2019. For the discussion in international relations, see Emanuel Adler and Vincent Pouliot (eds.), *International Practices* (Cambridge: Cambridge University Press, 2011).

[5] For an extensive discussion of these problems, see Friedrich Kratochwil, *The Status of Law in World Society: Meditations on the Role and Rule of Law* (Cambridge: Cambridge University Press, 2014).

[6] See, for example, David Kennedy and his plea for the disenchanted professional who relies less on (questionable) claims to expertise in a given area and more on his skills as mediator in bringing people together. David Kennedy, *A World of Struggle: How Power, Law, and Expertise Shape Global Political Economy* (Princeton: Princeton University Press, 2016).

[7] See, for example, Wouter Werner, Marieke de Hoon, Alexis Galan (eds.), *The Law of International Lawyers* (Cambridge: Cambridge University Press, 2017).

[8] Paul Schiff Berman, *Global Legal Pluralism: A Jurisprudence Beyond Borders* (Cambridge: Cambridge University Press, 2012).

[9] Charles Ragin, Howard Becker (eds.), *What is a Case: Exploring the Foundations of Social Inquiry* (Cambridge: Cambridge University Press, 1992).

[10] Here the application of Rawls's *Theory of Justice* (Cambridge, MA: Harvard University Press, 1971) to international relations and his later work, *The Law of Peoples* (New York: Columbia University Press, 1999). See also Habermas's discussion of communicative action and his later *Between Facts and Norms*, transl. by William Rehg (Cambridge: Polity Press, 1997).

[11] For an excellent, crisp, overview of the discussions about 'theory' and the turn to practices, see Christian Bueger, Frank Gadinger, *International Practice Theory* (New York: Palgrave-Macmillan 2014).

[12] See, for example, David Held, *Cosmopolitanism: Ideals and Realities* (Cambridge: Polity Press, 2010).

[13] For an interesting alternative to the mainstream liberal argument of the 'development' of international law from a 'society' of states to a 'community' encompassing all humanity – thereby nicely inverting the sequence by which social 'progress' has been analysed – see William Twining,

international political theory,[14] as this would be like offering a type of (secular) religion at basement prices.

A second reason justifying such an examination shows – at least indirectly – that, for analysing *the practical problem of creating* order, an *ordo ordinans* conception is more useful since it *emphasizes the activity of ordering*, rather than relying on an ideal order (*ordo ordinatus*), which can be intuited by ascending to some Platonic forms, or which can be derived from incontrovertible assumptions. An *ordo ordinans* conception suggests, instead, that we first have to inquire into the constitutive characteristics of the realm of praxis.

From those two reasons it follows, third, that we have to address the problem of which type of knowledge *praxis* requires, instead of just 'assuming' that all knowledge is of one cloth and that this cloth has to be produced by the loom of 'theory'. Might it not be that the conjunctural element that places practical choices always in *specific situations* requires different skills, such as the power of 'judgment', or the diagnostic of what 'fits' a particular situation, rather than focusing on what is 'always' true, as specified by the theoretical criteria of necessity and universality?[15]

This sketch opens then a space to get at the problem of *discretion* and responsibility by foregrounding both the importance of making choices by selecting *ends* (not only strategies concerning the means for 'given' ends) and the realization that such selections involve then 'commitments' which require an alignment of our will and our emotions in embracing a goal and justifying our appraisals of the options as 'good and bad' (not only as 'true' and 'false'). Finally, such an awareness also counteracts the myopia of a disengaged 'view from nowhere', typical of theoretical constructs, and of the alleged need for 'value freedom' in social analysis, which is based on a fundamental misreading of Weber. Whether such a fuller account of choice[16] points us to the role of *attitudes and virtues* – honed by experience and by example – is a different question which goes beyond the topic of this chapter, and which can remain an open question. For the purposes of this chapter, it is sufficient to accept the insight that learning always presupposes some ways of 'unlearning' and of letting go of some old convictions that are comforting because they are so

---

General Jurisprudence: Understanding Law from a Global Perspective (Cambridge: Cambridge University Press, 2009).

[14] For a useful collection of essays that have structured the debate, see Thomas Pogge, Darrel Moelledorf (eds.), *Global Justice: Seminal Essays* (St. Paul, MN: Paragon, 2008).

[15] Aristotle, *Nicomachean Ethics*, Bk. I, chap. vii (1098a27-b12).

[16] For an extensive discussion of how my concern with *praxis* overlaps but differs from the present discussion in law and the social sciences by drawing on Aristotle, Hume, American pragmatist and ordinary language philosophy, see Friedrich Kratochwil, *Praxis: On Acting and Knowing* (Cambridge: Cambridge University Press, 2018).

Authority, Law, and Knowledge

familiar. So clearing up misconceptions is the first step in realizing our freedom and the responsibility that comes with it. As Hume put it, 'Generally speaking the errors of religion are dangerous, those of philosophy only ridiculous.'[17]

From these initial remarks the steps of the argument are the following. In Section 2.2 I want to examine the vocabulary of individual responsibility as it emerges from institutional action and from decisions in organizations. In the latter case, principal/agent issues, on the one hand, and questions of immunity and liability, on the other, represent the focal points. This raises then the further question of whether the different forms of responsibilities could profit from a general 'theory' of responsibility, which would ground all particular responsibilities. Although I deal with this problem only peripherally, I think such an argument relies on a mistaken understanding of what provides the action-guiding 'pull' in practical reasoning, as this force does not arise from a simple 'subsumption' of a fact pattern under a general law or norm. Rather, for choosing the principle under which a particular situation, or fact pattern 'fits', the first (normative) and the second premise (facts) have to do some work. To that extent, the reasoning process resembles more a hermeneutic circle than a subsumption of facts under the norm expressed in the first (major premise). This realization suggests that practical choices are badly understood if they are pressed into the logical scheme of theoretical reason.

Sections 2.3 and 2.4 take off from these distinctions, exploring their implications for our notions of order and ordering. Section 2.3 is devoted to the exploration of systems and creating order in accordance with the part/whole distinction, or with a plan, taking either 'production', or a *telos* as given and finding the 'necessary steps' through functional analysis, or from the *telos* through a process of backward induction. Section 2.4 pursues the doubts voiced in Section 2.2 concerning the desirability of a general theory of responsibility and of the notion that the practical issue *about ordering can be illuminated by an ideal model of order according to the order ordinatus* conception.

Section 2.5 is devoted to the examination of action if it concerns the making of practical choices rather than orienting itself on *techne* or on prophetic claims about the *telos* of humanity. Basing my discussion mostly on Aristotle, I try to show that there are twelve important differences that characterize practical choices, which make it problematic to press practical choices in a 'theory', in a model of production, or in a scheme of the 'progressive realization' of a *final telos*.

---

[17] David Hume, *A Treatise of Human Nature*, Bk. I, Part 4, sec. 7, ed. by David and Mary Norton (Oxford: Oxford University Press, 2007), at 177.

In Section 2.6, I flesh out some of the implications of these thoughts instead of simply summarizing the argument, or claiming that a solution can be found in a virtue ethics. While I am sympathetic to the argument of incorporating the *hexeis* into an analysis of choice and also giving emotions their due, since practical choices require appraisals in terms of approbations and disapprobations which bring our emotions into play, I want to consider this an open question, which I would like to take up at another time.

2.2 VOCABULARIES OF OBLIGATIONS TOWARDS OTHERS: CONTRACTS, PRINCIPAL–AGENT, LEGAL ENTITIES, HARMS, AND RESPONSIBILITIES

Let me begin with the first question raised above of what we 'owe' to others. Sometimes the answers are easy, such as when we ourselves have specified the obligations, or have agreed to a price in an exchange. But even in the relatively easy case of contractual obligations, difficulties quickly arise when we examine the 'framing' conditions of this institution, such as the capacity to contract, disclosure requirements, fraud, or error, unclear wording, or unforeseen events that might make a decision necessary regarding who has to shoulder the costs or make the contract voidable.

On the other hand, we also have obligations for which we have neither contracted nor interfered with some other's actions. In the first case, those are, for example, obligations *erga omnes* (even if the *omnes* are predominantly those who are members of my community, or those who have the right of sojourn) imposing on me the duty that my liberty as a free agent also implies my acceptance of the freedom of others. Consequently, if someone's 'ox is gored' I have to 'respond'. If I do not do so, by relying on the 'me first' principle, the law will come down on me, as we rely – for good reasons – on self-help, only in 'exceptional' circumstance, presupposing a clear and imminent danger. Fortunately, the obligations *erga omnes* are usually easy to meet since they concern mainly forbearances, while in other cases my *not doing* something is precisely what makes me liable, such as when I fail to provide necessary first aid and/or notify the fire department when a house is on fire, or when my cattle moves in on the crops of a neighbour because I was negligent in putting up or mending a fence.

Furthermore, we can already see additional difficulties when, through the availability of institutions and also of organizations, responsibilities *are assigned to actions* of actors, which do not involve intentional attributions (intent or negligence) to actions, but which are simply ascribed to the position one occupies. Thus, a lawyer acting for his client 'owes' special duties that are

Authority, Law, and Knowledge 57

different from the just 'plain and honest dealing' among private actors. These 'special duties' become even more pronounced when we act in organizational contexts. Here the test for 'responsible' action shifts to the question whether an action is within the discretionary powers with which the actor was 'vested' due to the position s/he holds. Issues of the actor's intentions or motives are then back-grounded – save in 'ultra vires' cases which might not only invalidate the decision but may establish – in cases of manifest abuses of powers – also personal responsibility, such as criminal sanctions for having misused funds. Furthermore, while the distinction between institutional action – such as availing oneself of the institution of promising – and organizational action is also often identified with the private/public distinction, the above example of 'professional duties' and the below discussion of organizational action show things are more complicated. For organizational decision-making I take the 'firm' as my initial paradigm, as it highlights the distinctions between institutional and organizational framings, which the traditional distinction between 'market exchanges' and 'imperative control' obscures.

Let us begin with the 'firm' which emerges from the classical labour contract in which not only an exchange takes place (labour vs. wage) but which issues a new authority relationship: the principal acquires the 'right' to employ the agent's labour power as he sees fit (when acting within the framing conditions of the institution).[18] This gives rise to the 'principal–agent' problematique and to 'self-help measures' on the principal's side – ranging from supervision to setting production goals to incentives – and, on the agent's side, to 'slacking', to work simply 'by the book' (but not caring much about its quality), to collective bargaining, or seeking to exercise 'voice' by being represented on the 'board' of the corporation.

There is, however, a second issue that quickly gains in importance, when the 'principal' can shield himself with the help of 'the law' from liability, such as by incorporating and creating a fictional entity. It serves now as the 'owner', which can transfer authority to management, but also limit claims of customers for redress when defective products are sold to them, or 'torts' are committed. What represents a tort crucially depends on what is recognized by law as such. Thus negative 'externalities' might be a nuisance, such as the loss of peace and quiet for those living in the neighbourhood of a factory, or the fouling of the stream nearby, but neither of them necessarily establishes a cause of action. This strategy becomes naturally still more important when corporations become the main players in the market and try to shield themselves even further by

---

[18] See Friedrich Kratochwil, 'The Limits of Contract', *European Journal of International Law*, 5(4) (1994), 465–91.

58 *Friedrich Kratochwil*

installing 'distributers', who actually deal with customers, so that no 'privity of contract' between the final user of the product and the producer exists.[19]

Of course, these jurisdictional issues are subject to legislative change and the developments of case law, and – not surprisingly – product liability limited certain 'sheltering' practices. In addition, effects on third parties become now – at least indirectly – relevant. In addition, 'new knowledge' showed that, for example, not all externalities are just necessary and that their non-inclusion in the pricing by the producer actually distorts the market. To that extent it delegitimized the argument that negative externalities were necessary for reaping the welfare gains, which are provided by a competitive market, which is, therefore, best left alone.

As the brief discussion shows, important distinctions emerge from the analysis, such as between institutional and organizational action, and – at the margins – from taking notice of unintended effects of actions on third parties. Nevertheless, the principal-agent model is too limited for exploring several issues of 'answerability' (if we take this as a term that accommodates both responsibility and liability). After all, it is 'the law', which – by 'overlooking' certain harms and creating 'immunities' for certain harmful actions – enables and condones the 'systematic' infliction of harm. Thus if I open a pizza place in a neighbourhood in which a competitor had for a long time enjoyed a virtual monopoly, I probably damage seriously the business of the original supplier, especially if he had just embarked on an expansion. But I cannot be blamed for the damage caused to the competitor's interests and have to answer to no one.

Now consider the issue of immunity resulting from the powers granted to an office. A judge who lets a suspected terrorist go, although 'the state' presented substantial evidence that this person is up to no good – given her public statements and her contacts with other 'known terrorists' – does nothing legally wrong when deciding that the evidence was not sufficient, since she is only exercising the authority vested in her. She is 'immune', although her assessment was obviously in error, when a few days later this person and some other known accomplices engineer a bomb-attack. In short, 'the law' does not only *not recognize* certain damages but by distributing rights and granting powers attached to the 'roles' or positions – be it as simple actors, as workers, artisans or tradespeople,[20] professionals, or as officers in a public or private organization – it also prevents the victims from obtaining redress.

---

[19] See Cardozo's opinion in MacPherson v. Buick Motors, 217NY 382, 11N.E. 19590 (1916); L.R.A. 1916F 696.

[20] Thus what the actual responsibility of a plumbing and heating tradesman is in a concrete case will be governed by the norms establishing his status as a 'master' tradesman, certified by the 'guild', by his duties as a teacher, training his apprentices, by some supervening authority of,

Authority, Law, and Knowledge

Things are even more complex when the principals of the organization created are states and usually bestow some form of immunity on their agents. To that extent it is not so surprising that the issue of responsibility of international organizations for the exercise of powers entrusted to them had, until Klabbers' treatise in 2002,[21] not received much scholarly attention, unlike principal–agent issues. This is evident both from the settlement of disputes arising out of employment contracts of the organization with its employees[22] as well as from the disagreement between countries (as principals) and international organizations (agents), charging them with 'politization', or leading even a few times to some 'exits' from international organizations.[23]

These points need not be rehearsed here at length save to call attention to several points that shall occupy us in our discussion of responsibility. Perhaps the most important point here is to correct the common perceptions that the above-shown 'darker side of law' results mainly from *the fragmentation* of responsibility. There is, as usual, something to this 'take' on the problem, as the example of the responsibility of the tradesman in the footnote 20 below shows. But such an interpretation is also problematic, since it seems to suggest that such issues could be taken care of by increasing the scope of responsibility and by deriving all partial responsibilities from a general theory of responsibility, or at least from some supervening responsibility in case of serious transgressions of *jus cogens*, or human rights.

But this might be too easy an answer, as some counter-examples suggest: would it make sense to hold, for example, a foreign firm – or even better its

---

for example, the architect, or by the failures attributable to some others – such as the bricklayer who drilled a hole in a wall helping the electrician who came afterwards and worked according to a design of the building. Unfortunately, the hole had however been drilled by the apprentice a couple of centimetres to the left, an error that neither the master, nor the architect nor the plumbing inspector had noted and which afterwards caused a short circuit – as the PVC water pipe started leaking – leading to a fire, which devastated the basement.

[21] Jan Klabbers, *An Introduction to International Organizations Law*, 3rd ed. (Cambridge: Cambridge University Press, 2015). See also Jan Wouters, Eva Brems, Stefaan Smis, Pierre Schmitt (eds.), *Accountability for Human Rights Violations by International Organizations* (Antwerp: Intersentia, 2010).

[22] The case law concerning disputes about the employment contract and the international organization goes back to the League and the creation of 'staff tribunals'. See Chittharanjan F. Amerasinghe, *The Law of International Civil Service: As Applied by International Administrative Tribunals*, 2 vols. (Oxford: Clarendon, 1994).

[23] See, for example, the Soviet withdrawal from the WHO in 1950, and that of Poland, Czechoslovakia, and Hungary from UNESCO, later followed by Indonesia's exit from the UN (1 January 1965) and the US withdrawal from UNESCO on 12 October 2017. See also the two advisory opinions of the ICJ: Reparations for Injuries Suffered in the Service of the UN, [1949] ICJ Reports 174; and Certain Expenses of the United Nations, [1962] ICJ Reports 151.

60 Friedrich Kratochwil

governing board and its shareholders – responsible for selling trucks in a foreign country, which are then used by the regime there to transport alleged 'criminals' to forced labour camps – even if, according to reliable reports – they have only committed the 'crime' of protesting against some of the policies of their governments? What would it take to either hold the entire population or a civilian of the country in question responsible, who has the bad luck of being abroad, because their government is waging 'aggressive war' against some third state? After all, everybody in the 'lawless state' is in a way implicated in dutifully supporting the government by paying taxes, knowing full well that some, perhaps even much, of it goes towards committing an 'international crime'? Would it not be a sign of 'justice' if a state – not involved in this conflict – would take up the duty of doing something against 'impunity'?

Whatever we might think of these examples, one thing is clear. Such a system could only work in 'theory' while in practice it would be putting even the historical empires to shame, which allowed for considerable 'disorder' by building on local and very imperfect orders. The reason for such policies might have been more due to a lack of wherewithal than to design, but it also quickly puts an end to speculations of a 'universal' order, in which everything is potentially also everybody's business. But there is something more to it: the universalist speculation might be incoherent. Since universal responsibility going all the way down is impossible – as such concerns become, already in states with 'limited' government, the domain of the rulers(s) or magistrates. They represent the 'whole' but are by design also 'opposing' and 'limiting' each other, that is, they interfere with a 'rational' hierarchical ordering. To that extent, the idea of creating a global order which no longer is reined in by a division of power, and by immunity and rights, does not seem – *pace* Kant – to be particularly attractive.

This point has also further implications for assessing practical questions through 'theoretical' lenses: *issues of realizability arise not only at the stage of implementing the conclusions supplied by an ideal 'theory', or by the clarification of principles, but have to be part of the definition of the problem. Since they are constitutive of the very 'question', arising problems cannot be left only to the 'implementation' stage after a theory or the universal principles have provided their findings.* Given furthermore the possibilities, which modern technologies provide, especially in terms of handling information and disciplining the subjects, one need not be an adherent of Foucault to realize the even darker sides of this universalism.

Already Kant feared the implications of such constructs, which led him to both reject such imperial speculations, advocating a 'league' of republics instead, and hope that enlightened rulers – preferably those representing 'republics' – and the principle of 'publicity' – entrusted to the 'learned' who should advise the sovereigns – would be sufficient.[24] Needless to say that leads to the strange disconnect we observe between Kant's 'theory' of action – in which the will determines itself in accordance with the universal precepts provided by reason – and his practical advice – to exclude the subjects from any participation in making political decisions, as their duty is simply to 'obey'.[25]

2.3 SYSTEMS AND PLANS

Without wanting to enter now the merits of such arguments, it is clear that there is obviously something amiss in these 'universalist' constructions and with the traditional subordination of praxis to theory. Applied to responsibility, this means that the issue seems not to be responsibility per se, but of the underlying conception that any order has to be 'systemic' where everything has found its place and can now 'function', requiring only occasional repairs when something 'breaks'. Here Lindahl's seminal analysis is helpful for a diagnosis of what the concept of order is in such constructs.[26] As adumbrated above the notion of *order* in such 'theories' is conceived as an *order ordinatus* of either a perspicuous system in which parts and whole fit, or it is conceived – if one gives a bit more dynamic to it when applying it to social systems – by an arrangement in which nobody has any incentives for moving by making a nonconform decision. This might be a good way of describing the 'entropy' of physical systems – although using this notion of an equilibrium seems already problematic when applied to 'nature' as a whole, given the advances in our understanding as reflected in modern biology and physics. Using it, however,

---

[24] Immanuel Kant, *The Contest of Faculties* [1798] in Hans Reiss (ed.) *Kant: Political Writings*, 2nd ed. (Cambridge: Cambridge University Press, 1991): 176–90.

[25] See Immanuel Kant raising this issue in terms of the limits of criticism. He distinguishes between 'private reason' by which we cannot be forbidden to reason and criticize the 'functioning' of our institutions, such as churches or the military, and 'public reason', which limits his freedom due to the duties owed to his superiors. Here Kant suggests that it is not unjustified for the ruler (and perhaps the members of the 'Republic of Letters' as suggested in his later Perpetual Peace) – but quite significantly not 'normal' persons – to follow the maxim in regard to the criticism received, for example, by his officers: 'Argue as much as you like and about whatever you like, but obey'. See Immanuel Kant, *What is Enlightenment?*, in Hans Reiss (ed.), *Kant: Political Writings*, 2nd ed., op. cit.: 54–60, at 59.

[26] Hans Lindahl, *Authority and the Globalization of Inclusion and Exclusion* (Oxford: Oxford University Press, 2018).

62

Friedrich Kratochwil

for the analysis of social systems, which have to reproduce themselves, is nothing short of making a heroic mistake, induced by conceptual stretches and the use of a wrong analogy.

Social orders are hardly ever in a stable equilibrium since even the 'theory' of rational choice tells us that there are usually several equilibrium points, each benefiting different actors differently, so that 'ordering' is a never-ending task, precisely because social reproduction is not like executing a design or producing an object, which is at one point 'finished' even if it had to undergo a process of production. Consequently, social order has therefore to be conceived differently: as an *ordo ordinans*, as an activity of ordering rather than as the implementation of a design or of producing something. This has important implications for both the 'fragmentation' of law issue and for looking for alternative ways of understanding the process of social reproduction.

As Scott Veitch's remarks, reflecting on law's darker side, illustrate

... the division of legal labour is not well understood as a fragmentation of responsibility ... they are not fragments of a once greater whole because they never were 'whole' or capable of being understood in a singular way in the first place. Nor are they best thought of as each referring back to some singular or platonic notion of 'pure' responsibility, of which they are merely instances or paler copies. Rather in the way in which we described role responsibilities more generally, they are each normative devices that correspond to particular needs expectations and interests and are instantiations of *these* dynamics, not some greater or singular notion of responsibility.[27]

Two further corollaries follow from this realization. Law, although having in modernity become the near-exclusive device for ordering, cannot do so by itself, as 'legalism' or the notion of an autopoietic system suggests – similarly to the impossibility that the reflexivity of the subject itself can serve as an incontrovertible foundation for all that counts as 'knowledge'. Law might have its own logic and it might be successful to pretend to be a complete and autonomous system by 'incorporating' other logics of ordering – be they customary, 'professional' standards, or moral principles. Nevertheless, it is dependent on individual and collective action for setting the parameters of choice, for 'making' certain problems a public concern, and for deciding what should be done. Here arguments from the sciences, ethics, technology, or history enter and provide support for conflicting political projects. That these issues are often – through still not exclusively – voiced in legal language and

[27] Scott Veitch, *Law and Responsibility: On the Legitimization of Human Suffering* (Abingdon, Engl.: Routledge–Cavendish, 2007), at 76.

Authority, Law, and Knowledge

that law seems to have the last word by invoking its own authority for specifying that particular actions are now required or forbidden, or that new ways of pursuing certain goals are now established, all this can be granted. But it should not seduce us to believe that some internal logic of law is thereby working itself out, or that its capacity of 'guiding' our individual and collective projects can be reduced to the elaboration of legal doctrines or even through judicial decisions of the (highest) courts by finding the 'one right' answer a la Dworkin.

Since I have dealt with this problem in another context,[28] I rather want to follow up on the problem *of how and why certain root metaphors are useful or misleading for our understanding of 'ordering'* and social reproduction. In this section I critically examine the role of some of the traditional root metaphors in the analysis of action, that is, that of ends/means, of 'function', of 'fit' either through adaption or design, of systems, and of an 'end' of 'history'.

The reasons for examining *these* metaphors more closely are that they are the main hindrance for an adequate 'theory' of action. Such a 'theory' would have to address not only the issue of 'acting well' (*eu prattein*) in the old Aristotelian sense, but also those of responsibility and of the justifiable exercise of discretion. Consequently, such a 'theory' cannot be reduced to either a technocratic assessment or to the 'prophetic' evaluation (is this move 'progressive' or reactionary?) of political choices by pretending to know the 'destiny of mankind'.

As opposed to these constructs I propose an examination of how we make actual decisions in the practical realm, and this exploration cannot begin with some assumptions, or with a method that has been imported in the world of praxis because of the alleged success in other domains, or by the unexamined prejudice that all that is worth knowing has to satisfy 'theoretical' criteria. But since such an examination has to begin 'in the midst of it', it cannot start with absolute foundations or a mythical absolute beginning (social contract) or from the *telos* of all humanity, it has to recognize that the practical world is not 'there' but is made through interactions and showing how it came about is not only of historical interest but part of our predicament. To that extent, we cannot simply dispense with the archaeology of our concepts and imaginaries we have created, which provide the meaning and the yardsticks for our actions.

2.3.1 *Responsibility and Its Archaeology*

As the discussion so far suggests, examining the issues between responsibility – both in individual and in organizational contexts – and policy is tantamount to

---

[28] See Friedrich Kratochwil, *Praxis: On Acting and Knowing*, op. cit., chap. 5.

entering a conceptual minefield, stretching over several domains and levels. If you believe that all knowledge is of one cloth, then theory or an ethics that satisfies theoretical criteria must be able to clarify the principles on which we base the 'applicable' norms that we use for the design of institutional structures, as much of ideal theory or the 'one right solution of law' have argued.

But if we think that such an order is not achievable since in the practical world we have to converge on *one* solution – which is in a way far more exacting than finding 'determinate solutions' exemplified in the multiple equilibria of game theory – the practical task is also much less 'perfect' than ideal theory suggests. Thus a different conception of social order is required, as already suggested by foregrounding the problem of ordering (*ordo ordinans*) – for which already in Antiquity Aristotle's critique of Plato's notion of ideas (ideal forms) provided the *locus classicus*.[29] But there are even further objections to the 'ideal' conception of order which the archaeology of order and responsibility, of knowing and acting, discloses. If all order 'comes' from God - either because he ordered the *kosmos* as Plato suggests in his Timaios[30] or because he created the universe *ex nihilo* - it is this creation that serves as the ultimate template for what is and what should be done,[31] as further developed in Stoic thought about the 'laws' pervading the *kosmos*.

Although the account in Genesis, stressing the creation *ex nihilo* sits uneasily with this Greek ontology, it coincides with it in that God 'finished' his work (like the Platonic *demiourgos*) and saw that everything was 'good' so that he could 'rest'[32] and view his creation as an eternal presence. It is then not surprising that later, when 'nature' displaced God, the Philosopher having turned epistemologist claimed the 'view from nowhere' that disclosed how things really were, as there is in this view no foreground, no background, no peripheral vision, and no distortion as everything is perspicuous to the observer.

While such a take on the order of things and knowledge as an unobstructed 'view of the whole' underlies much of the 'unity of science position' and thereby 'mainstream' social science, it is rather problematic, as it is incompatible with the scientific revolutions of Darwin, modern physics, and cosmology,

---

[29] For his criticism, see Aristotle, *The Ethics of Aristotle* (*Nicomachean Ethics*), ed. by J. A. K. Thompson (London: Penguin Books, 1955), Bk. I. chap. 6, 1096a5–1097a14.

[30] See, for example, Plato's *Timaios*, 28a–29a6.

[31] This thought was further developed by the Stoics who focused on the 'law' that pervades the whole *kosmos*.

[32] Genesis 1 and 2.

as the latter has its 'history' too. It is also based on a very partial reading of Genesis as that book also contains another part – actually it is its main part counting forty-six chapters out of fifty – for which the first three chapters covering the creation are only the prologue. The rest deals with God's intervention in the world, as his 'work' was not completed. The eating of the forbidden fruit – nowadays having lost its status as a symbol for the 'fall', having become instead the logo of a corporation, promising to lead us to a technological paradise – sets up the subsequent 'history'.[33] It records the fate of the 'chosen' ones and their tribulations, individually (Cain and Abel, Job, Abraham, Loth), as well as collectively (the division of the Salomonic empire, the exile and destruction of the second temple, etc.).

Here is obviously not the place to follow this narrative and its attempts of coming to terms with individual and collective disasters by trying to bestow some meaning on the reported deeds and events, save to note the importance of two themes for its construction: the issue of knowledge, and – prodded by the unexplainable 'why me, why us' – the question of how order can be restored by sacrifice and atonement.

Interestingly, both solutions refer to 'practices' revolving around specific actions, rather than providing an answer to the initial question. The first concerns instructions for a ritual, that is, doing certain things in certain ways – such as offering a perfect animal and uttering specific formulas – so that order can be restored. The second, concerns atonement and involves a more reflective approach to action, examining both ends and means in our choices, which – if done well – has a cathartic character in which the 'self' becomes an issue.

The question is then no longer why the ritualistic actions misfired – whether this occurred because they were not properly performed or could be ascribed without remainder to 'bad luck' or by the unexplainable rejection of the offerings by God – but sets in motion a critical examination of the self and its links to others and of the 'meaning' of one's life. This meaning is not just established by performing a sequence of actions at given times – since rituals increasingly lose their power as a spell that brings this questioning to a rest – but by raising instead the existential question of good and bad, of justice and righteousness, of failure and (in)dependence (grace, sin), and of being able to engage in 'ordering'.

This 'coming to terms' with those questions, in finding a way of endowing actions and events with meaning by telling a story, rather than pretending that

---

[33] According to the serpent, the eating of the fruit would not result in death 'for God knows that when you eat of it you will be like God, knowing good and evil' (Genesis 3, 5).

an entire 'life' can be represented by a 'plan' or design – is difficult enough for the individual. But it creates even greater difficulties in the case of collectivities. Although Christianity accepted God's role in the historical world either in terms of the *manus gubernatoris* – which only in the eighteenth century becomes the *unseen hand* of institutional structures – or in terms of 'restorative' rites, such as 'sacraments', or by accepting 'miracles' that could change the course of events; however, what counts as a miracle, or is a 'sign', or even a 'punishment' can often lead to fundamental disagreements. Then its meaning has to be established by proofs or a 'declaration' by what we nowadays would call a speech act of a recognized authority. This of course raises the problem of potentially competing authorities and the possibility of escalating conflict.

This became the central issue during the reformation, when in its most radical form individuals and their 'conscience' – and thus neither the clergy nor the traditional ruler representing the emerging 'state' – claimed to be the proper 'authority' for such a declaration. But as Hobbes wryly pointed out, those who invoked their conscience and claimed to have a personal and unmediated relationship to the creator left the bystanders with the problem that all they had to go by was a claim by those who received illumination or messages from their saviour. For those who were willing to make this leap of faith, there was no problem. But for sceptics, additional difficulties arose. Even if the 'message' was taken as a fact, it was by no means clear that it had come from God, that the receivers had understood God's directives correctly, or that they were reporting to us the 'whole truth and nothing but the truth', instead of supplying us only with something that was adulterated because of misunderstandings, forgetfulness, or even guile. This is why the sovereign was necessary not only because his control of the means of coercion was likely to keep all the disarmed subjects 'in awe', but also because his power as representative of 'public reason' derived from his being the 'fixer of signs'.[34]

However, this 'practical' solution to the problem of collective action proves in a way too much and it shows why the challenge to knowledge launched by the sceptics was even deeper, as it suggested that the notion of an *ordo ordinatus*, because it was only a special case of the more general problem that no ultimate foundation for knowledge could be found. To that extent, disagreement concerned not only the proposed solutions to recognized problems, but even the conceptions of what was a problem had to be re-thought, since there could not be *one* answer if there were several questions. Of course,

---

[34] See Thomas Hobbes, *Leviathan*, ed. by C. B. Macpherson (Harmondsworth, Engl: Penguin, 1971), chap. 37.

Authority, Law, and Knowledge   67

this opened the way for all types of sophisms as had been the case in antiquity and again in the seventeenth century.

So, while on the level of popular understanding the sceptics seemed to argue that there is no 'truth', the more appropriate characterization would be that there is not 'One Truth', because there is not 'One Question', or that the different questions we can raise are not all part of the One Question, so that the various answers could be made to fit together without reminder. Instead, what 'serves' as an answer cannot be answered without referring to the context in which the question arose. Thus, the question of 'was this a trespass or not' cannot be answered by reference to the periodic table, which supposedly shows us what really 'is'.

It is, however, precisely this illusion that the Cartesian 'answer' claims in maintaining that all knowledge could be founded on the certainty of the self-reflective subject without any support from 'sources' – considered to be authoritative – as otherwise, by taking the sceptical objections seriously, one had to 'withdraw' from such inquiries in order to gain some peace and quiet. For Descartes, on the other hand, certainty was not only possible but could be attained by, ironically, putting the most radical doubt into the service for finding in self-reflection the 'unshakable foundation' of all knowledge. In fact, much more than claimed was required, as it remained unclear how the certainty of my existence can tell me anything about the world 'out there'. Thus, Descartes had not only to postulate 'clear and distinct ideas' as well as a 'method', but even more problematically, he had to re-introduce God – similar to a *deus ex machina* in the theatre – as a guarantor for the match of 'concepts' and the external world so that we can arrive at the 'Truth'.

Although Descartes' catchy phrase of *cogito ergo sum* seemed to have convinced the public that the sceptics' challenge had been effectively rebutted,[35] the problematic nature of its necessary auxiliary assumptions and the further inference that the knowledge of the practical world could be based on the same 'scientific' method reaching the stringency of geometry turned out to be little more than a pious wish. Thus, Hobbes' claim in his *De Cive* (1642) to have provided a study of the social world 'in the geometric mode' (*more geometrico*) was never realized. Instead, he used in his *Leviathan* (1651) every 'rhetorical' trick he could find in order to persuade his audience,[36] and

[35] On this, see Richard Popkin, *The History of Skepticism from Savonarola to Bayle*, 3rd ed. (Oxford: Oxford University Press, 2003).

[36] See, for example, Johnston David, *The Rhetoric of the Leviathan: Thomas Hobbes and the Politics of Cultural Transformation* (Princeton: Princeton University Press, 1986); Quentin Skinner, *Reason and Rhetoric in the Philosophy of Hobbes* (Cambridge: Cambridge University Press, 1996).

68　　　　　　　　　　　　*Friedrich Kratochwil*

Spinoza's attempt of constructing an *Ethics* (1677) in which the superiority of this method was supposed to provide 'proofs' (*Ethica ordine geometrico demonstrata*) had the ironic flaw that it was also a major attack on Descartes, so that the 'method' obviously did not possess the power of arriving at determinate and unique solutions. Finally, as the religious wars showed, this method seemed to be powerless to counteract the *escalation of conflicts*, contrary to the assumption that unshakable foundations and an impeccable method were able to provide firm guidance for our practical choices and resolve deep-seated disagreements. Ironically, when settlements concerning the 'fundamental' social issues were reached, as in the Westphalian Peace (1648) and finally in England by the 'Glorious Revolution' (1688), it was not one for which any 'method' had provided the blueprint.

As a matter of fact, it was the investigation of this settlement in his *History of England* that provided further support for Hume's anti-Cartesian project, which he had commenced in his *Treatise* and the *Enquiry*, in which he had outlined a full-fledged alternative to Descartes epistemology. For Hume the world of *praxis* was different from nature and its laws, because it had to rely on norms and conventions and on learning through participation in social exchanges, rather than on speculative assumptions or universal laws, which can be applied to 'facts' across time and space. It is not a world that pre-exists so that what 'is' can be provided by our sense perceptions or even by theoretically informed observations. Instead, what 'is' becomes again – as it had been for Aristotle – a problem. Whether an action 'is' a murder rather than an accident depends on appraisals that necessarily contain normative elements. This social world is therefore not natural but requires action and commitment for its reproduction and that means also the will, and not only cognition. It is also a 'historical world', formed by our choices in contingent situations rather than by the fact that all the different experiences and 'solutions' can be derived from *a prioris* or be based on generalizations. Consequently, what a situation 'is' requires imagination and judgment, reasoning from case to case, seeing similarities and differences, so as not to submit either to barren and meaningless abstractions, or to being seduced by misleading analogies.

Indeed, as the American pragmatists more than a century later noted, it is precisely this 'quest for certainty'[37] that distorts already the way we go about investigating nature. But it misguides us even more when we try to understand the social world by taking this epistemology as the yardstick. Of course, the

---

[37]　John Dewey, 'The Quest for Certainty', in Jo Ann Boydston (ed.), *The Gifford Lectures at the University of Edinburgh 1929* (Dewey: The Later Works 1925–53, vol. IV) (Carbondale: University of Illinois Press, 1984).

Authority, Law, and Knowledge 69

Pragmatists were not like the sceptics before and they shared the confidence in the success of technology. This success provided the proof that all problems, including the seemingly intractable ones of politics, could be solved, if not analogously by applying theories or the proper techniques to the facts, then by organizing the 'finding' of solutions in a better way. Instead of adhering to the model of demonstration and logic, we have to consider the 'debate' among the community of scientists and their judgments the appropriate template. But, even among the pragmatists, those trying to revolutionize science by 'democratizing' its practices[38] were in the minority. For most of them and the enlightened public alike, progress was sufficiently evidenced by the feats of engineers and the success of applied sciences. Engineering and 'scientific management' now take the pride of place and shift the interest to the right techniques, only to be followed later by economics and its 'system' explanation, showing that order does not necessarily result from an overall design but from the aggregation of the choices of a large number and their unintended consequences – later explicated by a general equilibrium model.

Thus, the original notion of a system based on functional fit and design is now expanded as the price-mechanism becomes the *spiritus rector* of the system. In it, sentiments no longer play a role within which this human tendency to 'truck and barter' had remained embedded for the old economists of the 'Scottish enlightenment'.[39] Since these actions concern the mediated exchanges in a market, which in turn trigger 'productive actions' of anonymous suppliers, they cannot be the template for action *tout court* since neither exchange nor production exhausts the *problematique* of practical choice.

Such a systemic view is also far removed from the historical prophecies that arise from Kant's speculation about nature's design and the 'signs' which 'universal history' supplies showing us the way to a cosmopolitan order.[40] Although this 'prophetic' reading of Kant has become dominant during the past decades both in political theory and in international law, Kant himself remained strangely undecided whether this *telos* could be reached by human

---

[38] See William Caspari, *Dewey on Democracy* (Ithaca, New York: Cornell University Press, 2000); and Molly Cochran, 'Deweyan Pragmatism and Post-Positive Social Science in IR', *Millennium*, 31(3) (2008), 525–48.

[39] See, for example, Francis Hucheson [1728], *An Essay on the Nature and Conduct of Passions and Affects, with Illustrations of the Moral Sense* (Indianapolis: Liberty Fund, 2002); Francis Hutcheson [1724], 'Reflections on the Common Systems of Morality', in *Francis Hutcheson: On Human Nature*, ed. by Thomas Mautner (Cambridge: Cambridge University Press, 1993): 96–106.

[40] Immanuel Kant, *Idea of a Universal History with Cosmopolitan Purpose [1784]*, in Hans Reiss (ed.) *Kant: Political Writings*, op. cit., 41–53.

action and for which an *a priori* duty existed to bring this cosmopolitan order into existence,[41] or whether it works itself out through the *List der Natur*, which by pushing and shoving forced people to arrive at this point.[42]

Obviously, it is not the place here to follow the twists and turns of the various 'theoretical' debates concerning the (im)possibility of a science of the social world, save to examine the issue whether by avoiding the basic metaphors of production, system or the *telos* of history and focusing instead on 'what worked' in particular cases, attempting to distil from it some 'best practices' provides an alternative. This is after all what the present 'turn to practice' has in mind. While here no manifest 'functional design' or self-equilibrating system supplies the template, there is an equally problematic belief that following certain rules and routines will be able to accomplish the task.

A moment's reflection shows, however, that the informing model is still that of 'production' so that the easy transferability of practices from one domain to another (managerial techniques based on dates, targets, base lines, indicators, numbers taken from accounting) seems to be guaranteed, as 'numbers are numbers'. But as the experiences from 'complex' peace-making operations indicate – where medicine usually supplies the metaphor for justifying the 'intervention', but where the 'patients' have little to say, since the 'disease' has been diagnosed – that might be a hasty conclusion. Not only is there not one single thread that runs from book-keeping to peace keeping, but what worked in one case does not necessarily ensure success in another; worse, the 'lessons learned' were ironically often the major reason why the subsequent operations failed, as the 'learning from Yugoslavia' showed in the

---

[41] See, for example, the remarks in *Perpetual Peace*, op. cit., at 112: 'For if I say that nature *wills* that that should happen [i.e. political, international and cosmopolitan right. F.K.] that does not mean that nature imposes on us a *duty* to do it, for duties can only be imposed by practical reason, acting without any external constraint. On the contrary nature does it herself, whether we are willing or not'. Compare this to the argument in *The Contest of the Faculties*, op cit., at 183. Having laid out in the previous chapter that for onlookers who try to understand the meaning of the momentous 'deeds or misdeeds' of the French Revolution only a 'disinterested but universal sympathy' is able to disclose, or rather 'proves that mankind as a whole shares a certain character in common and it also proves (because of its disinterestedness) that man has a moral character or least the makings of it'. This leads him to claim in the next chapter, significantly entitled 'The Prophetic History of Mankind', at 184: 'In these principles, there must be something *moral* which reason recognizes not only as pure, but also (because of its great epoch-making influence) as something to which the human soul manifestly acknowledges a *duty*'.

[42] Kant, *Perpetual Peace*, op. cit., quoting rather uncritically Seneca (*Epistle* 107, at 11) as his source (*ducunt volentem fata, nolentem trahunt*: Fate lead the willing [but] drag the unwilling). Similarly, the support for his notion of the '*List der Vernunft*' is derived from the figure of speech used by Lucretius in his *De rerum natura*, Bk V, verse 234 (*natura daedala*).

Rwanda massacre.[43] Sending in peacekeepers is not like having a doctor take out a patient's gallbladder – notwithstanding the military dreams of the possibility of 'surgical' strikes; and dealing with marauding or well-organized armed groups is not like treating a great number of patients singly.

This is not to bad mouth 'standardization' and 'performance indicators' but the analogy to autonomous systems and decomposable machines that work with precision is misleading. Consider in this context the practice of playing soccer. The team certainly needs drills (standard situations) that have to be executed with unflinching precision and it has to meet certain targets – so as to keep the ball in its own possession – but making this a 'strategy' and not learning from experience is to court disaster, as Germany had to learn at the last World Cup. Rather, scoring requires teamwork and quick mutual adjustments among all players, who have to change their positions and recognize opportunities opening up during the game rather than sticking to the execution of a preconceived plan.

For that purpose I want to examine in the next section in greater detail what distinguishes the domain of praxis from that of nature or of production, so as to get further clues where to look when our efforts fail because we were tempted by false analogies and looked for remedies that were based on the notion that 'true' knowledge had to be of one cloth, applicable to *praxis* without much ado.

2.4 ACTING AS MAKING PRACTICAL CHOICES

The discussion above has shown that the semantics of action shows surprising variety depending on which is the root-metaphor. As we have seen, the notion of production – going back to the Aristotelian *techne*, of knowing how to fabricate something – has in modernity gained the upper hand. Similarly, the interpretation of action according to efficient causality and the ease with which this scheme seems to explain 're-actions' – such as when we jump out of the way in order to evade, for example, a falling rock – has then given rise to extreme behaviourism and its notion that every action should be understood as a result of 'conditioning' in accordance with the Pawlowian dog experiment or - in less strict fashion - to un-reflected 'habits'.[44]

---

[43] See, for example, Michael Barnett, *Eyewitness to a Genocide: The UN and Rwanda* (Ithaca: Cornell University Press, 2002).

[44] See, for example, Harry Collins, *Tacit and Explicit Knowledge* (Chicago: University of Chicago Press, 2010). His earlier *Changing Order: Replication and Induction to Scientific Practice* (Beverley Hills; London: Sage, 1985) was still written in a more Wittgensteinian fashion about rule-following in scientific practice.

There are, however, some difficulties with this pressing of action in a causal scheme as we act prospectively (i.e. in the hope of reaching a goal), while strict efficient causality relies on antecedent causes, that is, it is 'backward' oriented. Since the 'constant conjunctions' imposed by the mind on our observations are hard to find in the practical world – as action might misfire or actors might change their mind – reserving the notion of an explanation to efficient causes cannot be right, and that is not only because of those 'exceptions'. Rather, I think the standard transformation of the 'end' at which an action aims – which becomes, via the 'motive' of the actor, the antecedent cause – is fishy for two reasons. One: the actor becomes then simply the throughput, as the action is the consequence of the motive. Two: whatever the plausibility of such a conceptual move might be, it violates the criterion of independence, which both the antecedent cause and the outcome have to satisfy in an explanation invoking efficient causality.

Similarly, although the analogy between choosing (making choices) and making 'something' holds, especially since it seems to take 'time' into account, 'choosing' and 'making something' are different, even if they both use the term 'making'. Thus, even in a production process, different steps have to fit the elements together but they also have to occur in a particular irreversible sequence, as, for example, in cooking; not paying heed to that dimension and focusing only on the ingredients and their weight and shape might spoil the broth. Nevertheless, in its 'generative grammar', this 'process' remains beholden to 'work' and the techniques, which produce objects. I think that this analogy is seriously misleading. Plato's analogy of 'choosing' and 'steering' serves as my example for explaining the reasons.

On the surface, the analogy is just an extension of the old Socratic argument asking people, be they shoemakers, priests, or politicians, what they 'are good at', that is, by bringing about what they are supposed to, by calling themselves shoemaker, joiner, priest, or whatever. When the analogy is extended, however, to the captain who has to steer a ship, or when this analogy is even further stretched to 'clarify' what a politician, as a captain steering the 'ship of state', has to know, we are in trouble. Linking the captain's authority to make decisions to a particular expertise and 'know how' is apt as far as 'running the ship' is concerned. But the analogy leads quickly to faulty conclusions when it is extended. While a captain must possess some 'expert' knowledge, such as of navigation, the weather, and the currents, as well as the technology on board, s/he cannot claim expertise on the question of which destinations are to be selected or whether or for what purposes one should set out to sea.

Authority, Law, and Knowledge

To that extent, the recent focus on 'know how' and 'best practices' seems to repeat this Platonic mistake that reserves 'rule' to those 'in the know', only that the modern kings are no longer philosophers, but 'expert/managers'. The claim that the choice of an end – which nearly always *implies a selection among ends* – can be reduced to that of choosing the adequate means is simply faulty since the 'selection problem' *hinges on different degrees of satisfaction of conflicting values*, which practical choices entail. Similarly, while production processes do include time in that different actions are required at different intervals, *it is not time in its historicity that characterizes practical choices*. In that case, the selection of the 'end' is open-ended since the situations allow not only for new actors to enter or exit, but for transformative change in the 'situation itself' so that the goals that seem reachable become out of reach, or new opportunities arise. To that extent – if we extend the metaphor – what seemed like being in the midst of the production process of a sausage now suddenly turns out to be more like a tennis match or an opera performance. Since my task here is to look at some of the philosophical issues raised by such mistaken analogies, I want to highlight now more systematically the distinguishing features of acting in the world of praxis.

A dozen or so important differences come to mind here: *first*, contingency is introduced by the fact that actions take place in *time* and are thus characterized by (historical) conjunctures, privileging thereby the particular not the general, as generalities outside of 'types' usually are uninteresting since too much information is lost by 'normalizing' cases. Consequently, *second*, the knowledge necessary for deciding practical questions fits badly the logical model of inference that operates with a general major (universal) premise and a minor (factual) premise ensuring the validity of the conclusion, whereby the force of the conclusion is largely supplied by the major premise, containing a nomic law of nature, or a normative principle. To that extent, the conclusion in practical reasoning seems to 'follow' analogously to the inference that establishes the 'truth' of the conclusion.[45] I think, however, that this argument is problematic since more is going on in practical reasoning: both the factual premise and the major one are important for supporting the conclusion. A further proof supporting this hunch is provided through the reasoning from case to case, characteristic for common law, where precedents not principles guide the process. But then reasoning consists in finding and

---

[45] That would be the case in the standard example:
All men are mortal (nomic law),
Socrates is a man ('factual' finding),
Socrates is mortal (true conclusion).

74   *Friedrich Kratochwil*

justifying 'distinctions' that allow for the creation of new precedents without 'touching' the general principles that constitute the legal enterprise. Consequently, this type of reasoning is badly represented when it is seen as a deductive entailment or as an inductive inference.

This suggests that, *third*, an agent is neither served by logic alone nor helped by the knowledge of what is true in general. Rather, given time pressures, s/he needs a quick diagnostic identifying what best characterizes the present problem. This presupposes imagination and experience, as different possibilities have to be conjured up and be assessed by comparisons, whereby the multidimensionality of such a comparison cannot be passed over. This is why 'rationality' – which by the time of Hume had been reduced to an ends/means calculus – is for him not the most important part of 'the mind'. It is rather this 'productive' capacity of imagination, which gets us through in figuring out what to do, while reason can remain subordinate – the slave of passion – as Hume put it. Nothing could be farther from the notion of a *'felicific calculus'* that Bentham later recommends to the legislator and which 'liberalism' makes the general model of 'rational' action.

Fourth, since the actor is never confronted with exhaustively defined situations and complete knowledge of all the strategies available, the search for new information is costly and the choice problem in terms of a maximization criterion becomes indeterminate.[46] How long are we to search? This is why, in such situations, more important than maximization is the criterion of *completeness*, and of pattern recognition, that is, of not having overlooked something that might become important down the line. But this skill involves, *fifth*, experience, which guides analogical reasoning and hones the ability of judgment, when we make practical choices. But, as Kant points out, this is a different capacity and not simply part of logic and its operation, and neither is it subject to the criteria of 'theory'.

> if (logic) wanted to show how one should subsume, or distinguish whether something falls under a rule or not, this could be done only through further rules. But this again would require a new determination by the power of judgment (*Urteilskraft*) because a rule is involved. Thus it is evident that the understanding (*Verstand*) is capable of being instructed by supplying it with rules, but that the power of judgment is a special talent (*Talent*), which cannot be taught, but can be acquired only by practice. For that reason (this faculty) is a specific quality of common sense (*Mutterwitz*), whose lack no school can cure. Although schooling might be able to furnish rules

---

[46] John Conlisk, 'Why Bounded Rationality?', *Journal of Economic Literature*, 34(2) (1996), 669–90.

Authority, Law, and Knowledge 75

derived from the insights of others and might [even be able] to somehow 'implant' them in a limited mind, the capacity to apply them correctly must be in the 'apprentice' (*Lehrling*) himself. No rule, which we prescribe to him with this intention, is secure from abuse, if such a talent is missing.[47]

Sixth, given this predicament not only a quick heuristics but a flexible rather than a purely maximizing strategy is demanded, since choices often cannot be postponed and windows of opportunity open and close, that is, are not indefinitely available. This also necessitates, *seventh*, a sense of 'timing' as an important element[48] as well as having, *eighth*, a viable fall-back strategy,[49] if it turns out that one had misjudged the initial situation, or that the dynamic of interaction does not develop along the expected lines. Doing more of the same (much helps much) according to the metaphysical principle of the continuity of nature is then hardly a prudent and defensible strategy.

The *ninth* important point is that the grammar of 'acting well' not only comprises that we reach our goals, but also *in what fashion* we do this. As we have seen, new problems arise in this context, since we are likely to interfere in our pursuits with the goals of others and competition can quickly degenerate into conflict.

Therefore, *tenth*, there has to be a general respect for 'the law' which regulates such interferences – rehearsed by Aristotle's rule of law argument (*nomos basileus*) in his *Politics*[50] – and the specific allowances, prohibitions, exceptions, and exemptions for which the law provides. These become sedimented in codes or precedents that form a specific tradition[51] which, in turn, serve as the enabling as well as the constraining background for making choices and for 'deciding' authoritatively cases brought before a court.

Eleventh, since many actions we undertake are taken on behalf of others, who are our clients, patients, or students, we owe them particular fiduciary duties. The latter are important institutionally secured expectations but cannot be derived from the general obligations we owe to all humans, or even to all fellow citizens. When seen in this light, the standard argument for having first to find a general theory of obligation in which then moral and legal obligations are 'grounded' – although perhaps differently – seems like a giant

---

[47] Immanuel Kant, *Kritik der Reinen Vernunft*, A 134, 135; B 173,174.
[48] Here Aristotle already mentions the importance of the *kairos*.
[49] This point has been particularly made by Clausewitz in his controversy with von Buelow who wanted to formulate a comprehensive strategy for any war. See Peter Paret, 'Clausewitz', in Peter Paret (ed.), *Makers of Modern Strategy* (Princeton: Princeton University Press, 1986): 186–216.
[50] Aristotle, *Politics*, 1287 a 3–6.
[51] See Krygier, 'Law as Tradition', *Law and Philosophy*, 5(2) (1986), 237–62.

misstep, despite the popularity of such 'transcendental' moves. It seems that to search for such a theory is likely to be as futile as the attempt to ground each exception in a general 'theory of exceptions', even though having a name for it is not as useless as it perhaps seems. Nevertheless, an exception attains its meaning from its link to the concept of 'rule' upon which it is parasitic, since the exception neither 'refutes' the rule, nor does it become part of it by falling 'under it' (although referring to and reaffirming the rule).

Twelfth, by *experience* obviously one cannot mean that a person must have performed the very same actions and routines frequently, even if they are of crucial importance in the case of production (*techne*) or in modern 'normal' science. Rather, it suggests that the prudent person *must have been exposed to a variety of things, that s/he must have learned to compare situations and to find ways of 'going on'*, rather than being stymied by an instance that refutes traditional wisdom, or embarking on the task of 'normalizing' non-conform cases, in order to expand the database and prepare a hypothesis for a scientific test.

2.4.1 *So What? Some Further Thoughts (in Lieu of a Conclusion)*

The reader who has had the patience (or fortitude) to follow this argument might now ask what all this has to do with those questions and problems s/he has to face in daily life. To lay out the complexities of the *problematique* through an examination of the philosophical debates in the Western tradition might therefore be considered more anxiety-producing than helpful.

While I understand this reaction, the way out is not to deny this problem but to realize that coping with this anxiety is all that matters. After all, the mundane question of how to get on with one's research as mentioned above – whether to follow some standard procedure and 'massage' some data so that they conform – or to take the unexpected rather as a challenge is perhaps not an existential question of the order of what one should do with one's life. But it points us to the issue that much more is involved in making choices than the bare-bone notion of rational decision-making, modelled after a consumer's choice and then extended by auxiliary assumptions. To that extent, anxiety engendered by this complexity is an ineluctable part of the human condition. It is not only addressed in existential philosophy (Heidegger), having led, as we have seen, from the Platonic philosophy of forms to Descartes' 'answer' to seventeenth-century sceptics – as problematic as his response may be – to the Scottish enlightenment's concern with 'sentiments' which are constitutive for our moral and social life.

Authority, Law, and Knowledge

While all these proposals are not 'the' answer – in the sense of bringing our questioning and pondering to an end – they do provide pointers as to how to go on with life: finding *meaning within it* without having to wait for an answer to what the meaning *of life* is. That this recognition entails having to shed much of what we have thought and we were taught, and that we have a hard time letting go, is obvious. But then again, learning is also always accompanied by unlearning something. Perhaps the most difficult notion to grasp is that thinking and deciding are not simply 'individual affairs' and that, therefore, everything social has to be explained and justified in terms of aggregation. But this cannot be right. Feelings, like language, are of course the feelings of a person, as is the articulation of words. However, to assume therefore that speaking a language has to be treated as idiosyncratic or only a 'psychological' phenomenon is not. Similarly, emotions provide the 'common standards' for appraisal as both virtue ethics and the Scottish enlightenment in regard to 'sentiments' and their 'education' show. Here not only Aristotle's *Politics*,[52] Hume's discussion of 'justice' as an 'artificial' virtue,[53] or Smith's discussion of cultivation of sentiments,[54] but also Wittgenstein's[55] argument about feeling 'pain' provide the crucial texts for correcting this myopia.

The radical individualization of thought and feelings obscured their reciprocal influence, although we clearly see in 'moral education' that the 'dos' and 'don'ts' – originally transmitted by signs or commands – are increasingly accompanied by verbal glosses. They address not only cognitive issues but attempt to teach adequate emotional responses as well: not to get furious when things do not work out, to be 'brave' when we fall down and cry for sympathy, or giving up on sulking in a corner ('taking it out on others'). Those examples explode the myth that feelings are just irrational and 'private' responses. Rather, they are mediated and moulded by language, which makes it possible to distinguish a 'freak-out response' from the resentment we 'justifiably' feel when we have been wronged. Such appropriate behaviour characterizes not only a sane and mature person, but makes civilized life possible.

This can be seen from Aristotle's characterization of friendship and justice as 'political' virtues. But from the examples he uses when elaborating on what one would consider nowadays 'private' or merely personal virtues, such as courage, gentleness, or moderation, we realize that we are not monads.

---

[52] Aristotle, *Politics*, op. cit., Bks. VI and VIII.

[53] David Hume, *A Treatise on Human Nature*, op. cit., Bk 3, part 2, sec. 2.

[54] Adam Smith, *The Theory of Moral Sentiments* [1759], ed. by D. D. Raphael, A. L. Macfie (Oxford: Oxford University Press, 1976).

[55] Ludwig Wittgenstein, *Philosophical Investigations*, op. cit., para. 293 (the 'beetle in a box' argument in the context of his criticism of 'private' languages).

Friedrich Kratochwil

Prudence provides the most obvious link as it joins the actions of the agent with society at large. This is why the most important virtues were later called 'cardinal virtues' as they derive their meaning from *cardo*: door-hinge.[56] They are temperance, justice, prudence, and fortitude. To that extent, the virtues are not only personal dispositions which help us to act well, but link the project of becoming oneself with the 'political project' of a good society, which requires respect for others (moral equality) but also provides the pre-conditions for the development of one's own capacities.

This realization also solves some of the problems that come with rule-following: exercising discretion responsibly, and acting with circumspection, that is, seeing the larger picture, which entails circumventing two of the most common errors in making bad choices: to avoid situations which are not only risky but push us in the direction of compromising the standards we have embraced; and to realize that focusing too narrowly on a task at hand might be like not seeing the forest for the trees. Thus, to act virtuously entails being:

> ... a certain sort of person with a certain complex mind set. A significant aspect of this mindset is the wholehearted acceptance of a distinctive range of reasons for action. A honest person cannot be identified simply as one who ... practices honest dealing and does not cheat. If such actions are done merely because the agent thinks that honesty is the best policy, or because they fear being caught, rather than through recognizing 'to do otherwise would be dishonest' as the relevant reason, they are not the actions of an honest person. An honest person cannot be identified as one who, for example, tells the truth because it *is* the truth, for one can have the virtue of honesty without being tactless or indiscreet. The honest person recognizes 'That would be a lie' as a strong (though perhaps not overriding) reason for not making certain statements in certain circumstances, and gives due, but not overriding weight to 'That would be the truth' as a reason for making them.[57]

Furthermore, a virtuous person is not one shirking responsibility, an option that is not available to the anxious one. Having weathered several storms, the virtuous actor does not think that everything is out of her hands but that something can be done, even if success is not guaranteed. On the other hand, this confidence and sensitivity for opportunities works also in reverse, when, for example, the virtuous agent does not even consider options that are shameful or exaggerated. Thus, an honest person 'does not weigh the pros and

---

[56] Aristotle's list in the Rhetoric, Bk I, vii (1366b1–1367a21): justice, courage, temperance, magnificence, magnanimity, liberality, gentleness, prudence, and wisdom.

[57] Rosalind Hursthouse, Virtue Ethics, *Stanford Encyclopedia of Philosophy*, pub. 18 July 2003, substantive revisions 8 December 2016, para 1.1, at 2.

cons of a theft as a way of making money'[58] which is 'normal' for the average 'bankster' of today. Similarly, someone temperate will not gloat about his victory over the opponent, or go in for the 'kill', since this would be out of character - even if it might be satisfying in the moment of success - because it could make life easier in the future. As Aristotle argues:

> We are afraid, for instance or be confident, or have appetites, or get angry, or feel pity and in general have pleasure or pain, both too much or too little . . . But having these feeling at the right time, about the right things, toward the right people, for the right end and in the right way is the intermediate and best condition, proper to virtue.[59]

There are three further points that have to be considered in this context. One concerns the differences of such an approach to practical choice to other 'theoretically' oriented approaches. The other relates to the limitations of this approach particularly of acting within the framework of organizations and under conditions or rapid social change. Finally, a third point, that of 'politics' and organizational decision-making in an increasingly globalized and 'mediated' world, has to be mentioned.

But let us begin by contrasting this approach to other, more 'theoretically' oriented ones. As the brief discussion of virtues showed, nothing could be further from a Kantian as well as from a liberal 'Benthamian' approach: the first focusing virtually exclusively on the actor's motive when assessed from an unsituated position provided by reason and not moved by feelings,; the second on the consequences. In the above example, that could mean that I should gloat and go in for the kill since both immediate utility considerations as well as expected utility point in this direction. Similarly, the Kantian approach would not allow 'interest'[60] to play a role, while the utilitarian pretends to assess any choice according to a calculus that makes conflicting value-consideration solvable by an algorithm.[61] Both have, however, little to do

[58] Kieran Setiya, 'Why Virtue matters', in *Reasons without Rationalism* (Princeton: Princeton University Press, 2007), Part II, at 74.

[59] Aristotle, *Nicomachean Ethics* (1106b 19–24).

[60] Here the emergence of an 'inter-esse', of an opening that allows for two or more actors to cooperate that might then lead to a change in the 'self-interest' by the extension of sympathy, is ruled out and the conflict of duties is simply denied. Kant's own example shows this. According to Kant, I am not justified in telling a stalker a lie when he knocks on my door and wants to know whether my friend, who has asked me for help in providing shelter, is hiding in my house.

[61] The criterion of the 'greatest happiness for *the greatest number*' corrects that problem, but perhaps overall utility gets distorted by the perverse utilities of a few, which skews the overall assessment – as it is familiar from free trade arguments that might favour a few who can live in luxury but at the cost of depressing the overall economy. It also does not solve the problem of

with how we try to find our way in the practical world. There, as virtue ethics suggests, competence of how to act can only be acquired by 'being in the midst of it' and 'learning' by 'commerce and conversation', as Hume has it, rather than by believing that only a general theory of obligation, or an algorithm allowing for the calculation of benefits and losses,[62] can resolve the dilemmas.

This leads us, however, to the second problem, which has two parts. On the one side, there is the chicken and egg problem: how is one to 'learn' by participation if one lives in a world of turmoil. Here, Thucydides' analysis of the revolution in Coryra and the plague that visited Athens in 430 B.C. draws our attention to the fragility of political order when it has been struck by natural or manmade disaster:

> ... Athens owed to the plague the beginnings of ... unprecedented lawlessness. Seeing how quick and abrupt were the changes of fortune which came to the rich who suddenly died and those who had previously been penniless but now inherited their wealth, people now began to openly venture on acts of self-indulgence which before then they used to keep in the dark. They resolved to spend their money quickly and to spend it on pleasure, since money and life alike seemed equally ephemeral. As for what is called honour, no one showed himself willing to abide by the laws, so doubtful was it whether one would survive to enjoy the name for it. It was generally agreed that what was both honourable and valuable was the pleasure of the moment ... No fear of god or law of man had a restraining influence. As for the gods, it seemed the same thing whether one worshipped them or not, when one saw the good and the bad dying indiscriminately. As for offences against the human law, no one expected to live long enough to be brought to trial and punished.[63]

The second, less severe problem arises, however, even under conditions of seemingly normal circumstances, that is, acting in and on behalf of organizations. After all, part of the strength of organizations is their specialization, based on a division of labour and the limits of attention that this entails. As long as you do your job, that is all you can be held responsible for, for everything else *respondeat superior*. Unfortunately, even the leaders of organizations are not and perhaps cannot be free from such limitations. After all, they have to compete with other organizations so that where 'you stand

---

the comparability of individual utilities and the tradeoff issue the 'greatest number' vs. that of the overall greatest utility.

[62] Donald Livingston, *Philosophical Melancholy and Delirium: Hume's Pathology of Philosophy* (Chicago: University of Chicago Press, 1998).

[63] Thucydides, *Peloponnesian War*, transl. by M. I. Finley (London: Penguin, 1972), Bk. II, chap. 53, at 155.

Authority, Law, and Knowledge 81

depends heavily on where you sit' and the legitimacy of your actions and your discretionary power extends only so far as the writ of the empowering instrument reaches. True, the 'mission' even of an international organization might be stretched through interpretation and a more expansionary reading provided by functionalism or by the deals proposed by neo-functionalist technocrats whose skill lies in persuading the members that an 'upgrade' is in the common interest.[64]

But not everything will be accepted, and resistance can form. When, for example, Indian peasants 're-take their land' by occupying the fields of Monsanto, claiming that the cultivation of gene-modified seeds violates both their traditional mode of agriculture and 'sustainable development', these arguments will hardly be 'salient' for the WTO and its leadership.[65] After all, the latter's mission is circumscribed by 'free trade, functioning markets, and security of property rights' even though international organizations have all recognized the need for the 'owned character' of their regimes and the sustainability of economic activity. However, in the absence of a well-institutionalized legislative process which can set priorities and pass on the legitimacy of policies attempting to secure these 'ends' prescribed in the constitutional document, ordering through organizational decision-making in the international arena will always show enormous gaps, considerable incoherence, and the idiocy that comes not only with the banal, but even rather committed engagement of administrators who 'do their jobs' (whatever that might mean). While these circumstances do not prevent 'virtuous action' they certainly make it rather unlikely.

Here, finally, a third point needs to be raised, which concerns the nature of the political discourse concerning global problems. While formerly there was much hope – perhaps misplaced hope – for the emergence of a global public sphere analogous to the publics that came into existence accompanying the process of state-building, a similar development was taking place globally. Meanwhile, the hopes for a global 'civil society' establishing itself through the global media have been disappointed as many of these groups or organizations are rather uncivil, interested in selling our data, instructing us to build bombs for the fight of 'true believers', or just overwhelm the potential public with *kitsch* and drivel, making the 'human interest' story – invented or partially true – the dominant mode of communication, even when asking us sometimes to show our approval by 'likes' or 'emoji'.

---

[64] Ernest Haas, *The Obsolescence of Regional Integration Theory* (Berkeley: University of California Institute of International Studies, Research Series, No. 25, 1975).

[65] For a discussion of the Indian case, see Hans Lindahl, *Authority and the Globalization of Inclusion and Exclusion* (Oxford: Oxford University Press, 2018), chap. 1, sec 3–5.

In the end, the bitter truth seems to be that there is not even a language left for addressing political issues, since learning through participation has largely degenerated into a never-ending show, where 'being there' is the most important thing. Ironically, being present is mistaken for 'making present' (re-present) that which is not 'there' but has to be 'created'. To that extent, photo opportunities increasingly dominate our political agendas, but what they 'show' are mostly professions of faith in 'common values', and of assuring the audience that one is on the right path. Instead of vetting arguments, of following the contestations,[66] and dealing with the difficulties of creating loyalty to a common cause, the anxieties of the 'followers' are managed by techniques that make media experts, celebrities, corporate bosses, 'influencers' from civil society, and politicians part of an increasingly in-transparent 'governance' network. It is incessantly churning out messages, and documents, requiring further meetings and installing new boards for supervision and partnerships for delivering services. To call these frantic activities 'actions' is rather difficult since the 'choices' they entail are carefully camouflaged as functional and urgent necessities that do not allow for 'alternatives'.

But this *problematique* will have to be taken up at another time, save to ponder now the question: could it be that the politics of freedom and responsibility, which has probably run its course, has also reached its 'end' not by having ironically found an answer that ends all questions, but because nobody seems to care anymore about what should be the 'common thing', the *res publica*?

---

[66] One of the really rare investigations that does not press the study of norms in the straight jacket of the usual and rather trite 'norms research' is Antje Wiener, A *Theory of Contestation* (Heidelberg-New York: Springer, 2014).

3

Commitment to the Rule of Law

From a Political to an Organizational Ideal

Sanne Taekema

3.1 INTRODUCTION

International organizations such as the United Nations (UN) and the European Union (EU) present themselves as champions for the rule of law. In recent years, EU member states such as Hungary and Poland have taken questionable measures, replacing the top of the judicial branch, bringing media under political control, changing the electoral system. The EU has responded by employing the EU Treaty instruments for rule of law oversight.[1] The UN are less directly engaged in supervising the rule of law, but there are many documents and policies that confirm the UN concern for the rule of law in states.[2] What is much less obvious is how the UN and the EU think about the rule of law as a governing idea for themselves. The EU Treaty presents the rule of law as something to which it is committed in general. The UN discussions of the rule of law include reference to the rule of law as an international value, and include UN bodies as actors that need to commit to governance of international law. In both cases, however, the rule of law is primarily described as something that states need to uphold.

In 2010, UN peacekeeping forces in Haiti dumped raw sewage in the river that provided many Haitians with drinking water. For the first time in centuries, there was an outbreak of cholera in Haiti, killing thousands. Although the cause of the outbreak was clearly attributable to the UN troops' actions, the tort claim against the UN, submitted to a US judge, was dismissed

---

[1]   C. Closa and D. Kochenov (eds.), *Reinforcing Rule of Law Oversight in the European Union* (Cambridge: Cambridge University Press, 2016).

[2]   See, for example, Report of the Secretary-General. Delivering Justice: Programme of Action to Strengthen the Rule of Law at the National and International Levels (2012) UN GA A/66/749, and Report of the Secretary-General. Strengthening and coordinating United Nations rule of law activities (2014) UN GA A/68/213/Add.1.

84 *Sanne Taekema*

on the basis of the UN's immunity from national lawsuits.[3] The UN finally acknowledged responsibility in 2016, but compensation has been slow and limited. The Haiti cholera outbreak is an infamous example of lack of accountability. As such, it raises a number of legal and political questions. The question that interests me here concerns the relevance of the rule of law for international organizations themselves.

The critique on the lack of accountability of the UN in the Haitian case may be based on a rule of law ideal: is the rule of law not a value to which organizations such as the UN should aspire in their own policies and operations? In turn, this raises the theoretical question of what kind of rule of law ideal is suitable to be applied to international organizations. In this chapter, my main question is therefore: how can the rule of law ideal be given meaning as an organizational value?

In 2019, Amnesty International was criticized for its 'toxic working environment' in which bullying and discrimination by managers were commonplace.[4] In recent years, similar scandals have appeared about other civil society organizations that clearly do not live up to the standards to which they themselves hold others.[5] Thus, it seems that the problem of upholding public standards equally within and outside of the organization is not limited to public international organizations, but also affects non-governmental organizations. I will therefore treat the central question of the rule of law as an organizational value as extending to both public and private organizations.

In the context of this volume, the question then arises of how the rule of law as an organizational value relates to accounts of ethical leadership. More generally, the underlying question is how the value or ideal of the rule of law may relate to ethics. Is a rule of law approach contrary to an ethical approach or rather continuous with it? Many understand the rule of law as the particular legal mode of governance by formal rules. In such an understanding, rule of law appears as fundamentally different from moral or ethical values or principles. Restriction of the rule of law to formal-legal constraints is compatible with a strict separation between law and morality.[6] However, for a number of reasons, I hold the view that law and morality cannot be strictly separated. First of all,

---

[3] J. E. Alvarez, 'International Organizations and the Rule of Law', *New Zealand Journal of Public and International Law*, 14 (2010), pp.3–45, at 4–5.

[4] Karen McVeigh, 'Amnesty has toxic working culture, report finds', *The Guardian*, 6 February 2019.

[5] Examples include Oxfam in relation to sexual abuse on Haiti, and World Wildlife Fund in relation to human rights violations by park rangers in various locations.

[6] Joseph Raz, 'The Rule of Law and its Virtue', in *The Authority of Law: Essays on Law and Morality* (Oxford: Clarendon, 1979), pp. 210–229.

even in a formal rule of law theory, a plausible argument can be made that the rule of law is a matter of law's internal morality. This was Lon Fuller's argument, who saw the requirements of the rule of law or legality as formal but as the internal moral aspirations of law too.[7] Of course, there has been much debate on the strengths of Fuller's arguments on the links between law and morality, but these have not concerned the aspirational, or ideal, dimension of principles of legality. If that ideal or value dimension of law is granted, it is then not a far stretch to argue that law's values are not isolated but closely connected to broader moral concerns. Legality is tied to the ideal of justice, which in turn links to equality and respect for agency.[8] The basis for my account here is therefore the view that law's values are values that are in part specific to legal practices but in part also broader moral values that permeate social practices generally.

Why then single out the rule of law as the value to worry about? Indeed, one might argue that the rule of law is only one among many moral concerns in the practices of international organizations. More particularly, one may doubt whether rule of law contributes to ethical leadership. Is it not because the guiding power of formal rules and procedures runs out that we need to turn to the moral qualities of people within organizations? I will return to this issue later, in Section 3.2, and for now will just say that I see the value of rule of law as one particularly important element in what constitutes organizational practices, especially in organizations committed to public purposes. One of the tasks of leaders in such organizations is to uphold the rule of law ideal.

In order to tackle the central question, a vision of the rule of law needs to be developed that transcends the particular political relationship between a national state and its citizens. The first step then is to argue which rule of law conceptualization is most suitable for application both to the relationships between international organizations and other actors and to the conduct of the international organizations themselves. The theoretical base for this argument is found in socio-legal work that extends the rule of law ideal from public to private actors, particularly the theory of Philip Selznick. Using the teleological view developed by Martin Krygier on the basis of Selznick's work, I put forward a view of the rule of law as an ideal that governs practices within and between organizations. This changes the character of the rule of law from being a political to a moral ideal to which people within organizations need to be

---

[7] Lon L. Fuller, *The Morality of Law*, 2nd ed. (New Haven: Yale University Press, 1969), pp. 41–44.

[8] I have made such an argument previously in Sanne Taekema, *The Concept of Ideals in Legal Theory* (The Hague: Kluwer Law International, 2003), pp. 189–94.

86 Sanne Taekema

committed. As a moral ideal, the rule of law is linked to a broader set of moral values and practices. Linking the value of rule of law to organizational practices makes it possible to see it as contextually embedded, and this in turn leads to an examination of the conditions under which the ideal of rule of law can be upheld. In light of the work of Lauren Edelman on endogeneity of law, it seems plausible that rule of law as a value may suffer from the process of being absorbed and reconstructed in organizational contexts. The final step in the chapter is therefore to examine the normative appeal and limits of rule of law as an organizational and professional value. It depends on the character of the organization and its leaders whether the rule of law can really be meaningful for people working within and for it.

3.2 A VISION OF RULE OF LAW IN CONTEXT

In discussions on extending the rule of law from the national to the international context, many theorists make reference to at least two meanings of the international rule of law. Using Chesterman's phrasing, these can be called the 'international rule of law',[9] the rule of law as governing the relationships between actors in the international realm, such as states and international organizations, or the 'rule of international law',[10] subjecting conduct to international law norms with these having priority over national law. Chesterman distinguishes a third meaning, 'global rule of law', to refer to norms that apply to 'individuals directly without formal mediation through existing national institutions'.[11] What all of these versions of the international rule of law share is a focus on the governance of legal norms.

That understanding relates to the standard catchphrase of rule of law thinking. Although the phrase 'rule of law, not men' is ambiguous in its reference to 'law' – what does law mean here? – it is common to interpret this as governance by a formal legal framework of norms. Chesterman's extension of the domestic rule of law to an international rule of law remains firmly anchored in that idea. The same is true of others who have argued for an international or 'internationalized' rule of law:[12] the rule of law in its core is detectable if a system of norms is in place that governs or ought to govern.

---

[9] S. Chesterman, 'An International Rule of Law?', *American Journal of Comparative Law*, 56 (2008), pp. 331–61, at 355.

[10] Ibid.

[11] Ibid., pp. 355–56.

[12] Vesselin Popovski, 'From Domestic to International Rule of Law: A Long and Unfinished Journey', in V. Popovski (ed.) *International Law and Professional Ethics* (Farnham: Ashgate

I see two basic problems with this standard vision of the rule of law: the idea of law as governing, and the focus on having norms as rule of law's essence. The governance of law is problematic, as was pointed out by Palombella,[13] because law, taking it to refer to norms or a normative system, cannot rule by itself. Law can only rule through the uptake of legal rules by people: strictly speaking, someone needs to use a rule as a normative standard for it to govern. Of course, there are many different ways of achieving that, such as the use of force or threat or the internalization of the rule,[14] but what matters is that legal norms need practical support in order to govern. Without people acting in accordance with the law, law does not rule. The second problem, of seeing norms as rule of law's essence, sends us in the wrong direction. As discussions on the normative emptiness of 'rule by law' have shown, simply having a system of norms in place does not give us much. These norms may require awful conduct, condone atrocities, and in all kinds of ways fail to give their subjects normative direction. The problem is that the subjection to a normative system is a means to an end, and without keeping that end in view, definitions of the rule of law lack direction. Therefore, I prefer to follow Krygier in his teleological conception of the rule of law: the idea should be built upon the basis of its point or purpose rather than based on the way in which it can be implemented.[15] According to Krygier, the point of the rule of law is the prevention, limitation or tempering of the arbitrary exercise of power. Krygier in turn derives his core idea of rule of law from Selznick, who describes it as the reduction of arbitrariness in positive law and its administration.[16] The shift from the governance of law to reduction of arbitrariness may seem trivial: what else does governance of legal norms do other than reduce arbitrary conduct? The shift is significant, I believe, because it enables us to ask what may be achieved through pursuit of the rule of law and to review critically whether putting in place systems of

---

2014) pp. 5–18. André Nollkaemper, 'The Internationalized Rule of Law', *Hague Journal on the Rule of Law*, 1 (2009), pp. 74–78.

[13] Gianluigi Palombella, 'The Rule of Law as Institutional Ideal', *Comparative Sociology*, 9 (2010), pp. 4–39, at p. 10.

[14] Compare H. L. A. Hart, *The Concept of Law*, 2nd ed. (Oxford: Clarendon Press, 1994).

[15] Martin Krygier, 'Four Puzzles about the Rule of Law: Why, What, Where? And Who Cares?', in J. Fleming (ed.), *Getting to the Rule of Law* (New York: New York University Press, 2011), pp. 64–104, at p. 75; Martin Krygier, 'The Rule of Law: Legality, Teleology, Sociology', in G. Palombella and N. Walker (eds.), *Re-locating the Rule of Law* (Oxford: Hart, 2009), pp. 45–70.

[16] Philip Selznick, 'Sociology and Natural Law', *Natural Law Forum* 6 (1961), pp. 84–108, at p. 94; Philip Selznick (with P. Nonet and H. Vollmer), *Law, Society and Industrial Justice* (New York: Russell Sage, 1969), p. 12.

norms is the best way to do so. It may well be that adding to the body of rules in order to further the rule of law has an opposite effect; for instance, having strict rules rather than individual discretion may diminish a sense of moral responsibility, possibly leading to more arbitrary conduct rather than less.

The core of my understanding of the rule of law is therefore seeing it as the ideal of reducing arbitrariness in the exercise of power. This is an open conception, because it is not instantly clear what arbitrariness means. On my view, the following elements are key. First of all, arbitrariness attaches to decision-making in a broad sense, including policy decisions, deciding concrete cases, making rules and regulations. Such decision-making is arbitrary if it is a mere expression of the will of the decision-maker. Secondly, this implies that non-arbitrariness is the restraint of that will by something else. However, this restraining element is not just somebody else's will. Think of military command: the fact that a sergeant orders his squad to attack on the basis of a higher officer's command does not make the order non-arbitrary. Reduction of arbitrariness means limiting wilful decision-making to make it understandable and legitimate to those subject to the decision. This means that justifying a decision by reference to a pre-existing rule is a standard way of achieving reduction of arbitrariness, but so is a balanced decision on the basis of weighing interests and circumstances.[17] Non-arbitrariness is thus understood as a relational quality of the decision-making by powerful actors which is responsive to those affected.

There are two important theoretical implications in the shift to consider the rule of law in purposive terms. First, it clarifies that the rule of law needs to be regarded as an ideal or value. Discussions on the rule of law suffer from ambiguity in this respect: are we speaking of the rule of law as being in place or as something to strive for? Seeing the rule of law as an ideal makes it clear that, in any given context, there may be a certain degree of realization of the ideal. Moreover, since non-arbitrariness is a complex notion, in practice it is impossible to realize the rule of law fully.

Second, it makes clear that the pursuit of rule of law, or legality,[18] is one important social or political aim for which law is used, but there are other aims that are equally important. Whereas the rule of law sets limitation of power as

---

[17] The elements of non-arbitrariness will be further elaborated in Section 3.5.
[18] I follow Selznick and Fuller in equating rule of law with the value of legality. See Selznick, *Law, Society and Industrial Justice*, p. 11. Fuller refers to his list of eight criteria, which is usually taken as a standard formulation of the formal rule of law, as principles of legality: Lon L. Fuller, *The Morality of Law*, revised edition (New Haven: Yale University Press, 1969), p. 41.

the purpose, large parts of law are there to constitute power.[19] Law not only limits what legal actors can do, it creates some of these actors and specifies the legal powers they have. (Here, too, of course, people need to put these powers into practice.) Although this aspect of law is not my focus here, it is important to note, because the creation of powers enables arbitrary action, unless limitations are set at the same time. This is especially relevant in the bureaucratic context of organizations because creating new legal bodies is a trusted method for tackling governance problems.[20]

As I mentioned in the Introduction, such a purposive account also implies that the rule of law is to be seen as a moral value. My understanding of morality is practical, in the sense that morality concerns evaluative and prescriptive aspects of human action.[21] Put simply, it concerns the question of what to do. Of course, there are many different accounts of how that question should be addressed. Is it a matter of deontological principles, consequentialism, or virtuous character? If these different ethical perspectives are considered broadly, I would think attention for the value of the rule of law is compatible with each. Since the combination with a virtue ethical account is less obvious than with deontology or consequentialism, I will focus the argument on that. Moreover, ethical leadership is often described as a matter of character and virtue, which makes the link to virtue ethics more relevant. As Christine Swanton has argued, a standard way of seeing the relationship between value and virtue is to see the virtues as derivative, as no more than predispositions to realize value.[22] Swanton rightly rejects this view in favour of a pluralistic account of the bases of virtue, including values, but also persons, nature or relationships. However, when it comes to the rule of law, studying the connection between virtue and value does seem an apt route. Values are part of social moral practices, of the ways in which we interact and respond to each other's action. It makes sense to see a social process as envalued, that is, as being shaped by value commitments, which includes legal processes. A legal procedure needs to respect values of fair treatment and equal respect, for instance. Virtues also have a crucial role to play, as the character traits of the persons shaping these processes. For instance, judges need to be good listeners and wise decision-makers. In political and legal

---

[19] Palombella, Rule of Law as Institutional Ideal, p. 20.

[20] The EU provides a clear example of the trend of creating agencies; see Morten Egeberg and Jarne Trondal, 'Researching European Union Agencies: What Have We Learnt (and Where Do We Go from Here)?', *Journal of Common Market Studies*, 55 (2017), pp. 675–690.

[21] I follow the convention of seeing morality as part of practice and ethics as the study of morality. This would mean that strictly speaking I should refer to ethical leadership as moral leadership. Since this is rather uncommon, I also follow standard terminology here.

[22] Christine Swanton, *Virtue Ethics: A Pluralistic View* (Oxford: Oxford University Press, 2003), p. 35.

90   *Sanne Taekema*

settings, we then also expect the virtues of participants to align with the rule of law ideal. The relationship between the value of the rule of law and morality can be summarized as the rule of law being a moral value with particular relevance to political and legal practices, which make it a part of the value commitments of actors within these practices. This does not detract from other moral commitments and traits of such actors.

From here on, I will present the rule of law as an ideal or value to be realized, for which we use law as the primary means of achievement.[23] An important consequence of viewing the rule of law as a value to be realized is that the question of what means are to be used to realize that value needs to be answered contextually. This, I think, is the central insight of the socio-legal approach to the rule of law taken by Selznick and Krygier.[24] I follow their lead in seeing the rule of law as a pragmatic ideal that can be applied creatively in different contexts, including those in which we are not accustomed to speak about rule of law values. This view does not, however, imply that the rule of law can be transplanted in whatever way we fancy; the context to which it is applied needs to be taken seriously as the practical environment constraining the possibilities, not only of realizing the ideal but also of formulating an understandable conception of it.

3.3 FROM A POLITICAL TO AN ORGANIZATIONAL IDEAL

The view of the rule of law as an ideal to be applied contextually at the same time invites an investigation of the meaning of the rule of law in different settings and warns against divorcing the value from the cultural practices in which it needs to be embedded. For lawyers, the dominant legal-cultural environment for the rule of law is that of the institutions of the constitutional state. The rule of law is seen as a political ideal, because it constrains institutions of government in the interest of its subjects.[25] One of the consequences of this setting is that the vast majority of authors on the rule of law understand it as

---

[23] A brief note on terminology: in my understanding, ideal or value may be used interchangeably to refer to a state of affairs that is desirable but not yet realized. Theoretically, ideals may be distinguished from values as being unrealizable rather than realizable, but that distinction has little purchase in rule of law discussions. See Taekema, *Concept of Ideals*, pp. 40–41.

[24] Martin Krygier, 'Institutional Optimism and Cultural Pessimism and the Rule of Law', in Martin Krygier and Adam Czarnota (eds.), *The Rule of Law after Communism. Problems and Prospects in East-Central Europe* (Aldershot: Ashgate, 1999), pp. 77–105; Philip Selznick, 'Legal Cultures and the Rule of Law', in Martin Krygier and Adam Czarnota (eds.), *The Rule of Law after Communism. Problems and Prospects in East-Central Europe* (Aldershot: Ashgate, 1999), pp. 21–38.

[25] Raz, *Authority of Law*, p. 213.

limiting the powers of state institutions, preferably in the form of constraints laid down in the state's constitution. As a political ideal, the rule of law qualifies the relationship between the state and its citizens, and the relationship between state institutions themselves. It does not concern the relationship between citizens among themselves nor does it include transnational actors or institutions.

However, once the rule of law is formulated as the ideal of reducing arbitrariness in the exercise of power, and regarded pragmatically as applicable in different contexts, whether it must be a political ideal in this sense becomes an open question. For the purposes of this book, extending the rule of law to a different context should be the context of organizations. Fortunately, this is also a point on which the theory of Philip Selznick has laid the foundations. In his 1969 book *Law, Society and Industrial Justice*, Selznick investigated the meaning of legality or rule of law in private corporations.[26] His main claim in the book is that, mainly due to the democratization of society in the 1960s, workers' rights became important within corporations and this introduced a rule of law sensibility to that context. The broader question Selznick sought to answer was 'what it means to "legalize" an institution, that is, to infuse its mode of governance with the aspirations and constraints of a legal order'.[27] Selznick also starts from an ideal of legality or rule of law in a legal-political setting. However, in line with what was already discussed above, his understanding of rule of law is not standard. The reduction of arbitrariness is not to be equated with formal rules, because this forgets the danger of legalism, treating the means as more important than the end. Selznick sees non-arbitrariness as connected to both formal and substantive justice, and readily admits that this means that the notion of arbitrariness is ambiguous and complex.[28] This vision of legality is broad: it is not just found in designing ways to limit the arbitrary exercise of official power, it extends to the moral value of being a citizen in a legal order. Thus, it underlines a broader vision of responsibility for the rule of law.

The biggest step to take is to show how legality may become relevant within private organizations. The key move by Selznick is to see private sector organizations as dealing with the same problem as legal administrative agencies, leading to a 'common law of governance', which 'should apply wherever the social function of governing is performed, wherever some men rule and others are ruled'.[29] At first, it seems this idea can be applied to rather

---

[26] Selznick, *Law, Society and Industrial Justice*, p.11.
[27] Ibid., p. 8.
[28] Ibid., p. 13.
[29] Ibid., pp. 243 and 259, respectively.

too many situations: would that mean including all situations of authority, for instance including the family, in which parents set rules for children? No, it is more restricted: it means performing governmental functions or having such a position of power that this calls for similar responsibilities as those of public institutions.[30] Thus, the relative position of an actor as one-sidedly determining the position of others seems crucial, as well as the impropriety of arbitrary action. The latter point, that arbitrary action must be restrained, is not completely obvious in private organizations. One might say that it is necessary to be free to decide in the interests of the company and that it would go too far to restrain that freedom on the basis of legality principles. This is a valid point to make, but it almost equally applies to public government: there, too, situations appear in which restriction of conduct based on rule of law principles is not a good idea. Although there is less scope for managerial freedom in public administration than in private organizations, what Fuller calls 'managerial direction' has a proper place in both settings.[31] Rather than separate the political realm from the realm of private organizations, and see them as governed by different basic principles, we need to ask to what extent the public value of legality can be carried over to other contexts and become a value that transcends the public–private divide.

At this point, Selznick's theory needs to be taken a step further. He sees the value of legality and legalization as relevant whenever the private organization takes on political meaning, and thus becomes a polity.[32] I would suggest that it is more useful to focus on the locus of power and the opportunities for arbitrary conduct with adverse consequences for the interests of others. When Google forces users to give access to crucial personal data in exchange for a trivial service, it is a valid question whether this should be seen as abuse of its (market) power. For the effects on individuals, it does not matter whether the monopoly of providing a service is in public or private hands. In both cases, there is the need to restrict the scope for arbitrary action in order to protect individuals affected by it. Thus, the first step towards the rule of law as an organizational value is to see the exercise of power by actors other than state institutions as a matter of concern equal to state power. Looking at the character and consequences of action by private organizations, they are sufficiently similar to be made subject to the same normative framework, that is, the rule of law. If the extent of an organization's power and the

---

[30] Ibid., p. 260.
[31] Lon L. Fuller, *The Principles of Social Order* (K. Winston, ed.) (Durham: Duke University Press 1981), pp. 178–179.
[32] Selznick, *Law, Society and Industrial Justice*, p. 250.

possibilities of impacting the interests of others are made central, then the rule of law seems especially relevant to a category of actors that, though private, have an impact similar to states: multinational enterprises (MNEs). Although I cannot go into the precise character of the responsibilities of MNEs, the discussion of the Ruggie principles in the context of business and human rights shows how MNE responsibilities for legal values in the form of human rights have become a standard part of the conversation.[33] From the perspective taken here, a key feature of corporate responsibilities is that such acknowledgement gives attention to the adverse consequences of their one-sided actions to basic interests of others, which displays a rule of law sensibility.

In a similar vein, we may then argue that the internal conduct of powerful actors within organizations does not fundamentally differ from external action affecting the interests of others outside of the organization. Here, too, it is the use of a powerful position in an arbitrary way that is problematic. In the example of Amnesty International, a review of the workplace culture was held after two staff members had committed suicide.[34] The review reported persistent intimidation and racial and gender discrimination. The example shows not only the importance of arbitrary use of power within organizations but also the importance of upholding the same values outside and within the organization. For a civil society organization such as Amnesty International, these findings are especially painful, since their work is devoted to combatting human rights abuses. As an internal ideal for organizations, the rule of law thus also demands reining in exercise of power for the benefit of those affected by it.

Viewing the rule of law as an organizational ideal and looking for its realization inside organizations also gives guidance as to the more specific standards that need to be upheld. It seems that the aims of the organization play a central role here. If an organization holds others to account for substantive rule of law violations such as human rights abuses, the same standards need to apply to the organization itself, both within the organization and when it acts externally. This makes it easier to argue that international organizations such as the UN and EU, and civil society organizations such as Amnesty International and Oxfam must uphold the organizational ideal of the rule of law, since they are so explicitly committed. With commercial companies, the argument is less easy to make, unless they also profess to be devoted to

---

[33] The business and human rights literature is vast; for an insider's discussion of the developments, see John Ruggie, *Just Business: Multinational Corporations and Human Rights* (New York: Norton, 2013).

[34] In the investigations of these deaths, one of them was found to be linked to treatment at work. See McVeigh, *The Guardian*, 6 February 2019.

94 *Sanne Taekema*

rule of law values (which some companies do in the context of corporate social responsibility). In the commercial context, the aspect of power seems more crucial than the mission of the organization in order to decide on the extent to which an ideal of rule of law should govern. As argued above, minimal requirements of decent and equal treatment of those subject to power relations apply in the commercial context as well. We can therefore allow for variations in rule of law value realization and commitment without giving up the idea that governance by the powerful anywhere needs to be scrutinized in a minimal sense at least.

3.4 THE PRECARIOUSNESS OF INTERNALIZING VALUES

If the normative point made in Section 3.3, that the rule of law is to be regarded as a value for all organizations with variable specific demands, is granted, the question arises of how this may work. More specifically, there is the worry that relying on value commitments within organizations risks not achieving much at all, because it is difficult to change people's values. How may values be introduced and how is commitment to them built up? I will approach these questions through a discussion of Lauren Edelman's work on law and organizations. Edelman applies her socio-legal approach to organizations and investigates how law enters organizations, and how organizations in turn shape law. Building on Selznick's work on law and organizational culture, she introduces the idea of law's endogeneity: 'the meaning of law is determined largely within (rather than outside of) the social arena that it seeks to regulate.'[35] She also shows how by internalizing law, that is, 'by creating and formalizing internal policies that approximate the core principles of legality', organizations are able to legitimize their conduct and avoid interventions by public authorities.[36] Although in most of her work, Edelman does not specifically focus on legal values, her approach highlights the interaction between law and organizational values, and shows how mimicking formal legal institutions helps organizations to comply with law symbolically rather than substantively.[37] Thus, Edelman points out the strength of organizational cultures and the uncertain result of introducing new legal

---

[35] Lauren Edelman, 'Legality and the Endogeneity of Law', in Robert A. Kagan, Martin Krygier, and Kenneth Winston (eds.), *Legality and Community. On the Intellectual Legacy of Philip Selznick* (Lanham: Rowman & Littlefield, 2002), pp. 187–202.

[36] Lauren Edelman and Mark Suchman, 'When the "Haves" Hold Court: Speculations on the Organizational Internalization of Law', *Law and Society Review*, 33 (1999), pp. 941–91, at p. 946.

[37] Edelman, 'Legality and the Endogeneity of Law', p. 195.

values in them: 'as law flows into organizational fields, legal ideals tend to be fused with managerial ways of thinking, producing a "managerialization of law" that may, in subtle ways, weaken or undermine legality.'[38]

Legal values, such as legality, depend on a culture that fosters them for their realization, and even their survival. Selznick has argued that values are latent in social reality: they are not abstract ideas, but have a basis in social practices.[39] Because values emerge from social practices, the environment in the form of culture, beliefs, norms, and behaviour needs to support these values. Simply writing down that an organization is committed to the rule of law will not start the process of making that organization commit to the rule of law. The rule of law ideal needs to have a connection to practical concerns and cultural ideas that are already present in the organization. According to Selznick, leadership is a core element in bringing about change in organizations. In his early work, he emphasized that organizations may turn into institutions if they are 'infused with value' and that such processes demand leadership to take hold.[40] Thus, we may argue that a viable introduction of a rule of law ideal in organizations depends on the extent to which its leadership is willing to commit to the ideal and to further its embedding in the organization. Again, for such a value change it is not enough to proclaim that the value is important; it requires a belief of the leaders of the organization in the ideal's relevance and taking action to ensure it becomes so.

As the discussion of Edelman's ideas on endogeneity shows, difficulties may arise when the organizational culture is already institutionalized, but with a commitment to values other than legal ones. We can clearly see this in relation to companies: commercial success and achieving your targets may be at odds with attention for the arbitrary consequences of your actions, because that draws on resources. This tension often gives rise to superficial commitment to non-commercial values; think of the phenomenon of 'greenwashing', for instance.[41] However, the problem of dominant managerial values is not limited to the commercial sector; in many other organizational fields there is also a bureaucratic view that organizations must be flexible, 'lean and mean', based on similar principles of internal organization and resources

---

[38]   Ibid., p. 196.
[39]   Selznick, *Law, Society and Industrial Justice*, p. 10. For a discussion, see Taekema, *Concept of Ideals*, pp. 132–36.
[40]   Philip Selznick, *Leadership in Administration: A Sociological Interpretation* (Berkeley: University of California Press, 1984), p. 17, '"to institutionalize" is to *infuse with value* beyond the technical requirements of the task at hand' (emphasis original).
[41]   Referring to the pretence of sustainable and socially responsible activities for marketing or reputation purposes only, see William S. Laufer, 'Social Accountability and Corporate Greenwashing', *Journal of Business Ethics* 43 (2003), pp. 253–61.

96 *Sanne Taekema*

management as commercial enterprises.[42] In such settings, it may be very difficult to realize the ideal of legality. However, even in more classic bureaucratic organizations, which are Weberian in their commitment to rationality and formal decision-making, commitment to legality as a value cannot be taken for granted. As Edelman shows, there is a tendency within organizations not to give up their existing, 'managerial', ways of thinking, which may well be at odds with genuine commitment to legality.[43] The easy way out for organizations is to play by the formal rules or to proceduralize values. For instance, it is easy to create complaints procedures for discrimination without doing much to change the organizational culture that condones discrimination.[44] This implies that a real concern for the meaning of arbitrariness, and for avoiding it in decision-making conduct, need not become part of the organizational culture.

The problem is exacerbated by the ordinary meaning of the rule of law as governance on the basis of formal rules. This meaning positively invites organizations to interpret adherence to the value of the rule of law as adopting formal rules and procedures. Creating a culture in which leaders and others in positions of power genuinely try to act non-arbitrarily towards people ruled by them is a much vaguer prescription, neither easy to do nor to show being done. Even legal cultures may be more or less committed to the rule of law as a foundational value. As work on authoritarian regimes shows, legal institutions which we generally expect to uphold the rule of law may be compromised to such an extent that they have adopted foundational values with a very different character, such as deference to political will.[45] Whenever there are strong values to compete with the rule of law, and an interest of organizational leaders to favour these, we may expect rule of law commitment to be no more than lip service. I believe this holds for both political and organizational contexts.

Looking more closely at the make up of international organizations, these appear as organizations that are structured bureaucratically, in the classic

---

[42] This is how I understand the introduction of New Public Management in governmental organizations; compare Soma Pillay, 'A Cultural Ecology of New Public Management', *International Review of Administrative Sciences*, 74 (2008), pp. 373–94.

[43] Edelman, 'Legality and the Endogeneity of Law', p. 196.

[44] See Lauren Edelman, Christopher Uggen, and Howard Erlanger, 'The Endogeneity of Legal Regulation: The Grievance Procedure as Rational Myth', *American Journal of Sociology*, 105 (1999), pp. 406–54.

[45] Examples of research done in this direction: Nick Cheesman, 'The Rule of Law or Un-Rule of Law in Myanmar?', *Pacific Affairs*, 82 (4) (2009–2010), pp. 597–613; Kathryn Hendley, '"Telephone Law" and the "Rule of Law": The Russian Case', *Hague Journal on the Rule of Law*, 1 (2009), pp. 241–62.

Weberian sense.[46] Bureaucracies thrive on working with rules and procedures, which may derail into observing rules and procedures for their own sake rather than for the purposes for which they are instituted. With their focus on rational, impersonal decision-making processes, the bureaucracies of international organizations have a close affinity with the rule of law as a formal structure. To give the rule of law meaning as a legal and moral value, this sense of the value of observing procedure can serve as a starting point. The rule of law is a good base because it is close to the internal values of bureaucracies, but it should not be interpreted narrowly if it is to do good. This requires a sense of purpose of the leaders of international organizations who need to take the rule of law seriously. A positive example is the EU's foregrounding of the rule of law by having a vice-president dedicated to better regulation and rule of law. Such a brief enables leadership for the pursuit of a more integrated rule of law agenda. Such leadership may contribute to rule of law realization, but it is not enough: the value also needs to be embedded in the working practices of the organization.

3.5 PRACTISING A RULE OF LAW IDEAL

Examining organizational culture in relation to legal values may give the impression that there is little to be done: realizing legality in organizations seems to be a matter of patience and of hoping that a leader comes along who thinks legality is important. Although we should acknowledge that realization of legal values is difficult, in this section I aim to sketch the contours of a more positive normative vision. To that end, I return to the vision of the rule of law portrayed in Section 3.2 and elaborate this vision for organizational practice. Practising an ideal has an individual and a social component. As a matter of personal morality, the ideal of legality asks individuals to consider the impact of their actions on others in terms of arbitrariness. Of special concern is the personal morality of organizational leaders who need to worry about fostering moral conduct within the organization more generally, in addition to making sure their own conduct realizes legality. In terms of social morality, the ideal of legality requires forming practices together in which opportunities for arbitrary conduct are reduced. To get a better sense of both dimensions, the idea of non-arbitrariness needs to be specified further: what makes conduct and practices non-arbitrary? Within the context of legal organizations, Elaine Mak and I have argued that this requires rational justification of decisions,

---

[46] Michael N. Barnett and Martha Finnemore, 'The Politics, Power and Pathologies of International Organizations', *International Organizations*, 53 (1998), pp. 699–732, at 700.

predictability of rules, fairness in decision-making in concrete cases, and accountability to those affected in the form of participation and procedures.[47] These four dimensions of non-arbitrariness can each be seen as elaborating a specific value aspect of the relationship between powerful actors and the people affected by their decisions and conduct. All four value aspects presuppose that the powerful actor needs to understand its own actions as related to other people. This requires considering whether arguments can be provided that make sense to them, whether rules issued are understandable and fit for application, whether a decision does justice to the circumstances in which a person is situated, and whether people have genuine opportunities to voice their side of the argument and complaints.[48]

All of these aspects, it seems to me, have meaning for the organizational context. The first aspect of rational justification is at stake whenever the internal or external conduct of people within an organization does not uphold the legal values the organization professes to serve or promote. The example of Amnesty International referred to in the introduction illustrates this. Although there may be reasons that can explain the conduct of Amnesty's managers, such as the pressure of a sudden reorganization, or the spirit of criticism needed for holding others to account being turned inward,[49] these cannot justify discrimination of employees. The aspect of predictability of rules seems less of a problem, although in organizational contexts similar problems may arise: of rules being made that are not sufficiently clear or known to subjects, and a lack of matching conduct to the rules' requirements.[50] The way the UN handled the Haiti cholera case may illustrate the dimensions of both fairness and accountability: the lack of a readiness to take responsibility and provide meaningful and timely compensation shows a neglect of fairness, while the

[47] Elaine Mak and Sanne Taekema, 'The European Union's Rule of Law Agenda: Identifying Its Core and Contextualizing Its Application', *Hague Journal on the Rule of Law*, 8 (2016), pp. 25–50. These aspects are also helpful to understand the normative framework for judicial culture, as argued by Elaine Mak, Niels Graaf, and Erin Jackson, 'The Framework for Judicial Cooperation in the European Union: Unpacking the Ethical, Legal and Institutional Dimensions of "Judicial Culture"', *Utrecht Journal of International and European Law*, 34 (1) (2018), pp. 24–44.

[48] The fourth aspect of accountability receives the most separate attention in relation to international organizations. Finding other forms of accountability than democratic accountability is seen as highly necessary. See, for example, Ruth Grant and Robert Keohane, 'Accountability and Abuses of Power in World Politics', *American Political Science Review*, 99 (2005), pp. 29–43.

[49] Kavita Avula, Lisa McKay, and Sébastien Galland, *Amnesty International Staff Wellbeing Review*, ORG 60/9763/2019, January 2019, available at www.amnesty.org/en/documents/org60/9763/2019/en/.

[50] Compare Fuller, *Morality of Law*, pp. 33–39.

fact that there were no clear avenues to complain and ask for redress shows the lack of accountability.

Moving beyond the formal making of rules and procedures requires that individuals in positions of power are concerned about the relationship with others. That basic relational aspect may also give resources for changing the practices within organizations, because the individuals who are affected by this behaviour have their own role in the process. By demanding accountability, asserting their own interest, and being critical of leadership that is insufficiently aware of the effects on power relationships, individuals within an organization or those directly suffering the consequences may contribute to change. Of course, this may also be for better or worse. As Selznick writes, 'As human beings and not mere tools they have their own needs for self-protection and self-fulfilment – needs that may either sustain the formal system or undermine it.'[51] Because the burden of many decisions falls on those who were not responsible for taking them but were simply on the receiving end, the awareness of arbitrary consequences of conduct is more acute among them. This means that, in addition to being committed to the ideal of legality as such, that is, attempting to act and organize practices to minimize arbitrariness, people in powerful positions also need to be responsive. This includes literally listening to the views and complaints of those affected, but also demands an imaginative consideration of what it means to be in a position without power. This is an important reason why the ideal of legality needs an ethical commitment not only to the ideal itself, but also to sustaining practices and relationships that allow it to flourish.

To conclude then, legal ideals, and especially the rule of law or legality, have a relevance that extends beyond standard legal practices. The core notion of the rule of law, aiming to reduce arbitrary exercise of power, has normative force in all contexts in which relationships depending on power differences are central. Organizations are built upon such power differentials, and rely on formal structures and rules to give these shape and limit their negative effects. As an ideal, rule of law or legality makes demands beyond the formal structures: it asks people to work towards non-arbitrary practices. This is a difficult proposition, because organizational cultures have their own values and these may not always be easily combined with values of legality. However, there is room for optimism. Importantly, the international organizations that are the focus of this book all include rule of law as a crucial value to uphold. This should make it easier to extend the meaning of legality inwards, because commitment to the ideal is not alien to these organizations. If the leadership

[51] Selznick, *Leadership in Administration*, p. 8.

in these organizations takes up a richer, moral, understanding of the rule of law, genuine realization of the ideal is possible. However, even private organizations, most notably multinational enterprises, understand that they need to consider the adverse effects of their powerful position on others. Whether it is voluntary or under pressure of media and interest groups, they also engage in making legality-based procedures to embed attention for arbitrary consequences of their actions in their organization. Introducing such values into the work of MNEs is harder work than it is in public organizations, and it may easily fail because these values become subordinated to standard business concerns, but here too leadership makes a difference. If key actors within the organization persist in pointing out how legality is relevant, and if they are responsive to the needs and criticisms of people affected by the organization's activities, rule of law sensibilities may also develop there. Formal rule of law procedures are but a part of diminishing arbitrary exercise of power; for genuine realization, people need to care.

4

Exemplarism, Virtue, and Ethical Leadership in International Organizations

Amalia Amaya[*]

4.1 INTRODUCTION

This chapter develops an exemplarist virtue approach to ethical leadership in international organizations. An exemplarist virtue theory of ethical leadership endorses a virtue perspective on ethical leadership that assigns a prominent role to exempla. This approach involves two central commitments about the structure of a theory of ethical leadership: first, a commitment to the view that virtues, rather than rules or consequences, are the primary concepts in a theory of ethical leadership; and second, a commitment to the claim that exempla of ethical leadership occupy a central stage within the theory. The development of an exemplarist virtue approach to ethical leadership thus draws on two main, connected, traditions of moral theory: virtue ethics and exemplarism.

Virtue ethics was the principal approach to ethics for much of the history of moral thought. It became, however, marginalized in the eighteenth century, with the upsurge of Kantian and Utilitarian ethics. Since its revival, in the last decades of the twentieth century, it has steadily gained prominence and has become, alongside deontology and consequentialism, a major normative framework in contemporary ethical theory.[1] Another significant development in contemporary ethics has been the vindication of exemplarity as an important concept in moral theory.[2] This vindication may too be viewed as a recuperation, for exempla have figured prominently in the history of moral thought, most importantly, as central devices for moral education. Interestingly, the revival of

---

[*]   I am deeply thankful to Euan MacDonald, Pablo de Larrañaga, Claudio Michelon, Maria Varaki, Guilherme Vasconcelos, and Neil Walker for very valuable comments on an earlier draft.
[1]   The revival of virtue ethics was triggered by Elisabeth Anscombe's paper "Modern Moral Philosophy," *Philosophy*, vol. 33, 1958, reprinted in R. Crisp and M. Slote, *Virtue Ethics*, Oxford University Press, Oxford, 1997 (which also contains key papers in contemporary virtue ethics).
[2]   See L. Zagzebski, *Exemplarist Moral Theory*, Oxford University Press, Oxford, 2017.

Amalia Amaya

both virtue and exempla as important concepts in ethical theory goes hand-in-hand, as one of the main developments that sparked current interest on exemplarism was the proposal of an exemplarist version of virtue ethics.[3]

In the last few decades, both virtue theory and exemplarism have expanded beyond the domain of ethics to be applied to other disciplines, including law and politics. Virtue jurisprudence and virtue politics are currently extremely active fields of research and the relevance of exemplarism to legal and political theory have also begun to be explored.[4] As I will argue in this chapter, virtue ethics and exemplarism may also be profitably deployed to give an account of ethical leadership in the context of international organizations. Virtue ethics provides resources to develop a theory of ethical leadership that has some advantages over both consequentialist and deontological approaches. Exemplarism furnishes tools for explaining the roles that ethical leaders play within their organizations as well as their impact, mediated by the moral authority they enjoy, on the legitimacy of the institutions they lead. Thus, an exemplarist variant of virtue ethics, as I hope to show in this chapter, provides a promising perspective for addressing questions about ethical leadership in international organizations.

In order to develop an exemplarist virtue account of ethical leadership for global governance institutions, I shall draw on historical thought on leadership as well as on contemporary work on leadership in organizational studies, in which both virtue and exempla are prominent.[5] This account also builds on and extends recent virtue-oriented work in both international law and international relations.[6]

---

[3] See L. Zagzebski, "Exemplarist Virtue Theory," *Metaphilosophy*, 41, 2010.

[4] See L. Solum and C. Farrelly (eds.), *Virtue Jurisprudence*, Palgrave MacMillan, New York, 2008; A. Amaya and H. L. Ho (eds.), *Virtue, Law and Justice*, Hart Publishing, Oxford, 2012; and A. Amaya and C. Michelon (eds.), *The Faces of Virtue in Law*, Routledge, London, 2019. On virtue politics, see M. Lebar, "Virtue and Politics," D. C. Russell, *The Cambridge Companion to Virtue Ethics*, Cambridge University Press, Cambridge, 2013; C. Farrelly, *Justice, Democracy and Reasonable Agreement*, Palgrave MacMillan, New York, 2007; and L. E. Goodman and R. B. Talisse (eds.), *Aristotle's Politics Today*, State University of New York Press, Albany, 2007.

[5] For a brief and lucid discussion of the history of virtuous leadership, see P. Kaak and D. Weeks, "Virtuous Leadership: Ethical and Effective," Stan Van Hooft (ed.), *The Handbook of Virtue Ethics*, Routledge, New York, 2013. For virtue approaches to leadership in organizational contexts, see, among others, C. Caldwell, Z. Hasan, and S. Smith, "Virtuous Leadership – Insights for the 21st Century," *Journal of Management Development*, vol. 34, 2015; K. Cameron, "Responsible Leadership as Virtuous Leadership," *Journal of Business Ethics*, vol. 98, 2011; and G. Flynn, "The Virtuous Manager: A Vision of Leadership in Business," *Journal of Business Ethics*, vol. 78, 2008.

[6] For virtue approaches to international relations, see J. Gaskarth, "The Virtues in International Society," *European Journal of International Relations*, vol. 18(3), 2011; and K. Ainley, "Virtue Ethics and International Relations," unpublished manuscript. For virtue ethics perspectives on international law, see Jan Klabbers' seminal work in "Virtuous Interpretation," *Queen Mary Studies in International Law*, vol. 1, 2010; "Law, Ethics and Global Governance: Accountability in Perspective," *New Zealand Journal of Public and International Law*, vol. 11, 2014; "Doing Justice? Bureaucracy, the Rule of Law and Virtue Ethics," *Rivista di Filosofia del Diritto*, vol. 6, 2017; and

In addition, it is meant to add a layer to work in international organizations scholarship that examines character traits that are distinctive of successful leadership.[7] Last, this theory intersects nicely with the growing body of literature that aims to provide biographical accounts of executive heads of international organizations.[8] This work makes available an extremely valuable empirical input for the development of an exemplarist virtue approach to ethical leadership in international organizations which, in its turn, may provide a productive framework for theorizing the impact and contributions of the actors under study.

The structure of the chapter is as follows. In Section 4.2, I argue for a conceptualization of ethical leadership in international organizations in terms of virtue. Section 4.3 presents a proposal about the main traits of character that are virtues for international civil servants who are in leadership positions in the context of international organizations. Section 4.4 discusses several varieties of exemplarity that are relevant to ethical leadership in international organizations. In Section 4.5, I provide an account of the roles that exemplary ethical leaders, that is, international civil servants that possess and exercise a large share of the virtues of ethical leadership, play in the context of international organizations. In Section 4.6, I claim that exemplary ethical leaders enjoy moral authority, which is a source of legitimacy for international organizations. I conclude in Section 4.7 with some thoughts on how virtuous leadership in international organizations may be fostered.

4.2 A PLEA FOR A VIRTUE APPROACH TO ETHICAL LEADERSHIP

Leadership has a consequential moral dimension that has been recently constructed as "ethical leadership."[9] How could ethical leadership be conceptualized? Virtue concepts, I would argue, should figure prominently in a theory of ethical

---

"The Virtues of Expertise," M. Ambrus, et al. (eds.), *The Role of "Experts" in International and European Decision-Making Processes*, Cambridge University Press, Cambridge, 2014.

[7] See M. G. Schechter, "Confronting the Challenges of Political Leadership in International Organizations," *Comparative Political Leadership*, Palgrave, 2012; and J. Wouters and J. Odermatt, "Individual Leadership in Guiding Change in Global Governance Institutions: Theory and Practice," Leuven Centre for Global Governance Studies, 2016, pp. 6–8.

[8] For studies on the UN Secretary-General with a focus on the moral dimensions of this position, see K. Kille, *The UN-Secretary and Moral Authority: Ethics and Religion and International Leadership*, Georgetown University Press, Washington, 2007; and M. Frölich, *Political Ethics and the United Nations: Dag Hmmarskjöld as Secretary-General*, Routledge, New York, 2008. See also the IO-BIO project at www.ru.nl/fm/iobio (for the analysis of executive heads of other international organizations).

[9] For a useful introduction, see M. E. Brown and L. K. Treviño, "Ethical Leadership: A Review and Future Directions," *The Leadership Quarterly*, vol. 17, 2006. See also L. K. Treviño and

leadership for international organizations. Indeed, the idea that virtue is linked to leadership has a long ancestry. Virtue occupied a central place in the reflection on leadership in Plato and, more importantly, Aristotle. Interestingly, virtue was also at the core of Eastern perspectives on leadership, specifically, in Confucius. It remained pivotal in Roman thought on leadership and through Christendom, but was marginalized as virtue ethics began to lose its traction in modern moral thought.[10] Arguably, the rise of the modern state, which put expertise and administrative abilities at the forefront, and the adoption of effectiveness as a morally neutral criterion for assessing good leadership also contributed to the displacement of virtue in leadership theory. Recently, however, leadership studies have partaken in the recovery of virtue ethics as an important ethical framework. A virtue theory of leadership has been articulated and defended most prominently in the context of business organizations.[11] Virtue, I would argue, is also critical to give an account of ethical leadership in the context of international organizations.

A virtue ethical approach to ethical leadership in international organizations focuses on the individual leaders as the primary object of evaluation. Good ethical leadership, in this view, depends on the leader's virtues, rather than on the performance of acts identified as right on agent-independent principles, most importantly, consequentialist and deontological principles.[12] There are some reasons that make virtue theory, I would argue, an attractive moral theory to conceptualize ethical leadership.[13] First, virtue theory does not reduce – unlike principle-based approaches – good moral practice to rule-following. There does not seem to be any set of rules sufficient to give a determinate answer to the question of what a moral agent should do in a particular situation of choice. Similarly, good leadership is not strictly rule-based. Insofar as virtue ethics takes good judgment to be inextricably linked to the appreciation of the particular features of the situation of choice, it resists any attempt to simplify ethical leadership to mere rule-following.

M. E. Brown, "Ethical Leadership," *The Oxford Handbook of Leadership and Organizations*, D. V. Day (ed.), Oxford University Press, Oxford, 2014.

[10] See Kaak and Weeks, *op. cit.*, and J. Petifils, *Mos Christianorum: The Roman Discourse of Exemplarity and the Jewish and Christian Language of Leadership*, Mohr Siebeck, Tübingen, 2016.

[11] For references, see note 5 above.

[12] Different varieties of ethical leadership in organizations result from the application of different types of moral theory, so we could distinguish between virtue, consequentialist, and deontological approaches to ethical leadership. See M. Van Wart, "Contemporary Varieties of Ethical Leadership in Organizations," *International Journal of Business Administration*, vol. 5(5), 2014.

[13] For an analysis of some of the advantages of virtue theory, see L. Zagzebski, *Virtues of the Mind*, Princeton University Press, Princeton, pp. 22–23.

Second, virtue concepts are "thick," in Bernard Williams' well-known terminology, and so they not only allow us to express a positive or negative evaluation (as "thin" concepts such as "justified," "unjustified," "rational" or "irrational" do), but they also provide information about the way in which the moral agent behaved properly or improperly.[14] In this sense, virtue concepts provide an articulation of the ethical standards for assessing leadership behavior in international organizations that is richer in content than principle-based standards.

Third, virtue ethics embodies a moral ideal according to which moral agents aim not merely to avoid blameworthiness, but to achieve moral praiseworthiness. In this respect, virtue ethics critically departs from both deontological and consequentialist approaches, in which the basic evaluative concept is that of a right act, that is to say, an act that is permitted by the applicable rules. In contrast to this "morality of duty," a virtue ethics approach to ethical leadership puts forward a "morality of aspiration" as the proper moral horizon that should guide leadership behavior in the context of international organizations.[15]

Thus, a virtue approach to ethical leadership has some distinctive advantages over both deontological and consequentialist theories, for it provides normative standards for guiding and assessing leadership conduct that are sensitive to the specificities of the particular context, richly informative, and inspirational.

4.3 THE VIRTUES OF ETHICAL LEADERS OF INTERNATIONAL ORGANIZATIONS

A first step towards the development of a virtue theory of ethical leadership is the elaboration of an account of the leadership virtues. Which virtues are constitutive of ethical leadership in the context of international organizations? A main insight of virtue professional ethics is that the proper ends of the profession, which should involve a commitment to key human goods, provide a main criterion for identifying virtuous traits of character in the context of a particular role. For instance, the character of a virtuous doctor is constituted by those traits that serve the good of health, which is the proper end of the medical profession, and one that unequivocally contributes to a flourishing human life.[16] Thus, leaders of international organizations ought to have the traits of character that are instrumental to realizing the proper goals of their professional role, which should be shown to embody

---

[14] See B. Williams, *Ethics and the Limits of Philosophy*, Harvard University Press, Cambridge, 1985, pp. 128–30, 140–42, and 150–52.

[15] For the distinction between the morality of duty and the morality of aspiration, see L. L. Fuller, *The Morality of Law*, Rev ed., Yale University Press, New Haven, 1969, p. 5.

[16] See J. Oakley and D. Cocking (eds.), *Virtue Ethics and Professional Roles*, Cambridge University Press, Cambridge, 2009.

substantive human goods.[17] These may be identified as one of service to organizational ends, which contribute to securing distinctive human goods within the international community. That is to say, leadership virtues in international organizational contexts are those traits of character that help international organizations accomplish their mission.[18] Despite wide differences in mandate and objectives across international organizations, the advancement of organizational ends requires both an energetic internal leadership – which involves the social relations between the leader and other members within the organization – as well as a strong external leadership – which involves the relations between the international organization and the larger social environment.[19] Thus, ethical leaders in international organizational contexts should possess and display virtuous character traits both inwards – in their internally oriented actions – as well as outwards – in externally oriented leadership behavior.

In light of this teleological justification of the virtues of leadership in international organizations, I would like to suggest that ethical leaders in international organizations ought to have a large share of the virtues which, in fact, have been considered historically to be central to leadership, properly specified and reinterpreted to respond to the peculiarities of their institutional role and our age.[20] Some of the key virtues for ethical leadership in international organizations are the following ones:[21]

---

[17] Interestingly, these ends are not fixed, but the individuals who hold the office also have an impact on the way in which these ends are conceived. There is thus a dialectical relationship between the conceptualization of professional roles and the character traits that are virtuous in the context of these professional roles. See K. J. Kille, "Secretary-General Leadership Capacity," paper presented at the Second World Conference on Humanitarian Studies, Medford, 2011, p. 14 (arguing that "the answer to 'what is a Secretary General' depends upon who holds the office").

[18] It is important to note that the proposal to identify leadership virtues in the context of international organizations on the basis of the ends of the role does not necessarily involve a commitment to functionalism, for one could identify the ends of the role on a basis other than the ends of the organization. For an introduction to functionalism as a theory of international organizations, see J. Klabbers, "Theorizing International Organizations," A. Orford and F. Hoffmann (eds.), *The Oxford Hanbook of the Theory of International Law*, Oxford, 2016.

[19] On "internally directed management" and "externally oriented pursuit" as crucial for leadership in international organizational contexts, see B. Reinalda and B. Verbeek, "Leadership in International Organizations," *Oxford Handbook of Political Leadership*, 2014, pp. 597 and 600.

[20] There is an important continuity between historical ideals of leadership and contemporary ones, which allows, nonetheless, for culture-specific features. Just as — as James Petifils' insightful textual analysis shows — ancient Jewish and Christian notions of leadership appropriated and redeployed Roman ideals of leadership, contemporary work on leadership underscores characteristically historical leadership priorities and develops them in distinctive ways. See Petifils, *op. cit., passim*.

[21] The foregoing list is not meant to be exhaustive, but merely illustrative of the main character traits that are virtues in the context of the role of international civil servants occupying leadership positions.

Exemplarism, Virtue, and Ethical Leadership in International Organizations 107

1. Courage. This virtue figures prominently in classical accounts of virtuous leadership.[22] While leaders in international organizations do not need to have courage in the sense of martial prowess, there is indeed a need for courage in facing social criticism, advancing controversial agendas, defending the values of the organization, and confronting the opposition of powerful member states.[23]

2. Loyalty. Loyalty is indeed critical in the context of a legal institution that needs to be subjected, like any other, to the requirements of the rule of law. "Piety" was traditionally viewed as a key characteristic of good leaders, and it required not only obedience to religious precepts but, more generally, abidance to societal norms.[24] It is this secular meaning of the word, as an attitude that encompasses loyalty to the law, that retains an important place in a conceptualization of the ideal of ethical leadership in international organizations.[25]

3. Austerity. The relevance of personal frugality and one's proper attitude towards material goods has been traditionally understood as critical to good government and it is still central for virtuous leadership to effectively counteract the threats of corruption.[26]

4. Temperance. Self-control and moderation are also pivotal – as much now as then – to good leadership insofar as they have a positive impact in

---

[22] Courage was a central virtue in both Greek and Confucian thought, see Kaak and Weeks, *op. cit.*, pp. 353 and 354. It was also pivotal in Roman thought on leadership, and it continued to be so in Christian thought. See Petifils, *op. cit.*, pp. 68–75. Courage figures in contemporary accounts of virtuous leadership in organizational studies as well; see Caldwell et al, *op. cit.*, p. 6.

[23] Courage in using the office's capabilities to their fullest so as to promote and defend the values of the organization is viewed as a desirable feature for the secretary-general of the United Nations; see K. Kille, "Secretary-General Leadership Capacity: Arguments and Evidence from the UN Secretary-Generalship," *op. cit.*, p. 5. The need for courage for leaders of international organizations is also pointed out by J. Klabbers in "Controlling International Organizations: A Virtue Ethics Approach," *Helsinki Review of Global Governance*, vol. 2(2), 2011.

[24] See Petifils, *op. cit.*, pp. 86–87. This sense of piety – although related – is different from the virtue of filial pity, which is prominent in Confucian approaches to the virtues of leadership. See Kaak and Weeks, *op. cit.*, p. 354.

[25] A recognition of law's authority is thus central for leadership in international organizations, which imposes constraints that sometimes are in tension with moral requirements and, in extreme cases, may give rise to genuine moral dilemmas. For a discussion of the interaction between legal and moral authority, focused on Hammarskjöld's service at the UN, see G. F. Sinclair, "The International Civil Servant in Theory and Practice: Law, Morality and Expertise," *The European Journal of International Law*, vol. 26(3), 2015. See also M. J. Struett, "Ethics and Agency in International Organizations," *International Studies Review*, vol. 11, 2009, p. 766.

[26] Personal frugality also figured prominently in Roman views on leadership; see Petifils, *op. cit.*, pp. 80–86.

both the generation of a civil working climate, equanimity in decision-making and negotiation processes, and sobriety in undertaking institutional actions.[27]

5. Endurance. Perseverance in following a line of action, a disposition to bear difficulties and hard work, and persistence in the face of adversity are needed to carry important institutional projects and lead them to completion.[28]

6. Justice. A commitment to justice has been historically viewed as central to good leadership.[29] In the context of international organizations, justice, like any other leadership virtue, is a character trait that is expected to be displayed in both the internal and external dimensions of leadership. Thus, ethical leaders in international organizations should promote organizational justice, that is, the justice of procedures, outcomes, and interactions within the organization, as well as justice in the externally directed actions of the organization they lead.[30]

7. Humility. This virtue did not make it into the list of classical virtues but was regarded as central in Christian thought on leadership.[31] A contemporary reading, which sharply departs from the mainstream religious interpretation of this virtue as self-abasement, but that is, nonetheless, rooted in minority views held within the Christian tradition, understands this virtue as requiring a deep commitment to an egalitarian stance.[32] Humble leaders generate an egalitarian ethos and are also critical to fostering important pro-social values within the organizations.[33] Humility is also a key virtue for effective leadership in that it has a positive impact in

[27] Moderation is a key leadership virtue in both Plato and Confucius (see Kaak and Weeks, *op. cit.*, pp. 353–54) as well as in Cicero (see Petifils, *op. cit.*, p. 112). On the need for moderation for leaders of international organizations, see Klabbers, "Controlling International Organizations," *op. cit.*, p. 51.

[28] Endurance is a characteristically Roman ancestral virtue. See Petifils, *op. cit.*, p. 187. "Commitment," is taken to be a key virtue in contemporary studies on organizational leadership; see Caldwell et al., *op. cit.*, p. 6. See also J. Collins, "Level 5 Leadership, The Triumph of Humility and Fierce Resolve," *Harvard Business Review*, vol. 18(2), 2005.

[29] See Kaak and Weeks, *op. cit.*, p. 353. Justice is also a key virtue for global leadership in organizational scholarship; see A. Rego, S. Clegg and M. Pina e Cunha, "The Positive Power of Character Strenghs and Virtues," G. M. Spreitzer and K. S. Cameron (eds.), *The Oxford Handbook of Positive Organizational Scholarship*, Oxford University Press, Oxford 2011, p.368.

[30] Greenberg introduced the concept of organizational justice in J. Greenberg, "A Taxonomy of Organizational Justice Theories," *Academy of Management Review*, vol. 12, 1987.

[31] See Petifils, *op. cit.*, chapters 4 and 5.

[32] For a discussion and defense of an egalitarian conception of humility, see A. Amaya, "The Virtue of Judicial Humility," *Jurisprudence*, vol. 9, 2018.

[33] For a discussion of the social benefits of humility in the context of legal organizations, including international organizations, see A. Amaya, "Humility in Law," M. Alfano, M. Lynch, and A. Tanesini (eds.), *The Routledge Handbook of the Philosophy of Humility*, forthcoming.

Exemplarism, Virtue, and Ethical Leadership in International Organizations 109

performance and bolsters organizational outcomes.[34] Furthermore, insofar as humility enhances one's capacities to work in transcultural environments, it is a trait of character that is particularly necessary for ethical leadership in international organizations.[35]

8. Compassion. Central in Western approaches to leadership is the idea of love, which is, alongside humility, a Christian addition to the Greek-Roman tradition of virtuous leadership.[36] Love of humanity seems, however, overly unrealistic and possibly inappropriately strong. I would suggest that we turn, paradoxically, to Greek-Roman thought and recover compassion – as a concern for the well-being of one's fellow beings and care for their good – to give an account of the affective relationship leaders in international organizations may be expected to establish with those who are affected by their decisions.[37]

In addition to these moral virtues, ethical leaders ought to possess also a number of intellectual or epistemic virtues, most prominently, the virtue of practical wisdom, prudence or *phronesis*. This virtue, as Aristotle argued, is needed in order to have any moral virtue at all.[38] It is also required to determine the mean that virtue consists of, to arbitrate in cases in which the virtues demand conflicting courses of action, and to specify what that virtue requires in the particular case, with a view to putting in motion a unified course of action.[39] Other intellectual virtues which, unlike the virtue of practical wisdom, do not typically figure in historical accounts of leadership but are highly relevant for ethical leadership include epistemic humility,

---

[34] See Collins, *op. cit.* See also M. Howes, "Humility and Leadership," Alfano et al. (eds.), *op. cit.*

[35] On humility as a trait of character that helps navigate transcultural environments, see C. Foronda, M. M. Reinholdt, and K. Ousman, "Cultural Humility: A Concept Analysis," *Journal of Transcultural Nursing*, vol. 27(3), 2016; and E. Hamman, "Culture, Humility and the Law: Towards a More Transformative Teaching Framework," *Alternative Law Journal*, vol. 42(2), 2017. On the specific challenges facing leadership in cross-cultural contexts, see Rego et al., *op. cit.*

[36] See Petifils, *op. cit.*, chapters 4 and 5.

[37] Compassion plays a role in discussions of leadership in the context of the role of the UN's secretary-general; see Kille, *op. cit.*, p. 13. Compassion also figures among the central leadership virtues in contemporary work on organizational leadership; see Caldwell et al., *op. cit.*, p. 6.

[38] In Aristotle's view, it is possible to have "natural virtues" without phronesis, but virtue in a strict sense involves practical wisdom (NE, VI. 13, 1144b1-17). The relation is one of interdependence, for there is no phronesis either without the character virtues (NE, VI.13, 1144b1-17). For a clarifying discussion, see D. C. Russell, *Practical Intelligence and the Virtues*, Oxford University Press, Oxford, 2009, p. 25ff.

[39] On these functions of *phronesis*, see Zagzebski, *op. cit.*, pp. 219–32.

110 *Amalia Amaya*

open-mindedness to the arguments and views of others, intellectual autonomy to form one's independent views about the problem at stake and the ends to be pursued, intellectual sobriety to avoid jumping into unwarranted conclusions, resoluteness and decisiveness, impartiality in assessing reasons and positions, and intellectual integrity.[40]

Besides moral and intellectual virtues, good leaders should also possess – as has been acknowledged since the early writings on leadership – virtues of communication.[41] In international organizational contexts, a number of rhetorical virtues are needed to successfully deal with multiple constituencies, including member states, NGOs, interest groups, corporations, social movements, and the staff of the organization.[42] Besides rhetorical virtues, other traits of character are relevant to the communicative dimensions of ethical leadership. More specifically, the virtues of communication should also include virtues such as clarity and receptivity, dialectical virtues – for example, the disposition to modify one's position or to listen to others – which are vital to properly deal with disagreement and reach consensus, as well as a number of traits of character that bear on the ethics of communication, such as civility, kindness, and gentleness.[43] These traits of character are critical in that they foster a cordial and cooperative working environment and promote the background conditions needed to enable a productive team-work, sound group decision-making, and good inter-institutional relations.[44]

To be sure, there is more to good leadership in international organizations than the possession and exercise of the foregoing virtues. International civil servants in leadership positions certainly need to have a number of important managerial qualities and political abilities.[45] These, however, should not be

---

[40] For an analysis of some of these virtues, see, among others, N. Cooper, 'The Intellectual Virtues," *Philosophy*, vol. 69, 1994.; and R. Roberts and J. Wood, *Intellectual Virtues: An Essay in Regulative Epistemology*, Oxford University Press, Oxford, 2007.

[41] See Cooper, *op. cit.*, pp. 465–66.

[42] See Wouters and Odermatt, *op. cit.*, p. 8. The rhetorical virtues were also central in Roman conceptions of leadership; see Petifils, *op. cit.*, pp. 75–80.

[43] See J. M. Harden Fritz, "Communication Ethics and Virtue," N. Snow (ed.), *The Oxford Handbook of Virtue*, Oxford University Press, Oxford, 2018. Clarity also figures as a key virtue in leadership studies; see Caldwell et al. *op. cit.*, p. 6.

[44] See S. F. Aikin and J. Caleb Clanton, "Developing Group Deliberative Virtues," *Journal of Applied Philosophy*, vol. 27, 2010, pp. 415–20.

[45] These capacities are critical to properly fulfil the administrative and political roles that are characteristic of executive offices in international organizations. On this dual mandate, see J. Kim, "The UN Secretary-General 'Walking a Two-Scope Rope': An Analytic Approach to the Secretary-Generalship," *Korea Review of International Studies*, vol. 9(2), 2006. The relevance of these capacities also underwrites the "leader vs. clerk" and the "secretary vs. general" dichotomies, which is a main theme that runs through the literature on leadership in international organizations. See Wouters and Odermatt, *op. cit.*, p. 6.

thought of as desiderata for good leadership that are independent from virtue requirements. In order to perform appropriately their administrative and political function, leaders in international organizations should also exemplify a certain type of (moral) character. To begin with, virtuous leadership has been shown to positively influence effectiveness in organizations.[46] Moreover, the virtuous leader has a moral horizon in sight when acting in his political and managerial capacities.[47] A leader who was an insightful administrator and an able politician but who lacked virtue not only would perform worse than a virtuous one, but, more importantly, would not have the dispositions of character needed to register the moral import of her job and the resources necessary to successfully engage in the kind of moral reasoning at times demanded by her office. It is only, as I will argue later, the (relatively) recent fragmentation of authority, which resulted from an infatuation with technical and scientific expertise and the goods of bureaucracy, that made the thought that a good leader could be a bad person – a thought considered for much of human history to be obviously wrong – plausible in the first place.

4.4 VARIETIES OF EXEMPLARY ETHICAL LEADERSHIP

Ethical leaders who have a large share of the leadership virtues are exemplary and provide models for others to emulate. Exemplary leaders, due to the possession of virtue, are also admirable. Thus, in a virtue-based account of exemplarity, admiration is an emotion that is properly triggered by exemplars, rather than a criterion – as has been claimed by some prominent

---

[46] For a defense of the claim that leaders who are virtuous are effective, see Kaak and Weeks, *op. cit.* For arguments to the effect that virtue is positively linked to success and increased performance in business organizational settings, see A. Caza et al., "Ethics and Ethos: The Buffering and Amplifying Effects of Ethical Behavior and Virtuousness," *Journal of Business Ethics*, vol. 52, 2004; G. Flynn, "The Virtuous Manager: A Vision of Leadership in Business," *Journal of Business Ethics*, vol. 78, 2008; J. B. Ciulla, "Ethics Effectiveness: The Nature of Good Leadership," in D. V. Day and J. Antonakis (eds.), *The Nature of Leadership*, 2nd ed., Sage, London, 2012; and K. Cameron, "Organizational Virtue and Performance," in K. S. Cameron, J. E. Dutton, and R. E. Quinn (eds.), *Positive Organizational Scholarship*, Berret-Koehler, San Francisco, 2003. Virtue has also been claimed to be inextricably linked to competence in public service institutions; see M. Macaulay and A. Lawton, "From Virtue to Competence – Changing the Principles of Public Service," *Public Administration Review*, vol. 66(5), 2006.

[47] For example, Annan emphasized that all the reforms he did to the management and structure of the UN were never an end in itself, but were driven by the need to make the organization work more effectively. Annan said, when receiving the Nobel Peace Prize in 2001, "I have sought to place human beings at the center of everything I do." See Wouters and Odermatt, *op. cit.*, p. 16.

proponents of moral exemplarism – for identifying exemplars.[48] It is critical to clarify the place of admiration within a theory of exemplarity, particularly in the context of exemplarism about leadership. Certain accounts of leadership – such as charismatic leadership – naturally seem to fit with the claim that admiration is a test for exemplarity.[49] In contrast, a virtuous exemplarist approach to leadership, although it recognizes the important ways in which admiration is tied up with *exempla*, grounds exemplarity in virtuous character.[50]

Different kinds of exempla are useful for the purposes of modeling ethical conduct in the context of international organizations. In addition to "complete" exempla, that is to say, exempla who possess and exercise to an exceptional degree the leadership virtues, many exempla are only "partial" in that they embody certain leadership virtues, but not others. Even if they fall short of completeness, partial exempla are nevertheless important for ethical leadership. As some studies have shown, the attainability of a model is critical to its effectiveness.[51] Since partial exempla of virtuous leadership are likely to be judged as attainable, they may have a large impact on followers' behavior. This makes it the case that not only widely praised leaders of international organizations, such as Hammarskjöld, but also leaders who are found to be admirable in a specific respect – for example, Annan's compassion, as shown in the many calls for UN humanitarian intervention during his tenure[52] – are relevant for modeling moral behavior in international organizations.

In addition to partial and complete exempla, it is also important to distinguish between positive exempla and negative ones. Whereas a virtue exemplarist account of ethical leadership for international organizations focuses on positive

---

[48] See Zagbezki, *Exemplarist Moral Theory, op. cit.*, pp. 14ff.

[49] See J. W. Mitchell, D. L. Wallace, and R. A. Rawlings, "Charismatic Leaders: The Role of Admiration and System Justification," *Leadership and Organization and Developmental Journal*, vol. 34, 2013.

[50] Thus, the rejection of the claim that admiration provides the foundation for an exemplarist ethical theory does not amount to denying the critical roles it plays within the theory. For an analysis of such roles in the legal context, see A. Amaya, "Admiration, Exemplarity and Judicial Virtue," A. Amaya and M. Del Mar (eds.), *Virtue, Emotion and Imagination in Law and Legal Reasoning*, Hart Publishing, Oxford, 2020.

[51] On the importance of attainability and relevance to the effectiveness of role models see H. Han, J. Kim, C. Jeong, and G. L. Cohen, "Attainable and Relevant Moral Exemplars Are More Effective than Extraordinary Exemplars in Promoting Voluntary Service Engagement," *Frontiers in Psychology*, vol. 8, 2017. Attainability is also a relevant criterion for assessing the effectiveness of role models in professional contexts; see D. Moberg, "Role Models and Moral Exemplars: How Do Employees Acquire Virtues by Observing Others?", *Business Ethics Quarterly*, vol. 10(3), 2000.

[52] See Kille, *op. cit.*, p. 13.

Exemplarism, Virtue, and Ethical Leadership in International Organizations 113

exempla, that is, exempla who embody traits of character that are worthy of imitation and desirable to promote within the organization, it is also important to note that negative exempla may also play a role in virtue development within the organization, insofar as they provide models to be avoided rather than emulated.[53] An interesting question in this regard is the extent to which moral failure on the part of an ethical leader discredits him as a model.[54] Arguably, in light of the relevance of attainability to model effectiveness, that an otherwise virtuous ethical leader may turn out to have negative attributes as well or be shown to have failed to act virtuously – for example, alleged evidence of bias and partiality of Hammarskjöld in the Congo might be a case to the point – does not disqualify him from playing an important role in ethical modeling.[55]

"Ordinary" exempla, alongside outstanding exempla, such as heroes, sages, and saints, are also critical to modeling moral conduct. Oftentimes, one's moral outlook is more importantly fleshed out by the influence of those one knows more and has a closer interaction with, than by distant others who have performed extraordinary deeds and with whom it becomes more difficult to identify. Indeed, in (business) organizational contexts, it has been claimed that – notwithstanding the relevance of top managers, who are frequently valorized as "heroes,"[56] for setting the ethical climate within an organization – employees are most influenced by the people they work with every day.[57] Similarly, in the context of ethical leadership of international organizations, it is important to note that civil servants, other than executive heads, serve as important role models within their organizations.

Last, moral excellence may be exemplified in different ways, that is to say, there is a variety of types of exemplarity, each of which privileges a subset of

---

[53] On the value of negative models, see P. A. Haack, "Use of Positive and Negative Examples in Teaching the Concept of Music Style," *Journal of Research in Music Education*, vol. 20(4), 1972; and P. Lockwood et al., "The Impact of Positive and Negative Fitness Exemplars on Motivation," *Basic and Applied Social Psychology*, vol. 27(1), 2005. Negative exemplars have also been shown to play important roles in professional development. Gibson has shown that middle and late-stage career individuals are more likely to see role models as sources of negative rather than positive attributes. See D. E. Gibson, "Developing the Professional Self-Concept: Role Model Construals in Early, Middle, and Late Career Stages," *Organization Science*, vol. 14(5), 2003, p. 591. On the potential educational value of negative exemplars of ethical leadership, see Treviño and Brown, *op. cit.*, p. 536.

[54] See Treviño and Brown, *op. cit.*, p. 537.

[55] In fact, mixed models (i.e. those who have both positive and negative attributes) have more enduring inspirational effects. See Moberg, *op. cit.*, p. 682.

[56] See Rego et al., *op. cit.*, p. 367.

[57] See G. R. Weaver, L. K. Treviño, and B. Agle, "Somebody I Look Up To: Ethical Role Models in Organizations," *Organizational Dynamics*, vol. 34, 2005.

114   *Amalia Amaya*

relevant virtues. The saint, the hero, and the sage embody different models of moral exemplarity, as the brave, the caring, and the just do.[58] The point also holds, I would argue, as far as ethical leadership in international organizations is concerned. Different sets of moral virtues may be possessed and exercised by ethical leaders, who are exemplary in different ways. Distinct leadership styles – the manager, the visionary, and the strategist may be a useful classification for these purposes – may give rise to diverse models of exemplarity for ethical leadership in international organizations.[59]

4.5 THE ROLE OF EXEMPLARY ETHICAL LEADERS IN INTERNATIONAL ORGANIZATIONS

Exempla virtutis, in their different varieties, who occupy leadership positions play a number of important roles in the context of international organizations.[60] First, exemplary leaders provide models worthy to be imitated by civil servants within the international organization. A virtuous leader, as Alfarabi already said, is "someone to be copied in his ways of life and his action."[61] Through imitation – triggered by the emotion of admiration – civil servants may come to develop a virtuous moral outlook. Imitation thus results – when successful – in a transformation of character.[62] This impact on character formation goes beyond the individual level to reach the group level. There is a "cascading effect" of virtuous leadership so that a certain style of doing and behaving permeates through different levels within the organization.[63] Thus,

---

[58] See L. Zagzebski, *Exemplarist Moral Theory*, *op. cit.*, pp. 96–99; and L. J. Walker and K. H. Hennig, 'Differing Conceptions of Moral Exemplarity: Just, Brave and Caring," *Journal of Personality and Social Psychology*, vol. 86, 2004.

[59] On these three leadership styles, see K. J. Kille, *From Manager to Visionary: The Secretary-General of the United Nations*, Palgrave-Macmillan, New York, 2006.

[60] I am focusing here on the role that exemplary executive heads play within the organizations they lead. However, it is important to note that ethical leadership may be exercised at any level within the organization. This makes it important to expand current research on the executive heads of international organizations, most prominently, the UN Secretary-General, to cover other institutional roles.

[61] See Alfarabi, *The Political Writings*, Cornell University Press, Ithaca, 2001, p. 27 (cited in Kaak and Weeks, *op. cit.*, p. 354).

[62] There are several ways, however, in which the process that goes from admiration of exemplars to virtue development may go wrong. I have discussed some of these in "Admiration, Exemplarism and Judicial Virtue," in Amaya and Del Mar, *op. cit.*, pp. 31–34.

[63] It has been found that executive heads reach lower- level-employees through the ethical leadership practiced by supervisors, who are influenced by them. See D. M. Mayer et al., "How Low Does Ethical Leadership Flow? Test for a Trickle-down Model," *Organizational Behavior and Human Decision Processes*, vol. 108, 2009.

virtuous leaders have an important role in forming an international organization's ethical culture.

Secondly, morally exemplary leaders are public figures and as such their influence as models to be imitated transcends the limits of the organization they lead. They play, accordingly, an important role in shaping legal and political culture. This impact may be more evident as far as the legal and political climate at the international level is concerned. However, the extent to which they may also have an effect on public political morality and public deliberation should not be underestimated. Erasmus was acutely aware of the impact of leaders' behavior on public morals. "Turn the pages of history – he claimed – and you will always find the morality of an age reflecting the life of its prince."[64] Erasmus' views, I would argue, are applicable to international leaders in our time. Their moral commitments and behavior – as much now as then – have a strong influence in setting the moral sensibilities of a given society. Furthermore, given the unexpected escalation of social communication, the power of exemplary leaders of international organizations to imprint on international legal and political actors and reach, more broadly, the public at large is unprecedented.[65]

Third, exemplary leaders in international organizations – given the high authority which, as I will argue below, they possess – are particularly well positioned to contribute to the evolvement of international law and policy through the advancement and transmission, via imitation, of novel forms of thinking, behaving, and acting in the international arena.[66] As Tomasello and others have shown, imitation plays a critical role in the evolution of human culture. The unique cumulative form of the evolution of human culture is the product of a "ratchet effect" that allows modifications and improvements to stay rather easily in the population until further changes ratchet things up.[67]

---

[64] Erasmus, *The Education of a Christian Prince*, edited by L. Jardine, Cambridge University Press, Cambridge, 1997, p. 21.

[65] As Wouters and Odermatt say, "Executive heads, who are present at leaders' summits and international organizations, have visibility in the international media and are more than ever in the public eye." See Wouters and Odermatt, *op. cit.*, p. 4.

[66] Indeed, the relevance of the executive heads of international organizations for the development of law and policy is a recurrent theme in the literature. See Wouters and Odermatt, *op. cit.*; J. L. Dunoff, "The Law and Politics of International Organizations," in J. K. Cogan, I. Hurd, and I. Johnstone (eds.), *The Oxford Handbook of International Organizations*, Oxford, 2017, p. 69; I. Johnstone, "The Secretary-General as Norm Entrepreneur," in S. Chesterman (ed.), *Secretary or General? The UN Secretary-General in World Politics*, Cambridge University Press, New York, 2007; and Sinclair, *op. cit.*, pp. 748–49.

[67] See M. Tomasello, *The Cultural Origins of Human Cognition*, Harvard University Press, Cambridge, 1999; and C. Tennie, J. Call, and M. Tomasello, "Ratching Up the Ratchet: On the Evolution of Cumulative Culture," *Philosophical Transactions of the Royal Society Biological Sciences*, vol. 364, 2009.

116 *Amalia Amaya*

This process relies on inventiveness and, critically, on faithful imitation. A similar mechanism, I would argue, drives the evolution of legal culture, and, more specifically, international legal and political culture. International legal and political culture is also cumulative and its development depends, to a large extent, on the creation of novel readings of traditional rules, original ways of addressing global problems, legal innovations and new policies, and the refinement and improvement of legal and political concepts as well as their preservation, so that they form a platform for future developments. Hammarskjöld's impact on the formulation of several legal innovations, including preventive diplomacy and peacekeeping, Annan's reforms in the UN management structure, and Boutros-Ghali's efforts to promote democracy, are examples of the long-lasting impact on international law and policy of exemplary ethical leaders.[68]

Fourth, exemplary leaders are important tools for theorizing virtuous leadership in international organizations. Exemplary ethical leaders do not merely illustrate the leadership virtues, but they contribute, in various ways, to fleshing out a conception of virtuous leadership.[69] To begin with, in light of an analysis of exemplary leaders, we may come to improve our views of what the best ethical leadership practice consists of. In addition, a careful examination of exemplars may prompt questions that help advance a theory about how ethical leadership should be conceptualized.[70] For example, what distinguishes the exemplary leaders' response to the moral dilemmas they face from the responses of other leaders? Which contextual factors may help bring about exemplary ethical leadership? What is the contribution of diplomats, legal counselors, and other functionaries within the international organization on exemplary individual ethical leadership? Another way in which the study of exemplars may advance a theory of leadership is by revealing connections between the leadership virtues and relations between private and public

---

[68] See C. Stahn and H. Melber (eds.), *Peace Diplomacy, Global Justice and International Agency: Rethinking Human Security and Ethics in the Spirit of Hammarskjöld*, Cambridge University Press, Cambridge, 2014; M. Müller, *Reforming the United Nations: The Quiet Revolution*, Martinus Njihoff Publishers, 2001; and S. Roushton, "The UN-Secretary General and Norm-Entrepreneurship: Boutros Boutros-Ghali and Democracy Promotion," *Global Governance*, vol. 14(1), 2008.

[69] Thus, exempla do not simply "represent traits of character in our imagination" but they are rather "the vessels through which we construct those traits." See S. Clark, "Neoclassical Public Virtues: Towards an Aretaic Theory of Law-making and Law Teaching," in Amaya and Ho, *op. cit.*, p. 88.

[70] A. Olberding, "Dreaming of the Duke of Zhou: Exemplarism and the *Analects*," *Journal of Chinese Philosophy*, vol. 35(4), 2008, p. 188.

Exemplarism, Virtue, and Ethical Leadership in International Organizations 117

virtue.[71] Finally, the detailed analysis of a rich set of relevant exemplars, across different organizational settings and levels, may lead to the construction of more refined versions of the leadership virtues.[72]

Last, exemplary ethical leaders of international organizations represent normative ideals that play a critical role in guiding and evaluating conduct. Hammarskjöld provides an example of the relevance of exemplary leaders as normative ideals. "Even today – says Hammarskjöld scholar Jones – when people are faced with international crises, it is to Hammarskjöld's words and actions that they turn to for guidance. He has, in fact, become *the* model for international leadership."[73] In addition to setting a normative ideal for guiding conduct, the example of Hammarskjöld also provides a normative ideal for evaluating it. As Sinclair writes, when discussing Hammarskjöld's extraordinary legal prowess, "For a generation (and perhaps more) of international lawyers, that prowess established a benchmark against which all other Secretaries-General would be measured."[74] Besides establishing normative standards for guiding and evaluating conduct, exemplary ethical leaders have an inspirational value as well.[75] They are models who motivate international civil servants to expand their moral horizons and ambitions, imagine better "possible selves,"[76] and reach higher levels of moral and professional excellence.[77]

To sum up, exemplary leaders play critical roles within international organizations. They shape the institutional ethos and, more broadly, the international legal and political culture. In addition, they play a pivotal role in legal and policy development in the international domain. They also help envision how the best exemplary practice in ethical leadership at international organizations

---

[71]   See Zagzebski, *Exemplarist Moral Theory, op. cit.*, p. 119ff.

[72]   See Clark, *op. cit.*, p. 49. See also Olberding, *op. cit.*, pp. 631 and 635.

[73]   See D. Jones, "International Leadership and Charisma," in S. Ask and A. Mark-Jungkvist (eds.), *The Adventures of Peace: Dag Hammarskjöld and the Future of the UN*, Palgrave Macmillan, New York, 2005.

[74]   See Sinclair, *op. cit.*, p. 751.

[75]   On the claim that outstanding others – under certain conditions – provoke inspiration, see P. Lockwood and Z. Kunda, "Increasing the Salience of One's Best Selves Can Undermine Inspiration by Outstanding Role Models," *Journal of Personality and Social Psychology*, vol. 76, 1999.

[76]   See H. Markus and P. Nurius, "Possible Selves," *American Psychologist*, vol. 41, 1986. On this notion, and the related one of "provisional selves," in the context of role-modeling in the professions, see H. Ibarra, "Provisional Selves: Experimenting with Image and Identity in Professional Adaptation," *Administrative Science Quarterly*, vol. 44(4), 1999.

[77]   This does not necessarily imply that moral exemplars also increase the level of moral obligation. Cf. V. Carbonell, "The Ratcheting-Up Effect," *Pacific Philosophical Quarterly*, vol. 93(2), 2012.

118 *Amalia Amaya*

could be conceptualized. Finally, they set up valuable normative standards for guiding and assessing ethical conduct within international organizations that provoke inspiration and moral improvement. Thus, exemplarist virtue ethics – I hope to have shown – is a productive framework for theorizing the roles that ethical leaders play within the context of international organizations. It also provides, as I will argue in the next section, a useful perspective for examining the nature of authority in international global institutions.

4.6 EXEMPLARY LEADERS AND *AUCTORITAS* IN INTERNATIONAL ORGANIZATIONS

International organizations have extensively expanded their functions, powers, and influence in the recent decades, and this makes questions about their legitimate exercise of authority a central concern in both international law and international relations.[78] A virtue exemplarist approach to ethical leadership in international organizations provides a distinctive viewpoint on issues of legitimate authority of global governance institutions. Exemplary leaders, I would argue, enjoy *auctoritas* and this translates into a greater legitimacy of the institutions they lead. Two theses are involved here: the claim that the exemplarity of a leader confers upon her authority and the claim that such individual authority, which emanates from virtuous leadership, is a contributing factor to institutional legitimacy. I take them up in turn.[79]

The claim that the authority of civil servants occupying leadership positions is (partly) a matter of virtuous character runs indeed against the spirit of our times. In modernity, the idea that moral standing is a pivotal element upon which the authority of an occupation relies on has fallen into disrepute as a result of the professionalization and bureaucratization of social life.[80] The thought has steadily taken hold that expertise is the main source of authority so that a good civil servant – like a good doctor, a good judge, or a good politician – is someone who has the expertise relevant to the domain and that character is,

---

[78] For a useful overview, see D. Bodansky, "Legitimacy in International Law and International Relations," in J. Dunoff and M. A. Pollack (eds.), *Interdisciplinary Perspectives in International Law and International Relations*, Cambridge University Press, Cambridge, 2013.

[79] A thorough defense of these claims is beyond the scope of this chapter; here I will merely provide the main outline of the arguments in support of them, with a view to showing that a virtue approach to ethical leadership provides a productive framework for addressing questions of authority and legitimacy in international organizational contexts. A fuller argument will have to await another occasion.

[80] To these, Shapin adds "secularization". See S. Shapin, "The Way We Trust Now: The Authority of Science and the Character of the Scientists," in P. Hoodbhoy, D. Glaser and S. Shapin (eds.), *Trust Me, I'm a Scientist*, British Council, London, 2004.

Exemplarism, Virtue, and Ethical Leadership in International Organizations 119

consequently, irrelevant to his being a good professional or to his performing well his functions.[81] This professionalization goes hand-in-hand with bureaucratization in that good professional practice is thought to consist of the display of expert knowledge in accordance with the rules that regulate the profession. As a result, authority – as much in international civil service as in any other professional domain – is viewed as rooted in expertise and rule-abidance to the detriment of moral character.

The neglect of individual morality as a basis for professional authority is, however, problematic. There is an important distinction between "knowing more" and "doing the right thing" that collapses under the view that authority can be conveniently de-moralized.[82] In order to trust a professional, it is necessary not only that he possesses the relevant expert knowledge, but also that he can be relied on to know what is the best thing to do in the particular case, which is a practical matter.[83] Thus, in addition to technical expertise, a certain type of moral character is necessary for good professional practice. This is particularly so for professions that involve taking decisions of high moral import. Judges' struggles to find a way to honor law's commitments while avoiding an unjust outcome, doctors' dilemmatic choices concerning end-of-life care, or scientists' determinations of whether a promising line of inquiry should be pursued despite its troubling potential applications are examples to the point. Good decision-making in these cases requires factoring in a variety of reasons, including, prominently, moral reasons. This makes the segregation of "spheres of authority" – that is, the modern idea that types of authority, legal, moral, and technical, can be isolated from each other – unfit to portray the complexity of professional authority.

Like these professionals, civil servants occupying leadership positions in international organizations are similarly called on to engage in moral reasoning when discharging their functions. A UN Secretary-General has to decide whether or not he should propel armed peace-keeping operations; the executive head of the WTO needs to determine whether he should question a well-settled interpretation of the founding charter with a view to take decisive actions in a severe financial crisis; a bureaucratic leader of the ILO, in the face of hard political pressure, struggles to decide in a way that is mindful of the relevance of political compromise for effective action but that does not merely hews to the wishes of major political actors; and a UN executive officer is bound to decide whether or not she should implement a unpopular social

---

[81] We live now, as Shapin says, in a "postvirtuous" culture, in which trust takes an "impersonal form" and is given to institutions on account of the expertise that is attributed to them. See S. Shapin, *A Social History of Truth*, The University of Chicago Press, Chicago, 1994, p. 412.
[82] On this distinction, see Shapin, "The Way We Trust Now," *op. cit.*, p. 48.
[83] Ibid., p. 49.

program which might affect her chances of staying in office – and thus her capability to implement other valuable social changes in the long run. Given the moral dimensions of their task, the authority of international civil servants, no less than the authority of a scientist, a jurist, or other professionals, partly depends on moral character.

Thus, views of authority that are invested in legality and expertise and disengaged from personal virtue fail to give an adequate account of the authority of leaders in international organizations. When technical expertise, shielded by the law, is severed from virtuous character – and thus from knowledge of what it is that makes their office and the international institution they lead socially valuable, which is needed to determine the right decision in the particular case – their authority is eroded. Beyond having the relevant expertise and following the applicable legal rules and procedures, their moral character is an important source of authority.[84] Exemplary ethical leaders best embody the type of character that may be claimed to be a worthy repository of *auctoritas* in international civil service. This *auctoritas*, and its associated prestige, consideration, and influence, is essential – more even so in the flexible normative context in which international organizations operate, for leaders of international organizations to successfully perform their roles and, ultimately, for the success of the international organization.[85]

Critically, the *auctoritas* of exemplary leaders is not only of consequence for the effectiveness of the international institutions they lead, but – and this is the second claim advanced here – it also has an important impact on the legitimacy of these institutions. The moral character of those in leadership positions in international organizational contexts – on which, as argued, their individual authority partially depends – increases the legitimacy of the institutions they lead.[86] Two main senses of legitimacy should be

---

[84] Expertise and legal rationality are generally viewed as important sources of authority in international organizational contexts; see A. Peters and S. Peter, "International Organizations: Between Technocracy and Democracy," in B. Fassbender and A. Peters (eds.), *The Oxford Handbook of the History of International Law*, Oxford, 2012, pp. 193–94; and M. N. Barnett and M. Finnemore, "The Politics, Power and Pathologies of International Organizations," *International Organizations*, vol. 53, 1999, p. 707ff. Morality is considered by some scholars to be a source of authority in international organizational contexts as well; see Kille, *The UN Secretary-General Moral Authority, op. cit.* Critically, however, a "fragmented" conception of authority, which conceives moral authority as separable from other forms of authority, is prevalent in the literature. For an exception, see Sinclair, *op. cit.* (arguing for the need to study the complex interactions of expert, legal and moral authority in international civil service).

[85] I thank Natalia Saltalamacchia for this suggestion.

[86] In fact, arguably, the positive effects of the moral authority of leaders on both the efficacy and the legitimacy of the international organizations they lead are not unconnected, since the

Exemplarism, Virtue, and Ethical Leadership in International Organizations 121

distinguished: a sociological and a normative one.[87] Whereas the former refers to the issue of whether an international organization is believed to exercise authority properly, the second refers to the question of whether the international organization's exercise of authority is in fact justified. The authority of exemplary ethical leaders is arguably a contributing factor to both the social and the normative legitimacy of international organizations.

To begin with, the social legitimacy of institutions of global governance is importantly affected by the moral character of their leaders. Despite the fact that standards for evaluating professional performance, as argued, have come to be viewed as disconnected from the moral domain, the demoralization of the professions is less than complete, as there is still a strong connection between public trust in institutions and the integrity of the individuals working in them, and specially, of those in leadership positions.[88] Shapin writes, with regard to the crisis of legitimacy in science:

> For an indicator of the extent to which a 'trust society' has not yet been dissolved, and to which technical experts are held to higher-than-ordinary standards of conduct, look no further than the extent to which both the public and many of our experts respond to occasions of scientists' materialism, malfeasance, corruption and insensitivity with displays of shock and dismay.[89]

Evidence of misbehavior on the part of scientists decreases people's beliefs that scientific authority has been properly exercised and erodes public trust in the institution of science.

Shapin's analysis is equally apposite for institutions other than science and, more specifically, for institutions of global governance.[90] Indeed, political capture, corruption, rampant indifference in the face of human suffering, fraud, patronage, lack of a firm response to staff's criminal conduct, evasion of responsibility, abuse of power, opulence, and frivolity in the management of international organizations generates a deep loss of legitimacy in the eyes of

---

capacity of international organizations to deliver has been shown to be conditioned on their legitimacy; see J. Tallberg and M. Zürn, "The Legitimacy and Legitimation of International Organizations: Introduction and Framework," *The Review of International Organizations*, vol. 14, 2019, pp. 581–82. See also Peters and Peter, *op. cit.*, p. 194.

[87] For this distinction, see A. Buchanan and R. O. Keohane, "The Legitimacy of Global Governance Institutions," *Ethics and International Affairs*, vol. 20, 2006, p. 405.

[88] Shapin, "The Way We Trust Now," *op. cit.*, p. 59.

[89] *Ibidem.*

[90] Media interest in corporate scandals speaks to the fact that there is an expectation of ethical behavior on the part of business organizations too. See L. K. Treviño, G. R. Weaver, and S. J. Reynolds, "Behavioral Ethics in Organizations," *Journal of Management*, vol. 6, 2006.

member states and bureaucratic staff and is met with public outcry.[91] Thus, even if personal virtue has given way to expertise and legal rationality – as much in the context of international institutions as in any other modern institution – moral character is still pivotal to institutional prestige. Hollande said, in the context of announcing new measures to combat corruption and tax fraud, that "the exemplarity of the Republic is the condition of its authority."[92] Similarly, the social acceptance of the authority of international organizations importantly rests on the exemplarity of its leaders. The possession and display of the virtues that are constitutive of ethical leadership confers upon them *auctoritas*, which is a source of social legitimacy in international organizational contexts.

Finally, the authority of exemplary ethical leaders, I would argue, is also relevant to attributions of normative legitimacy in international organizational contexts. The extent to which the rules and procedures followed by international organizations as well as the results they reach embed morally relevant values is a critical factor upon which the normative legitimacy of these organizations is claimed to depend.[93] In addition to the moral properties of rules, processes, and outcomes, the moral properties of agents – especially those on leadership positions – also have an important bearing on the issue of whether the authority of an international organization is properly exercised. There is, as argued above, no system of general rules or procedures that suffices to capture good moral choice. Correct practical reasoning involves an appreciation of the reasons for action that obtain in a particular case – which virtue enables. This makes virtuous individual judgment indispensable to sound decision-making – as much in international organizational contexts as in any other practical domain. Given the relevance of virtuous features of agents to correct decision-making whether an international organization's claim to authority is justified partly depends on whether those leading institutional action possess the right sort of character. Individual virtue – in addition to

---

[91] Indeed, public scandals involving individual misconduct in international organizations are taken to damage the reputation of the affected international organization. See I. Lehmann, "The Political and the Cultural Dynamics of United Nations Media Scandals: From Waldheim to Annan," LSE Electronic Working Papers, no. 22, London, 2011; and T. Capelos and J. Wurzer, "United Front: Blame Management and Scandal Response Tactics of the United Nations," *Journal of Contingencies and Crisis Management*, vol. 17(2), 2009.

[92] L. Marlow, "Hollande announces new measures to combat corruption and tax fraud," *The Irish Times*, 10 April 2013.

[93] International relations scholars usually distinguish between input-legitimacy, which depends on procedures, and output-legitimacy, which is a matter of results. In contrast, international lawyers focus more on the legitimacy of rules and rules-systems. See Dunoff, *op. cit.*, p. 75.

Exemplarism, Virtue, and Ethical Leadership in International Organizations 123

organizational one – is thus central to establishing the normative legitimacy of international organizations.[94]

4.7 WORKING VIRTUOUS LEADERSHIP IN INTERNATIONAL ORGANIZATIONS

Thus far, I have argued that an exemplarist virtue approach to ethical leadership provides an appealing account of the concept, functions, and authority of ethical leaders in international institutions. This approach, however, could be objected to on the grounds that the ideal of virtuous leadership is unrealistic given the complex political circumstances that international civil servants in leadership positions ought to navigate. Regardless of the merits it might have in other domains, given the hard choices that executive heads of international organizations have to make and the political dimensions of their office, an exemplarist variant of virtue ethics – so the objection goes – fails to provide a normative theory that may be put to work in international organizational settings.[95]

Skepticism about the feasibility of applying an exemplarist virtue ethics to the context of ethical leadership for international organizations may, however, be counteracted. Virtuous leadership has some features that make it a normatively relevant ideal for ethical leaders of international institutions. In contrast to other normative ideals, exempla of virtuous leadership are embodied and concrete and do not abstract away from human limitations and capacities. Thus, they impose on civil servants attainable moral demands and thereby have a direct normative relevance. They also have an indirect normative relevance, in that they are moral ideals towards which international civil servants ought to strive. Thus, even when unsatisfied, they retain normative relevance as an ideal that they may able to approximate.[96] In addition, insofar as the leadership virtues – as much as any other professional virtues –

---

[94] For an argument to the effect that to be legitimate global governance institutions must possess certain epistemic virtues, see Keohane and Buchanan, *op. cit.* The relationship between virtue at an individual level and virtue at an organizational level is complex. For an examination of this issue in the context of business organizations, see G. Moore and R. Beadle, "In Search of Organizational Virtue in Business: Agents, Goods, Practices, Institutions and Environments," *Organization Studies*, vol. 27, 2006; and T. A. Wright and J. Goodstein, "Character is not 'Dead' in Management Research: A Review of Individual Character and Organizational-Level Virtue," *Journal of Management*, vol. 33, 2007.

[95] The problem of "dirty hands" is probably the most recurrent version of this objection. I thank Euan MacDonald for drawing my attention to this problem. For a discussion of this problem in the context of virtue ethics, see D. Thillyris, "After the Standard Dirty Hands Thesis: Towards a Dynamic Account of Dirty Hands in Politics," *Ethical Theory and Moral Practice*, vol. 19, 2016.

[96] For the distinction between direct and indirect normative relevance, see L. Zynda, "Coherence as an Ideal of Rationality," *Synthese*, vol. 109, 1996, p. 175.

are identified and specified in a way that is sensitive to the distinctive features of the professional role, exemplary virtuous leaders provide normative ideals that are fit to guide, regulate, and assess behavior in the real circumstances that international civil servants are likely to encounter in the exercise of their functions.[97]

Furthermore, virtuous leadership is not only an appropriate normative ideal in international organizational settings, but also one that may be translated into practice. Indeed, there are a number of venues through which international servants in leadership positions may come to attain, or at least, approximate, the ideal of virtuous leadership. A first important way in which the virtues constitutive of ethical leadership may be instilled is by means of education. It is important that educational curricula and professional training be designed with a view to foster among students of international law and international relations as well as international civil servants the leadership virtues.[98] One way in which this might be done is by putting in place specific ethical training programs that aim at virtue development. Training interventions have proved to be useful for enhancing moral reasoning as well as for promoting forms of leadership that have an important moral dimension, such as transformational leadership. Arguably, similar interventions could be designed with a view to promoting the virtues necessary for ethical leadership.[99]

Given the centrality of imitation for virtue development, a most important educational means for fostering virtuous leadership is role-modeling. It seems critical to generate contexts of interaction, such as, for example, internships and guest speakers, so that students and professionals become acquainted with virtuous ethical leaders. Fortunately, the models from which one may learn virtue are not restricted to real people one can have first experience of. Virtue may also be inculcated through the imitation of fictional as well as real, but distant, models. Some educational tools – well known since antiquity – such as literary narratives of excellent leaders, historical narratives as well as biographies of contemporary admirable leaders and case studies may be used to provide

---

[97] Not only are professional virtues, as argued before, identified on the basis of the ends distinctive of the profession, but they are also specifications of general, "prototype," virtues that are responsive to the particular features of the professional role. See C. Swanton, "Virtue Ethics, Role Ethics, and Business Ethics," in R. L. Walker and P. J. Ivanhoe (eds.), *Working Virtue*, Oxford University Press, Oxford, 2007.

[98] On the claim that the education of future leaders should not only focus on developing competencies but also in building a virtuous character, in the context of business organizations, see Neubert et al., "The Virtuous Influence of Ethical Leadership Behavior: Evidence from the Field," *Journal of Business Ethics*, vol. 90, 2009, p. 166; and Brown and Treviño, *op. cit.*, 536.

[99] On these interventions, see Brown and Treviño, *op. cit.*, p. 609.

Exemplarism, Virtue, and Ethical Leadership in International Organizations 125

prospective and actual international civil servants with a larger set of models worthy of imitation.[100] Furthermore, as argued before, partial, mixed, and negative exempla also have educational value, and this further extends the range of models that may be useful for the purposes of inculcating the leadership virtues.

Besides education, virtuous leadership may also be propelled by explicitly incorporating virtuous standards for leadership in the strategies, mandates, and ethical codes of international organizations.[101] The inclusion of the language of virtue in these instruments is important for explicitly stating the extent to which the international organization values the virtues of ethical leadership, takes them to be central to its normative identity, and is committed to fostering them. Although limited as tools for virtue development, professional codes of conduct may also be useful for promoting the virtues of ethical leadership in that they play an important role in providing standards for assessing professional conduct as well as enabling criticism and discussion of core professional values. Much more controversial, however, are suggestions to incorporate virtuous standards of leadership in ethics audits and performance management processes, so that ethical leadership weighs in promotion and compensation decisions. These measures may provide perverse incentives for virtuous behavior that, instead of resulting in enhanced ethical leadership, may turn out to be detrimental to virtue development.[102]

Last, virtuous leadership may also be nudged through institutional design.[103] One can structure decision-making and management within international organizations in ways that promote virtuous behavior. Importantly, these structural solutions do not rely on incentives, sanctioning, or coercing. Rather, the objective of nudging strategies is to design the institutional environment in ways that facilitate virtuous behavior. For example, a way to give equal weight to opinions, uncontaminated by racial, gender bias, etc. and thereby to promote impartiality (as well as to secure that one benefits from all the relevant information available) is the Delphi Method, which consists in

---

[100] The "mirror for princess" genre or the book of exempla are classical examples of these educational tools. See Kaak and Weeks, *op. cit.* See above note 8, for contemporary work on exemplary figures in international organizations, which may be profitably put to use for educational purposes.

[101] See, in the context of business organizations, Neubert et al., *op. cit.*, p. 159. Ethical role-modeling might also be profitably fostered through formal means; for an argument to this effect, see Weaver et al., *op. cit.*, p. 326ff.

[102] For the suggestion that ethical leadership be incorporated into performance management processes, see Weaver et al., *op. cit.*, pp. 327–28; and Brown and Treviño, *op. cit.*, p. 610.

[103] On structural ways to develop virtue, see E. Anderson, "Epistemic Justice as a Virtue of Social Institutions," *Social Epistemology*, vol. 26, 2012, p. 168.

126   *Amalia Amaya*

leaders asking people to state their opinions anonymously before deliberation.[104] Thus, there are several structural mechanisms that can be used to foster, at least, behavior in accordance with virtue on the part of leaders in international organizations, which may be a path towards the development of genuine virtue.

4.8 CONCLUSIONS

In this chapter, I have examined ethical leadership in international organizations through the lenses of exemplarist virtue ethics. After providing some reasons why virtue ethics may provide a productive framework for analyzing ethical leadership, I have proposed an account of the leadership virtues, that is, the traits of character that are necessary to properly achieve the ends that are constitutive of international civil service, as a distinctive professional role. Ethical leadership, I have argued, requires the exercise of a number of moral virtues as well as a set of intellectual and communicative virtues that have moral import. In addition, managerial and political abilities, which, as argued, are not unconnected to virtuous traits of character, are also needed for good leadership.

International civil servants that possess a large share of the leadership virtues are exemplary. In addition to complete models of virtue, I have claimed that partial, negative, and ordinary exempla also have an important place within an exemplarist virtue account of ethical leadership for international organizations. There are, moreover, different ways in which ethical leaders may be claimed to be exemplary. Exempla, in their different varieties, play a number of significant roles. Most importantly, as argued, they contribute to create a valuable ethical climate within the organization, shape the international legal, political, and moral culture, prompt the revision and refinement of ideals of virtuous global leadership, and set up normative standards for guiding and evaluating ethical conduct in the context of global governance institutions.

In addition to providing a productive framework for examining the concept and roles of ethical leaders in international organizations, virtue exemplarism, as argued, brings to light the relevance of ethical leadership to questions of international authority. Exemplary ethical leaders in international organizations enjoy authority, which is thus viewed as partly a matter of moral character. Such authority, I have claimed, translates into a greater legitimacy of the institutions they lead. The vigorous ethical leadership that is embodied in

---

[104]   See C. Sunstein and R. Hastie, *Wiser: Getting Beyond Groupthink to Make Group Smarter,* Harvard Business Review Press, Cambridge, 2015, chapter 6.

exempla of virtue has a positive impact on societal perceptions of the legitimacy of international organizations. In addition, it is also a source of normative legitimacy, which is thus claimed to depend not only on the properties of the processes, outcomes, and rules that structure international organizations but also on the properties of the agents that work within those institutional environments.

Last, I have argued that ethical leadership that is exemplary from a virtue ethics perspective is a relevant normative ideal that is not doomed to remain in the realm of the impossible, rather than the actual, for there are a number of educational tools, normative instruments, and institutional means through which it may be brought about in international organizational contexts. To be sure, rethinking education and professional training in a way that promotes the virtues of ethical leadership among students and international civil servants, forging virtue-oriented normative frameworks for international organizations, as well as designing international institutions that foster virtuous behavior pose tremendous challenges. However, if the claims advanced in this chapter as to the relevant roles that exemplary ethical leaders of international organizations play and the impact that their authority has on the legitimacy of the institutions they lead is on the right track, there seem to be good reasons for engaging in the difficult work that goes into imagining alternative ways in which one could reconceive education as well as normative and institutional structures with a view to promoting virtuous leadership in international organizational contexts.

PART II

ETHICAL NARRATIVES AND ORGANIZATIONS

5

Virtue in Algorithms?

Law and Ethics in Algorithmic Governance

René Urueña

5.1 INTRODUCTION

Two central transformations occurred in the second decade of the twenty-first century. The first is a whole new level of access to information about peoples' habits. This is the 'big data' revolution: never before had it been possible to gather so much information about so many people, with such accuracy[1] – specially gathered by huge online service providers such as Facebook, Google, or Amazon, which record each action of their users.[2] Thus, while marketing strategists or political campaigns have always sought to know the preferences of particular segments of the population, big data makes possible a truly high-resolution profiling of behaviours, which reflects the habits of specific individuals, and not only of demographic groups or certain geographical areas.

The second new transformation is the exponential increase in the computational capacity of the last decade. One way to think about such transformation is Moore's law, named after Intel's founder, who in 1965 correctly observed that microprocessor capacity would double every two years.[3] This exponential growth (which may already be changing[4]) entails that a microprocessor of 2017 had almost nine times more capacity than one from 2010, or 511 times

---

[1] Amir Gandomi and Murtaza Haider, 'Beyond the Hype: Big Data Concepts, Methods, and Analytics', *International Journal of Information Management*, 35(2) (2015), 137–44.

[2] See John Cheney-Lippold, *We Are Data: Algorithms and the Making of Our Digital Selves* (New York: New York University Press, 2017). Pp. 37–50.

[3] Gordon E. Moore, 'Cramming More Components onto Integrated Circuits', *Electronics*, 38(8) (1965), 114.

[4] Tom Simonite, 'Moore's Law Is Dead. Now What?', *MIT Technology Review*, 23 May 2016.

132 René Urueña

more capacity than one from the year 2000.[5] Never has there been such a capacity to process information, and never before, as we saw, was it possible to gather such large amounts of information on human beings.

These two changes have increasingly captured the attention of legal scholarship. The way in which information is gathered, stored, analysed, and used may create a conflict with the right to privacy[6] and intimacy.[7] Such was the case of the political consultancy firm Cambridge Analytica, who improperly

---

[5] Source: Karl Rupp, '42 Years of Microprocessor Trend Data', accessed 15 February 2018, www.karlrupp.net/2018/02/42-years-of-microprocessor-trend-data/. These proportions are correlated, in general terms, with those in Ray Kurzweil, *The Singularity Is Near: When Humans Transcend Biology* (New York: Viking, 2005). P. 234.

[6] See Omer Tene and Jules Polonetsky, 'Big Data for All: Privacy and User Control in the Age of Analytics', *Northwestern Journal of Technology and Intellectual Property*, 11 (2013), 239–74. While I was writing this text, the Supreme Court of the United States was about to decide a critical case for the relationship between privacy and big data. In *Carpenter v United States* (Docket No. 16–402), Carpenter is, ironically, a cell-phone thief who was captured because his cell-phone service provider gave the FBI his location for 127 days, without a previous judicial order but under the Stored Communications Act. This law is applicable to user communications' information stored by third parties (like a cell phone or internet provider), and it establishes a lower standard of proof to justify the disclosure of stored information by third parties to the authorities than the proof standard established by the Fourth Amendment to authorize search warrants. The important question posed before the Court is then: what is the threshold of this 'third party rule' and, in consequence, if the cell phones' geographic location record without judicial order breaches the Fourth Amendment. The Court's decision was that the 'third party rule' does not apply and that, consequently, acquiring the physical location information of a cell phone is in effect a search. For the Court, '[...] we decline to grant the state unrestricted access to a wireless carrier's database of physical location information. In light of the deeply revealing nature of CSLI ("cell site location information") its depth, breadth, and comprehensive reach, and the inescapable and automatic nature of its collection, the fact that such information is gathered by a third party does not make it any less deserving of Fourth Amendment protection. The Government's acquisition of the cell-site records here was a search under that Amendment' (at 22).

[7] See Ana Garriga Domínguez, *Nuevos retos para la protección de datos personales en la Era del Big Data y de la computación ubicua* (Madrid: Dykinson, S.L., 2016). Pp. 75–88. On the Inter-American system of Human Rights, see Inter-American commission on Human Rights-Special Rapporteur on Freedom of Expression, 'Freedom of expression and Internet' OEA/ Comisión Interamericana de Derechos Humanos – Relatoría Especial para la Libertad de Expresión, 'Libertad de expresión e Internet' OEA/Ser.L/V/ii, cidh/rele/inf. 11/13 (31 December 2013). Pp. 130–137. Special Rapporteur of the CIDH on Freedom of expression and Special Rapporteur of the UN for the Promotion and Protection of the Right to Freedom 'Joint Declaration about surveillance programs and their impact in Freedom of Expression', 21 June 2013. Special Rapporteur of the UN on Freedom of Opinion and Expression, Agent on Media's Freedom of the OSCE, Special Rapporteur of the CIDH on the Freedom of Expression and Special Rapporteur on Freedom of Expression and Access to information of the CADHP 'Joint Declaration on Freedom of Expression and Answers to Conflict Situations', 3 May 2015. In the Universal system, it is of paramount importance the conceptual framework of the UN Office of the High Commissioner for Human Rights, 'The Right to Privacy in the Digital Ages' A/HRC/27/37 (30 June 2014). In addition, the UN Human Rights Council created

Virtue in Algorithms? Law and Ethics in Algorithmic Governance

used the information of millions of Facebook users in order to provide services to their clients influencing the elections of United States, United Kingdom, Nigeria, India, Brazil, and Colombia, among others.[8] And yet, crucially important as it is, data management and privacy are only the beginning of the conversation regarding big data. Even if data is collected and stored appropriately, these recent changes have created the conditions for the appearance of new ways of exercising power, with particular characteristics.

Such an exercise of power is transnational by nature. On the one hand, providers of algorithmic services are often multinational corporations, and algorithmic decision-making often has transnational effects – for example, in the form of Google search results directly affecting the rights of millions of individuals across jurisdictions. Moreover, international organizations are also increasingly relying on big data in their very own decision-making processes.[9] Thus, for example, Google helps process massive amounts of information for monitoring the UN's Sustainable Development Goal.[10] Similarly, humanitarian and development aid are increasingly relying on big data to adopt decisions, and direct scarce resources with potential impacts on the lives of the most vulnerable populations in the globe.[11] Leadership in international economic institutions, such as the World Trade Organization, is also increasingly reliant

in 2015 a Special Rapporteur on the Right to Privacy, designating the Maltese professor Cannataci, who presented the preliminary report in October of 2017. See Joseph A. Cannataci, 'Report of the Special Rapporteur of the Human Rights Council on the Right to Privacy', UN Docs. A/72/540, 19 October 2017. The General Assembly has, likewise, enacted three resolutions of great importance on the right to privacy in the digital era: 68/167 of 18 December 2013, 69/166 of 18 December 2014, and 71/199 of 19 December 2016.

8   Matthew Rosenberg, Nicholas Confessore, and Carole Cadwalladr, 'How Trump Consultants Exploited the Facebook Data of Millions', *The New York Times*, 17 March 2018, sec. Politics.

9   See the example in Fleur Johns, 'Data, Detection, and the Redistribution of the Sensible in International Law', *American Journal of International Law*, 111(1) (2017), 57–103.

10 See Ronald Jansen, 'Planet and Google are ready to help the United Nations in the data work behind the 2030 Agenda for Sustainable Development'. Available at: https://unstats.unorg/bigdata/blog/2019/planet-google.cshtml. For a similar discussion on SDGs in the health sector, see Eduard J. Beck, Wayne Gill, and Paul R. De Lay, 'Protecting the Confidentiality and Security of Personal Health Information in Low- and Middle-Income Countries in the Era of SDGs and Big Data', *Global Health Action*, 9(1) (2016), 1–7.

11 For the use of big data by international organizations in humanitarian and development work, see generally David Le Blanc and Jean-Marc Coicaud, 'Information Revolution and International Organizations: Three Challenges for the Way Ahead', *Global Policy*, 6(1) (2015), 72–75. Mikkel Flyverbom, Anders Koed Madsen, and Andreas Rasche, 'Big Data as Governmentality in International Development: Digital Traces, Algorithms, and Altered Visibilities', *The Information Society*, 33(1) (2017), 35–42. John Karlsrud, 'Peacekeeping 4.0: Harnessing the Potential of Big Data, Social Media, and Cyber Technologies', in *Cyberspace and International Relations: Theory, Prospects and Challenges*, ed. Jan-Frederik Kremery Benedikt Müller (Berlin, Heidelberg: Springer, 2014), 141–60.

on big data,[12] and, in general, the turn of international law towards increased reliance in new technologies is now a fact widely observed.[13]

Algorithmic decision-making is thus quickly becoming a crucial part of the overall landscape of international leadership, posing difficult questions in terms of ethics and accountability. In that context, scholarship and policy makers have turned towards law, or law-like mechanisms, to create the conditions of possibility for such accountability to emerge. Two mindsets seem to dominate the discussion of legal accountability in big data: the human rights/human dignity framework, and the transparency mindset. This chapter argues that such two mindsets are not enough to achieve their purpose of accountability. On the one hand, the human rights/human dignity framework merely imports the limits of the human rights language on to the problem of algorithmic regulation. On the other hand, even if requirements of transparency are indeed adopted, they will only go so far to 'explain' the decision-making process underlying an algorithmic decision facing these limitations. This chapter proposes that virtue ethics may prove to be a useful complement for 'traditional' modes of algorithmic accountability. In particular, it argues that virtue ethics is useful to move from ex-post regulation to an ex-ante approach, and turn the spotlight on developers and users of algorithms, and define the sphere of diligence that could be expected of them – be it as individual professionals, as corporate actors, or as information fiduciaries of society as a whole.

To advance that argument, this contribution partially builds on existing literature that supports a virtue approach to computer ethics, yet differs from it in three important senses. First, the argument here seeks to make a contribution to the legal approach to algorithmic accountability, and seeks to complement legal reasoning, as applicable to algorithmic authority, with virtue ethics. The contribution is limited to legal reasoning, and does not seek to outline a wider ethics of computing. Second, the argument here does not intend to deal with the ethics (virtue or otherwise) *of* algorithmic entities – that is, the possible ethical standards applicable to autonomous decision-makers.[14] And, third, this intervention does not deal with the ethical presuppositions underlying legal reasoning as applicable to algorithmic

---

[12] See generally Wolfgang Alschner, Joost Pauwelyn, and Sergio Puig, 'The Data-Driven Future of International Economic Law', *Journal of International Economic Law*, 20(2) (2017), 217–31.

[13] Johns, 'Data, Detection, and the Redistribution of the Sensible in International Law'. Fleur Johns, 'Data Territories: Changing Architectures of Association in International Law', in *Netherlands Yearbook of International Law* 2016 (The Hague: T.M.C. Asser Press, 2017), 107–29.

[14] For example, in Kari Gwen Coleman, 'Android Arete: Toward a Virtue Ethic for Computational Agents', *Ethics and Information Technology*, 3(4) (2001), 247–65.

Virtue in Algorithms? Law and Ethics in Algorithmic Governance   135

authority (for example, whether the law in itself reflects a consequentialist mindset), nor with the internal ethics of law (for instance, à la Fuller), as applied to algorithmic authority.[15]

The chapter proceeds in the following way. Section 5.2 briefly introduces automated decision-making systems – those with some knowledge of this issue can safely skip that section. Section 5.3 describes the two dominant approaches to algorithmic accountability: human rights, and transparency. These two approaches, valuable as they are, feature important limits, which are explored in sections 5.4 and 5.5. Section 5.6 then describes the ways in which virtue ethics might complement existing frameworks of algorithmic accountability, by defining the sphere of diligence of algorithm designers and users in terms of professional ethics, corporate action, and information trust-worthiness. Section 5.7 concludes.

5.2 UNDERSTANDING AUTOMATED DECISION SYSTEMS

As suggested in the introduction, the first step to understand automated decision-making systems is to underscore the importance of big data. While no term of art, it is possible to characterize big data as information of very high volume (tera or even petabytes), which is gathered rapidly (that is, created almost in real time), and that is diverse in its variety (formed by organized and unstructured information). It is exhaustive (in the sense that it seeks to capture populations or entire systems), of high definition (because it allows indexing with relative ease, and maintains the accuracy of the information even on a granular level). Big data, moreover, is relational in its characteristics (as it allows information to be related with that contained in other databases).[16] Thus, what is new and different in big data is not only its sheer *volume* (extraordinary in and of itself), but also (and, especially) what can be *done* with the information at a very low cost.

Data feeds algorithmic operations. Algorithms are organized and finite groups of operations that enable the resolution of problems. Thus, a cooking recipe, for example, may be considered an algorithm. In the digital context, operations are done by computers, which follow instructions reflected in the 'code' – the latter being nothing different than the specific expression, in a certain programming language, of abstract algorithm operations. At the

---

[15]   See in this volume, Jan Klabbers, 'Re-visiting *Rainbow Warrior*: Virtue and Understanding in International Arbitration', Ch. 9.
[16]   For these characteristics, see Rob Kitchin, 'Big Data, New Epistemologies and Paradigm Shifts', *Big Data & Society*, 1(1) (2014), 1–12.

same time, algorithms describe operations that will be executed on the compiled data (the 'input'), which is, by definition, external to the program.

Algorithms may consist of a series of instructions that repeat themselves statically: if you want to get result X, you must first follow step one, then step two, finally step three and so on, always. But the algorithm may also include instructions so that the program seeks to improve its performance in achieving result X. The algorithm may modify the steps in order to get there. In this sense, the program 'learns', because its performance with regards to certain task improves with repetition. This is the idea of 'machine learning' or 'independent learning', in which the algorithm is ordered to analyse the data and 'decide' the next step, with the goal of improving the performance.

The expression 'machine learning' has been used since 1959, and, since then, techniques have been developed that are able to achieve, in one way or another, the learning process previously described.[17] The recent transformation appears, once again, by virtue of big data and the increase in computational capacity. To a large extent, independent learning occurs today through pattern recognition: the program is capable of finding patterns in a database, and automatically deploys those patterns in other databases in order to make a 'decision', or make a prediction. An example is music streaming services: the program analyses my previous musical selections and, based on that information, looks for artists that have the same characteristics, suggesting an artist that I do not know but might like. Therefore, the richer the database is (in the example, the more songs I 'like'), the more the program may 'learn', and it becomes better in achieving its objective (i.e. the suggestions will be more accurate).

---

[17] See Arthur L. Samuel, 'Some Studies in Machine Learning Using the Game of Checkers', *IBM Journal of Research and Development*, 3(3) (1959), 210–29. In 1950, Alan Turing submitted his famous test, based on an imitation game, in which a human (judge) interacts with another human and a computer, without knowing which of these was the human and which the computer. If the judge confuses the computer with the human, the computer wins the game (Alan M. Turing, 'Computing Machinery and Intelligence', *Mind*, 59 (1950), 433–60). In that text, Turing names the theoretical characteristic of a "learning machine", which may win the imitation game. Nonetheless, Turing's test refers to general artificial intelligence (AI), in which computers apply their capacity to any sort of problem, like a human (for example, C-3PO in *Star Wars*, or *Terminator*). On the contrary, the scenario opened by Samuel, which is the issue important for our purposes here, is the possibility of a limited AI, in which the machine learns in order to fulfil a discrete function allocated by a human (for example, winning a chess game). In order to learn more about the difference between general AI and limited AI, see John O. McGinnis, 'Accelerating AI', *Northwestern University Law Review*, 104 (2010), 1253–70. Pp. 1256–1260.

Perhaps the most important recent developments in the independent learning genre is 'deep learning'. This process is based on a structure built up by several layers of algorithms called 'artificial neural networks', inspired in the biological structure of the neurons in the human brain. In this network, the data goes through the algorithm's layer, which transforms it and sends it to the next layer, which likewise transforms it in order to achieve its task – hence the name 'deep learning': the more algorithmic layers, the 'deeper' the neural network will be. The important thing about the neural network, however, is that it does not take 'decisions' by recognizing patterns given by the programmer (as machine learning does), but through examples, from which it autonomously extracts patterns in order to apply them into a new database.

Imagine we want a program that 'knows' how to autonomously recognize images of cows and birds. In machine learning, the algorithm is fed a large database of images of cows and birds, and is 'taught' to identify in them characteristics chosen by the programmer as belonging to each animal: for example, 'horns' and 'beaks'. The program hence 'learns' to identify images of cows and birds within large databases such as Facebook or satellite images. In deep learning, on the contrary, the programmer does not provide the characteristics that must be identified in the database ('horns'), but rather feeds directly the training images,[18] and the program automatically extracts those characteristics in order to apply them into a new database, different from the training data. Consequently, the programmer does not need to know the characteristics of the cow's or bird's image: the program will identify them and 'learn' autonomously, and the program will be able to make predictions over a new database regarding the appearance of a cow or a bird.

5.3 ALGORITHMIC ACCOUNTABILITY AND THE LAW

It is quite obvious that the potential use of algorithmic decision-making is limitless, and it is perhaps self-evident that some form of legal regulation is required. Two dominant models of regulation have emerged, which try to tackle some of the challenges posed by algorithmic accountability: (a) the human rights/human dignity framework, and (b) the transparency mindset. We now explore each of these models, and the next section will explore some of its limits.

---

[18] In my example, the images would be extracted from CIFAR-100 dataset that contains thousands of free training images, gathered in 100 classes and 20 super classes (available at: www.cs.toronto.edu/~kriz/cifar.html). In practice, the images' bases will be owned by a supplier (such as Facebook or Google), provided "voluntarily" by their users, which concerns a problem that will be discussed later.

138 René Urueña

5.3.1 *The Human Rights/Human Dignity Framework*

The first model of regulation is human rights. If it is true that algorithmic decision-making is a form of power, then it makes sense to subject such an exercise of power to human rights norms. This is the dominant strategy in, for example, cases of algorithmic discrimination. In the United States, for example, algorithms are frequently used to calculate the risk of recidivism of people convicted in criminal proceedings.[19] These tools, the most famous of which is COMPAS, of the company Northpointe, essentially asks defendants about their age, crime, and previous convictions (but, importantly, not about their race), as well as other information concerning the defendant's life ('Has your father ever been arrested?', 'Were you suspended or expelled from your school?'[20]), and assigns a certain score that reflects the likelihood of recidivism, which is reported to judges at the time of establishing the sentence.

For obvious reasons, the use of these tools has been controversial. On the one hand, some have claimed that the algorithm gives worse scores to black men (that is, it gives them a greater chance of recidivism[21]), while others maintain that COMPAS fails to bring anything new to the table, as compared to predictions that a human with a minimum level of information could make.[22]

In possible situations of discrimination, such as these, the default reaction has been to apply human rights – in this case, anti-discrimination law. Thus, for example, the challenges posed by COMPAS might be tackled through algorithmic affirmative action, which would push algorithmic designers and users to consider race (or other possible categories of discrimination) in order to define

---

[19] See Sarah Desmarais and Jay P Singh, 'Risk Assessment Instruments Validated and Implemented in Correctional Settings in the United States', 27 March 2013, https://csgjusticecenter.org/reentry/publications/risk-assessment-instruments-validated-and-implemented-in-correctional-settings-in-the-united-states/.

[20] An example of the COMPAS questionnaire can be found at: www.documentcloud.org/documents/2702103-Sample-Risk-Assessment-COMPAS-CORE.html.

[21] See Julia Angwin and Jeff Larson, 'Machine Bias', *ProPublica*, 23 May 2016. However, questioning these results, see Anthony W. Flores, Christopher T Lowenkamp, and Kristin Bechtel, 'False Positives, False Negatives, and False Analyses: A Rejoinder to "Machine Bias: There's Software Used Across the Country to Predict Future Criminals. And it's Biased Against Blacks"', 2017, www.crj.org/assets/2017/07/9_Machine_bias_rejoinder.pdf. Against this latter critique, see Avi Feller et al., 'A Computer Program Used for Bail and Sentencing Decisions Was Labeled Biased against Blacks. It's Actually Not That Clear', *Washington Post*, 17 October 2016, sec. Monkey Cage.

[22] Julia Dressel and Hany Farid, 'The Accuracy, Fairness, and Limits of Predicting Recidivism', *Science Advances*, 4(1) (2018), eaao5580.

Virtue in Algorithms? Law and Ethics in Algorithmic Governance   139

whether a given algorithm is having, in effect and not necessarily by design, a disproportional effect on a particular group – such as black males.[23]

A similar line of argument, building on human rights, mobilizes the principle of human dignity, in order to create a category of decisions that simply cannot be subject to autonomous decision-making processes, even if they are technically automatable.[24] These would be non-automatable decisions, as a matter of principle. Such may be the case, for example, of completely autonomous lethal weapon systems – that is, weapon systems with the ability to choose their objectives and eliminate them independently of the human.[25]

The principle of dignity requires that each person be considered as unique. However, an autonomous decision-making process necessarily prevents the person to be killed from being considered as unique, since it requires that it be considered as a case of a rule previously designed by the programmer, or as an expression of the pattern extracted autonomously by the algorithm. In either case, the act of killing is done following some steps defined before the lethal encounter, when it was not known who the person to be killed is. Therefore, the consideration of the specific person who is going to be killed is logically impossible, so that the link of humanity is not generated, which makes lethal autonomous weapons inherently contrary to human dignity.[26] In this sense, there may be an external constitutional limit to accept certain autonomous decisions (even if they are

---

[23] See Anupam Chander, 'The Racist Algorithm', *Michigan Law Review*, 115 (2017), 1023–46.

[24] See, for example, Eyal Benvenisti, 'EJIL Foreword: Upholding Democracy Amid the Challenges of New Technology: What Role for the Law of Global Governance?', Global Trust Working Paper, 2018, https://papers.ssrn.com/abstract=3106847. Pp. 65–66.

[25] This is the definition adopted by the Department of Defense of the United States, which does not require that the weapon system be activated autonomously. Even if the activation depends on the human, the system will be autonomous if it chooses and eliminates the objective without human intervention. See US Department of Defense, 'Autonomy in Weapons Systems' (Directive 3000.09, 21 November 2012). Pp. 13–14. The same definition is adopted by Human Rights Watch and the ICRC. See Human Rights Watch, 'Losing Humanity. The Case against Killer Robots', 19 November 2012. P. 1; ICRC, 'Autonomous Weapon Systems: Technical, Military, Legal and Humanitarian Aspects. Expert meeting, Geneva, Switzerland, 26–28 March 2014', 1 November 2014, www.icrc.org/en/document/report-icrc-meeting-autonomous-weapon-systems-26–28-march-2014. P. 3.

[26] See Christof Heyns, 'Human Rights and the Use of Autonomous Weapons Systems (AWS) During Domestic Law Enforcement', *Human Rights Quarterly*, 38(2) (2016), 350–78. Pp. 370–71. There are, of course, other arguments, both deontological and consequentialist, against lethal autonomous weapons that do not derive from the principle of dignity, which will not be explored here. See, for example, Daniele Amoroso and Guglielmo Tamburrini, 'The Ethical and Legal Case Against Autonomy in Weapons Systems', *Global Jurist; Berlin*, 17(3) (2017), 1–20. In international humanitarian law, there are also arguments in this regard, for example, see Dustin Andrew Lewis, Gabriella Blum, and Naz Khatoon Modirzadeh, '*War-Algorithm Accountability*' (Harvard Law School Program on International Law and Armed Conflict – PILAC, 2016), http://nrs.harvard.edu/urn-3:HUL.InstRepos:28265262. Pp. 66–76.

technically possible), as has been posited by thousands of experts, jurists and technology entrepreneurs, who called, in 2015 and in 2017, for a complete ban on autonomous lethal weapons.[27]

5.3.2 *The Transparency Mindset*

The second strategy to deal with algorithmic authority is focused on transparency. The challenge, in general, has been posed in terms of the algorithmic 'black box'.[28] Autonomous decision-making processes are opaque, in the sense that input and result are known, but the process that carries from one to another is not known in a specific way. This opacity, coupled with the fact that the algorithmic process features its result with a veil of objectivity and inevitability, have triggered a call for greater transparency, an 'open the algorithm' plea/campaign, so that algorithmic decisions are explained, and humans can understand it – for example, by allowing the algorithmic decision-making to be traceable and reproduced ex post facto by a human.[29] Such is the option, for example, adopted by the European General Data Protection Regulation (GDPR), which establishes that, in addition to the right to know and question stored information (standard in matters of *habeas data*), people have the right to receive an 'explanation' of the 'decision' adopted by creating profiles (in the terms of recital 71), and to receive significant information regarding the 'logic applied' in certain automated decisions that affect their rights (in the terms of articles 13.2.f and 14.2.g).

5.4 THE LIMITS OF THE CURRENT HUMAN RIGHTS/TRANSPARENCY FRAMEWORK

It goes without saying that both human rights and transparency must be protected in the context of algorithmic decision-making. However, while necessary, they can be complemented by a tighter framework of algorithmic accountability. This section explores the limitations of the current human rights/transparency approach, and the next section explains why virtue ethics might be a useful complement to the current approach.

---

[27] See the public letters in: 'Autonomous Weapons: An Open Letter from AI & Robotics Researchers', 2015, https://futureoflife.org/open-letter-autonomous-weapons/; and 'An Open Letter to the United Nations Convention on Certain Conventional Weapons', 2017, https://futureoflife.org/autonomous-weapons-open-letter-2017/.

[28] See Frank Pasquale, *The Black Box Society: The Secret Algorithms That Control Money and Information* (Cambridge: Harvard University Press, 2015). Pp. 1–19.

[29] For a non-technical introduction to, and further examples of, initiatives seeking to 'open' algorithms, see Cliff Kuang, 'Can A.I. Be Taught to Explain Itself?', *The New York Times Magazine*, 21 November 2017, sec. Magazine.

Let us begin by exploring the limits of the human rights/human dignity approach. While necessary, it merely imports the limits of the human rights language on to the problem of algorithmic regulation. This is not the place to rehearse such limits;[30] the point, however, is that, by resorting to human rights law, we have to be mindful that law is 'not enough'[31] to deal with the structural challenges posed by algorithmic decision-making. Of course, this is not to imply that human rights language, and arguments based on human dignity, are irrelevant in dealing with possible injustices deriving from the use of algorithmic decision-making. They create a framework and a range of argumentative possibilities that are indeed helpful in certain cases.

However, it is also clear that human rights law comes with baggage, and a set of built-in limitations, that makes it a less than ideal one-stop answer to controlling algorithmic authority. In particular, as Klabbers has suggested with regards to international law in general,[32] human rights have a problem with actors, in the sense that they fail to directly bind the very institutions that exercise algorithmic authority – namely, multinational corporations. Thus, for example, even if one were to establish an individual right to transparency in algorithmic decision-making under international law, this right would in any case not be directly binding on Google or Facebook, but would instead create the duty on states to hold them accountable – at least according to the conventional international legal consensus.[33] Second, human rights have a problem with sources, in the sense that they fail to register much of the normative utterances that are key to algorithmic authority – such as guidelines, industry-wide software design blueprints, quality standards, among others. Human rights instruments are both too inflexible and too blunt: on the one hand, they too struggle to adapt to new challenges, relying mostly on tools like the evolutive interpretation of treaties in order to adapt to new social realities[34] and, on the other, they fail to penetrate the finer grain of algorithmic

---

[30] See, for example, Martti Koskenniemi, 'Human Rights, Politics, and Love', *Mennesker & Rettigheder*, 4 (2001), 33–45 and David Kennedy, 'The International Human Rights Movement: Part of the Problem?', *Harvard Human Rights Journal*, 15 (2002), 101–25.

[31] Samuel Moyn, *Not Enough: Human Rights in an Unequal World* (Cambridge, Mass.: Belknap Press of Harvard University Press, 2018).

[32] Jan Klabbers, 'Law, Ethics and Global Governance: Accountability in Perspective', *New Zealand Journal of Public and International Law*, 11(2) (2013), 309–321.

[33] See, generally, Surya Deva, 'Human Rights Violations by Multinational Corporations and International Law: Where from Here', *Connecticut Journal of International Law*, 19 (2003–2004), 1–57.

[34] See, generally, Julian Arato, 'Subsequent Practice and Evolutive Interpretation: Techniques of Treaty Interpretation over Time and Their Diverse Consequences', *The Law and Practice of International Courts and Tribunals*, 9(3) (2010), 443–94.

design, thus providing guidelines that hardly translate into workable blueprints. Third, human rights and the concept of human dignity have a problem with indeterminacy, in the sense that their use begs the question of interpretative discretion, which has been widely explored in critical legal scholarship.[35] As is well known, legal texts in general, and human rights in particular, cannot in and of themselves determine the outcomes of a case. Thus, the specific meaning of 'transparency' or 'privacy' is indeterminate, always factoring in the politics of interpretation in order to acquire meaning in a specific context.[36] And, finally, applying human rights to algorithmic decision-making also poses the problem of 'accountability fragmentation', in the sense that different stakeholders will have different views (and different venues) to achieve accountability. Shareholders owning stock in corporations are certain to have a different view of accountability from that of users, or even non-users. Moreover, human rights might also entail conflicting courts with overlapping jurisdictions (or no jurisdiction at all), and conflicting standards contained in diverging treaties, or domestic legislations.

In this context, the human rights framework is necessary, but not sufficient, to tackle the challenges of algorithmic accountability. Just as international law faces structural challenges when dealing with global governance, so too do human rights face difficult limitations when deployed to frame accountability in algorithmic decision-making. Something similar occurs, in turn, with the second important strategy deployed to regulate such authority: transparency – to which we now turn.

The instinct behind the claim for greater transparency is understandable. In the same way that the exercise of informal authority led to the requirement of standards of transparency in global governance, so too the algorithmic authority must be subject to standards of transparency.[37] And, of course, just as *habeas data* standards in terms of data collection and storage are a necessary guarantee, the possibility of knowing, to the extent possible, the process of data analysis is also a key guarantee for algorithmic accountability.

However, transparency, in the sense of knowing the 'logic' underlying the results of an autonomous decision, is quite problematic. As we have seen, the machine learning processes and, above all, deep learning consist of millions of

---

[35] See, generally, Duncan Kennedy, *A Semiotics of Legal Argument* (New York: Plenum Press, 1989).

[36] For the radical indeterminacy thesis in general international law, see Martti Koskenniemi, *From Apology to Utopia: The Structure of International Legal Argument*, 2nd ed. (Cambridge: Cambridge University Press, 2005). Pp. 60–66. In human rights in particular, see Koskenniemi, 'Human rights, politics, and love'. Pp. 83–84. Jarna Petman, 'Human Rights, Democracy and the Left', *Unbound: Harvard Journal of the Legal Left*, 2 (2006), 63–90.

[37] See Benedict Kingsbury, Richard B. Stewart, and Niko Krisch, 'The Emergence of Global Administrative Law', *Law and Contemporary Problems*, 68 (2005), 15–61.

operations whose 'logic' can hardly be described to the human. Such is precisely the point of pattern recognition: detecting what the human cannot detect. Requiring direct transparency, like one would expect of a regulatory agency that adopts a decision, would seem to be a solution that is just not a good fit for several instances of algorithmic decision-making.

Think, for example, of a case of algorithmic discrimination. COMPAS, the recidivism prediction platform discussed above, systematically pointed to black men as more prone to recidivism.[38] The process of recognizing Google photos, a typical example of machine learning, categorized photos of black people as 'gorillas'.[39] And Google's ad algorithm tended at one point to show women fewer ads for the best-paid jobs.[40]

In these examples, the call for direct transparency can eliminate a first layer of discriminatory practices. It is, of course, possible that a bigoted programmer would have reflected his racial or gender biases in some set of classification criteria in the training database of Google Photos or Google Ads. But this is unlikely, and would be irrelevant in deep learning processes, where the algorithm 'learns' from huge databases of examples.

Most likely, then, discrimination is not intentional, but derives from patterns in databases that reflect structures of discrimination in society. Of course, the absence of intention does not prevent the result of the autonomous decision-making process from being discriminatory, which reflects the state of the art in current anti-discrimination law, and makes human rights law relevant to solve some of these problems. However, the absence of intention does imply that a call to direct transparency seems ineffective in solving this problem. A neutral algorithm can generate discriminatory effects by virtue of the database from which it 'learns' – which is the result of the continuity between structures of social power and algorithmic decision-making, discussed later on in this chapter.

There is at least one precedent that shows the limitation of a direct concept of transparency. In Wisconsin, United States, Eric Loomis, a detainee whose sentence had been decided in part on the basis of a COMPAS report, sought to challenge the constitutionality of the use of the algorithm, claiming that it violated his due process, as he did not know how it calculated the score.[41]

---

[38] Angwin and Larson, 'Machine Bias'.

[39] Alistair Barr, 'Google Mistakenly Tags Black People as "Gorillas," Showing Limits of Algorithms', WSJ (blog), 1 July 2015, https://blogs.wsj.com/digits/2015/07/01/google-mistakenly-tags-black-people-as-gorillas-showing-limits-of-algorithms/.

[40] Amit Datta, Michael Carl Tschantz, and Anupam Datta, 'Automated Experiments on Ad Privacy Settings', *Proceedings on Privacy Enhancing Technologies*, 1 (2015), 92–112.

[41] See, in first instance, *State v. Loomis* 881 N.W.2d 749 (Wis. 2016). In appeal: *Loomis v. Wisconsin*, 137 S. Ct. 2290 (2017). *Certiorari* was not granted by the Supreme Court.

Since the algorithm was protected by intellectual property rights, Northpointe, the company that produces the algorithm, refused to deliver the information. Faced with this refusal, the detainee sought (among other things) that Northpointe revealed the COMPAS code, that is, the expression of the algorithm in a programming language. The point, though, is that Eric Loomis knew what information COMPAS had about him (he had filled out the questionnaire), but he did not know how the score assigned to him was derived from that information.[42] The Court denied his claim, arguing, among other things, that due process had not been violated, because Loomis had the right to access and verify the information on him that fed into the algorithm – a typical argument of transparency.[43]

Faced with these challenges of transparency, a first strategy is to encourage a culture of intelligibility in algorithms – a strategy that should be encouraged. Despite the difficulties in the practical implementation of the European General Data Protection Regulation, the development of techniques to make deep learning processes understandable, at least by experts, constitutes important progress.[44] However, this progress does not generate greater hope in terms of algorithmic accountability. Even important initiatives explicitly tailored to make certain techniques more understandable (such as the visualization of neural networks[45]) seem to be beyond the technical expertise that can reasonably be asked of a judge, or a citizen. The same applies to the possibility of external audits of independent decision processes: even if intellectual property rights were not an obstacle to the idea of 'open algorithms', this process would require the auditor to train the audited program and seek to interpret what the program did in its decision-making process, which triggers the aforementioned difficulties.

---

[42] See Ellora Israni, 'Algorithmic Due Process: Mistaken Accountability and Attribution in State v. Loomis', *JOLT Digest – Harvard Journal of Law & Technology*, 31 August 2017, http://jolt.law.harvard.edu/digest/algorithmic-due-process-mistaken-accountability-and-attribution-in-state-v-loomis-1.

[43] The Court, though, did underscore its scepticism regarding the indiscriminate use of the tool. It prohibited judges from basing a decision exclusively on the score of the algorithm and demanded that, from then on, when the scores were to be used, language was to be introduced to warn that the private nature of the algorithm prevents knowing how the scores were calculated, noting also that studies have suggested that scores disproportionately classify convicts belonging to minorities as more prone to recidivism. See *State v. Loomis*, Pp. 757–69.

[44] For a description on the culture shift with regards to algorithmic transparency, see Kuang, 'Can A.I. Be Taught to Explain Itself?'

[45] Chris Olah, Alexander Mordvintsev, and Ludwig Schubert, 'Feature Visualization', *Distill*, 2 (11) (7 November 2017), e7.

Ultimately, the deeper challenge to transparency is that autonomous decision-making processes exist precisely to extract patterns of certain information. Those patterns may reflect suspicious categories of discrimination (such as race or gender), even if the explicit criteria that is programmed, or the training data in deep learning cases, do not. Thus, autonomous decision-making processes can predict the gender of a person based on their purchasing habits, and might allow for discrimination based on a suspicious category (gender). But this is not an error: it is exactly what the autonomous decision-making process is supposed to do – namely, what the human cannot do.

Similarly, certain processes of deep learning in facial recognition have been able to predict the sexual orientation of men with 91% success and of women by 83%.[46] Thus, five photos per person, without any mention of sexual orientation, are enough for a classification based on a forbidden category of discrimination, with obvious effects on human rights. And the same is true of ethnicity, socio-economic status, and housing addresses in recidivism prediction algorithms: a trained algorithm with historical data from recidivist geolocations may assign higher probability of recidivism to people living in predominantly poor neighbourhoods, or to Latinos or immigrants, thus generating discrimination against people in these categories – even if they do not appear in the code, nor in the training data.[47]

Direct transparency is, in much the same line as human rights, necessary but not enough for algorithmic accountability. Even if requirements of transparency are indeed adopted, the fact is that they will only go so far to 'explain' the decision-making process underlying an algorithmic decision – a reality that has already dawned on those who are responsible for implementing the recent European regulation.[48]

These limitations are intimately linked to a specific view of algorithmic decision-making, which interposes the algorithm as an independent agent, and obscures the role of the humans involved in the process. In a way, the human rights mindset has a paradoxical result: while it strives to find accountability of 'decision-making', it is unable to find such 'decision-making' in some of the most controversial processes of algorithmic decision-making. Human rights thus leave us with an accountability system built on the reproach to a 'human' decision-maker – and no human in sight to plausibly reproach.

---

[46] Yilun Wang and Michal Kosinski, 'Deep Neural Networks Are More Accurate Than Humans at Detecting Sexual Orientation from Facial Images', *PsyArXiv*, 7 September 2017, https://psyarxiv.com/hv28a/.

[47] See Chander, 'The Racist Algorithm'.

[48] See Alison Cool, 'Don't Follow Europe on Privacy', *The New York Times*, 15 May 2018, www.nytimes.com/2018/05/15/opinion/gdpr-europe-data-protection.html.

146 *René Urueña*

Facing these limitations, the last section of this chapter proposes a different vocabulary that might complement both the human rights and transparency frameworks. That language, this chapter argues, is virtue ethics, which could expand the vocabulary deployed to achieve algorithmic accountability.

5.5 THE MISSING LINK: ACCOUNTABILITY OF HUMANS BEHIND THE ALGORITHM

The limits of both human rights and transparency point to a basic difficulty with framing, in legal terms, accountability for the exercise of algorithmic authority. Ultimately, algorithmic accountability through human rights or transparency tends to keep humans out of the equation, focusing instead on the 'algorithm' as an independent entity to be held accountable. The absence of the human poses a specific doctrinal problem in terms of algorithmic accountability through law. Both human rights and transparency focus on the algorithm. On the one hand, the best work on human rights focuses on the effects of the algorithm, while search for transparency also seeks to unpack the algorithm itself – both accepting, ultimately, that the search for accountability of humans behind the algorithm is a lost cause.

This move is, of course, understandable: as we have seen, it is quite hard to link specific human decisions to algorithmic outcomes. Thus, unless we are faced with a clear problem of biased programming, programmers tend to be thought of as removed from algorithmic outcomes. This means that there is a missing link: humans (those developing the algorithm, and those who use it) whose accountability is hard to factor into the language of human rights, or of transparency.

Interposing the algorithm as an independent agent frames automated decision-making as outside societal structures of power.[49] This is, however, incorrect. While algorithms are a specific vehicle of power, the power that is exercised through them is no different from power that arises from existing social structures beyond the use of algorithms.

This difference between power (in general) and 'algorithmic authority' (specifically) implies that the relationships of power established through algorithms merely reflect the power differences that already exist in the society where algorithms are used. Automatic decision-making processes take their

---

[49] It is not, then, a wider exercise of power (an "algorithmic governance") that would imply a diffuse exercise of the power of influence in the preferences of the individuals. Regarding this reading of algorithms as a social organizer, see Natascha Just and Michael Latzer, 'Governance by Algorithms: Reality Construction by Algorithmic Selection on the Internet', *Media, Culture & Society*, 39(2) (2017), 238–58.

Virtue in Algorithms? Law and Ethics in Algorithmic Governance 147

data ('learn') from an already existing description of reality – whether it is given by the programmer, or reflected in raw data. Thus, the criteria of a human programmer, or the processes of deep learning, will draw from materials existing in the reality already developed by humans (photos, texts, videos, or sound recordings) that will 'educate' the programs. The algorithm will 'learn' the differences of power that are reflected in the materials provided, or stem from the prejudice of the programmer. A male chauvinist society produces male chauvinist data (for example, pornography), from which independent 'learning' processes will extract male chauvinist patterns, which will be employed afterwards in a new database in order to draw male chauvinist conclusions. Thus, it is wrong to think that 'an algorithm is male chauvinist': because male chauvinism results from the interaction between humans and therefore the society in which the algorithm functions – which is in turn reflected by the automated 'learning' process.

Underscoring this continuity between deep power structures and algorithms prevents us from incurring in the so-called 'fallacy of the homunculus', according to which there is an 'agent' taking the autonomous 'decisions' of the programme: a kind of little person, a *Golem*, reaching conclusions that are good or bad.[50] But there is no such little person: the algorithm is not an agent to be held accountable. The reproach arises with respect to the type of human interaction that is created by the autonomous decision-making process: even if the automated decision-making process has particular characteristics, its exercise reflects and is inseparable from the power structures in human society. Only in the context of human society does algorithmic accountability make sense. Consequently, legal doctrines that imply a title of imputation of accountability or responsibility based on some type of reproach of conduct (such as fraud or guilt in criminal law, negligence in civil law, or failure of service in administrative law) cannot be used to hold accountable the

---

[50] The homunculus fallacy is usually traced to Wittgenstein's argument about the possibility of attributing to a part of the creature characteristics that correspond only to the whole (for example, saying that certain parts of the brain 'see' is fallacious, because it is the person who does it). In Philosophical Investigations, it is held '(. . .) only of living human beings and what resembles them (behave similarly) can one say that they have sensations, they see, they are blind, they hear, they are deaf, they are conscious or unconscious', Ludwig Wittgenstein, *Investigaciones filosóficas* (Mexico D.F: UNAM, 2003). Para 281. Although Wittgenstein's argument is mereological, since it never speaks of the fallacy implying that there was a little person in the brain who 'sees', it is also clear that the mere fact of assigning to the part the attribute of a person ('To see') implies affirming that the part is also a person, reason why this deceit also implies to affirm that in the part there is a homunculus that does what the whole (the person) also does. For this reading of the fallacy, see Anthony John Patrick Kenny, 'The Homunculus Fallacy', in *The Legacy of Wittgenstein*, ed. Anthony John Patrick Kenny (Oxford; New York: Blackwell, 1984), 125–36.

148 *René Urueña*

algorithm itself, but the human who develops it, or the human who uses it. Algorithmic autonomy, although certainly existing, does not imply a non-human addressee of ethical or juridical reproach.

Of course, sometimes there will be an ideological incentive to 'blame' the algorithm: the homunculus fallacy allows what Balkin has called the 'substitution effect',[51] by which the public debate focuses on a fetishized autonomous decision-making process, as if it were an 'agent' with the magical power to affect the lives of humans, instead of focusing on the profound power differences that the algorithm reflects. The analogy to the fetishism of commodities proves useful at this point. Due to the fetishism of commodities, the alienated worker inhabits a phantasmagoric world populated by objects she made, but that are foreign and belong to someone else.[52] Likewise, the fetishism of the algorithm places us in a world of 'thinking machines' that are alien to the human community – and we are all potential victims. But this description is ideological, as it involves the mobilization of meanings for the perpetuation of structures of domination:[53] the supposed 'thinking machines' actually operate in terms of human relations of power. Focusing on their 'autonomy' and obsessing over the 'rise of the machines' only serves to distract from the power relations that underlie algorithmic decision-making.

It is humans that create social processes of inequality, discrimination and arbitrariness. Automatic decision-making processes just recreate power relationships that already exist. The effects of the algorithmic authority will always be in human relationships.[54] However, current focus on transparency and human rights makes it difficult to see those underlying structures of power, because they interpose the algorithm and obscure the human. They are, in consequence, not enough to think about accountability of those humans who are involved in the interaction – be they developers or users of algorithmic decision-making.

5.6 VIRTUE IN ALGORITHM?

What are the legal tools available to think of this kind of human accountability in algorithms, that complements both human rights and transparency? Virtue

---

[51] Jack Balkin, 'The Path of Robotics Law', *California Law Review Circuit*, 6 (2015), 46–60. Pp. 55–59.

[52] See Jon Elster, *Making Sense of Marx* (Cambridge; New York; Paris: Cambridge University Press; Editions de la Maison des sciences de l'homme, 1985). Pp. 56–58.

[53] John B. Thompson, *Studies in the Theory of Ideology* (Berkeley: University of California Press, 1984). P. 4.

[54] Jack M. Balkin, 'The Three Laws of Robotics in the Age of Big Data Lecture', *Ohio State Law Journal*, 78 (2017), 1217–42. P. 1234.

ethics might prove useful to complement standard approaches to controlling algorithmic decision-making. As Klabbers has argued, referring to international organizations, 'what is missing here is the consideration that accountability may be better seen as a social relation where learning and adaptation are at least as important as carrots and sticks, and what is also missing here – and quite fundamentally so – is the consideration that rules are not always reliable and airtight guideposts for political action.'[55] Indeed so. The limits of both the human rights and transparency-based approaches to algorithmic accountability might warrant a different, complementary, approach to decision-making. This section argues that virtue ethics might be just what is needed.

Klabbers' insight speaks to the 'vacuum' of ethics in computer science. In an early contribution to the debate on ethics in computing, Moor argued that the key problem with ethics in new technology is that it allows us to do things that were just impossible before.[56] Therefore, it was impossible to consider whether we *should* do them. In much the same sense, algorithmic authority allows some decision-makers (be they algorithm designers, or its users) to do things that were not possible just a few years earlier – hence, there is a 'policy vacuum', in Moor's terms, concerning what should be done by humans acting through algorithms.

This ethical vacuum leaves us with little guidance as to what is expected of a good behaviour of *humans* in the context of algorithmic decision-making – a question that is answered by neither human rights nor transparency. These two mindsets are necessary, but insufficient, to tackle this question. By focusing on the algorithm as an independent entity, they fail to provide us with criteria to evaluate the behaviour of humans who design, or use, the algorithm.

To be sure, this vacuum presents a wide set of challenges to develop a vocabulary to ethically assess algorithmic decision-making.[57] I am, however, interested in one specific dimension of these challenges: the vacuum of human accountability that is left by the interposition of algorithm; in particular, lack of a title to find humans accountable for algorithmic decision-making. This poses a specific legal problem – and virtue ethics, in conjunction with existing efforts based on human rights and transparency, may be useful to solve it.

---

[55] Jan Klabbers, 'Controlling International Organizations: A Virtue Ethics Approach', *International Organizations Law Review*, 8(2) (2011), 285–89. P. 287.

[56] James H. Moor, 'What Is Computer Ethics?', *Metaphilosophy*, 16(4) (1985), 266–75. P. 286.

[57] See Brent Daniel Mittelstadt et al., 'The Ethics of Algorithms: Mapping the Debate', *Big Data & Society*, 3(2) (2016), 1–21.

5.6.1 *Virtue Ethics and Algorithmic Decision-Making*

As is well known, virtue ethics seeks to escape from the 'law conception of ethics' that fails to make sense without a belief in divine commands,[58] and from consequentialism. The basic idea behind virtue may be perhaps better grasped if one drops the label 'virtue' (which is often misleading in contemporary language) and frame it as *good-sense ethics*.[59] From that perspective, the question posed is: has this person acted in good sense? And acting in good sense is fundamentally a matter of practical wisdom: how should one behave in a given context, to live in excellence?[60]

This line of ethical thought has proven useful in the context of computer science. In an early key contribution, Moor proposed an Aristotelian view of computing, in which virtues would be useful to fill the 'ethical gap' created by computer advancement – mainly through ethical training of computer professionals.[61] Similarly, Grodzinsky has argued that virtue is part of the solution to re-examine how to handle the micro-basis of moral agency in computer ethics,[62] and, more recently, Stamellos has applied Plotinus' ethics to computing, directing us to change our emphasis from a normative aspect of computer ethics, and the bipolar social-constructive interaction between the individual and society, to a more self-centred, psychodynamic form of the moral agency and to a character-based development of the moral self.[63] Against this view of virtue ethics as being useful for computing, though, Floridi and Sander argue that virtue ethics 'remains limited by its subject-oriented approach and its philosophical anthropology, failing to provide, by itself, a satisfactory ethics for a globalized world in general and for the information society in particular'.[64]

Most of this work focuses on the ways in which virtue ethics may guide computing science, in general, and algorithmic decision-making, in particular.

---

[58] See, generally, G. E. M. Anscombe, 'Modern Moral Philosophy', *Philosophy*, 33(124) (1958), 1–19.

[59] I take this idea from C. M. Coope, 'Modern Virue Ethics', in T. Chapell, *Values and Virtues: Aristotelianism in Contemporary Ethics* (2006). P. 21.

[60] For a notoriously convincing elaboration, see A. MacIntyre, *After Virtue: A Study in Moral Theory* (London: Duckworth, 1981).

[61] James H. Moor, 'If Aristotle Were a Computing Professional', *SIGCAS Computers & Society*, 28(3) (1998), 13–16.

[62] Frances Grodzinsky, 'The Practitioner from Within: Revisiting the Virtues', *ACM SIGCAS Computers and Society*, 29(1) (1999), 9–15.

[63] Giannis Stamatellos, 'Computer Ethics and Neoplatonic Virtue. A Reconsideration of Cyberethics in the Light of Plotinus' Ethical Theory', *International Journal of Cyber Ethics in Education*, 1(1) (2011), 1–11.

[64] Luciano Floridi and Jeff W. Sanders, 'Internet Ethics: The Constructionist Values of Homo Poieticus', in *The Impact of the Internet on our Moral Lives*, ed. R. Cavelier (Albany, New York: State University of New York Press, 2005), 195–214. P. 199.

However, it fails to account for the dominant efforts of ethical assessment of algorithmic decision-making; that is, deontological efforts based on human rights and transparency. To apply virtue ethics to algorithms will, by necessity, require an interaction with a generally deontological framework of legal regulation. How can these two approaches complement each other? A valuable starting point is the contribution of van der Sloot who specifically focuses on big data and privacy, and has argued that a shift towards virtue ethics could strengthen privacy protection in the age of big data. He asks whether a rights-based approach to privacy regulation suffices to address the challenges triggered by new data-processing techniques – answering of course in the negative.[65] Instead, he argues, virtue ethics is useful, as it is necessary to base privacy protection not only on the question of respect for the rights of citizens but also on the broader question of whether the actions of an agent are the actions a virtuous agent would perform.[66]

In that sense, virtue ethics emerges as a mindset that complements deontological approaches: while accountability in algorithmic decision-making requires that human rights and transparency standards are applied, it could also benefit from assessing the behaviour of the algorithm's designer, and its users, on the basis derived from the latter's own community, featuring a sensibility to the professional experience of those engaged in the particular activity to be assessed. That is where virtue ethics comes in. It gives us the substantive criteria to mobilize the title of imputation of responsibility in order to find the human accountable, and not the algorithm – and it does so by defining the sphere of diligence that can be reasonably expected, as we will see below, from the individual IT professional, from the corporation and from online service providers as information fiduciaries. Virtue ethics allows us to pose the question of whether algorithmic designers and users are acting in *good sense* – not only according to a deontological standard that may be perceived as foreign and uninformed, but according to what in their very own community is considered to be virtuous.

---

[65] Bart van der Sloot, 'Privacy as Human Flourishing: Could a Shift towards Virtue Ethics Strengthen Privacy Protection in the Age of Big Data', *Journal of Intellectual Property, Information Technology and Electronic Commerce Law*, 5 (2014), 230–44. In the same sense, Bart van der Sloot, 'Is the Human Rights Framework Still Fit for the Big Data Era? A Discussion of the ECtHR's Case Law on Privacy Violations Arising from Surveillance Activities', in *Data Protection on the Move: Current Developments in ICT and Privacy/Data Protection*, ed. Serge Gutwirth, Ronald Leenes, and Paul de Hert (Dordrecht: Springer, 2016), 411–36.

[66] Bart van der Sloot, *Privacy as Virtue: Moving Beyond the Individual in the Age of Big Data* (Cambridge, UK: Intersentia, 2017).

152 René Urueña

This form of complementing deontological forms of regulation with virtue-ethics substance seems promising. In particular, virtue ethics may provide the conceptual basis to turn legal regulation towards the algorithm developer, and the algorithm user, thus opening new spaces for algorithmic accountability through law. Virtue ethics provides criteria to evaluate the behaviour of developers and users of algorithms, such as jurists, academic, journalists, among others, thus complementing legal standards of diligence in the exercise of algorithmic authority.

This complement may occur in three dimensions: professional ethics, organizational compliance procedures, and online service providers as information fiduciaries. In what remains of this chapter, I will explore each of these dimensions. The last section will conclude.

5.6.2 *Virtue Ethics and Professional Ethics*

The first, and perhaps most traditional, approach to virtue ethics is professional ethics. An important body of work on virtue ethics features a teleological structure, in which the desirable traits of characters are those that allow for the achievement of a certain goal – ultimately, the traits of character that allow humans to flourish and achieve their goal. As such, virtue ethics are a good fit for professional ethics, as they describe some of the traits to be held in order to be a good professional. To be sure, as we will see below, professional ethics are often expressed in the form of codes, thus prompting some commentators to classify them as inherently deontological.[67] However, the fact that professional ethics describes the end of a certain profession (justice in lawyering,[68] say, or minimizing distress in nursing[69]), and describes traits of character that are conducive to that end (fairness, for example), makes professional codes of ethics a natural space for the discussion of virtue ethics.

In the context of computing, certain professional ethics, and virtues associated with algorithmic design, have been a common staple. The goal is to produce meta-level ethical orientations to data collection and data use in decision-making, distinctively based on certain professional virtues. To that effect, professional virtue ethics may be highly informal, and take the form of individual pledges of virtue, such as the 'Critical Engineer Manifesto', whose authors consider being 'critical'

---

[67] See, for example, Jan Klabbers, 'The Virtues of Expertise', in *The Role of 'Experts' in International and European Decision-Making Processes*, ed. Monika Ambrus et al. (Cambridge, UK; New York: Cambridge University Press, 2014), 82–102.

[68] Justin Oakley and Dean Cocking, *Virtue Ethics and Professional Roles* (Cambridge: Cambridge University Press, 2001). P. 75.

[69] Sarah Banks and Ann Gallagher, *Ethics in Professional Life* (London: Palgrave Macmillan, 2009).

Virtue in Algorithms? Law and Ethics in Algorithmic Governance   153

as a key attribute for responsible engineering today.[70] Piecemeal approaches also emerge often in the context of algorithmic design, as a form of bottom-up call for virtuous algorithmic design. Such is the case, for example, of the notion of 'fair by design',[71] which tries to factor in fairness concerns to the design process of the algorithm, thus creating, in effect, an ethical duty on behalf of engineers to be 'fair' and 'diligent' in their algorithmic design. To be sure, 'fair by design' does not guarantee that an ethical outcome will necessarily emerge. Ultimately, it has to be acknowledged that no deontological standards are available to guide this process, which rather relies heavily on the communicative practices of the community.[72] However, 'fair by design' does point to a significant shift, as it opens an *ethics-striving* space, in which the debate of what constitutes an ethical behaviour, on the basis of the good sense of a specific community, becomes relevant.

Professional ethics often also takes the form of codes. In the context of computing, the best example of professional codes is the work of the Association for Computer Machinery (ACM), which adopted the 1999 Software Engineering Code of Ethics and Professional Practice, as the product of the ACM/IEEE-CS Joint Task Force on Software Engineering Ethics and Professional Practices. The Software Engineer Code provides insights into what kind of virtues are expected of an engineer: for example, to 'accept full responsibility for their own work' (section 1.01), to 'be fair and avoid deception' (1.06), to 'identify, define and address ethical, economic, cultural, legal and environmental issues related to work projects' (3.03), and to 'temper

---

[70] See https://criticalengineering.org/en.

[71] See, for example, Francesco Bonchi et al., 'Exposing the Probabilistic Causal Structure of Discrimination', *International Journal of Data Science and Analytics*, 3(1) (2017), 1–21 and Sara Hajian, Francesco Bonchi, and Carlos Castillo, 'Algorithmic Bias: From Discrimination Discovery to Fairness-Aware Data Mining', in *Proceedings of the 22nd ACM SIGKDD International Conference on Knowledge Discovery and Data Mining* (ACM, 2016), 2125–26. In the context of machine learning, Niki Kilbertus et al., 'Avoiding Discrimination Through Causal Reasoning', in *Advances in Neural Information Processing Systems*, 2017, 656–66. On this 'internal' regulation of algorithmic design, the best introduction is Batya Friedman and Helen Nissenbaum, 'Bias in Computer Systems', *ACM Transactions on Information Systems (TOIS)*, 14(3) (1996), 330–47.

[72] I draw this insight from constructivist international relations scholarship, particularly from the notion of communities of practice and the work that explores their relevance in international law. From this perspective, it is possible to derive normatively relevant statements from the practice of a community, as long as certain agreed-upon criteria are met. On communities of practice generally, see Emanuel Adler, *Communitarian International Relations: The Epistemic Foundations of International Relations* (London; New York: Routledge, 2005). For the relevance of communities of practice in international law, see Stephen J. Toope and Jutta Brunnée, *Legitimacy and Legality in International Law: An Interactional Account* (Cambridge: Cambridge University Press, 2010).

all technical judgments by the need to support and maintain human values' (4.06), among many others.

Moreover, the ACM has also developed its Code of Ethics and Professional Conduct, which applies to a wider set of professionals. Moreover, the ACM has also developed in 2008 its Code of Ethics and Professional Conduct, which applies to a wider set of professionals, and is structured in four sections ('general moral principles', 'professional responsibilities', 'professional leadership principles', and 'compliance'). The Code also puts forward a set of virtues regarding computer professionals that seem crucially relevant for algorithmic accountability: 'be honest and trustworthy', 'be fair and take action not to discriminate', 'respect privacy', and 'honor confidentiality', among others.

The most direct connection between these individual virtues of the engineer and algorithmic accountability is, of course, education. Teaching IT professionals the virtues that make for non-biased algorithms is the focus of much of virtue ethics scholarship focused on engineering. Beyond education, though, professional ethics interacts with legal reasoning in varied forms. Many of these statements of professional virtue are enforced by professional bodies, as is the case of medical doctors and lawyers. Moreover, these virtues are also applied directly by courts as causes of legal action – again, the example of lawyers comes to mind.

More interesting, though, is the use of these virtues to establish a standard of care or duty owed to another by the professional.[73] This use seems particularly useful for the purposes of algorithmic accountability. While the algorithm itself may end up being obscure, there is something to be said in favour of turning the spotlight on to the conduct of the algorithm designer, and asking whether she acted as required to achieve the purpose of her profession – regardless of the result. In this context, it is the virtues of the good professional that define the sphere of obligation that can be demanded of the IT professional that works with algorithms. This behaviour can (and should) be triggered by the appropriate education in the virtues. Legal reasoning, though, applies in this case as a test of diligence, and virtue ethics serves as the substantive content that fills the otherwise empty standard of responsible engineering.

5.6.3 Virtue Ethics and Organizational/Corporate Diligence

Unlike professional ethics, streamlined ethics procedures apply to the organization as a whole (for example, the corporation) and are less focused on the

---

[73] In the US, see, for example, Criton A. Constantinides, 'Professional Ethics Codes in Court: Redefining the Social Contract between the Public and the Professions Symposium: Cruzan and the Right to Die', *Georgia Law Review*, 25 (1991), 1327–74.

individual behaviour of the IT professional, but rather focus on the collective action of the organization. Here, virtue ethics can be useful as well for creating spaces for algorithmic accountability. However, the first question that emerges is whether virtue ethics is relevant for collective bodies, such as a state or a corporation. Is a collective entity capable of behaving in a virtuous manner? There are, at least, two possible answers. One possibility is to accept 'organizational virtue'. While it is clearly the case that much of virtue ethics literature focuses on individuals, it is also the case that certain virtues might be attributable to corporate entities when they act as such – for example, it is not unreasonable to say that a corporation or a state is 'honest' or 'fair'. Another option is denying 'organizational virtue', as virtues (in terms of means to human flourishing) can only be predicable of natural persons. In that latter case, organizations may be thought of as spaces that foster (or hinder) individual virtues. In both scenarios, then, ethics at the organizational level is a crucial space for the interaction between law, virtue, and algorithmic accountability.

Now, corporate ethics may also take different forms. As is the case with professional ethics, corporate ethics may consist of informal statements. Think, for instance, in the *uber*-famous 'don't be evil' motto at Google, which was then changed to 'do the right thing' at Alphabet, Google's new parent company. This motto, though, provides a good insight into the limits of open-ended virtue ethics at the corporate level. The 'don't be evil' motto was, in fact, originally intended to be applicable in the very narrow context of online ads: 'don't be evil' meant, essentially, 'don't insert ads into search results',[74] which is definitely underwhelming in terms of virtue ethics. Ultimately, 'don't be evil' seems more like an empty PR stunt than an actual framework for ethical corporate decision-making.

Given the limits of informal ethical pledges, more formalized forms of corporate ethics have been adopted outside algorithmic decision-making, for example, in the context of anti-corruption regulation. During the last twenty years, several international initiatives, standards, and principles have been developed to provide guidance for companies on how to fight corruption in their operations, by upholding enhanced integrity standards. In this context, a whole cottage industry of ethics and compliance programmes has emerged, creating different procedures and guidelines to create a streamlined structure of incentives, information procedures, and collective action mechanisms to prevent corporate corruption.

---

[74] See Siva Vaidhyanathan, *The Googlization of Everything: (And Why We Should Worry)* (Berkeley: University of California Press, 2011). See also Steven Levy, *In the Plex: How Google Thinks, Works, and Shapes Our Lives* (New York: Simon & Schuster, 2011).

In a way, though, this approach is the exact opposite of a virtue ethics approach. It turns virtues into procedures and checklists, bringing the form to the fore as a proxy for ethical commitment. Even when anti-corruption procedures have been complied with, it is still the case that the organization has not engaged in virtuous behaviour leading to its flourishing as an honest broker in the market. However, it is *also* the case that these kinds of compliance procedures may create incentives towards the emergence of virtue. Still in the context of anti-corruption, one may make the deontological argument that international bribery is wrong because it is against a legal or moral norm, or because it is against my own interest, as my corporation might end up having high reputational or market access costs. But international bribery might also be simply *dishonest*. This attachment to *honesty* may come as the result of a good education of the individual in the virtues (either personal or, as we have seen earlier, professional), but it may also come from an organized set of incentives and procedures that lead to a growing attachment to honesty.

Such a strategy of 'nudging virtue'[75] poses the key problem of intention: determining the effects of this kind of regulation on a person's character is an imprecise exercise. We can measure people's changes in behaviour, but not whether those changes reflect an altered inner state across the course of their life by having adopted and acquired virtues.[76] This is, though, a problem of evidence of regulatory effectiveness and not one of principle in terms of virtue – it is possible (even probable) that the appropriate set of incentives inspires an attachment to a set of virtues, just as the appropriate educational environment is likely to have the same effect. In this sense, compliance procedures are an acceptable proxy for the virtues in a particular organization.

Now: algorithmic decision-making is intimately linked to nudging, in the sense that the former can be mobilized in order to achieve the latter. From fitness watches to apps that help users smoke less, or eat better, big data is often thought of as the perfect complement for well-meaning Cass Sunstein-style regulation that seeks to nudge people into better behaviour – and eventually the internalization of such behaviour in a form that becomes virtuous.[77] For others, though, this sounds like a scary prospect – particularly if the data is in the hands of the Facebooks of this world.

My argument, though, highlights a *different* link between nudging and algorithms. Organized procedures of compliance in organizations (which

---

[75] Kiran Iyer, 'Nudging Virtue', *Southern California Interdisciplinary Law Journal*, 26 (2017), 469–92.

[76] Ibid. P. 478.

[77] See Cass Sunstein and Richard H. Thaler, *Un pequeño empujón (nudge): El impulso que necesitas para tomar las mejores decisiones en salud, dinero y felicidad* (Madrid: Taurus, 2009).

nudge people into virtuous behaviours) are useful to define the reasonable sphere of diligence that corporate algorithm developers and users can be expected to fulfil. Just as corporate anti-corruption compliance procedures are proof of diligence in many jurisdictions (for example, as a defence in criminal cases) so too could algorithmic design and use be subject to procedures that reflect a set of virtues. It is possible to think, for example, of fairness and non-discrimination: procedures could deal with the question of whether a corporation has been fair when designing or using an algorithm, and promulgate guidance for developing algorithms that meet those standards[78] – just as other procedures have dealt with the equally hard question of corporate attitude towards transnational corruption, with a certain degree of success. In line with the OECD programme on Anti-Corruption and Compliance, one might even think of an OECD programme of Algorithmic Ethics, under which procedures would be suggested that may nudge organizational structures towards the virtues that are desirable in terms of algorithmic decision-making.

5.6.4 Virtue Ethics as a Complement of Information Fiduciary Obligations

Finally, corporations that engage in algorithmic decision-making are often depositaries of vast amounts of our data. In that sense, they can be thought of as information fiduciaries that have a duty to act in a certain way towards their customers. The idea of online service providers as information fiduciaries was first proposed by Balkin,[79] and builds on the idea that certain contract and service relations (such as the relation of a client with her lawyer, or a patient with his doctor) are characterized by an underlying link of trust, from which legal obligations emerge, beyond the specific obligations of the primary contractual relation. These 'implicit' obligations are typically called 'fiduciary' obligations, which derive from the special relation of trust and confidence that exists between the parties. The fiduciary, Balkin explains, must take care to act in the interests of the other person, who is sometimes called the principal, the beneficiary, or the client.

Our relationship with online service providers is very similar to these relationships of deep trust. First, according to Balkin, end-users' relationships with many online service providers involve significant vulnerability, because

---

[78] Andrew Tutt, 'An FDA for Algorithms', *Administrative Law Review*, 69 (2017), 83–109.

[79] Jack M. Balkin, 'Information Fiduciaries and the First Amendment Lecture', *U.C. Davis Law Review*, 49 (2016), 1183–234.

service providers have considerable expertise and knowledge and end-users usually do not. Second, we find ourselves in a position of relative dependence with respect to these companies. Third, in many cases, online service providers hold themselves out as experts in providing certain kinds of services in exchange for our personal information. And, fourth, online service providers know that they hold valuable data that might be used to our disadvantage – and they know that we know it too.[80]

An ethics of virtue may prove to be particularly useful in giving content to such fiduciary obligations of online providers – complementing their obligations in the design and use of algorithms discussed above. As fiduciaries, online service providers have two basic duties: care and loyalty towards the client.[81] In some cases, these fiduciary duties overlap with some of the duties emerging from professional ethics, as is the case with lawyers and medical doctors. In other cases, where the extent of these duties of care and loyalty is less defined, a virtue ethics approach might prove useful.

The fiduciary duties imposed depend on the nature of the relationships involved. Doctors, for example, have a duty of care towards their patients. On the other hand, it might be reasonable that online service providers exert a different kind of care towards their clients – perhaps not a duty to prevent someone from posting self-damaging information, but a general duty to prevent underage or mentally disabled users from using certain services.

Of course, by definition, the business of online service providers is gathering information. A virtue ethics approach to information fiduciaries must take into account that reality. However, the kind of virtues to be promoted, and the intensity with which such virtues can be demanded in a legal framework, must also balance the underlying duty of care and loyalty emerging from fiduciary obligations.

Balkin suggests that we should think of these kinds of online service providers as 'special-purpose information fiduciaries', in the sense that 'the nature of their services should guide our judgments about what kinds of duties it is reasonable to impose. We should connect the kinds of duties that information fiduciaries have to the kinds of services they provide'.[82] This makes perfect sense, and virtue ethics is precisely the kind of flexible language of normative assessment that may give substantive content to the general notion of fiduciary obligations.

---

[80] Ibid.
[81] Ibid.
[82] Ibid., P. 1229.

5.7 CONCLUSION

This chapter proposed that virtue ethics may prove to be a useful complement to 'traditional' deontological modes of algorithmic accountability – such as human rights and transparency. Virtue ethics is useful to turn the spotlight on to developers and users of algorithms and define the sphere of diligence that could be expected of them – be it as individual professionals, as corporate actors, or as information fiduciaries of society as a whole.

Professional ethics helps define the virtues that contribute to the achievement of the goal of a given profession, and by doing so, it helps also to define the sphere of diligence that could be expected of individual professionals when designing or using algorithms. Similarly, organizational compliance procedures could attain the same goal at the corporate level. And, finally, virtue ethics can contribute to a wider societal definition of fiduciary obligations, not only by reference to the corporation and its stakeholders, but to society as a whole. In that way, at the individual, corporate, and societal spheres, virtue ethics can complement the existing framework of regulation, focused on human rights and transparency, and help create a more flexible (and potentially more resilient) regime of algorithmic accountability.

6

Ethics in International Sporting Institutions

Lorenzo Casini[*]

6.1 THE SPORTS LEGAL ORDER AND INTERNATIONAL SPORTING INSTITUTIONS: A PRIVATE LEGAL REGIME WITH PUBLIC TRAITS?

Dealing with law and ethics in the field of sports requires several caveats, premises, and clarifications.[1]

The most compelling one would probably be to keep in mind that international sporting institutions are formally private institutions.[2] There is one important exception, however, that is the World Anti-Doping Agency (WADA), an interesting case of global hybrid public and private body, which adopts the World Anti-Doping Code (WADC).[3] Beside WADA, international sporting bodies, such as the International Olympic Committee (IOC), the Court of Arbitration for Sport (CAS), and the dozens International Sports Federations, are genuinely private entities and, in most cases, it is Swiss civil law that regulates them.

Yet, in spite of their private nature, international sporting institutions often display a degree of "publicness", which cannot be ignored. In the case of the IOC, for instance, there are international treaties mentioning it; the UN recognizes such committee; and the Olympic Games may be seen as a sort of global public good

---

[*] The author warmly thanks Sabino Cassese, Maria Luisa Catoni, Giulio Napolitano, and Serena Stacca for their comments to an earlier version of this chapter. All the usual disclaimers apply.

[1] K. Foster, *Global Sports Law Revisited*, in 17 *The Entertainment and Sports Law Journal* (2019), 4; J. A. R. Nafziger and S. F. Ross, *Handbook on International Sports Law*, Northampton, Edward Elgar, 2011.

[2] F. Latty, *La lex sportiva. Recherche sur le droit transnational*, Leiden-Boston, Brill, 2007; and L. Casini, *The Emergence of Global Administrative Systems: The Case of Sport*, in Glocalism, Issue 2015, 1.

[3] L. Casini, *Global Hybrid Public-Private Bodies: The World Anti-Doping Agency (WADA)*, in 6:2 *International Organizations Law Review*, 2009, 421 "et seq".

under the IOC monopoly.[4] This public element does play a significant role, as we will see, when we consider the role of ethics in international sporting institutions.

Another important premise to be made, therefore, refers to the very essence of sports law and of the sports legal order more generally. As a matter of fact, "sports law is not just international; it is non-governmental as well, and this differentiates it from all other forms of law".[5] Sports rules are genuine "global law", because they reach across the entire world, involve both international and domestic levels, and directly affect individuals (such as athletes): this is, for example, the case of the Olympic Charter, a private act with which all States comply; or of the above-mentioned WADC, a document that provides the framework for harmonization of anti-doping policies, rules, and regulations within sports organizations and among public authorities.

These rules include not only transnational norms established by the IOC and International Federations (IFs) – that is, "the principles that emerge from the rules and regulations of international sporting federations as a private contractual order"[6] – but also "hybrid" public–private norms approved by WADA and international law (such as the UNESCO Convention Against Doping in Sport). Sports law is highly heterogeneous, and, above all, it is "global": it consists not only of norms adopted by States, but also of the regulations of central sporting institutions (such as the IOC, IFs, and WADA) and of national sporting bodies (such as National Olympic Committees and National Anti-Doping Organizations). Sport has thus generated a set of institutions and rules that amounts to an autonomous legal corpus, which legal scholarship has varyingly referred to as "International Sports Law", "Global Sports Law", and *lex sportiva* (here drawing a patent analogy with the *lex mercatoria* governing international trade).[7]

---

[4] See J.-L. Chappelet, B. Kübler-Mabbott, *The International Olympic Committee and the Olympic System: The Governance of Sport*, London, Routledge, 2008, and A. M. Mestre, *The Law of the Olympic Games*, The Hague, T.M.C. Asser Press, 2009.

[5] M. Beloff, T. Kerr and M. Demetriou, *Sports Law*, Oxford, Hart, 1999, 5. According to these authors, the term "sports law" is "a valid description of a system of law governing the practice of sports". They also note that "the public's limitless enthusiasm for sport and its importance to our cultural heritage makes sports law more than mere private law" (*ibidem*, p. 4).

[6] K. Foster, *Is There a Global Sports Law?*, in 2 *Entertainment Law* (2003), p. 1, who describes "global sports law" as a "transnational autonomous legal order created by the private global institutions that govern international sport", "a contractual order, with its binding force coming from agreements to submit to the authority and jurisdiction of international sporting federation" and not "governed by national legal systems" (*ibidem*, p. 2). This author considers "global sports law" a significant example of spontaneous global law without a State, according to the definition provided in *Global Law Without a State* (Gunther Teubner, ed., Dartmouth, Aldershot, 1997), and Gunther Teubner (2001), *Un droit spontané dans la société mondiale*, in C.-A. Morand (ed.), *Le droit saisi par la mondialisation*, Bruxelles, Bruylant, p. 197.

[7] On these issues, see R. C. R. Siekmann and J. Soek (eds.), *Lex Sportiva: What is Sports Law*; The Hague, T.M.C. Asser Press, 2012, and J. A. R. Nafziger and S. F. Ross (eds.), *Handbook on*

162   *Lorenzo Casini*

Within this context, the issue of ethics in international sporting institutions also allows dealing with how an autonomous legal order as a whole may use (virtue) ethics and put it into practice. Sport and its law in fact offer a clear example – perhaps one of the most ancient – of a genuine global legal order:[8] first, sports norms and rules are mostly produced by a legal institution above the level of the nation state (e.g. IOC, WADA, International Sports Federations); second, sports norms and rules are directed to legal institutions inside nation states (and in many cases such domestic institutions are public entities, as it happens in the anti-doping regime); and third, sports norms and rules are produced in recognizable legal forms, to the extent that a sophisticated (quasi-)judicial system has been built to enforce those norms.[9]

The complexity of the global sports legal order thus will show that ethics may intervene in the decision-making processes not only of the socalled executive institutions, but also of the (quasi-)judicial bodies, such as the Court of Arbitration for Sport (CAS).

The aim of this chapter, therefore, is to demonstrate that ethics – in all its facets and its meanings, and whether it is related to the concept of morality – is inherently connected with sports and sporting institutions, which are "global" *per se*: every athlete or every team dreams of winning

---

International Sports Law, Cheltenham, Edward Elgar, 2011. See also J. A. R. Nafziger, *International Sports Law*, New York, Transnational Publishers, 2004; J.-P. Karaquillo (2006), *Droit international du sport*, in *Recueil des Cours – Collected courses of the Hague Academy of International Law*, The Hague, 2004, tome 309; A. Wax, *Internationales Sportrecht: Unter besonderer Berücksichtigung des Sportvölkerrechts*, Berlin, Duncker & Humblot, 2009, p. 173; M. Greppi and E. Vellano (eds.), *Diritto internazionale dello sport*, Torino, Giappichelli, 2010,; formerly, M. S. Giannini (1996), *Ancora sugli ordinamenti giuridici sportivi*, in M. S. Giannini, *Scritti*, IX, 1991–1996, Milano, Giuffrè, 2006, p. 441, who wrote that the term "international" refers, in sport, to a "diritto super-statale", such that it does not mean the "diritto proprio di un ordinamento giuridico a sé", but "una normativa interstato e superstato" (p. 444).

8   Since the 1920s, Italian legal scholarship has applied to the case of sport the notion of "legal order" with all its features – namely those identified by Massimo Severo Giannini in elaborating the hypothesis originally conceived by Santi Romano – that is, plurality of actors/addressees, organization, and norms. Sports law thus became one of the best fields for investigating the theory of legal orders; see S. Romano, *L'ordinamento giuridico*, Pisa, Vannucchi, 1918; W. Cesarini Sforza (1933), *La teoria degli ordinamenti giuridici e il diritto sportivo*, in *"Foro italiano"*, c. 1381 et seq.; and M. S. Giannini (1950), *Sulla pluralità degli ordinamenti giuridici*, now in M. S. Giannini, *Scritti*, vol. III, 1949–1954, Milano, Giuffrè, 2003, p. 403 et seq.; and M. S. Giannini (1946), *Prime osservazioni sugli Ordinamenti giuridici sportivi*, ibidem, p. 83 et seq.; F. Modugno, *Ordinamento giuridico (dottrine generali)* and *Pluralità degli ordinamenti*, both in *Enciclopedia del diritto*, XXX, Milano, Giuffrè, 1980, p. 678 et seq. and XXXIV, Milano, 1983, p. 32 et seq.; and F. P. Luiso, *La giustizia sportiva*, Milano, Giuffrè, 1975, particularly p. 363 et seq.

9   See T. Halliday and Gregory Shaffer (eds), *Transnational Legal Orders*, Cambridge, Cambridge University Press, 2015; F. Latty, *La lex sportiva. Recherche sur le droit transnational*, Leiden-Boston, Brill, 2007; and L. Casini, *Il diritto globale dello sport*, Milano, Giuffrè, 2010.

the world championship; and the very essence of competition tends to go beyond local or national borders. Lastly, investigating the role of ethics within the sports legal order and sporting institutions can contribute to the general discourse about international law and ethics.[10]

6.2 SPORTS, ETHICS AND INTERNATIONAL SPORTING INSTITUTIONS

"There was a little trickery [une petite magouille]. We did not spend six years organising the World Cup to not do some little shenanigans [petites magouilles]. Do you think other World Cup hosts did not? . . . France-Brazil in the final, it was the dream of everyone."[11] With this statement made to the press in May 2018, Michel Platini, former President of the European Union of Football Associations (UEFA) from 2007 to 2015, confessed that the draw for the 1998 International Federation of Football Associations (FIFA) World Cup was fixed. Before that, sporting authorities had already banned Platini for four years for a corruption case, because he violated the FIFA Code of Ethics. In June 2018, the Swiss prosecutor dismissed the case: according to Swiss criminal law, Platini was innocent. The ban, however, still remains because of the autonomy of sport justice.

There is an inextricable linkage between sports, ethics, and law.[12] And this comes from a long time ago, from the famous chariot race narrated by Homer in the Iliad: *"And thereby [Achilles] set as an umpire godlike Phoenix [. . .] that he might mark the running and tell the truth thereof."*[13] Michel Foucault dedicated beautiful pages to this literary episode, focusing on the very concept of judicial avowal.[14] The Homeric story is well known: Achilles decides to hold games to honour the memory of his beloved Patroclus, killed by Hector; such games include a chariot race, which has its rules and its umpire, Phoenix; but when the race starts, first gods and then racers start "cheating" . . . . We do not have to follow Foucault's reflections in all detail, but this example testifies that sport, since ancient times, offers an anthropological space where strife takes place – the "good" and competitive form of strife among the two kinds of strife

---

[10] D. E. Childress (ed.), *The Role of Ethics in International Law*, New York, Cambridge University Press, 2012.

[11] www.theguardian.com/football/2018/may/18/michel-platini-world-cup-1998-brazil-france-draw-trickery (last visited on March 15, 2020).

[12] A. L. Caplan and B. Parent (ed.), *The Ethics of Sport. Essential Readings*, Oxford, Oxford University Press, 2017.

[13] *Iliad*, book 23, v. 360. The scene related to the chariot is from verses 257 to 650.

[14] M. Foucault, *Wrong-doing, Truth-telling: the Function of Avowal in Justice* (1983), Chicago, University of Chicago Press, 2014.

("Ἔρις") described by Hesiod[15] – and it is a space where strife must have its own rules. Rules in sport are needed before we start playing: if there are no rules, there will be no game. And some rules can be non-written, because they belong to an ethical dimension. You must not only respect the rules, you must also play fair: this is why, for instance, we expect that players in the field stop playing if there is an opponent lying down on the ground. And this explains why fair play is so important in all sports and why WADA's motto is "play true".

The ethical dimension of sports is extremely complex and variegated. There are several themes, which overlap and interact with legal issues: drugs; match-fixing; corruption; age limit; gender discrimination; youth and young athletes; athletes with disabilities; professionals vs. amateurs (a theme well known if we go back to the case of Paavo Nurmi); use of animals; use of technological devices.[16] And many of these items present other legal and ethical problems legal and ethical problems: in doping issues, for instance, we have questions related to control (when and where, respecting athletes' personal life) or to the therapeutic use of certain prohibited substances.

But how do ethics legally affect organizations and activities of international sporting institutions?

6.2.1 *The Constitutional Dimension of Ethics*

The Olympic Charter is the instrument of "constitutional nature" ruling the world of sport.[17] The Charter sets the basis of global sports governance and it is the statute of the IOC.

According to the Charter Preamble:

---

[15] *Works and Days*, vv. 11–24: "So, after all, there was not one kind of Strife alone, but all over the earth there are two. As for the one, a man would praise her when he came to understand her; but the other is blameworthy: and they are wholly different in nature. For one fosters evil war and battle, being cruel: her no man loves; but perforce, through the will of the deathless gods, men pay harsh Strife her honour due. But the other is the elder daughter of dark Night, and the son of Cronos who sits above and dwells in the aether, set her in the roots of the earth: and she is far kinder to men. She stirs up even the shiftless to toil; for a man grows eager to work when he considers his neighbour, a rich man who hastens to plough and plant and put his house in good order; and neighbour vies with is neighbour as he hurries after wealth. This Strife is wholesome for men. And potter is angry with potter, and craftsman with craftsman, and beggar is jealous of beggar, and minstrel of minstrel."

[16] J. Bowen, R. S. Katz, J. R. Mitchell, D. J. Polden, and R. Walden, *Sport, Ethics and Leadership*, New York, Routledge, 2017; J. L. Pérez Triviño, *The Challenges of Modern Sport to Ethics. From Doping to Cyborgs*, Plymouth, Lexington Books, 2013; see also A. Epstein and B. Niland, *Exploring Ethical Issues and Examples by Using Sport*, in 13 *Atlantic Law Journal* (2011) 19.

[17] The text of the Charter is available at: www.olympic.org/documents/olympic-charter (last visited on March 15, 2020). See A. Duval, *The Olympic Charter: A Transnational Constitution Without a State?*, in 45 *Journal of Law and Society* (2018) 245.

1. *Olympism is a philosophy of life, exalting and combining in a balanced whole the qualities of body, will and mind. Blending sport with culture and education, Olympism seeks to create a way of life based on the joy of effort, the educational value of good example, social responsibility and respect for universal fundamental ethical principles.*
2. *The goal of Olympism is to place sport at the service of the harmonious development of humankind, with a view to promoting a peaceful society concerned with the preservation of human dignity. [. . .]*

Moreover, article 2 of the Olympic Charter states that the Mission of the IOC is also *"to encourage and support the promotion of ethics and good governance in sport as well as education of youth through sport and to dedicate its efforts to ensuring that, in sport, the spirit of fair play prevails and violence is banned."* But we may find (virtue) ethical values in the majority of IOC functions listed by the Charter: the role of this institution includes, for instance, *"to cooperate with the competent public or private organisations and authorities in the endeavour to place sport at the service of humanity and thereby to promote peace"*; *"to act against any form of discrimination affecting the Olympic Movement"*; *"to encourage and support the promotion of women in sport at all levels and in all structures with a view to implementing the principle of equality of men and women"*; *"to encourage and support measures relating to the medical care and health of athletes"*; *"to oppose any political or commercial abuse of sport and athletes"*; *"to encourage and support the efforts of sports organisations and public authorities to provide for the social and professional future of athletes"*; *"to encourage and support a responsible concern for environmental issues, to promote sustainable development in sport and to require that the Olympic Games are held accordingly"*; *"to encourage and support initiatives blending sport with culture and education"*; *"to promote safe sport and the protection of athletes from all forms of harassment and abuse"*.[18]

We may see here a first legal dimension of ethics. Ethics is meant as a set of fundamental values, which serves as the basis of the overall sports movement.[19] The wording adopted in the Charter is self-explanatory. Ethics delivers here a constitutional function: such strategic role of ethics also appears whenever international organizations – for example, the Council of Europe – promote and foster ethical values in sport.[20] Another evidence of this approach comes from the Olympic Solidarity Programme, aimed at providing assistance to

---

[18] Article 2 of the Olympic Charter.
[19] M. MacNamee and J. Parry (ed.), *Olympic Ethics and Philosophy*, Abingdon, Routledge, 2013.
[20] D. Bodin and G. Sempé, *Ethics and Sport in Europe*, Strasbourg, Council of Europe, 2011; see also the Resolution on ethics in sport (adopted by the 11th Council of Europe Conference of Ministers responsible for Sport, Athens, Greece, 10–12 December 2008).

National Olympic Committees for *"athlete development programmes, in particular those which have the greatest need of it"*: this requires, for instance, launching actions for promoting the Fundamental Principles of Olympism or for supporting athletes who are refugees.

Therefore, (virtue) ethics represents the very basis of the overall sporting movement, from both internal and external perspectives. On the one hand, virtue ethics – which here supports values like fairness, correctness, respect, to name but a few – is, or should be, the keystone of sport success on a global scale. On the other hand, such good qualities make sport a prime example for strengthening worldwide other public policies, like education and public health.

Such constitutional dimension of ethics of course does not limit its scope to the Olympic Charter, since the global sport system is the product of the interaction between a large number of institutions creating different regimes, each of which features both a superior body located at the international level and domestic terminals operating at the national level. Moreover, the increasing political, social, and economic significance of sporting institutions has triggered a rise in the number of functions performed by these bodies and a rise in the corresponding rate of procedures: the case of the Olympic Games' bidding process is emblematic in this respect. Lastly, the increase in norms, institutions, functions, and procedures in the sports context inevitably requires review mechanisms and dispute-settlement bodies to be instituted, to face the ever-more frequent (and complex) number of controversies. Thus, the sport system developed tools for reviewing the decisions taken by sports institutions and arbitration or (quasi)-judicial bodies.

In conclusion, the role of ethics in sports is not simply a matter of how (virtue) ethics may or may not affect the decision-making process of international institutions. It also includes problems such as how ethics may operate in an autonomous legal order and how it may (virtuously) affect the norms-making process and their interpreting. This dynamic is triggered by the features of the global sports organizational structure, which began to develop around the Olympics at the end of the nineteenth century. This organization has the IOC at its apex and International Federations (IFs) and National Federations (NFs), on the one hand, and National Olympic Committees (NOCs), on the other hand, at its base. For both of these substructures, there is only one "monopolistic" regime respectively, as the IOC recognizes only one IF per sport, and one NOC per country. And National Federations (also founded upon the principle of monopoly) are associated with each IF. Such a structure has been portrayed as a "double pyramid", one comprising the IOC and National Committees, and the other the International

Ethics in International Sporting Institutions

and National Federations.[21] However, the structure may be better described as a "network" of several pyramids: in addition to the pyramid of IOC and NOCs, there are as many pyramids as international sports federations (i.e. about one hundred); furthermore, each pyramid is connected to the rest by multiple institutional relationships, of both vertical and horizontal nature.

6.2.2 Ethics as a Legal Instrument

A second dimension of ethics is when it is meant as a genuinely legal instrument, equipped with dedicated rules, bodies, and enforcement mechanisms, designed to ensure full compliance at least within the sport movement. Here again the Olympic Charter may offer useful instances. Article 22 regulates the IOC Ethics Commission. And this provision must be read together with article 59 of the Charter, which expressly mentions the IOC Code of Ethics.

The IOC Ethics Commission is *"charged with defining and updating a framework of ethical principles, including a Code of Ethics, based upon the values and principles enshrined in the Olympic Charter of which the said Code forms an integral part. In addition, it investigates complaints raised in relation to the non-respect of such ethical principles, including breaches of the Code of Ethics and, if necessary, proposes sanctions to the IOC Executive Board."*[22]

The IOC Code of Ethics states rules related to the fundamental principles of Olympism, the integrity of conduct, the integrity of competitions, good governance and resources, and candidatures. In particular, the Code demands the IOC Ethics Commission implement its norms. The Commission adopts decisions on the election of the IOC president, the conflict of interests affecting the behaviour of Olympic parties, candidature for the Olympic Games, preventing manipulation of competitions, and the rules applicable in case of breach of ethical principles.

The IOC is the world governing body of sport. Each sport has its own international federation, which sets the rules of the games. Most of them have their own code of ethics, disciplinary code, and code of conduct. There is some homogeneity, due to the role of IOC, the Court of Arbitration for Sport (CAS), and to the Olympic Charter and the IOC Code of Ethics provisions; similarly, the WADC and WADA ensure a certain degree of uniformity in the case of doping. All Olympic parties, indeed, including international sports federations, must comply with such provisions, including the WADC.

---

[21] M. R. Will (1994), *Les structures du sport international*, in P. Cendon (ed.), *Scritti in onore di Rodolfo Sacco*, Milano, Giuffrè, 1994, p. 1211 et seq.

[22] Article 22 of the Olympic Charter; see also article 59 on sanctions.

Amongst the over sixty existing international sports federations, FIFA offers a prime example. Such international federation has its own Code and its Ethics Committee.[23]

The function of the FIFA Ethics Committee *"shall be governed by the FIFA Code of Ethics. It is divided into an investigatory chamber and an adjudicatory chamber. The adjudicatory chamber shall pass decisions if at least three members are present. The chairperson may pass decisions alone in specific cases."*[24]

The FIFA Code of Ethics was extensively reviewed in 2018,[25] not without critiques and attacks,[26] and updated in 2019. The Code lists the general rules of conduct, related to the duty of neutrality, loyalty, confidentiality, report, cooperate, conflicts of interest, offering and accepting gifts and other benefits, commission, discrimination and defamation, protection of physical and mental integrity, forgery and falsification, abuse of position, involvement with betting, gambling or similar activities, bribery, misappropriation of funds, and manipulation of football matches or competitions.

The FIFA Code of Ethics is more detailed than the IOC one. Sanctions are: (a) warning; (b) reprimand; (c) compliance training; (d) return of awards; (e) fine; (f) social work; (g) match suspension; (h) ban from dressing rooms and/or substitutes' bench; (i) ban on entering a stadium; (j) ban on taking part in any football-related activity.

The FIFA Ethics Committee is particularly active.[27] Only in 2018 and 2019, the Committee banned from any football-related activities, in different procedures, over twenty former or current high officers, including the President of the Brazilian football association (who was banned for life in April 2018[28]). Nonetheless, the Committee itself experienced a case of resignation in November 2018 because of an investigation for corruption against one of its members.[29]

Finally, FIFA also has its own Code of Conduct, last revised in December 2017, which states rules on fair play, team spirit, diversity and sustainability, transparency,

[23] See FIFA Statutes, available at https://resources.fifa.com/image/upload/the-fifa-statutes-2018 .pdf?cloudid=whhncbdzioo3cuhmwfxa (last visited on March 6, 2020).

[24] Article 54 of FIFA Statutes.

[25] The Code is available here: https://resources.fifa.com/image/upload/fifa-code-of-ethics-2019-version.pdf?cloudid=la3f5yqsox5cns9oypkg (last visited on March 6, 2020).

[26] Here, for instance, FIFA responses against critiques raised in August 2018, when the revised Code entered into force: www.fifa.com/about-fifa/who-we-are/news/clarification-concerning-the-revised-fifa-code-of-ethics (last visited on March 6, 2020).

[27] See www.fifa.com/governance/independent-ethics-committee/index.html (last visited on March 6, 2020).

[28] See www.fifa.com/who-we-are/news/fifa-appeal-committee-confirms-ban-imposed-on-marco-polo-del-nero (last visited on March 6, 2020).

[29] See www.fifa.com/who-we-are/news/sundra-rajoo-resigns-from-fifa-ethics-committee (last visited on March 6, 2020).

Ethics in International Sporting Institutions

and innovation.[30] FIFA says in the Code that the Association is *"driven by the aspiration to become a leader in international sports by embodying the highest ethical values and beliefs"*.[31] Any breach of the Code *"may result in appropriate sanctions under applicable employment law, as well as other disciplinary measures, up to and including termination of the employment relationship"*.[32]

FIFA is of course only one example, probably the most known even outside the sport world. But almost all of the other international sports federations display similar provisions in their statutes and regulations, not least because they must comply with the Olympic Charter and with the Fundamental Principles of Olympism. For instance, the World Athletics, formerly known as the International Association of Athletics Federations (IAAF), expressly states in its own 2019 Constitution that it should commit to *"protect the integrity of Athletics and by developing and enforcing standards of conduct and ethical behaviour and implementing good governance"*.[33] Moreover, the World Athletics regularly updates its Code of Ethics, which sets anti-doping rules, rules against betting, manipulation of results and corruption, rules concerning candidacy for IAAF Office and the conduct of elections, rules of conduct applicable to members and candidate cities wishing to host World Athletics Series Competitions and other International Competitions organised by the IAAF, and rules concerning conflicts of interest of IAAF officials.[34]

In other terms, the global sports network – made up of the multiple pyramids mentioned earlier – enhances the interactions between the Olympic Charter, the IOC rules, and all the legal documents and codes adopted by International Sports Federations. The result is that ethical values are largely used in the legal context of sporting institutions, where there are also plenty of compliance committees or commissions called to monitor and sanction any breach of such values.

6.2.3 *The Multiple Dimensions of Ethics in Sport*

Ethics, as a set of moral values, therefore represents the core of sport and sporting institutions, serving a "constitutional" function.[35] The linkage between games,

---

[30] The FIFA Code of Conduct is available at https://resources.fifa.com/image/upload/fifa-code-of-conduct-2929214.pdf?cloudid=wfomatimtwtql2kogyxr (last visited on March 6, 2020).

[31] The FIFA Code of Conduct, p. 2.

[32] The FIFA Code of Conduct, p. 5.

[33] Article 4.1, letter e), of the World Athletics 2019 Constitution, available at www.worldathletics.org/about-iaaf/documents/book-of-rules (last visited on March 6, 2020).

[34] See www.iaafethicsboard.org/code-of-ethics (last visited on March 6, 2020).

[35] An analysis of the relationship between ethics and constitution-making process is developed in B. Gershman, *Constitutionalizing Ethics*, in 38 *Pace Law Review* 40 (2017), which focuses on the case of the New York's Constitution.

rules, and ethics is "ontological" and comes before any possible form of explicit regulation. Ethics is at the very basis of sport and this is why it serves as the fundamental principle of Olympism and the overall Olympic movement. This implies that the sport legal order as a whole relies on a set of ethical values.

As a consequence of this constitutional dimension of (virtue) ethics, sporting institutions tend to follow ethical principles in order to reach their decisions and to manage their resources (as the earlier mentioned case of the Olympic Solidarity Programme clearly illustrates). This often happens with the awards issued by the Court of Arbitration for Sport (CAS), but also when the IOC itself is called to take important measures. In the famous case related to the Russia doping scandal, for example, the IOC, while suspending the Russian National Olympic Committee, decided to allow individual Russian athletes to participate in the 2018 Olympic Winter Games under the name "Olympic Athlete from Russia (OAR)".[36] By doing so, the IOC looked for a just balance between the need to sanction an NOC and the right of athletes to compete in the Games: such decision might of course appear driven by IOC politics, but it also relies on the quest for a just solution coherent with the spirit of the Olympic Charter.[37]

Furthermore, ethics may also be transformed into a legal instrument equipped with institutions and specific sanctions, serving regulatory, administrative and procedural functions. Codes of Ethics adopted by International Sports Federations are legal instruments with their norms, procedures, sanctions, and 'judicial' bodies. From this perspective, sports norms offer an interesting example of how ethical principles can not only be effective in terms of compliance, but they can also be expressly formalized in written provisions. This is what happens with sports codes of ethics, where even the lexicon is forged by virtue ethics. Although this dynamic of norm-making may happen for any organized group, the case of sport seems to show something special. In fact, the self-legalization of customs and ethical values of a given "group" or "society" seems to have an added value, that is, to transform rules of conduct and ethical principles into mandatory norms that are not only accepted, but also shared and considered as the very essence of sport itself.

Lastly, there may be norms, such as in the case of fair play, which leave room for ambiguous interpretations; but there might also be cases where ethical

---

[36] The decision taken by the IOC Executive board is available here: https://stillmed.olympic.org/media/Document%20Library/OlympicOrg/IOC/Who-We-Are/Commissions/Disciplinary-Commission/IOC-DC-Schmid/Decision-of-the-IOC-Executive-Board-05-12-2017.pdf#_ga=2.142200368.386106920.1583272566–1397182691.1565190145 (last visited on March 6, 2020).

[37] Article 6, para. 1, of the Olympic Charter states that '*The Olympic Games are competitions between athletes in individual or team events and not between countries*".

Ethics in International Sporting Institutions 171

principles are not enough, such as in the famous episode related to the use of cannabis during the 1998 Winter Olympic Games. On that occasion, the Gold Medal Winner, a Canadian snowboarder, tested positive for marijuana in a doping control, but at that time such drug was not included in the list of doping substances. The IOC decided to sanction in any event the athlete, who appealed against such decision before the CAS. And the latter observed that:

> We have been told that the decision to sanction R. was reached after difficult deliberations at the level of the IOC Executive Board as well as at that of its Medical Commission. Our own decision is not difficult. Although we have taken pains to explain our reasoning in some detail, and although we understand that the ethical aspects of the question have given pause as to appropriate sanctioning policies – and may result in further reflection in this regard – the existing applicable texts leave us no alternative whatsoever. It is clear that the sanctions against R. lack requisite legal foundation.[38]

6.3 LEGITIMACY AND ACCOUNTABILITY OF SPORTS GOVERNANCE THROUGH ETHICS

Can therefore the ethical dimension of sports and of international sporting institutions contribute to the more general discourse of ethics in international law? We may identify three significant issues here.

The first one refers to ethics as a source of legitimacy.[39] International sporting institutions allow us to recall the Max Weber concept of "charismatic" legitimacy. We may simply consider how many sports champions have become leaders within sporting institutions: Platini was one of them, since he was the first former player elected as UEFA President. But this does not apply only in sports: Finland had the case of Urho Kekkonen, for instance, who was able to bring his charisma beyond the sporting institution. Thus, ethics in sporting institutions often serves as a powerful source of legitimacy for leaders.

This issue also shows the limits of virtue ethics when it becomes the main – if not the sole – basis of power. Records show that not all sport champions became virtuous ethical leaders, as the story of Michel Platini clearly illustrates.

---

[38] Court of Arbitration for Sport (CAS) *ad hoc* Division, OG 98/002 6 R./IOC award of 12 February 1998.

[39] Legitimacy here can be broadly understood as a "generalized perception or assumption that the actions of an entity are desirable, proper, or appropriate within some socially constructed system of norms, values, beliefs, and definitions": M. C. Suchman, *Managing Legitimacy: Strategic and Institutional Approaches*, in 20 *The Academy of Management Review* (1995), pp. 571 *et seq.* See also A. Buchanan and R. O. Keohane, *The Legitimacy of Global Governance Institutions*, in 20 *Ethics & International Affairs* (2006) 414.

Nevertheless, the role of charismatic legitimacy within sporting institutions is still significant; at least if we look at how frequent former champions hold leading positions at different levels (and such approach is sometimes adopted also when sporting institutions call or hire famous people - from cinema, TV shows, or even politics - in order to increase their credibility and visibility). Moreover, the very institutional basis of the IOC and sporting institutions is anchored to "charisma", in so far as their legal status is mainly that of associations of people. And it is in order to limit such trait that the IOC composition combines members selected through co-optation (up to a maximum of seventy) and other more democratic and representative mechanisms of elections (forty-five).[40] In any event, the importance of ethical values for the Olympic movement is further testified by the wording of the "oath" that new members must take when they agree to fulfil their obligations.[41]

The second issue is related to the accountability mechanisms adopted by international sporting institutions and by organizations more generally.[42] The linkages between sports and ethics are tight and strict to the extent that we could add them to the plethora of types of accountability detected by political scientists and lawyers: the case of sporting institutions brings to the fore a type of accountability based on ethics, meant here as respect of fundamental values on which the very essence of sport is based. Sporting institutions build their identity and their accountability through ethical and moral values.[43]

This issue explains why the IOC and WADA, for instance, are very strict whenever they must defend sports values. Sometimes their decisions are severe to the extent that the CAS, that is, the Supreme Court for Sport, must amend them and make them more proportionate. It happened, for instance, when the IOC tried to ban from the Olympic Games any athlete who was ever sanctioned – even

---

[40] See Article 16 of the Olympic Charter.

[41] See again Article 16 of the Olympic Charter: "*Honoured to be chosen as a member of the International Olympic Committee, I fully accept all the responsibilities that this office brings: I promise to serve the Olympic Movement to the best of my ability. I will respect the Olympic Charter and accept the decisions of the IOC. I will always act independently of commercial and political interests as well as of any racial or religious consideration. I will fully comply with the IOC Code of Ethics. I promise to fight against all forms of discrimination and dedicate myself in all circumstances to promote the interests of the International Olympic Committee and Olympic Movement.*"

[42] R. W. Grant and R. O. Keohane, *Accountability and Abuses of Power in World Politics*, in 99 American Political Science Review (2005), pp. 29 et seq.; and R. B. Stewart, *Remedying Disregard in Global Regulatory Governance: Accountability, Participation, and Responsiveness*, 108 American Journal of International Law (2014) 211.

[43] See J. Klabbers, *Controlling International Organizations: A Virtue Ethics Approach*, 8 International Organizations Law Review 285 (2011); and Id., *Law, Ethics and Global Governance: Accountability in Perspective*, 11 New Zealand Journal of Public and International Law 309 (2013).

only once – for doping: the CAS here stated that "*A rule prohibiting doped athletes from participation in the next Olympic Games provides for a period of ineligibility (non-participation) that is not provided for under Article 10 of the WADA Code. In so doing, the rule constitutes a substantive change to the WADA Code, which Signatories of the WADA Code have contractually committed themselves not to do and which is prohibited by Article 23.2.2 of the WADA Code.*" Thus, because "*the Panel has found that the rule prohibiting doped athletes from participation in the next Olympic Games is not in compliance with the WADA Code, and because the WADA Code has been incorporated into the Olympic Charter, the rule is not in compliance with the IOC's Statutes, i.e. the Olympic Charter.*"[44]

The third and final issue refers to normative pluralism and institutional plurality.[45] The case of sporting institutions illustrates these phenomena at several levels.

As for the regulatory dimension, we have a high number of codes of ethics, the IOC one and those adopted by International Federations. These norms are provided with sanctions and enforcement mechanisms before sporting bodies and sporting "courts". There are plenty of cases (over a hundred only before the CAS). At least formally, the case of sporting institutions represents an intense development of ethics as a technique to prevent corruption and ensure integrity in institutions. Ethical norms operate from a dual perspective: one is individual; the other one is related directly to institutions (according to the dedicated OECD and UN Conventions, although we are talking about private bodies).

As for the institutional dimension, there are several ethics or disciplinary committees in the world of sporting institutions. Such bodies – with their different names: committees, commissions, tribunals, or courts – exercise different powers. FIFA has an investigatory and an adjudicatory body, for instance. This growing number of institutions, offices, and bodies at international level is also a common trend of several global regulatory regimes.[46]

6.4 THE FUTURE OF ETHICS IN SPORT

If ethics is so deeply related to sports and if international sporting institutions and their acts are full of references to ethics, why do we have so many cases of corruption?

---

[44] Arbitration CAS 2011/O/2422 United States Olympic Committee (USOC) v. International Olympic Committee (IOC), award of 4 October 2011, available at https://jurisprudence.tas-cas.org/Shared%20Documents/2422.pdf.

[45] J. Klabbers and T. Piiparinen (ed.), *Normative Pluralism and International Law*, New York, Cambridge University Press, 2013.

[46] C. Closa and L. Casini, *Comparative Regional Integration: Governance and Legal Models*, Cambridge, Cambridge University Press, 2016.

In December 2017, for instance, a US Federal Court found two top international soccer officials guilty for their role in a web of corruption that extended across several continents and involved dozens of men, with a traffic of millions of dollars.[47] Match fixing is still a serious problem in sports competitions, and doping cases are still numerous – see the Russian case mentioned earlier – in spite of the enormous progress made by WADA and the success reached by the anti-doping investigations and techniques (such as the case of the famous cyclist Lance Armstrong, where many ethical issues were also raised).[48]

The easiest and most immediate response is that sports and sporting institutions are genuinely human . . . . Recent years, however, show a positive trend. It was the FIFA Ethics Committee, for instance, who sanctioned its former President, Joseph Blatter: the lack was therefore in preventing, not in investigating and sanctioning.[49]

How can this be improved? We have at least two lessons from the past. The first one is that ethics is more effective when it works at different levels: constitutional, regulatory, administrative, procedural, and judicial. We have here the examples of the IOC and FIFA. In the case of the Olympic Games, for instance, after the 2002 Salt Lake City bribery scandal, the IOC not only profoundly revised its rules for the Olympic bid, but also launched a huge programme reform based on ethics. In the case of the FIFA World Cup, such lesson was learnt some years later, and it was only after the scandals emerged in the middle of the 2010s that FIFA started to improve the degree of transparency and openness of the World Cup bids.[50] Another example of how FIFA is trying to improve the ethical dimension of football is the fight against match manipulation, which it brought to a significant number of cases decided in the last two years.[51] However, the most significant case of how necessary it is to design sound and sophisticated (legal) mechanisms in order to pursue and enforce (virtue) ethical values comes from anti-doping policies: in the 1990s, when the sports world failed to effectively fight against

---

[47] See www.nytimes.com/2017/12/22/sports/soccer/fifa-trial.html (last visited on March 6, 2020).

[48] See, for instance, M. E. Osei-Hwere, G. G. Armfield, E. S. Kinsky, R. N. Gerlich, K. Drumheller, *Ethical Implications of Lance Armstrong's Performance-Enhancing Drug Case*, in 17:1 Journal of Legal, Ethical and Regulatory Issues (2014).

[49] Arbitration CAS 2016/A/4501 *Joseph S. Blatter v. Fédération Internationale de Football Association (FIFA)*, award of 5 December 2016.

[50] As for those scandals, see C. J. Boudreaux, G. Karahan and R. M. Coats, *Bend it like FIFA: corruption on and off the pitch*, in 42:9 Managerial Finance (2016) 866; B. W. Bean, *An Interim Essay on Fifa's World Cup of Corruption: The Desperate Need for International Corporate Governance Standards at Fifa*, 22:2 ILSA Journal of International & Comparative Law (2016), 1.

[51] www.fifa.com/who-we-are/legal/integrity/leading-cases/ (last visited on March 6, 2020).

the "plague" of doping, States stepped in; as a consequence, governments, together with the IOC, created one of the most sophisticated global hybrid public and private regimes ever established, that is, the World Anti-Doping Programme fostered by the WADA.

The second lesson is that in some cases private actors or private institutions cannot solve highly problematic issues without the intervention of public powers. And this is exactly what happened at the end of the twentieth century in the case of doping, with the establishment of the WADA. Some scholars, such as Miguel Maduro and Joseph H. H. Weiler, suggested that a similar public intervention should happen in the case of FIFA, that governments should be more involved and an independent international agency should be established.[52] There is justified scepticism around such proposals, but if law and ethics do not accomplish their mission, as they should, arguments against this "call" for public powers will risk appearing too weak.

That is why it is crucial for sporting institutions to strengthen their ethical dimension at every level and with every possible instrument: from this perspective, sporting institutions represent a good example of how (virtue) ethics may be operationalized.[53]

---

[52] They wrote in an article published in December 2017 in one of the most important Italian newspapers, *Corriere della Sera*, available at www.corriere.it/digital-edition/CORRIEREF C_NAZIONALE_WEB/2017/12/28/28/solo-la-ue-potra-cambiare-il-calcio_U43410104505928 AKC.shtml (last visited on March 15, 2019). This proposal finds its reasons also in the scandals which FIFA has undergone in recent years; see J. Sugden and A. Tomlinson, *Football, Corruption and Lies: Revisiting 'Badfellas', The Book FIFA Tried to Ban*, Abingdon, Routledge, 2017.

[53] J. Klabbers, *Towards a Culture of Formalism; Martti Koskenniemi and the Virtues*, 27 Temple International and Comparative Law Journal 417 (2013), especially 424 *et seq.*

7

Modes of Acting Virtuously at the Universal Periodic Review

Jane K. Cowan

7.1 INTRODUCTION

The call for ethical leadership in international organizations is intuitively persuasive. We need – or at least, we want – leaders to 'model' ethical values: to profess them and, ideally, to be guided by them. This is not simply an issue of public perception about international organizations. In numerous conversations over many years with individuals who worked professionally in the vast system of organizations that comprise 'international Geneva' – including senior civil servants in the United Nations (UN) and International Labour Organization (ILO) systems, civil society activists, members of diplomatic delegations, and young interns to all of these positions – I found that many were emphatic that good leaders made an enormous difference. This may be particularly important for the staff of international organizations: many of them come to these organizations with a deep sense of idealism and a desire to 'make the world a better place'[1] and they believe that such leaders need to set an example.

Of the virtues normally cited as important to leadership – including integrity, honesty, courage, responsibility, humility – my interlocutors were not of one mind regarding which should be prioritized. But courage and integrity were consistently emphasized. Significantly, virtue was more noticed in its breach than in its observance: when a leader was found to be lacking in whatever virtues were thought crucial, they told me, this bred disillusionment, demoralization, bitterness, and cynicism among the staff.[2]

---

[1] Billaud, J., & Cowan, J. K. (Eds.) (2020). The bureaucratisation of utopia: Ethics, affects and subjectivities in international governance processes. *Social Anthropology/Anthropologie Sociale*, **28**(1), 6–16.

[2] Stoyanova, D. (2018). The ethics of the international civil service – the human stories. In J. Klabbers, M. Varaki, & G. V. Vilaça, eds., *Towards Responsible Global Governance*, Helsinki: Helsinki University Press, pp. 95–109.

Modes of Acting Virtuously at the Universal Periodic Review 177

At the same time, there are examples of prominent individuals who displayed ethical leadership – particularly those virtues of courage and integrity – who have been treated badly and even ousted from the organization, because their actions threatened the interests of powerful parties. Examples can be drawn from human rights officers working internationally in the field: they include the Head of Office in Bosnia of the UN Office of the High Commissioner for Human Rights, Madeleine Rees, and her colleague, the UN human rights investigator, Kathryn Bolkovac, who uncovered and blew the whistle on the UN's complicity and implication in forced prostitution and sex trafficking in Bosnia in the early 2000s.[3]

Individuals in the highest positions at the UN have also spoken out. In the early 2000s, Mary Robinson, United Nations High Commissioner for Human Rights, vociferously criticised US government actions in its War on Terror, for which she was, she believed, 'forced out' of her UN position.[4] In 2003, Rubens Ricupero, Secretary-General of the United Nations Commission on Trade and Development (UNCTAD), roundly condemned the United States (US) government's massive cotton subsidies to its own large-scale farmers to the detriment of peasant cotton farmers living in extreme poverty in poor African developing countries,[5] as well as its own small farmers. Not only did US actions contravene WTO agreements, their hypocrisy was breathtaking, given US claims to be concerned about tackling extreme poverty in developing countries.[6] Having uttered such inconvenient truths, Ricupero found that his mandate was not renewed in 2004, despite his wish to extend his term of office. In all of the above cases, the leaders were arguably 'just doing their job' in denouncing injustice. They would have been aware that they took risks in doing so, and all paid the price.

These examples indicate the professional perils for leaders of acting ethically in the UN, when doing so challenges the vested interests of powerful countries

---

[3] Bolkovac, K., & Lynn, C. (2011). *The Whistleblower: Sex trafficking, military contractors and one woman's fight for justice*, St Martin's Griffin; Prügl, E., & Thompson, H. (2013). The Whistleblower: An interview with Kathryn Bolkovac and Madeleine Rees. *International Feminist Journal of Politics*, 15(1), 102–109.

[4] Burkeman, O. (2002, July 31). "America forced me out," says Robinson. *The Guardian*; Preston, J. (2002, September 12). Vigilance and memory: United Nations; Departing Rights Commissioner faults U.S. *The New York Times*. www.nytimes.com/2002/09/12/us/vigilance-and-memory-united-nations-departing-rights-commissioner-faults-us.html

[5] Although I recognize that the terminology of development, distinguishing 'developed' from 'developing' countries, is problematic both conceptually and politically, this terminology is currently in everyday use in the UN; where appropriate, I use it here.

[6] Ricupero, R. (2003, June). Promoting an integrated approach to rural development in developing countries for poverty eradication and sustainable development. Statement by Mr. Rubens Ricupero, Secretary General of the UNCTAD, 234–238. Presented at the High-level Segment of the United Nations Economic and Social Council, Geneva. Retrieved from https://www.un.org/en/ecosoc/docs/pdfs/an_integrated_approach_to_rural_development.pdf

(interestingly, the US figures in all four of these examples). Even so, the courage and honesty of such individuals has prompted admiration and respect among UN staff. In this ambiguous context, recent efforts within the UN to institutionalize a specific kind of ethical leadership in the context of human rights governance warrant attention. In the mid-2000s, as a consequence of what Secretary-General Kofi Annan described as the 'declining credibility and professionalism'[7] of the UN Commission on Human Rights, the UN human rights system was reformed. The Universal Periodic Review (UPR) was designed as a holistic review of a state's human rights situation and launched in 2008.

Although the 'origins' of the UPR are, in fact, rather complex,[8] one important logic that it incorporates is that of peer review, a characteristic mode of a distinctly modern form of power that involves both a horizontal assessment of peers, by peers, and also a core element of self-assessment.[9] Importantly, in the context of ongoing complaints that the Commission on Human Rights habitually scrutinized some countries for human rights violations, while allowing other countries to escape scrutiny altogether, the UPR was claimed to create a 'level playing field' in which the human rights situation of all states would be reviewed. The Institution-Building package agreed by UN member states mandated the new mechanism to develop a monitoring practice that was 'objective, transparent, non-selective, constructive, non-confrontational and non-politicised' that guaranteed 'universal coverage and equal treatment of all states'.[10]

Universal rather than selective, the UPR started from the premise that, in the words of a British diplomat, 'none of us is perfect, we've all got something to learn'.[11] It thus aimed to replace 'naming and shaming' with the encouragement of cooperative learning on how to address human

---

[7] Annan, K. (2005). In larger freedom: Towards security, development and human rights for all. Report of the Secretary-General of the United Nations for decision by Heads of State and Government in September 2005. (United Nations General Assembly No. A/59/2005), New York: United Nations.

[8] Alston, P. (2006). Reconceiving the UN human rights regime: challenges confronting the new UN Human Rights Council. *Melbourne Journal of International Law 185*, 7(1), 185–224; Gaer, F. D. (2007). A voice not an echo: Universal Periodic Review and the UN treaty body system. *Human Rights Law Review*, 7(1), 109–139.

[9] Barry, A. (2001). *Political machines: Governing a technological society*, London and New York: Athlone Press; Cowan, J. K. (2014). The Universal Periodic Review as a public audit ritual: An anthropological perspective on emerging practices in the global governance of human rights. In H. Charlesworth & E. Larking, eds., *Human rights and the Universal Periodic Review: Rituals and ritualism*, Cambridge: Cambridge University Press, pp. 42–62; Rose, N. (1999). *Powers of freedom: Reframing political thought*, Cambridge: Cambridge University Press.

[10] United Nations Human Rights Council. (2007, June 18). HRC Resolution 5/1, Institution Building of the United Nations Human Rights Council.

[11] Cowan, J. K., & Billaud, J. (2015). Between learning and schooling: the politics of human rights monitoring at the Universal Periodic Review. *Third World Quarterly*, 36(6), 1175–1190.

rights issues through promoting 'dialogue' and 'sharing best practice'.[12] Although the mechanism is not explicitly presented in such terms, it can be seen as an effort to develop ethical leadership within the UN's human rights monitoring practices, in that it seeks to cultivate virtuous sovereign subjects who acknowledge not only their own human rights 'challenges' but who are also willing to 'constructively criticise' other states and help them to improve. Moreover, it adopts a 'learning' approach[13]; it explicitly relies on the modelling of good practice by exemplary, although always imperfect, states (informally dubbed as the 'good students') which less adept states will strive to follow.[14]

In this chapter I draw on an ethnographic study of the UPR that I carried out in collaboration with fellow anthropologist Julie Billaud.[15] In that work, I have theorised the UPR as an example of what Marilyn Strathern has called 'audit culture', in which actors are enrolled, through myriad micro-practices, to provide an account of themselves and of others: in this case, in relation to the project of human rights.[16] As an anthropologist of performance, I have been especially interested in the UPR's public manifestations in front of the community of states, which I conceptualize as 'public audit rituals'.[17] Here, I take up the challenge of

[12]   Charlesworth, H., & Larking, E. (2014). Introduction: the regulatory power of the Universal Periodic Review. In *Human rights and the Universal Periodic Review: Rituals and ritualism*, Cambridge: Cambridge University Press, pp. 1–21; Dominguez-Redondo, E. (2012). Is there life beyond naming and shaming in human rights implementation? *New Zealand Law Review*, 4, 673–706.

[13]   Dominguez-Redondo, Is there life beyond naming and shaming in human rights implementation?; Klabbers, J. (2011). Controlling international organizations: A virtue ethics approach. *International Organizations Law Review*, 8, 285–289.

[14]   Cowan & Billaud, Between learning and schooling.

[15]   The research project, 'International Human Rights Monitoring at the Reformed Human Rights Council: An Ethnographic and Historical Study' (BR100028), was funded by the British Academy, whose support I gratefully acknowledge. The grant supported research in Geneva (from October 2010 to September 2011) during the final year of the UPR's first cycle; since then, we continue to follow UPR developments and remain in contact with a number of our interlocutors at the UN.

[16]   Cowan, The Universal Periodic Review as a public audit ritual; Power, M. K. (1999). *The audit society: Rituals of verification*, Oxford: Oxford University Press, and Power, M. K. (2003). Auditing and the production of legitimacy. *Accounting, Organizations and Society*, **28**, 379–394; Cowan & Billaud, Between learning and schooling; Strathern, M. (Ed.). (2000). *Audit cultures: Anthropological studies in accountability, ethics and the academy*, London: Routledge.

[17]   Cowan, The Universal Periodic Review as a public audit ritual; Cowan & Billaud, Between learning and schooling. Cowan, J. K., & Billaud, J. (2017). The "public" character of the Universal Periodic Review: Contested concept and methodological challenge. In R. Niezen & M. Sapignoli, eds., *Palaces of hope: The Anthropology of global organizations*, Cambridge: Cambridge University Press, pp. 106–126.

180 *Jane K. Cowan*

adopting an 'ethical leadership' lens on the UPR, and specifically ask: what does it mean to act virtuously in the UPR?

For the remainder of the chapter, I proceed as follows: I begin by setting out my approach to questions of virtue in the UPR. I then explain the design and modalities of the UPR and clarify its specificity in relation to other human rights mechanisms. Following this, I present some key features of UPR practice by the end of the first cycle, based on my in-depth ethnographic and historical research for ten months in 2010–2011, with a focus on the UPR Working Group. In the course of my analysis of the UPR, I explore the problem of acting virtuously in this context.

7.2 EXAMINING VIRTUE IN THE UPR

Anthropology has recently seen a turn towards questions of ethics and virtue.[18] If this work overwhelmingly focuses on 'ordinary' ethics, much of it also strongly retains a methodological focus on the individual, staking out a theoretical position that is anti-Durkheimian while drawing on Foucault's late writings, particularly on the care of the self.[19] The primary concern is to investigate the individual as she or he faces everyday ethical choices or engages in self-making through the conscious cultivation of virtuous conduct. I have not, until now, found these discussions especially relevant to my work on human rights practice within international institutions. Not only are my questions rather different but the methodological individualism characteristic of this work poses particular difficulties. Yet having been asked to consider virtue and ethical leadership at the UPR, I recognize that they offer useful lenses for exploring hitherto less developed dimensions of my UPR materials.

---

[18] Among others, see Das, V. (2007). *Life and words: Violence and the descent into the ordinary*, Berkeley, Calif.: University of California Press; Das, V., & Kleinman, A. (2000). Introduction. In V. Das, A. Kleinman, M. Ramphele, & P. Reynolds, eds., *Violence and subjectivity*, Berkeley, Calif.: University of California Press, pp. 1–18; Laidlaw, J. (2002). For An anthropology of ethics and freedom. *The Journal of the Royal Anthropological Institute*, 8, 311–332; Laidlaw, J. (2013). *The subject of virtue: an anthropology of ethics and freedom*, Cambridge: Cambridge University Press; Lambek, M. (2010). *Ordinary ethics: Anthropology, language, and action*, New York: Fordham University Press; Mahmood, S. (2003). Ethical formation and politics of individual autonomy in contemporary Egypt. *Social Research*, 70(3), 837–866.

[19] Foucault, M. (1986). *The care of the self*. (R. Hurley, Trans.), Vol. 3, New York: Pantheon Books.

Modes of Acting Virtuously at the Universal Periodic Review 181

In addressing questions of virtue at the UPR, I will be focusing on practice ('acting virtuously') rather than possession ('having' virtue) or essence ('being' virtuous). Examining this practice, I have identified not simply one, but, indeed, three distinctive modes of acting virtuously within the UPR, which I label as liberal, subaltern, and parrhesiastic. I intend to argue that, although diplomats share a common diplomatic language as well as learned habits of diplomatic etiquette and ways of working, their modes of acting virtuously as representatives of states within the UPR are largely relational and a function of their country's position. That is to say: the modes they adopt reflect the positioning of the states they represent within geopolitical relations; they further manifest the state's ways of navigating these relations while asserting a specific sovereign identity.

I must nonetheless admit to a certain reticence about adopting a virtue approach to the UPR; this is because, in my view, a certain analytical awkwardness is inevitably entailed when employing an approach that is, by definition, methodologically individualist – that focuses on virtues as they are manifested in an individual's behaviour – for an intergovernmental process in which diplomats speak not as individuals, but in their role as representatives of states. Indeed, we can go further: in the UPR (as in all the bodies of the UN system), these individuals speak 'as' states, something explicitly articulated in the language of these forums and in the reports of their proceedings ('Greece stated that', 'Algeria commended'). At the same time, diplomats are, of course, well aware that individuals have distinct personalities, and they frequently insisted that an individual's specific, idiosyncratic qualities were crucial to his or her status and effectiveness as a diplomat, even as he or she had to speak in the voice of the state. In discussions with diplomats on this issue, I found that many were, indeed, fascinated by their own double persona. They offered stories of occasions when a diplomat was compelled by her government to take a stance or express a view with which she personally disagreed, as well as other (much rarer) stories of diplomats who resigned rather than carry out their government's instructions.[20]

This topic is worthy of investigation in its own right; however, my focus in this chapter is primarily on *the sovereign subject*, the subject position that it

---

[20] In August 2012 as the conflict in Syria intensified, Syria's highest-level diplomat to the UN in Geneva resigned 'because he no longer felt able in that position to do anything for the Syrian people' ('Syria's rep to UN human rights council joins opposition' 2012, *The Journal.Ie.*). Similarly, when I visited Geneva in early 2017, a few months after Donald Trump's election, in order to attend a short course on 'Leadership in the Human Rights Council', I was told by the course leader, herself a former diplomat, of a slew of resignations at the United States Mission in Geneva by diplomats who found it impossible to serve under the Trump administration.

occupies and the ways of acting virtuously that it adopts. Within UN contexts, the state is treated linguistically as a person, personified by the diplomat.[21] Moreover, as I observed in my fieldwork at the UN, each state – what I am calling the sovereign subject – was deemed to have a distinctive public face, formed out of its history and its policies, to which a 'personality' and even a 'moral character' was often attributed, irrespective of the diplomat who was representing it, by actors inhabiting the UN institutional space. Thus, almost any UN insider could recount the kinds of positions that 'Norway', 'Cuba', 'Nigeria' or 'the US' would take in debates, and even the rhetorical styles in which they expressed themselves.[22]

That we might find different understandings of what constitutes ethical behaviour among states and thus different modes of acting virtuously in the UPR should not in itself be surprising. Anthropologist and legal scholar Marie-Bénédicte Dembour has discerned deep disagreements about the meanings of another supposedly universal concept: human rights; she has identified four 'schools' of human rights whose proponents vary in their views on where human rights come from and what they are for.[23] As she admits, calling them 'schools' somewhat over-formalises what are generally implicit positions and also implies an internal conceptual homogeneity, when the writings of a single scholar may in fact express several schools of thought. Similarly, the three modes of acting virtuously that I examine here are analytical abstractions used to name patterns that I observed at meetings and public sessions of the UPR. UN actors would, I believe, recognize the patterns I describe, but my point is that they differ in the ways that they evaluate them, in part depending on their (that is, their state's) positionality. I want to be clear that this is not primarily an argument about cultural relativism. Culture does play a part, among other things in the ways that it informs norms of diplomatic sociability.[24] However, my argument is primarily about structural differences and inequalities between states, rather than cultural ones, and how these may

---

[21] We should recall that 'person' in Latin means 'mask', referring originally to the masks worn in Roman theatre that signified the social role being performed.

[22] See Cowan & Billaud, Between learning and schooling.

[23] Dembour, M.-B. (2010). What are human rights for? Four schools of thought. *Human Rights Quarterly*, **32**(1), 1–20.

[24] Thus, several diplomats from the Middle East that we interviewed complained that the UPR time restrictions on country statements, usually less than two minutes, inhibited the elaborate greetings that they considered obligatory etiquette for state-to-state encounters, while the North American and Western European diplomats we spoke to tended to favour directness; many advocated reducing or even excising these state-to-state greetings so as to give time to the 'more important' substance of the statement, especially the recommendations.

Modes of Acting Virtuously at the Universal Periodic Review 183

lead to different strategies in performing the sovereign subject 'self', as well as in performing the relation to the State under Review.

Acknowledging the existence of three distinctive modes of acting virtuously in the UPR is particularly important because UPR practice is overwhelmingly evaluated through a single liberal lens. Many actors participating in the UPR, or observing it, regard the liberal mode of acting virtuously as praiseworthy and rightfully normative (the 'right way' to do UPR), while deeming the subaltern mode as corrupt game-playing and the parrhesiastic mode as irritating distraction. I argue, to the contrary, that each of these modes – liberal, subaltern, and parrhesiastic – is informed by ethical principles, although the latter two require actors to engage in what we could call, adopting a Foucaultian frame, forms of 'counter-conduct' that evade or resist the formal rules.[25] By exploring these three modes of acting virtuously, I challenge the hegemonic view. I insist that the practice of virtue in international organizations must be assessed within an analysis of the complex social relations among states within the international system; even more importantly, it can only be understood in light of the power relations of that system.

7.3 UNIVERSAL PERIODIC REVIEW: ITS DESIGN AND MODALITIES

A new element within the 2006 reform of the UN human rights system, the Universal Periodic Review (UPR) was designed to avoid some of the problems that had allegedly plagued the Commission on Human Rights which preceded it, such as politicization, selectivity, and double standards. Rejecting the naming and shaming approach, it is instead conceived as a cooperative process where human rights improvement occurs through dialogue, the sharing of best practice, and mutual learning. By the end of the first cycle, all 192 UN member states had been reviewed, and the UPR was being described as a 'success story' and even 'the jewel in the crown' of the new system.

Organised as a four-and-a-half-year cycle,[26] the UPR has four phases. In the first phase, information is gathered and the three reports on which the review is based are prepared: the State under Review writes its National Report, and the Office for the High Commissioner for Human Rights (OHCHR) Secretariat

---

[25] I am inspired here by Bal Sokhi-Bulley's (2016). Re-reading the riots: Counter-conduct in London 2011. *Global Society*, **30**(2), 320–339 analysis of the 2011 London 'riots' as examples of counter-conduct which are better interpreted as forms of political insurgency, rather than as mere criminal behaviour.

[26] Originally the UPR cycle was four years. Since the second cycle, it has been four and a half years.

drafts the Compilation (relevant extracts of reports by UN bodies such as treaty bodies) and the Stakeholder Summary (from submissions by civil society, the National Human Rights Institution, and other multilateral bodies such as the UN High Commission for Refugees, the European Union, and the International Organization for Migration).

The second phase is the public review, a series of what I call 'public audit rituals', the most important of which is the 3.5-hour review[27] conducted by the collectivity of UN member states, officially called the UPR Working Group. During this public session, the State under Review opens the proceedings by presenting its 'achievements' and 'challenges' and answering any advance questions. This is followed by an 'interactive dialogue', where Participating Governments – with the first chosen by lot and, subsequently, one by one in alphabetical order according to the French name of the state – offer short oral statements of greeting, congratulations, condemnations, observations, concerns, questions, and the all-important recommendations: that is, suggestions for improving the State under Review's human rights practices which that state is free to accept or reject. As the session unfolds, the State under Review can pause the flow of Participating Government statements in order to answer questions and present new information, and then does a final summing up. When this session finishes, the delegation of the State Under Review, OHCHR Secretariat staff, and members of 'the Troika', a team of three states who assist in the review, prepare the Draft Report which summarizes the interactive dialogue and lists all recommendations received, distinguishing between those accepted, noted,[28] and still to be decided upon. The Draft Report is presented at 'The Adoption' (i.e. of the Draft Report of the Working Group), a public meeting of the same constituents convened about forty-eight hours later, in which 'technical issues' can be resolved. The final Report is presented and adopted several months later, at the plenary of the next Human Rights Council under Item 4. The final Report on the Working Group on the Universal Periodic Review for that country is allocated thirty minutes, divided equally between the State under Review, other Participating Governments and Civil Society, this being the first and last opportunity for members of Civil Society to speak publicly.

The third phase is a roughly four-year phase of implementing the accepted recommendations. Finally, the cycle culminates in the next review (the fourth

---

[27] The UPR Working Group review originally lasted three hours, but from the second cycle onwards, from May 2012, the time has been increased to 3.5 hours.

[28] During the first cycle, recommendations that the State under Review did not accept were described as 'rejected'. At some point in the second cycle, under civil society pressure, the terminology shifted to 'noted', referring to the fact that the recommendations were recorded in the official record, even if they were not accepted by the State under Review.

Modes of Acting Virtuously at the Universal Periodic Review

phase) where – ideally – the Working Group monitors how well the State under Review has implemented previous recommendations, while also offering new recommendations, thereby simultaneously launching the first phase of the new cycle.

7.4 THE UPR IN RELATION TO OTHER COMPONENTS IN THE UN HUMAN RIGHTS SYSTEM

The UPR is one component within the UN human rights system established to monitor compliance with the international treaties and agreements that UN member states have accepted. The UN system involves two types of human rights monitoring mechanisms: charter-based and treaty-based. The UPR is a charter-based mechanism, along with the Human Rights Council (created in 2006 to replace the Commission on Human Rights), the Complaints Procedure, the Advisory Committee, and the Special Procedures, which include both thematic and country mandates. These are contrasted to the treaty-based mechanisms, in which committees of experts monitor each individual state's compliance with the international treaties (mostly called 'conventions') that it has signed: one treaty at a time, and one country at a time. For instance, the Convention on the Elimination of All Forms of Discrimination Against Women (CEDAW) is monitored by the Committee on the Elimination of Discrimination Against Women, while the International Covenant on Civil and Political Rights is monitored by the Human Rights Committee.[29]

The component elements within the UN human rights system are complementary. Through the various monitoring bodies, a range of actors in various configurations engage with human rights compliance in different ways, with different foci. Although there are commonalities across the different monitoring bodies in terms of documentary forms and practices, working relations, and languages used, there are also distinctive elements specific to each component. Interestingly, among UN-based actors, the UPR tends to be compared to, or talked about in relation to, two of these: the treaty bodies and the Human Rights Council.

---

[29] See Halme-Tuomisaari, M. (2017). Meeting "the world" at the Palais Wilson: Embodied universalism at the UN Human Rights Committee. In R. Niezen & M. Sapignoli, eds., *Palaces of hope: The anthropology of global organizations*, Cambridge: Cambridge University Press, pp. 127–151; Kelly, T. (2009). The UN Committee Against Torture: Human rights monitoring and the legal recognition of torture. *Human Rights Quarterly*, **31** (3), 777–800; Merry, S. E. (2006). *Human rights and gender violence: Translating international law into local justice*, Chicago: University of Chicago Press.

In Geneva human rights circles, particularly in the early years of the UPR, human rights lawyers and activists often compared the UPR unfavourably with the treaty bodies. They faulted, in particular, the absence of human rights 'experts' within the UPR who were knowledgeable in human rights law and willing to examine in depth the state's compliance with a specific human rights treaty. They also worried that the state-centred rituals of the UPR led to recommendations that were 'either weak in comparison with those coming from the treaty bodies, or which actually contradict[ed] a state's obligations under international human rights law'.[30] Yet not all practitioners concurred with this evaluation. An Amnesty International senior staff member that I interviewed in March 2011 captured the key points of difference between the two mechanisms, noting the UPR's 'energy' and 'political buy in' from states:

> For us, the UPR is a very different space from, say, the treaty bodies . . . . It's a state space, one where states feel much more in the driving seat than they do in some of these other procedures, where they are facing a group of experts who are – sometimes perhaps not in the most helpful way – lecturing to them. I think that's rarely a good way of getting people to do what you want them to do. [The UPR] is a very different animal . . . it's much more rough and ready, it's political, it's sometimes dirty, as well, but there's a lot of energy in the UPR. It's much cruder, interventions are made in the space of two-minute slots, whereas the treaty bodies will pontificate at length, you know, for days: long concluding observations and so on. The UPR is quick and dirty: you've got to say what you want to say in these two minutes. The UPR has that kind of energy, it has the political buy-in.

In addition to comparisons with the treaty rights bodies, the UPR is also often compared and contrasted with the Human Rights Council. Notwithstanding the comments above about the 'rough and ready' and 'sometimes dirty' nature of the UPR, my interlocutors frequently identified the Human Rights Council as much more contentious and adversarial than the UPR. They cited the bloc politics, the frequent polarizations over particular issues and the metaphorical finger-pointing and sometimes literal desk-pounding that not infrequently emerged in Council debates.

UPR norms, they told us, with their emphasis on the constructive 'sharing of best practice', required more 'friendly' diplomatic modes. For instance, a member of the British delegation explained that while he might consciously

---

[30] Collister, H. (2014). Rituals and implementation in the Universal Periodic Review and the treaty rights bodies. In H. Charlesworth & E. Larking, eds., *Human rights and the Universal Periodic Review: Rituals and ritualism*, Cambridge: Cambridge University Press, p. 109.

and intentionally refer to 'Burma' when that country was being discussed in the more confrontational context of Human Rights Council debates – thereby signalling the British Government's disapproval of the ruling military junta by refusing to use the junta's preferred term for the country, 'Myanmar' – his delegation would, in fact, refrain from using the term 'Burma' in the UPR, most often by simply referring to 'the government'. Bloc politics, commonplace in the Human Rights Council, were also much more muted in the UPR: although in the UPR's first cycle, states friendly to the State under Review might make Herculean efforts to be first in the queue to sign up for the speakers' list for the interactive dialogue, and thus be able to offer 'friendly' recommendations while ensuring that more 'critical' states spoke later, or not at all (if time ran out), this kind of stage management is no longer possible. Since the beginning of the second cycle in March 2012, Participating Governments now speak in alphabetical order (with only the first state to speak being selected randomly), with the available time for speakers divided equally by the number of delegations that have signalled their wish to speak.

7.5 REPETITION, RESPONSIBILIZATION, AND CONSTRUCTIVE CRITICISM IN THE UPR

Key to the UPR's power and persuasiveness as a mechanism is its relentless repetition. Scholars of ritual have long observed the significance of repetition; more recently, Judith Butler has identified repetition as central to the performativity of gender. For her, the repetitive execution of mundane, gendered postures and gestures are the primary means by which gender is made real in the world[31]; my own study of the construction of gender in social dancing events in northern Greece similarly emphasized the ongoing effects for everyday experience of sensually intense, repeatedly performed celebratory 'embodiments' of gender.[32] In analogous fashion, through participating in dozens of reviews of fellow states (up to 192 of them in any single cycle), and then performing from the podium themselves for their own review, delegates of states are enrolled in concrete, embodied ways into the project of human rights improvement and compliance. Importantly, UPR is what I have called 'a ritual of state responsibilisation in relation to human rights'[33]: repetition

---

[31] Butler, J. (1990). *Gender trouble: Feminism and the subversion of identity*, London: Routledge.
[32] Cowan, J. K. (1990). *Dance and the body politic in northern Greece*, Princeton, New Jersey: Princeton University Press.
[33] Cowan, The Universal Periodic Review as a public audit ritual, p.60.

188 *Jane K. Cowan*

makes the discourse of state responsibility for human rights habitual and normal. Not surprisingly, recommendations directed to any other party besides the state (e.g. the request for international assistance through 'technical assistance') are deemed 'weak' and are discouraged.[34]

One of the far-reaching innovations of the UPR has been to cultivate sovereign subjects who are willing to perform their human rights responsibility not only in front of a panel of human rights experts in a closed meeting room – the standard format for treaty-body sessions – but publicly, in front of the entire collectivity of UN member states (and, via the online webcast, to anyone in the world). Most obviously, the UPR asks the sovereign subject – in its role as the State under Review – to self-report, announcing achievements and acknowledging 'challenges', and saying how it intends to do better in the future. Although this is something it already does in front of treaty bodies, this now becomes a public performance in front of the international community of states. Yet the UPR calls on the sovereign subject in a second way, as well, in an innovation whose novelty and significance has largely escaped notice. It asks the sovereign subject – this time, in its role as a Participating Government – to 'participate': mainly by taking an active role in monitoring fellow states in the public audit ritual of the Working Group.

This very public, other-monitoring role is a new role and something that diplomats found perplexing at first. In the Human Rights Council, where (as discussed above) a regional bloc politics reigns, certain delegations – e.g. United States of America, China, Egypt – habitually take the lead in denouncing other states (occasionally named, more often alluded to), and other delegations fall quietly into line behind them. The UPR demands something different: that the Participating Government acts individually vis-à-vis the State under Review: as a peer, rather than an ally, adversary, donor, or client. Rather than choosing between support and denunciation, the Participating Government is asked to offer an altogether novel amalgamation of support and criticism: 'constructive criticism', in the form of recommendations. Moreover, the recommendations that, for instance, India makes to Australia are conceptualized as 'bilateral': this one-to-one peer relationship implicates only the recommender and the receiver.

7.6 THREE MODES OF ACTING VIRTUOUSLY

'Ethics' and 'virtue' were not words I heard very often in talk about the UPR at the UN in Geneva: more commonly, accounts of the discrepancies between

---

[34] Ibid., pp. 59–62.

Modes of Acting Virtuously at the Universal Periodic Review 189

what should happen and what actually did happen tended to be phrased in terms of rules, responsibility, and accountability, or, alternatively, in terms of learning, setting an example, and persuading.[35] Those participating in the UPR process seemed to understand themselves as operating within a rule-based and norm-based framework, albeit one that was explicitly being reframed as a context for cooperative learning. Yet ethical issues were and continue to be at play in the UPR in a number of ways that the intrinsically 'righteous' character of human rights thinking makes difficult to see.

Asking 'what does it mean to act virtuously in the UPR context?' I have discerned on the basis of my fieldwork three different modes of acting virtuously, though others might be further delineated. I call the first one 'liberal virtue': it is the dominant, hegemonic mode that is normally taken as self-evidently good, but that tends to remain oblivious to its privilege and power. It contrasts with another mode that I call 'subaltern virtue' that is grounded in, and must be seen in terms of, a vulnerable, dependent, and encumbered positionality. Both of these modes of acting virtuously could be observed on a daily basis at the UPR. But there was a third mode of acting virtuously that could be observed only occasionally. The second, subaltern mode recognizes that the so-called 'level playing field' of the UPR is a myth, given the continuing effects of historical domination and political and economic inequality, but it tends to remain silent. The third mode of acting virtuously makes these inequalities visible and explicit. I call this third kind of virtuous performance 'parrhesia' or 'fearless speech', drawing on the work of Foucault and other scholars, because it defies the procedural norms and insists on naming what everyone understands but will not say.[36] In the pages that remain, I briefly elaborate on the first two modes of acting virtuously. Then, using the reviews of Greece in 2011 and 2016, I bring out the problem of the UPR frame and the silences it produces, and give an example of the third mode of being virtuous through fearless speech.

---

[35] Gaskarth, J. (2011). The virtues in international society. *European Journal of International Relations*, 18(3), 431–53, p. 432 has observed that very little of the literature on ethics in international relations mentions 'virtues'; rather, writers 'focus on the normative structure of international relations rather than individual virtues exhibited by participants in world politics'.

[36] Anderson, A. (2019). Parrhesia: Accounting for different contemporary relations between risk and politics. *Journal of Sociology*, 55(3), 495–510; Billaud, J. (2014). Keepers of the truth: Producing "transparent" documents for the Universal Periodic Review. In H. Charlesworth & E. Larking, eds., *Human rights and the Universal Periodic Review*, Cambridge: Cambridge University Press, pp. 63–84; Folkers, A. (2016). Daring the truth: Foucault, Parrhesia and the genealogy of critique. *Theory, Culture and Society*, 33(1), 3–28; Foucault, M. (1997). What is enlightenment? In S. Lotringer, ed., *The politics of truth*, Los Angeles: Semiotext(e); and Foucault, M. (2001). *Fearless speech*, Los Angeles: Semiotext(e).

7.7 ACTING VIRTUOUSLY IN THE LIBERAL AND SUBALTERN MODES

The first mode of acting virtuously entails, for a start, setting a good example as a self-critical State under Review. The state should show 'sincere and genuine engagement' with all the various phases. According to numerous actors in the UPR, the engagement of the State under Review is demonstrated by the quality and transparency of its reports, its comprehensive consultations with civil society, the high-ministerial level of representatives it sends to Geneva, and its frank acknowledgement of its own strengths and weaknesses. The UPR of the USA in November 2010 epitomized, for some diplomats and members of civil society, this first mode of virtue: the assembled participants in Room XX at the Palais des Nations watched as a rainbow delegation – African American, Korean American, European American, male and female – took their seats at the podium. Assistant Secretary Esther Brimmer emphasized 'making the participation of citizens and civil society a centrepiece of our UPR process', while Assistant Secretary Michael Posner, quoting Martin Luther King, insisted that, despite his country's frequent failure to live up to its ideals, 'the arc of our history is long but it bends toward justice'. After a vigorous and frequently combative series of statements in the interactive dialogue, Yale Law Professor Harold Koh accepted the large number of recommendations, although he dismissed those that were 'mischievous' or made in bad faith. I asked a US diplomat after the review how his delegation felt things had gone: 'Pretty ecstatic, actually . . . very proud that we did what we should in setting a good example'.[37]

Acting virtuously in the liberal mode involves not only a sincere performance as the State under Review; it also requires taking the role of the constructive critic seriously. In the first cycle (2008–2012), the Western and Others Group (WEOG) energetically took up the challenge of constructive criticism, making the most recommendations overall (40 per cent), while the other four regional groups each made between 11–16 per cent of the total recommendations. If one looks at each Region under Review, one sees the same pattern: for the reviews of African countries, WEOG made 43 per cent of the recommendations, while the Africa group made 18 per cent; for the reviews of Asian countries, WEOG made 42 per cent of the recommendations, and the Asia Group 21 per cent.[38]

---

[37] For a fuller account, see Cowan, J. K. (2013). Before audit culture: A genealogy of international oversight of rights. In B. Müller, ed., *The gloss of harmony: The politics of policy-making in multilateral organisations*, London: Pluto Press, pp. 118–120.

[38] McMahon, E. R. (2012). The Universal Periodic Review: A work in progress – An evaluation of the first cycle of the new UPR mechanism of the United Nations Human Rights Council. In *Dialogue on Globalisation Report*, Geneva: Friedrich Ebert Stiftung.

Diplomats that we interviewed from the WEOG group (US, UK, Belgium, Norway) told us their delegations were trying to 'set an example' through their diligent and tough recommendations, good attendance, fair play and collegial manners. They stressed that they tried to do this consistently for all States under Review.

Developing countries, by contrast, tended to calibrate their recommendations, at least in part, according to their position in relations with the State under Review. This has likewise been observed by US political scientist Edward McMahon.[39] He reports that an African diplomat that he interviewed 'suggested that African states view UPR as a means to "protect" and "support" each other, especially in the face of criticism emanating from mainly WEOG states. He would think twice before producing a criticism of western states who are donors, such as the U.S. and the U.K.'.[40]

Occasionally, a developing country might be audaciously defiant towards a former colonial power. In the United Kingdom's first review in April 2008, Sri Lanka recommended that it 'consider holding a referendum on the desirability or otherwise of a written constitution, preferably republican, which includes a bill of rights'.[41] More typically, though, diplomats of historically subordinated countries expressed worry over the hidden traps of this now putatively egalitarian 'peer' relationship. During an informal meeting in spring 2011 about possible changes to UPR modalities attended by diplomats and civil society, when the norm of constructive criticism was being discussed, a North African diplomat remarked: 'If you're a developing country receiving aid from a donor country, are you going to criticize it? Let's be frank. You will not do something that will affect bilateral relations. We have to be realistic'.[42]

Remarkably, the regional bloc system evident in the Human Rights Council, and in UN contexts generally, was commonly presented as a *cause* of dysfunction, rather than a symptom of a larger problem: a problem that Martti Koskenniemi identified as the 'sharp division' between a prosperous, powerful and organized North and a poor and disorganized South.[43] Diplomats of the Global North acting virtuously in the liberal mode rarely connected their ability to 'set an example' (e.g. to admit that 'we are not

---

[39] Ibid.

[40] Ibid., p.16.

[41] United Nations Human Rights Council (2008). *Report of the Working Group on the Universal Periodic Review, United Kingdom of Great Britain and Northern Ireland* (No. A/HRC/8/25), Geneva, p. 17.

[42] Cowan, The Universal Periodic Review as a public audit ritual, pp. 58–59.

[43] Koskenniemi, M. (2005). *From apology to utopia: The structure of international legal argument*, Cambridge: Cambridge University Press.

perfect', to give tough recommendations to all) with their countries' power, privilege, wealth, and thus relative invulnerability to reprisal. Rather, they saw their autonomy as naturally given and their fair-minded and even-handed compliance with the mechanism's rules as virtues that diplomats of all countries could choose to cultivate and deploy. Thus, for them (as for civil society activists generally) one of the most frustrating problems of the UPR modalities was the frequent transformation of the Working Group review into what some ruefully called a 'Mutual Admiration Society': the practice whereby the State under Review invited, or compelled, its 'friends' to rally round with 'easy' recommendations, blocking out the more critical ones.[44]

Diplomats from the Global South acknowledged the practice; some even defended it as legitimate protection of their colleagues against hostile criticism.[45] Even while insisting on their formal equality as sovereign states, they knew, like George Orwell, that some states were more equal than others.[46] They were all too aware of the constraints they worked within and the difficulties of navigating the competing pressures coming from regional bloc leaders, colleagues from their regional or thematic groups, donor countries, international financial institutions, and their own domestic publics. They could not afford to act virtuously in the liberal mode, even if they wanted to. For them, virtuous action entailed, instead, loyalty to and solidarity with similarly encumbered colleagues (from their regional group, fellow Non-Aligned Movement [NAM] countries or Least Developed Countries [LDCs]) and prudence towards donors.

7.8 ACTING VIRTUOUSLY THROUGH FEARLESS SPEECH: REVIEWING GREECE AT THE UPR

Already we have seen evidence of two modes of acting virtuously in the UPR. A third mode, although far more rare, was manifested during Greece's second Universal Periodic Review in 2016. Telling this third story requires a brief sketch of the historical and political context of Greece's deteriorating human rights situation since the onset of the global financial crisis in 2007. A key

---

[44] Critics of this practice typically associated it with certain Global South countries, though a Norwegian diplomat told me he saw European Union countries as similarly 'too soft' on each other in their recommendation practices.

[45] McMahon, E. R. (2012). The Universal Periodic Review: A work in progress – An evaluation of the first cycle of the new UPR mechanism of the United Nations Human Rights Council. In *Dialogue on Globalisation Report*, Geneva: Friedrich Ebert Stiftung.

[46] In George Orwell's *Animal Farm*, the pigs who take over the farm adapt the commandment to read: 'All animals are equal but some animals are more equal than others.'

Modes of Acting Virtuously at the Universal Periodic Review   193

moment in this very Greek drama was the revelation by the newly elected PaSoK[47] Prime Minister Georgios Papandreou, soon after taking power in October 2009, of the huge hole in Greece's finances that the previous government (led by the conservative New Democracy party) had kept hidden: a deficit of 12.7% of GDP, more than four times the Eurozone limit, and a public debt of $410 billion.[48]

Greece's debt was, in part, a complex legacy of long-term national processes, including underdevelopment, a history of political patronage and corruption on the part of both leftwing and rightwing governments since the 1980s and before, and endemic tax avoidance over many years by many Greek citizens.[49] More fundamentally, however, the dramatic expansion of the debt was a consequence of Greece's position within European,[50] as well as global, economic, and political processes. Greece joined the Eurozone in 2001, aided by Goldman Sachs;[51] it shared a disadvantageous position on the Eurozone periphery with countries such as Portugal, Italy, Ireland, Spain, and Slovenia.[52] From the early 2000s onwards, the public and private sectors of these peripheral countries were the object of profit-seeking speculative lending from the Eurozone's centre. In the case of Greece, French and German

[47] Pan-Hellenic Socialist Movement (in Greek: Πανελλήνιο Σοσιαλιστικό Κίνημα).
[48] Toussaint, E. (2017, January 9). Banks are responsible for the crisis in Greece: Debts claimed from Greece are odious. Retrieved from www.cadtm.org/Banks-are-responsible-for-the#nb2-3
[49] Lyrintzis, C. (2011). Greek politics in the era of economic crisis: reassessing causes and effects. *Hellenic Observatory Papers on Greece and Southeast Europe* (GreeSE Papere No 45); Mouzelis, N. P. (1978). *Modern Greece: Facets of underdevelopment*, London: Macmillan; Varoufakis, Y. (2017). *Adults in the room: My battle with Europe's deep establishment*, London: The Bodley Head.
[50] I mean, here, European in both the regional and the institutional senses. German economist Kunibert Raffer places primary responsibility for Greece's sovereign debt crisis at Europe's door, describing it as 'an EU-inflicted crisis' (2017).
[51] Hired by the Greek government to assist it in its bid to join the Eurozone, a team led by Lloyd Blankfein from Goldman Sachs Bank 'helped Greece hide the true extent of its debt, and in the process almost doubled it' (Reich, R. B. [2015, July 18]. How Goldman Sachs profited from the Greek Debt Crisis. *The Nation*. Retrieved from https://www.thenation.com/article/goldmans-greek-gambit/). Many commentators have noted that EU bureaucrats were generally aware of Greece's shaky finances prior to 2001 but that most turned a blind eye; see Raffer, K. (2017). Greece: An EU-Inflicted Catastrophe. In J. P. Bohoslavsky & K. Raffer, eds. Sovereign debt crises: what have we learned?, Cambridge: Cambridge University Press, pp. 65–83; Varoufakis, Y. (2017). *Adults in the room: My battle with Europe's deep establishment*, London: The Bodley Head.
[52] Lapavitsas, C., Kaltenbrunner, G., Lambrinidis, G., ... Teles, N. (2010). *The Eurozone between austerity and default* (RMF Occasional Report), Research on Money and Finance. Retrieved from www.researchonmoneyandfinance.org; Toussaint, E. (2017, January 9). Banks are responsible for the crisis in Greece: Debts claimed from Greece are odious. Retrieved from www.cadtm.org/Banks-are-responsible-for-the#nb2-3

banks in particular, but also Belgian, Dutch, Luxembourgian, and Irish, as well as Swiss and US banks, loaned heavily to Greek government and Greek banks; the latter, in turn, encouraged Greek businesses and households to borrow more than ever, to enjoy the fruits of European integration but also to keep up with the higher costs of living.

As banks across the globe began to fail, however, starting with Lehman Brothers in September 2008, governments ostensibly committed to capitalist principles seemed to fear a rerun of the 1929 stock market crash and its aftermath. Rather than allowing banks to reap the consequences of their own risky investments, a series of Western governments rescued banks from the brink of bankruptcy, bailing them out from the public purse and then shackling their own citizens with the debt, to be paid for through years of austerity policies. Facing a crisis that was only partly of its own making, Greece was not in a position to repay its lenders, which Papandreou's revelations made even more evident. When in early 2010 the true extent of Greece's debt became clear, financial rating agencies immediately downgraded Greece's sovereign debt to junk status. Papandreou turned to Europe for help.

Greece's first Universal Periodic Review was carried out in May 2011, a full year after the signing in May 2010 of its first Memorandum of Understanding with the so-called 'Troika' (the European Union, the European Central Bank, and the International Monetary Fund). In exchange for funds to 'rescue' the Greek economy from bankruptcy and to enable the Greek government to pay off some of its lenders, generally referred to as 'creditors' (predominantly French private banks), the Troika had imposed a series of 'reforms' that required the Greek government to reduce pensions, weaken labour rights, and radically cut health and education spending and housing support. As widely reported in the press, these austerity measures led to plummeting living standards, soaring unemployment, homelessness, and months of street demonstrations.[53]

As I watched Greece's May 2011 review unfold, I was extremely surprised to observe that 'the Greek financial crisis' was barely mentioned by Participating Governments, NGOs, or the Greek government itself. In the interactive dialogue, Greece received 124 recommendations: not a single one addressed rights to health, housing, water, or labour rights.[54] Apart from recommendations to sign treaties or optional protocols, and a few on hate speech, police

[53] See also the contributors to Dalakoglou, D., & Agelopoulos, G. (Eds.) (2017). *Critical times in Greece: Anthropological engagements with the crisis*, London: Routledge and Papailias, P. (2011, October 10). Beyond the "Greek crisis": Histories, rhetorics, politics. *Editors' Forum: Hot Spots, Society for Cultural Anthropology*.

[54] United Nations Human Rights Council (2011). *Report of the Working Group on the Universal Periodic Review: Greece* (No. A/HRC/18/13), Geneva.

brutality, gender-based violence, and Roma, the vast majority concerned migrants and refugees. There was almost no mention of the effects of the austerity measures on the socio-economic rights of all Greek citizens and residents.

How could this dramatic situation go unremarked? What was this silence about? This particular silence is an obviously complex phenomenon. Significantly, though, Greece's 2011 National Report itself hardly mentioned the crisis; other UPR actors then followed the Greek government's lead. Yet the reasons for the Greek government's silence were unclear. Was it an attempt to be virtuous in the first mode: that is, was the Greek government acting responsibly by 'owning' its own crisis? Alternatively, did it signify a reluctance on the Greek government's part to admit to the seriousness of the crisis? Was its seriousness even recognized?

Whatever its causes, the government's stance puzzled me. In January 2016, I visited the Greek Ministry of Foreign Affairs to try to find out why the government-authored 2011 National Report had ignored the crisis. I interviewed a high-level civil servant who I shall call Mr T., who had been a primary author of Greece's UPR report (and many of the Greek government's other human rights reports). He would not criticize the 2011 National Report for failing to mention the crisis, and he further exonerated the Participating Governments for failing to ask pertinent questions to Greece about the effects of the crisis. 'It was too early [in the crisis], too early for administrations of other states to prepare questions', because, as he explained, the preparation of questions is a long process and reflects what already exists; here, he was referring to the temporalities of the human rights system's committee and report-writing cycles.[55] But the second National Report for Greece's 2016 review, currently being written, 'will be totally different', he assured me. It was to be framed by the economic crisis and its effects. There would be three main themes, he said: first, socio-economic rights; second, refugees; and third, racism and xenophobia.[56]

At a certain point, I asked: 'How can UPR help you?' Mr T. answered: 'Through dissemination of recommendations . . . .which will help us push for

[55] Halme-Tuomisaari, M. (2020). Guarding utopia: law, vulnerability and frustration at the UN Human Rights Committee. *Social Anthropology/Anthropologie Sociale*, 28(1), 35–49.

[56] It is, of course, not irrelevant that the government in power during Greece's 2011 review was the socialist PaSoK, led by Georgios Papandreou, while Syriza, The Coalition of the Radical Left (in Greek: Συνασπισμός Ριζοσπαστικής Αριστεράς), which had campaigned on a vehemently anti-austerity platform, came to power in January 2015; its coalition government was led by Alexis Tsipras. Syriza was in government during Greece's second review in May 2016 as well as for the period of preparation.

changes internally. Also, we can use them in discussions with our partners in European institutions. We want them to recognize our human rights obligations, and theirs.' Very delicately, Mr T. was insisting that 'European partners needed to be reminded that they also have human rights obligations in relation to the Greeks.

Greece was reviewed for a second time on 3 May 2016. Greece's National Report was indeed framed by the three themes promised by Mr T. In the oral presentation launching the review, Mr Kostis Papaioannou, Secretary-General for Transparency and Human Rights in the Syriza government and head of the Greek delegation, described the effects of Greece's double crisis – the coincidence of the Greek economic crisis with the refugee crisis – with unflinching directness. He noted that, due to 'extreme and horizontal' austerity cuts, in 2014 36 per cent of the population were at risk of poverty or social exclusion; GDP fell by 25 per cent; unemployment rate reached 24.4 per cent and youth unemployment 49.8 per cent; and that excessive cuts in the health service were 'killing the nurse and doctor before treating the patient'.[57] In relation to the refugee crisis, he emphasized that 'it is only through international cooperation and burden sharing that a solution ensuring respect for human rights can be reached' and he expressed his view that this principle was 'not shared by all our European friends'.

In terms of the frankness and tone of Mr Papaioannou, the contrast with the 2011 Greek review could not be sharper. There was no question this time about the bureaucratic visibility of the human rights violations arising from extreme austerity measures imposed by the Troika: in other words, by European institutions, thus implicating European member states. So, what happened in the interactive dialogue that day in May 2016?

It is customary in the UPR for the delegations of Participating Governments to include in their short prepared statements (in the case of Greece's 2016 review, each state was given 1 minute, 20 seconds) greetings, congratulations or condemnations, concerns, comments, questions, and recommendations. Unlike the 2011 review, when not a single Participating Government mentioned the economic crisis, this time many delegations offered, in their introductory greetings, sympathy for Greece's difficulties and praise for its heroic efforts in confronting both austerity measures and the refugee crisis. But again, there was very little acknowledgement of the enormity of the

---

[57] Papaioannou was here quoting from UN Independent Expert Juan Pablo Bohoslavsky's report from his mission to Greece (*The Independent Expert on the effects of foreign debt and other related international financial obligations of States on the full enjoyment of all human rights, particularly economic, social and cultural rights on his mission to Greece* (No. A/HRC/31/60), United Nations).

devastation for Greek society as a whole. Moreover, most of the 207 recommendations concerned the refugee crisis – the second of Greece's double crisis – and primarily asked Greece to provide 'more': more protection, better facilities, more adequate food, shelter, and security. When delegations mentioned austerity, they asked Greece to mitigate the effects 'for the most vulnerable' – not for everyone.

There were a few delegations, nonetheless, that pushed against the spirit of UPR as a 'ritual of national responsibilisation for human rights',[58] to insist on the responsibility of other parties. Those delegations included Armenia, Poland, and the Islamic Republic of Iran. The most forceful statement, however, came from Iceland, so I reproduce in full the initial section of that statement:

> Iceland welcomes the delegation of Greece and acknowledges the high standards Greece has maintained in human rights despite confronting 'two simultaneous crises' and strict austerity measures at the same time. Iceland notes the concerns of the Greek National Commission for Human Rights on the impact of austerity policies on the social welfare system of Greece. These concerns are also shared by the Independent Expert of Foreign Debts (sic) who concludes that the measures have been particularly severe for the most vulnerable sectors of the populations: the poor, young people, older persons, pensioners, women, children, people with disabilities and immigrants.
> Mindful of its own recent situation,[59] Iceland would like to stress the importance of keeping the social fabric of the society intact. For Greece it is not only the task of the Greek authorities but also its creditors. Let me in this regard refer to the Resolution on the Basic Principles of Sovereign Debt Restructuring Processes adopted by the General Assembly last September. It promotes orderly, transparent constructive debt structuring process, with durable results. Such an approach is in favour of all stakeholders and upholds the enjoyment of social and economic rights.
> On refugees and migrants, my Delegation is concerned by the poor living conditions at reception facilities, the detention of unaccompanied children

---

[58] Cowan, The Universal Periodic Review as a public audit ritual, p. 60.

[59] Iceland's three largest banks, which had grown highly profitable during the 2000s, ignored warnings of impending crisis in 2006 and collapsed in 2008. However, Iceland faced its banking crisis very differently from nearly all other countries: it held its elected leaders to account, while relying on its excellent social welfare system to help its citizens absorb the shock. Bohoslavsky, J. P. (2017). Iceland: A human rights-sensitive approach to deal with financial crises. In J. P. Bohoslavsky & K. Raffer, eds., Sovereign debt crises: What have we learned?, Cambridge: Cambridge University Press, pp. 103–122.

and disturbing reports of xenophobic violence and attacks. Iceland neverthe-less acknowledges Greece's disproportionate share of the responsibility to meet humanitarian needs and a burden that Greece should not face alone. We are all in this together.

[Iceland's recommendations followed]

Whereas other delegations 'express[ed] their concern' and 'ask[ed]' Greece to 'ensure', 'improve', or 'address', Iceland's delegate identified 'the creditors' as sharing with the Greek authorities 'the task' of 'keeping the social fabric of the society intact'. He referred to collective agree-ments (the Resolution on the Basic Principles on Sovereign Debt Restructuring Processes) and collective responsibility for humanitarian needs ('a burden that Greece should not face alone; we are all in this together'). Even if he did not name the authors of the Troika-imposed austerity policies, he named their obligations.

I see this as manifesting what Foucault called the virtue of *parrhesia*: 'fearless speech', which for him entailed 'an engaged sense of truth-telling that requires some risk'.[60] In this instance, his statement was not flagrant or extreme; it retained the form and etiquette of Participating Government statements, demonstrating the skill and discipline informing this diplomat's truth-telling.[61] But it pushed these conventions, transgressing the norm that the State under Review should be the sole addressee, and reminding those watching and listening what the UPR frame occludes: actors and processes beyond the state which bear upon – indeed, which in many cases cause – human rights violations.

7.9 CONCLUSION

In his 2005 'Epilogue' to his book *From Apology to Utopia: The Structure of International Legal Argument*, Martti Koskenniemi wrote of his intuition that 'the most serious problems of the international world are related to its sharp division into a relatively prosperous and peaceful north and a conflict ridden South'. He challenged us to consider 'how our practices, institutions and conceptual frameworks [of international law] somehow

---

[60] Pickup, A. (2016). Critical inquiry as virtuous truth-telling: implications of phronesis and parrhesia. *Critical Questions in Education (Special Issue)*, 7(3), 178–196, p. 178.

[61] For an astute and detailed account of the practice of parrhesia among the OHCHR staff engaged with the UPR, see Billaud, J. (2014). Keepers of the truth: Producing "transpar-ent" documents for the Universal Periodic Review. In H. Charlesworth & E. Larking, eds., *Human rights and the Universal Periodic Review*, Cambridge: Cambridge University Press, pp. 63–84.

Modes of Acting Virtuously at the Universal Periodic Review 199

help to sustain it'.[62] Agreeing with Koskenniemi, I believe that a good place to start such an investigation is with Susan Marks' important article on the difficulties of addressing root causes of human rights violations.[63] Marks accepts Naomi Klein's[64] contention that the early human rights movement of the 1970s focused on documenting human rights violations while saying almost nothing about their causes. Subsequently, however, this changed, and in Marks' view, 'the question of the causes, indeed the "root causes", of violations has become a central and very conspicuous element of discussions within civil society and, perhaps most strikingly, the United Nations'.[65]

Yet Marks judges that those involved in these discussions 'have grappled only partially and rather problematically with the question of why abuses occur, how vulnerabilities arise and what it will take to bring about change'.[66] She identifies three principal problems: first, 'the investigation of causes is halted too soon'; second, 'effects are treated as though they are causes'; and third, 'causes are identified, only to be set aside'.[67] What accounts for these problems? In Marks' view, they are a consequence of the 'arrangements' in which UN institutions and officials operate: for her, 'the issue is how the international system of human rights protection, at least as currently configured, may itself limit the possibilities for revealing the reasons behind violations'.[68]

The first and second reviews of Greece at the UPR offer clear illustrations of Marks' insights. They reveal how the institutional structure of the UPR limited what was sayable and how it diverted attention away from the root causes of human rights violations. The national framing of the review, the tight time-frame of the public audit ritual of the UPR Working Group and the resulting focus on concise, pragmatic recommendations for improvement left no discursive space for addressing broader root causes; in the case I have just presented, these indisputably included not only long-standing dysfunctions internal to the Greek state, but also the operations of the global financial system and the decisions of the Troika (European Union, European Central Bank, and International Monetary Fund) from 2010 onwards to prioritize the

---

[62] Koskenniemi, M. (2005). *From apology to utopia: The structure of international legal argument*, Cambridge: Cambridge University Press.
[63] Marks, S. (2011). Human rights and root causes. *The Modern Law Review*, 74(1), 57–78.
[64] Klein, N. (2007). *The shock doctrine*, London: Penguin, pp. 118–128.
[65] Marks, Human rights and root causes, 59.
[66] Ibid., p. 70.
[67] Ibid.
[68] Ibid., p. 71.

interests of private creditors over the well-being of Greek citizens and inhabitants.[69]

A small number of country delegations resisted the single-nation framing in Greece's 2016 UPR review, as in other country reviews, by calling for the international community to offer Greece support. Iceland's statement went further: it called for acknowledgement of collective responsibility, for recognition that 'keeping the [Greek] social fabric intact' was a task that had to be shared 'by the Greek government and the creditors', in other words, by European states as well as by the European Central Bank and the International Monetary Fund. Although the language deployed remained diplomatically courteous and the accusations were largely implicit, Iceland's statement was courageously subversive in refusing to confine responsibility for remedying human rights violations to the State under Review. In this sense, it manifested parrhesiastic virtue.

The UPR was created to encourage states to improve their capacities to respect, protect, and fulfil human rights. Within this mechanism, ethical leadership has been envisaged as proceeding through a kind of modelling process, in which the more confident 'good students' of the UPR should 'set an example' and share best practice.[70] Yet, if virtue in the UPR tends to be equated with compliance to the frame, its values and modalities, the virtue of parrhesia – of fearless speech – by states who transgress also remains essential if the UPR is to remain alive. Thus, fearless speech in the context of whistleblowing speaks the language of human rights, whereas fearless speech in the context of the UPR recalls what the frame excludes, and hints at the silences and dark sides of hegemonic virtue.[71]

Recognising that there are different ways of being virtuous within the UPR allows us to take a step back from the assumptions of a singular understanding of

---

[69] Bohoslavsky, J. P. (2016). *Report of the Independent Expert on the effects of foreign debt and other related international financial obligations of States on the full enjoyment of all human rights, particularly economic, social and cultural rights on his mission to Greece* (No. A/HRC/31/60), United Nations; Bohoslavsky, J. P., & Raffer, K. (Eds.) (2017). *Sovereign debt crises: What have we learned?*, Cambridge: Cambridge University Press; Galbraith, J. K. (2016). *Welcome to the poisoned chalice: The destruction of Greece and the future of Europe*, New Haven: Yale University Press; Linarelli, J., Salomon, M. E., & Sornarajah, M. (2018). *The misery of international law: Confrontations with injustice in the global economy*, Oxford: Oxford University Press; Raffer, K. (2017). Greece: An EU-inflicted catastrophe. In J. P. Bohoslavsky & K. Raffer, eds., *Sovereign debt crises: What have we learned?*, Cambridge: Cambridge University Press, pp. 65–83; Varoufakis, Y. (2017). *Adults in the room: My battle with Europe's deep establishment*, London: The Bodley Head.

[70] Cowan & Billaud, Between learning and schooling.

[71] My phrase is an obvious nod to David Kennedy's influential text (2004) *The dark sides of virtue: Reassessing international humanitarianism*, Princeton, NJ: Princeton University Press.

Modes of Acting Virtuously at the Universal Periodic Review 201

the good, the just, and the virtuous embedded in the 'compliance' framework. It asks us to acknowledge the continuing effects of historical domination and subordination, and of political and economic inequality, on the so-called 'level playing field' of the UPR. I have shown that the new expectation that states actively monitor fellow states is, in some instances, defended as a gesture to hold accountable and facilitate improvement (expressing liberal virtue) and, in other instances, resisted as politically risky or as an unacceptable attempt to undermine solidarity (expressing subaltern virtue). Using the case of Greece, I have also shown that, while the UPR invites Participating Governments to monitor achievement, suggest improvements, and even offer aid to the State under Review, it simultaneously deflects attention away from human rights harm caused by parties beyond the state, including the actions of states that are acting as monitors. In the 2016 review of Greece, this deflection provoked a sense of injustice for diplomats of several Participating Governments and elicited the virtuous performance of 'parrhesia', fearless speech, by the delegate of Iceland.

Any serious consideration of virtue and ethical leadership in international organizations needs to look at the shape of the institutional architecture and ask whose interests it serves: who benefits from institutional modalities that lock in a conception of human rights as solely or primarily a state responsibility and that make the responsibilities of others difficult to articulate, much less enforce? Who benefits when discussions of human rights and of economic issues are kept institutionally separated? When the configuration of the international human rights system so starkly shapes what can be said, it is not enough simply to focus on the virtuous behaviour of individual actors.

Tellingly, even the Icelandic delegate's remarks in Greece's 2016 review have not been captured in the written record; this is because they were not articulated as a recommendation. The full oral statement of each Participating Government is included in the webcast of each review, but only recommendations, frequently in edited form, are captured as a numerated list in the final Report of the Working Group. Like the greetings, congratulations, condemnations, concerns, observations, questions, and comments with which Participating Governments pepper their statements in the interactive dialogue, and that are so central to the sociability, the negotiation of norms, and the institutional memory of UN processes, the occasional flashes of fearless speech leave hardly a trace in the official record.

ACKNOWLEDGEMENTS

I warmly thank Julie Billaud, Marie-Bénédicte Dembour, Charles Gore, Andrew Graan, Jonathan Mair, Agathe Mora, Eleni Papagaroufali, Samuel Shapiro, Bal Sokhi-Bulley, Guilherme Vasconcelos Vilaça, Maria Varaki and

Alice Wilson, as well as the participants at the conference on 'Ethical Leadership in International Organizations: Concepts, Narratives, Judgment and Assessment' at the University of Helsinki, June 2018, for their lively engagement with earlier versions of this chapter. I had presented a version of the final section on Greece's UPR review at a British International Studies Association (BISA) seminar on 'Ethics and World Justice' at the University of Sussex in January 2018, and I thank the participants for stimulating and helpful feedback, particularly Myriam Fotou, Joe Hoover, David Karp, Zdenek Kavan, and Louiza Odysseos. I also gratefully acknowledge the financial support of the British Academy, which funded my research at the Universal Periodic Review in Geneva in 2010–2011, the much-valued long-term support from the University of Sussex, and the equally treasured support of my research and writing during academic year 2018–2019 of the Helsinki Collegium for Advanced Studies at the University of Helsinki, when I held the Jane and Aatos Erkko Visiting Professorship in Studies on Contemporary Society.

PART III

JUDGMENT AND ASSESSMENT OF ETHICAL NARRATIVES AND LEADERSHIP

8

Imaginary Leadership and Displacement

A *Laboratory of Dilemmas?*

Maria Varaki

Without reflection, without mercy, without shame, they built strong walls and high, and compassed me about.

C. P. Cavafy, Walls.

8.1 INTRODUCTION

The Greek Pavilion in the 57 Venice Biennale of Art hosted an exhibition titled *Laboratory of Dilemmas*. As the informative note explained at the entrance of the site:

> Laboratory of dilemmas is a narrative video installation based on Aeschylus' theatre play Iketides (Suppliant Women) and the dilemmas it poses between saving the Foreigner or maintaining the safety of the Native, which attempts to expose the anguish, puzzlement and confusion of individuals and social groups when called upon to address similar dilemmas.[1]

According to the note: Iketides

> is the first literary text in history that raises the issue of a persecuted group of people seeking asylum . . .. The King is faced with a major dilemma . . . If he doesn't help them he will be breaking the sacred laws of hospitality and violating the principles of Law and Humanism, leaving the Suppliants to the mercy of their pursuers who might well destroy them.[2]

The Greek installation reflected the overall theme of the 2017 Biennale, which according to its curator, Christine Macel, was 'an Exhibition inspired by humanism. . .. [i]n this type of humanism, the artistic act is

---

[1] http://laboratoryofdilemmas.gr (accessed 1 February 2020).
[2] *Ibid.*

contemporaneously *an act of resistance*, of *liberation* and of *generosity*.'[3] One could add that the title of the Biennale reflected the challenges and 'crisis'[4] of its era, an era overwhelmed with demanding policy dilemmas about forced displacement.[5] The war in Syria had forced millions of people to abandon their country and find refuge in other neighbouring countries and Europe. Greece and the Aegean Sea became a sea of despair. The Mediterranean sun and landscape, the way Camus described it,[6] could not enlighten the lives of desperate human beings who fled war and poverty.

Within this context three main images captured the attention of the world. On 2 September 2015 the picture of the drowned body of the three-year-old Alan Kurdi, lying on the Turkish coastline, triggered tears, shame, silence but also an outcry. Alan's family was Syrian of Kurdish origin, living in Kobane, and they were trying to reach Canada via Europe. They did not manage to complete their trip. Their boat capsized in the Aegean Sea and the image of the red t-shirt the little boy wore haunted even, temporarily, political leaders and common people all over the world. The Turkish hashtag in twitter, *Humanity Washed Ashore*, illustrated vividly the tragedy.

The second image depicted a five-year-old boy, Omran Daqneesh, who had been rescued from the rubble of his house after an airstrike in Aleppo, Syria.[7] The boy sat still and bloodied in an ambulance looking in shock, without crying, only staring. According to *The New York Times*, Omran's image generated so much reaction because it could be simply '*Every Child*', or as the text of the article highlighted: 'it may be the relatively familiar look of Omran's distress that allows a broader public to relate to it'.[8]

The third image derived from Yarmouk, the largest Palestinian Refugee camp in a suburb of Damascus.[9] Yarmouk was under siege and, when representatives

---

[3] At: www.labiennale.org/en/art/2017/57th-international-art-exhibition (accessed 1 February 2020).

[4] For the critique of the word *crisis*, see Marion Panizzon & Micheline van Riemsdijk, 'Introduction to Special Issue: "Migration Governance in an Era of Large Movements: A Multilevel-Approach"' (2019) 45 *Journal of Ethnic and Migration Studies*, 1225, whereas for an analysis of the contribution of migration law towards the creation of crisis, see Jaya Ramji-Nogales, 'Migration Emergencies' (2017) 68 *Hasting Law Journal*, 609.

[5] For the purposes of this chapter, the notion of forced displacement is understood to cover mixed movement both of refugees and migrants. It is beyond the focus of this intervention to provide an analysis of the different legal terminology, its implications, and controversies.

[6] Albert Camus, *The First Man* (Penguin Random House, 1994).

[7] www.theguardian.com/world/2016/aug/18/boy-in-the-ambulance-image-emerges-syrian-child-aleppo-rubble (accessed 5 February 2020)

[8] www.nytimes.com/2016/08/19/world/middleeast/omran-daqneesh-syria-aleppo.html (accessed 5 February 2020)

[9] www.theguardian.com/news/2015/mar/05/how-yarmouk-refugee-camp-became-worst-place-syria (accessed 5 February 2020)

Imaginary Leadership and Displacement 207

from the United Nations Relief and Works Agency for Palestine Refugees (UNRWA) managed to enter and deliver food, a photographer took a picture of thousands of people appearing from the ruins. Most of them suffered from malnutrition and were in desperate need of assistance while starving to death.

These three pictures, to a different extent, triggered global calls for assistance and some kind of action. Arguably there are several conflicting views regarding the power of an image especially when it stems from a conflict. For example, Susan Sontag in her work on images of war and atrocities has stressed that the image creates a distance from suffering that prohibits genuine empathy.[10] On the other side, the late acclaimed war photojournalist Yannis Behrakis has supported that

> Photography can leave people speechless with its power and beauty. It can send a message to the audience, make people cry or laugh or both. It can make people feel guilty – or give money for a good cause. And it can make people think twice before pulling the trigger.[11]

When he was further questioned about his work, he replied that 'My mission is to tell you the story and then you decide what you want to do. My mission is to make sure that nobody can say: "I didn't know".'[12] On this last note, it could be argued that the three images succeeded *at least* not to allow anyone to say, I didn't know . . ., or as the aunt of the first little boy (Alan Kurdi) said, 'It was one of those moments when the whole world seems to care.'[13]

From 2015 onwards, the phenomenon of forced displacement became the key policy topic that experts and politicians were called to address, within a political environment of anxiety and polarization. A daunting challenge that triggered unprecedented pressure upon national entities and the international polity. Whether one can attribute it to security reasons, humanitarian concerns, or a combination of both, a vivid public exchange of opinions intensified. This debate took place (and continues to do so) in what Seyla Benhabib years ago described as the 'paradox of democratic legitimacy'; thus '[t]he tension between universal human rights claims and particularistic cultural and national identities'.[14] Or as several other commentators have identified, between the idea of state

---

[10]   Susan Sontag, *Regarding the Pain of Others* (Farrar, Straus and Giroux, 2003).

[11]   www.theguardian.com/artanddesign/ng-interactive/2015/dec/21/photographer-of-the-year-2015 -yannis-behrakis (accessed 10 February 2020)

[12]   www.theguardian.com/media/2019/mar/03/pulitzer-prize-winning-reuters-photographer- yannis-behrakis-dies-aged-58 (accessed 10 February 2020)

[13]   BBC news: Alan Kurdi's aunt: 'My dead nephew's picture saved thousands of lives, www.bbc.com/news/blogs-trending-35116022, (accessed 10 February 2020)

[14]   Seyla Benhabib, *The Rights of Others* (Cambridge University Press, 2004), at 44.

sovereignty and the ideal of humanity.[15] In this framework, the challenge of forced displacement has been addressed as a question of open, closed, porous, or shifting borders.[16] Several fine scholars have strongly advocated both in favour and against a right to immigrate and a subsequent duty of acceptance that goes beyond temporary hospitality as Kant famously prescribed.[17] The same scholars have tried to explore the limits of sovereignty before grave necessity and they have developed various theories that justify an exceptional practice,[18] whereas others have tried vigorously to identify the legal responsibility of states for human rights violations while externalizing migration control.[19]

The current chapter, while acknowledging the normative significance and policy relevance of these thorny questions, does not purport to directly address them. Instead, the aim of this modest contribution is to explore paradigms of ethical leadership[20] (according to my own sensibility), as a counter compass of governance and normative resilience in times of great dilemmas. This latter front will draw upon an Aristotelian understanding of aretaic leadership that argues in favour of particular virtues those in decision-making positions should carry, such as the virtues of phronesis, empathy, imagination, but also moderation. It is contended that those virtues provide a different channel of apprehension and

---

[15] In this regard, see Betts & Collier (eds.), *Refuge: Transforming a Broken Refugee System* (Penguin Random House, 2017), Aleinikoff & Zamore (eds.), *The Arc of Protection* (Stanford University Press, 2019), Joseph Carens, *The Ethics on Immigration* (Oxford University Press, 2013), David Miller, *Strangers in Our Midst* (Harvard University Press, 2018), Ayten Gundogdu, *Rightsless in an Age of Rights, Hanna Arendt and the Contemporary Struggles of Migrants* (Oxford University Press, 2015), Michael Walzer, *Spheres of Justice* (Basic Books, 1983), Fine & Ypi (eds.), *The Ethics of Movement and Membership* (Oxford University Press, 2016), and most recently the work of Itamar Mann, *Humanity at Sea* (Cambridge University Press, 2015), who provides a novel understanding of the imperatives of sovereignty when balanced with the right of human encounter, and Jeremy Waldron, 'Exclusion: Property Analogies in the Immigration Debate' (2017) 18 *Theoretical Inquiries in Law*, 469, where he distinguishes between an *'ownership conception'* of sovereignty contrary to a *responsibility one* he prefers.

[16] Ayelet Schahar, *The Shifting Border, Legal Cartographies of Migration and Mobility* (Manchester University Press, 2020), where she proposes a further expansion of the extraterritorial application of human rights based on the concept of effective control.

[17] Seyla Benhabib, *The Rights of Others* (Cambridge University Press, 2004) at 25–48.

[18] In this regard, see Joseph Carens, *The Ethics on Immigration* (Oxford University Press, 2013), David Miller, *Strangers in Our Midst* (Harvard University Press, 2018), Ayten Gundogdu, *Rightsless in an Age of Rights, Hanna Arendt and the Contemporary Struggles of Migrants* (Oxford University Press, 2015), Michael Walzer, *Spheres of Justice* (Basic Books, 1983), Fine & Ypi (eds.), *The Ethics of Movement and Membership* (Oxford University Press, 2016).

[19] One characteristic example is the latest special issue guest-edited by Cathryn Costello and Itamar Mann, 'Border Justice: Migration and Accountability for Human Rights Violations' (2020) 21 *German Law Journal*, 3.

[20] For a fine introduction to the leadership notion and discourse, see Nannerl O. Keohane, *Thinking about Leadership* (Princeton University Press, 2010).

Imaginary Leadership and Displacement

deliberation that neither condones the 'middle way' nor solely resorts to expertise or techniques that several times appear to be of non-satisfactory if not problematic use. Those virtues enhance the idea of what I call *imaginary leadership* that can be empathetic, phronetic, and moderate in a context-specific framework.

This intellectual endeavour will unfold around a series of developments on the displacement front. I assert, that this area of forced displacement, operates as an aspirational platform to test the Aristotle inspired idea of imaginary leadership, because it depicts those perennial dilemmas that transcend human nature, time (*kairos*) and space (*topos*). However, the current chapter will not delve into a thorough discussion of virtue ethics, nor will it deliver strong judgments of what is a virtuous behaviour and who is a virtuous person.[21] Contrary to this later grandiose approach, the contribution here aims to shed some light on concrete behaviours via the reflective angle of the particular virtues I mentioned above; the ones of empathy, phronesis, and moderation. The reason I opt for a cautious and less ambitious approach lies primarily on the acknowledgment of the complexity of the intellectual debate surrounding the limits and contradictions of the theory of virtue ethics.[22] On a second level, my personal encounter with virtue ethics develops around a narrow sensibility, inspired by specific admirable actions before tragic dilemmas. In other words, I am trying to explore how different and variable shades of the virtues of empathy, moderation, and phronesis might have instigated concrete decisions and actions in different contexts and times. This narrow exercise appreciates the plurality and elusiveness of the virtues themselves,[23] while at the same time abstains from a risky claim of strong causation based on a purist or even modified understanding of virtue ethics

---

[21] In this regard, see the *agent-based approach* of Michael Slote, *Morals from Motives* (Oxford University Press, 2001), the *qualified-agent account* by Rosalind Hursthouse, *On Virtue Ethics*, (Oxford University Press, 1999), and the *target-centred* account by Christine Swanton, *Virtue Ethics, A Pluralistic View* (Oxford University Press, 2003). But see Ramon Das, 'Virtue Ethics and Right Action: A Critique', in Besser-Jones and Slote (eds.), *Routledge Companion to Virtue Ethics* Routledge, (2015). Of particular interest is also the exchange between Bernard Williams and Rosalind Hursthouse in Heinaman, (ed.), *Aristotle and Moral Realism* (Westview Press, 1995) at 13–34. For a comparative overview of the three approaches, see Van Zyl, 'Virtue Ethics and Right Action', in Russell (ed.), *The Cambridge Companion to Virtue Ethics* (Cambridge University Press, 2013).

[22] See characteristically Martha Nussbaum, 'Virtue Ethics, a Misleading Category?' (1999) 3 *The Journal of Ethics*, 163, Svensson & Johansson, 'Objections to Virtue Ethics', in Snow (ed.), *Oxford Handbook of Virtue* (Oxford University Press, 2018), criticizing the lack both of a rightness criterion and of concrete practical guidance.

[23] But see Martha Nussbaum, who has vigorously criticized a *relativist* understanding of virtues at least in its Aristotelian version, *Non Relative Virtues, An Aristotelian Approach* (1988) 13 *Midwest Studies in Philosophy*, 32.

that could legitimately be contested.[24] To conclude here, my personal understanding of virtues neither evolves around an ultimate *telos*, nor embraces a holistic approach of virtuous life. If I could be slightly poetic, I would add that the virtues I refer to appear to function as a kind of compass that accommodates the challenging human journey through islands of tragedy.

In this regard, this chapter will initially explain in a selective mode the significance of virtue ethics and in particular the virtues of phronesis, empathy, and moderation. It will continue by providing a generic overview of the relevant socio-political context and assess the effect of the phenomenon of populist sovereignty upon migration policies and discourses. And then it will proceed on two fronts: First, it will narrate and unfold from a virtue sensibility different behaviours especially at the peak of the 'Mediterranean crisis' until the adoption of the Global Compact for Migration. The reason I chose to focus solely on the Compact for Migration derives from the fact that it is the very first comprehensive response to the phenomenon of mixed forced displacement.[25] Second, the chapter will question, the added value of the virtue ethics approach while examining the importance of soft law in the further development of legal normativity within the contested area of forcible displacement. In other words, how could these extra-legal assets strengthen the normativity of international law while confronting a systemic attack on against its basic premises.

8.2 OF ARISTOTLE AND VIRTUES

Somewhere else I have also argued that the word crisis originates from the Greek word κρίσης which means judgment and thus discretion.[26] Every crisis

---

[24] See in particular Ramon Das, 'Virtue Ethics and Right Action: A Critique', in Besser-Jones and Slote, (eds.), *Routledge Companion to Virtue Ethics* (Routledge, 2015), but also Daniel Russell's critique to Slote's theory, in *Practical Intelligence and the Virtues* (Oxford University Press, 2009), questioning his defiance of the necessity of phronesis, Karen Stohr, 'Virtuous Motivation', in Snow, (ed.), *The Oxford Handbook of Virtues* (Oxford University Press, 2018).

[25] In this regard, a series of scholars from various disciplines have highlighted the importance of the GCM as the most comprehensive and multilevel attempt to understand migration; compared to the pre-existing centralized legal framework for refugee protection, Colleen Thouez, 'Strengthening Migration Governance: The UN as "Wingman"' (2019) 45 *Journal of Ethnic and Migration Studies*, 1242, Vincent Chetail, *International Migration Law* (Oxford University Press, 2019).

[26] See Maria Varaki, 'Quest for Phronesis in Holy Land', in *Towards Responsible Global Governance*, Klabbers, Varaki, & Vilaça (eds.,), (University of Helsinki, 2018) citing Florian Hoffman, 'Facing the Abyss, International Law before the Political', in Goldoni and McCorkindale (eds.), *Hannah Arendt and the Law* (Hart Publishing, 2012) 175.

Imaginary Leadership and Displacement

according to Hannah Arendt could be translated into a new beginning, yet at the same time it requires the exercise of krisis or judgment.[27] Within this framework I pursue the course of questioning the role of politicians when they exercise discretion and make judgments. How can they exercise imaginative and wise assessment balancing between reason and emotions? My modest response to those dilemmas is that one possible way to do that is by returning to virtue ethics. The reason for refocusing on the normative theory of virtue ethics lies in the importance it carries for human agency, emphasizing the particular traits those in positions of influence should have, especially in an era where 'robotic' applications of rules appear to lose relevance.[28]

In addition, I concur with those who embrace the Arendtian proposition that in critical moments a sense of common responsibility should be further developed.[29] The migration dilemmas I try to explore here necessitate this sensibility of common responsibility, as it will be further argued. This aggravated sense of responsibility derives, as Arendt stresses, from the human capacity to think and make judgments.[30] In order to respond to this call for common responsibility, especially in face of migration policies, I contend that the world would likely be a better place if politicians demonstrated the virtues of phronesis, empathy, and moderation.

---

[27] *Ibid.*, at 173.

[28] Since the mid-1950s, there has been a revival of interest in virtue ethics; see in particular G. E. M. Anscombe, 'Modern Moral Philosophy', 33 *Philosophy* (1958) 1, Alasdair MacIntyre, *After Virtue: A Study in Moral Theory* (Bloomsbury Publishing, 2013), Rosalind Hursthouse, *On Virtue Ethics* (Oxford University Press, 1999); Lawrence Solum, 'Virtue Jurisprudence: Towards an Aretaic Theory of Law', in Huppes-Cluysenaer and Coelho (eds.), *Aristotle and the Philosophy of Law: Theory, Practice and Justice* (Springer, 2013) 1, Michael Slote, 'Agent-Based Virtue Ethics' (1995) 20 *Midwest Studies in Philosophy*, 83. It is beyond the purpose of this piece to present a thorough and comprehensive discussion of virtue ethics, yet other indicative articles and books include Farrelly and Solum (eds.), *Virtue Jurisprudence* (Palgrave, 2008); Crisp and Slote (eds.), *Virtue Ethics* (Oxford University Press, 2007); Jennifer Welchman (ed.), *The Practice of Virtue: Classic and Contemporary Readings in Virtue Ethics* (Hackett Publishing, 2006); Amaya & Hock Lai (eds.), *Law, Virtue and Justice* (Hart, 2013), Julia Driver, *Uneasy Virtue* (Cambridge University press, 2001), and Julia Annas, *Intelligent Virtue* (Oxford University Press, 2011), which describes virtues as not static but active and reliable dispositions of a person, like a 'practical skill'.

[29] In this regard, see Jan Klabbers, 'Possible Islands of Predictability: The Legal Thought of Hannah Arendt' (2007) 20 *Leiden Journal of International Law* 1, and Jan Klabbers, 'Hannah Arendt and the Languages of Global Governance', in Goldoni and McCorkindale (eds.), *Hannah Arendt and the Law* (Hart Publishing, 2012) at 246.

[30] Arendt throughout her work paid full attention to the importance of thinking, willing but also judging. Unfortunately, the last component of her work was not fully articulated due to her death. In this regard, see Elisabeth Young-Bruehl, *Why Arendt Matters* (Yale University Press, 2006) and her analysis of the 'standard of the self' and the importance of 'reflective judging' in relation to others.

The virtue of phronesis has been developed in book VI of Aristotle's *Nicomachean Ethics*, where he analyses the intellectual virtues.[31] The Aristotelian theory of *phronesis* does not condone the 'middle way' but requires choices and judgment in hard cases of indeterminacy and discretion.[32] My own proposition of *phronesis*, as I have developed elsewhere, is very much based on the notion of common sense,[33] and in particular of a dialectic format based on the interpretation Outi Korhonen has described.[34] *Phronesis* is the next step of intellectual wisdom, that assesses the entirety of the context and moves from the general to the particular and backwards, and in that sense *phronesis* is 'dialogic', whereas *tekhne* is 'dogmatic knowledge'.[35] *Phronesis* understood this way provides simultaneously the means for deliberation and liberation while strengthening the capacity of the decision-maker to assess the particularities of a situation, before making a choice.[36] The essence of phronesis also rests with the lack of predetermined criteria that can secure a phronetic judgment.[37] Instead, when we exercise *phronesis*, 'a family of skills',[38] the conflict between the particular and the global reaches its maximum and the 'mean' becomes the key element of *phronesis*.[39]

Phronesis, I argue, should be accompanied by the virtue of courage when a responsible person exercises her judgment and decides upon challenging policies. Mainly, though, I would say that phronesis requires imagination: imagination to place yourself in unprecedented situations, or to try to imagine the conditions affecting others. In this sense, responsibility as depicted by Arendt

---

[31] See Aristotle, *Nicomachean Ethics* (1976, Thomson trans.). See also Aristotle, *The Eudemian Ethics* (2011, Kenny trans.); D. Russell, 'Phronesis and the Virtues', in Ronald Polansky (ed.), *The Cambridge Companion to Aristotle's Nicomachean Ethics* (Cambridge University Press, 2014) 203; and Jamie Gaskarth, 'The Virtues of International Society' (2012) 18 *European Journal of International Relations*, 431.

[32] R. Kamtekar, 'Ancient Virtue Ethics': An overview with an Emphasis on Practical Wisdom', in Daniel C. Russell (ed.), *The Cambridge Companion to Virtue Ethics* (Cambridge University Press, 2013) 29, at 34–35, citing *Nicomachean Ethics*.

[33] For Arendt also the exercise of judging was developed around the notion of common sense, see Jonathan P. Schwartz, *Arendt's Judgment* (University of Pennsylvania Press, 2016) 151.

[34] See the seminal work of Outi Korhonen, 'New International Law: Silence, Defense or Deliverance?' (1996) 7 *European Journal of International Law* 1, on situationality.

[35] Id.

[36] Rosalind Hursthouse, 'Practical Wisdom: A Mundane Account' (2006) 106 *Proceedings of the Aristotelian Society* 1; Daniel Russell, *Practical Intelligence and the Virtues* (Oxford University Press, 2009); and Bronwyn Finnigan, 'Phronesis in Aristotle: Reconciling Deliberation with Spontaneity', 91 *Philosophy and Phenomenological Research* (2015) 674.

[37] As Macintyre argues, 'the exercise of such judgment is not a routinizable application of rules' (*After Virtue*, supra note 28 at 176), whereas later he attributes the lack of criteria to the interrelationship of virtues (*After Virtue*, at 182).

[38] Russell, 'Phronesis and the Virtues', *supra* note 31 at 206.

[39] MacIntyre, *After Virtue*, *supra* note 28 at 180–181.

Imaginary Leadership and Displacement

means 'representative thinking'.[40] By situating yourself in the shoes of other people, the particularities of the context can accommodate an imaginary deliberation that entails empathy[41] and understanding. This deliberation purports to constantly appease tension and consolidate bridges of communication and action. And today we need those bridges contrary to the erection of walls that became the new normal. In that sense imagination can be seen as the complementary side of phronesis, where the latter is the initial step in the exercise of judgment and the former completes this intellectual exercise with a meta step. Or else, phronetic judgment operates either as a restraining or accelerating exercise of discretion, but imaginary judgment completes the picture while creating the foundation for something else than the expected one. If understood this way, then imaginary judgment provides not only wisdom but also inspiration and thus becomes a paradigm of exemplarism.

Finally, my understanding of imaginary leadership entails moderation. In ancient Greek, moderation can be translated as μέτρο, or else fine balance. Aristotle speaks of virtue as the mean between excesses.[42] Albert Camus, who was massively infatuated with Greek tragedy and the dilemmas it raises for human nature,[43] spoke of '*la pensée de midi*', or else his conceptualization of a mediterranean sensibility of measure and acknowledgment of limit.[44] In *The Rebel*, Camus further highlighted the value of moderation by courageously writing that:

> In 1953, excess is always a comfort and sometimes a career. Moderation, on the one had, is nothing but pure tension. It smiles, no doubt and our convulsionists, dedicated to elaborate apocalypses, despise it. But its smile shines brightly at the climax of an intermidable effort: it is in itself a supplementary source of strength.[45]

---

[40] See John Shotter & Haridimos Tsoukas, 'In Search of Phronesis: Leadership and the Art of Judgment' (2014) 13 *Academy of Management Learning and Education*, 224.

[41] For a case study of negative empathy, see Jan Klabbers, 'Doing Justice? Bureaucracy, the Rule of Law and Virtue Ethics' (2017) VI *Rivista di Filosofia del Diritto*, 27, and for more positive aspects, see the work of Michael Slote, *Morals from Motives* (Oxford University Press, 2012), and 'Empathy, Law and Justice', in Amaya and Ho Hock Lai (eds.), *Law, Virtue and Justice*, (Hart Publishing, 2012) 279–291.

[42] Aristotle, *Nicomachean Ethics* supra note 31.

[43] For a fine inquiry on the ethical dilemmas in Greek Tragedy, see Martha Nussbaum, *The Fragility of Goodness* (Cambridge University Press, 1986).

[44] Robert Zaretsky, *A Life Worth Living, Albert Camus and the Quest for Meaning*, Robert Zaretsky (Harvard University Press, 2013). Tony Judt also highlights the significance of measure for Camus, in Tony Judt, *The Burden of Responsibility* (The University of Chicago Press, 1998), 122–126. For Camus, see also Jan Klabbers, 'The Passion and the Spirit, Albert Camus as Moral Politician' (2016) *European Papers*, 13.

[45] Albert Camus, *The Rebel* (Penguin Random House, 1992).

I argue that moderation here is perceived as a crucial component of imaginary responsibility that resists not only dogmatism but also 'excess of imagination, of aspiration, of exertion',[46] in times of great challenges and dilemmas. In an more artistic way, I would add that my sense of moderation is vividly depicted by Kandinsky's description of the circle. For the great artist, '[t]he circle is the synthesis of the greatest oppositions. It combines the concentric and the eccentric in a single form and in equilibrium.'[47]

8.3 DISPLACEMENT DILEMMAS DURING CHALLENGING TIMES

Martti Koskenniemi, nine years ago, wrote that sovereignty 'articulates the hope of experiencing the thrill of having one's life in one's own hands'.[48] Yet, the recent backlash[49] against liberal ideas and institutions of global governance whose mission is the further promotion of human rights protection, the strengthening of international criminal justice, and the dissemination of the rule of law framework has triggered a vivid discussion among various experts and scholars regarding the causes and dynamics of this new crisis.[50]

Especially after the election of President Trump, the Brexit decision, and the rise of authoritarian leaders in various parts of the world, who not only opt for politically incorrect language but also adopt policies that threaten domestically civil and political liberties and target institutional fora of global cooperation and security, the notion of backlash has become the most recurrent research question.[51]

Yet, this time it is not only the usual suspects: traditionally authoritarian regimes or isolated undemocratic states that fight the western 'establishment'. Instead, an orchestrated backlash has been initiated by democratically elected

---

[46] Judith Shklar, *Political Thought and Political Thinkers*, Foreword (University of Chicago Press, 1998).

[47] KANDINSKY, TASCHEN PORTFOLIO (2003).

[48] Martti Koskenniemi, 'What Use for Sovereignty Today?' (2011) 1 *Asian Journal of International Law*, 61.

[49] Leslie Vinjamuri, 'Human Rights Backlash', in Hopgood, Vinjamuri & Snyder (eds.), *The Futures of Human Rights* (Cambridge University Press, 2017) 120–121.

[50] See characteristically Philip Alston, 'The Populist Challenge to Human Rights' (2017) 9 *Journal of Human Rights Practice*, 1, J. Michael Ignatieff, *The Ordinary Virtues, Moral Order in a Divided World* (Harvard University Press, 2017), Karen Alter, 'The Future of International Law', iCourts Working Paper Series, No. 101, 2017.

[51] James Crawford, 'The Current Political Discourse Concerning International Law' (2018) 81 *Modern Law Review*, 1, where he questions the 'susceptibility' of international law in the current context of defiance by political practice.

Imaginary Leadership and Displacement

actors inside the so-called West[52] that oscillates between tactical and strategic backlash as Leslie Vinjamuri has highlighted.[53] This new era is characterized by an axiomatic consensus between the 'old' West or North and the former 'orientalist' East or South that transcends the traditional conceptual divisions that prevailed in the academic scholarship until now.

Populist sovereignism stands between the statists and globalists understanding of sovereignty.[54] This kind of sovereignism contains six common characteristics;[55] it is founded on the binary between the people v. the elite, the strongman represents the will of the 'real' people, the strongman reflects the anti-establishment, national interests take priority (America First), national law supersedes international law, and finally it opposes the erosion of state sovereignty in favour of intergovernmental organizations. In other words, this sovereignism fights to reassert both popular and state sovereignty in the domestic and international front.

Within this context, populist sovereignism as defined above appears to gain ground worldwide. Undoubtedly, migration dilemmas lie at the heart of sovereignty. This issue has been meticulously explored by a variety of scholars long time ago, whether in historical, political, or socio-legal terms.[56] Vincent Chetail has stressed, while explaining why international migration law is not properly developed, that 'This is probably due to the common belief that admission of non-citizens is 'the last major redoubt of unfettered national sovereignty'.[57] Or, as Catherine Dauvergne has highlighted in her early work

---

[52] The same claim is made by Garavito in César Rodriguez-Garavito & Krisna Gomez, (eds.) *Rising to the Populist Challenge, A New Playbook for Human Rights Actors* (Dejusticia, 2018).

[53] Leslie Vinjamuri, 'Human Rights Backlash' supra note 49, 2017.

[54] This term has been introduced in a study conducted by the Hague Institute for Strategic Studies titled The Rise of Populist Sovereignism, What It Is, Where It Comes From, And What It Means For International Security And Defense, The Hague Centre for Strategic Studies (HCSS) 2017.

[55] *Id.*

[56] In this sense, see characteristically Catherine Dauvergne, 'Sovereignty, Migration and the Rule of Law in Global Times' (2004) 67 *The Modern Law Review*, 588, Vincent Chetail, 'Sovereignty and Migration in the Doctrine of the Law of Nations: An Intellectual History of Hospitality from Vitoria to Vattel' (2016) 27 *European Journal of International Law*, 901, Chantal Thomas, 'What Does the Emerging International Law of Migration Mean for Sovereignty?, Cornell Law School research paper No. 13–72 and Itamar Mann, *Humanity at Sea: Maritime Migration and the Foundations of International Law* (Cambridge University Press, 2016), and of course the pioneer work of Seyla Bnhabib.

[57] Vincent Chetail, 'The Transnational Movement of Persons under General International Law – Mapping the Customary Law Foundations of International Migration Law', in Chetail & Bauloz (eds.), *Research Handbook on International Law and Migration* (Elgar, 2012);

on migration and globalization, 'migration law is being transformed into the last bastion of sovereignty'.[58]

At the same time, right-wing xenophobic parties gained power all over Europe, some of them with clear neo-Nazi ideology, while in the United States, the election of President Trump unleashed dangerous extreme forces of white supremacist rhetoric and violence.[59] Within the European Union, President Orbán declared his goal to make Hungary a migrant-free zone opposing an 'invasion',[60] several countries raised fences and closed their borders, whereas others defied the quotas for relocation of asylum seekers from the front-line countries of the EU.[61] The quest for 'solidarity' challenged the foundation of the European project even more than the financial crisis of the 2010s.[62]

On one hand, there was (and remains) the instrumentalization and exploitation of migration for political purposes. On the other hand, the depiction of migrationary flows by several media as a threat to national security and identity exacerbated the polarization of discourse and the rise of fear.[63] Vincent Chetail has summarized this sentiment of hostility arguing that:

> Racism and xenophobia have become so mainstream that calling for an evidence-based approach to migration is viewed at best as partisan and at worst as an affront to democracy. In such a politically toxic climate, there is more than ever a crucial need to develop a pedagogy of migration. This is essential to not only better understand the normality of being a migrant, but

---

[58] Catherine Dauvergne, *Making People Illegal: What Globalization Means for Migration and Law* (Cambridge University Press, 2008) 169.

[59] In August 2017, in Charlottesville, Virginia white supremacists rallied in the city, chanting racial insults, and clashed with anti-right-wing groups, and a woman was killed when a car ran into a crowd of protesters. President Trump did not immediately denounce the violence of far-right extremists but condemned 'hatred, bigotry and violence on many sides.' Forty-eight hours later and under severe criticism, he delivered a clear condemnation. www.nytimes.com/2017/08/13/opinion/trump-charlottesville-hate-stormer.html?smid=fb-share (accessed 20 February 2020)

[60] www.theguardian.com/world/2018/mar/15/hungarian-leader-says-europe-is-now-under-invasion-by-migrants (accessed 20 February 2020)

[61] https://curia.europa.eu/jcms/upload/docs/application/pdf/2020–04/cp200040en.pdf?fbclid=I wAR2qztvsoL7CZZk2-nJDyVP4aZwNdjjSq_tzwZPoCo5QijJzBYmqEoWdjwQ

[62] For a detailed account, see Eleni Karageorgiou, 'The Distribution of Asylum Responsibilities in the EU Dublin, Partnerships with Third Countries and the Question of Solidarity' (2019) 88 *Nordic Journal of International Law*, 315.

[63] In this regard, see the special issue by M. Krzysanowski, A. Trandiafyllidou & R. Wodak, 'The Mediatization and the Politicization of the "Refugee Crisis" in Europe' (2018) 16 *Journal of Immigrant and Refugee Studies*; Heaven Crawley & Dimitris Skleparis, 'Refugees, Migrants, Neither, Both': Categorical Fetishism and the Politics of Bounding in Europe's "Migration Crisis"' (2018) 44 *Journal of Ethnic and Migration Studies*, 48.

Imaginary Leadership and Displacement 217

also to inform public debate and dispel the current manipulation surrounding the dominant discourse. Developing a rational and objective narrative about migration has become a critical endeavor; otherwise, demagogues will continue to hijack democracy.[64]

His observations for a rational narrative and evidence-based approach can also be also translated as an urgent call for political action. It seems though that this is not a new appeal. During the same period described above, a series of developments took place between different countries and continents, where various actors acted differently before concrete challenges and dilemmas, as will be further explored later.

8.3.1 *From NY to Marrakesh*

Despite the fact that forced displacement received various degrees of attention within the global framework,[65] one could argue that the so-called forced displacement 'crisis' that reached its peak during 2015–2016 paved the way for the adoption of the UN New York Declaration for Refugees and Migrants.[66] The Declaration was the result of a High Level Meeting on Large Movements of Refugees and Migrants held in New York, securing the commitment of States to produce two Compacts: one on responding to the refugee crisis, and the other one on formulating a common managerial scheme for safe orderly and regular migration. The UN New York Declaration operated as a high-level political platform of officially acknowledging the complexity of human mobility and the need for coordinated action.[67] The UN High Commissioner for Refugees, Filippo Grandi, characteristically stressed that 'The Declaration marks a political commitment of unprecedented force and resonance. It fills what has been a perennial gap in the international protection system – that of truly sharing responsibility for refugees.'[68]

As the declaration itself highlights, state sovereignty remains important but, in our er of a globalised world, the new challenge of mixed migration movements can be addressed only via continuous cooperation and 'shared responsibility' among the relevant stakeholders.[69] In this context, the states are committed to respect international law and human rights, and produce two compacts of

---

[64] https://graduateinstitute.ch/sites/default/files/2020–03/globe25_0.pdf?fbclid=IwAR2TVCEl-lQ3NxAjnbRAKNQnIrw7iijoJXU_1W-dopBeRo-mfoJl3_MZb90 (accessed 15 March 2020)

[65] For an excellent historical and normative overview of the evolution of the migration framework, see Vincent Chetail, *International Migration Law* (Oxford University Press, 2019).

[66] A/71/L.1*, NY Declaration for Refugees and Migrants, 13 September 2016.

[67] *Ibid.*

[68] www.unhcr.org/new-york-declaration-for-refugees-and-migrants.html

[69] Par. 11–21.

understanding for refugees and migrants.[70] For a leading commentator, the Declaration represents a *'milestone'* since *'it is the most comprehensive soft law instrument'* in the field of mixed migration movements both of refugees and of migrants.[71] Despite its shortcomings, that derive from its inherently compromisory nature, while oscillating between the notion of state sovereignty and humanity, the Declaration facilitated the production of two Compacts, one for refugees and the other one for migrants, whereas the International Organization for Migration (IOM) was elevated to a *related agency* within the UN system.[72] The production of two separate Compacts was justified upon the premises of a preexisting differentiated legal regime for refugees, that should not be jeopardized, and the insistence of some countries to reaffirm their control over their borders.[73] Similarly, the development process of the two Compacts reflected this diversity of vision and purpose. The Compact for Refugees was produced by the UNHCR, whereas the Compact for Migration was formulated within an intergovernmental framework with significant participation of various stakeholders.[74]

The UN Global Compact for Migration (GCM) was negotiated for two years after several rounds of consultations among several stakeholders and it was scheduled for adoption in a major intergovernmental conference in Morocco.[75] The GCM is founded upon a set of guiding principles and a vision of collective commitment to enhance further cooperation.[76] As it is emphasized, the Compact *'[s]ets out our common understanding, shared responsibilities and unity of purpose regarding migration, making it work for all'.*[77] While the cross-cutting

---

[70] Prof. Guild has emphasized how *human rights oriented* is the NY Declaration mainly due to the work of several UN agencies in Guild & Grant, 'Migration Governance in the UN: What is the Global Compact and What does it mean?', Queen Mary University of London, School of Law, Legal Studies Research Paper No. 252/2017.

[71] Vincent Chetail, *International Migration Law* supra note 65 at 323.

[72] For an initial critical comment on the nature of the IOM as a 'non-normative' organization, see Guild et al., 'IOM and the UN: Unfinished Business', Queen Mary University of London, School of Law, Legal Studies Research Paper No. 255/2017.

[73] Vincent Chetail, International Migration Law, supra note 65 at 323.

[74] https://refugeesmigrants.un.org

[75] Global Compact on Migration, A/Res/ 73/195 January 2019.

[76] For an introductory analysis on the genesis and final shape of the GCM, see, Michele Klein Solomon and Suzanne Sheldon, 'The Global Compact for Migration: From the Sustainable Development Goals to a Comprehensive Agreement on Safe, Orderly and Regular Migration', (2018) 30 *International Journal of Refugee Law*, 584, Kathleen Newland, 'The Global Compact for Safe, Orderly and Regular Migration: An Unlikely Achievement', (2018) 30 *International Journal of Refugee Law*, 657 and Elspeth Guild, 'The UN Global Compact for Safe, Orderly and Regular Migration: What Place for Human Rights?' (2018) 30 *International Journal of Refugee Law*, 661, Guild, 'The UN's Search for a Global Compact on Safe, Orderly and Regular Migration' (2018) 18 *German Law Journal*, 1779.

[77] Global Compact on Migration, A/Res/73/195 January 2019.

and interdependent guiding principles of the Compact are listed as: Being people-centred, based on international cooperation, with respect of national sovereignty (in conformity with international law), adherence to rule of law, implementation of the 2030 Agenda for Sustainable Development, protection of human rights, being gender-responsive and child-sensitive and finally being developed around a *whole of government* and *whole of society approach*.[78] In this context, the Compact sets up 23 specific objectives, prescribes a follow-up and review process, and thus it departs from previous soft law instruments since it endorses a holistic vision, despite the lack of a design framework.[79] Yet, what is of equal significance is that the GCM is not a legally binding document and does not create new legal obligations for the state parties, as repeatedly highlighted in its text.

However, despite all these assurances that the Compact reflects solely political commitment, a series of countries decided not to sign up the UN Global Compact for Migration just before its adoption in Marrakesh on 10–11 December 2018.[80] The United States of America had opened pandora's box already in 2017, with President Trump stating that the 'Global Compact would undermine the sovereign right of the United States to enforce our immigration laws and secure our borders'.[81] The United States were followed by many others such as Australia, Israel, Brazil, including a considerable number of European Union countries.[82] In some EU countries, the Compact triggered a political crisis,[83] notwithstanding the relatively unified position adopted by the EU during the consultation period.[84] The UN Special Representative for International Migration, Louise Arbour, expressed her

---

[78]   *Ibid.*

[79]   This critical point has been raised by Chetail, whereas Aleinikoff and Martin speak of a *'laundry list of worthwhile objectives'* in 'Making the Global Compacts Work, What Future for Refugees and Migrants?', Policy Brief, 2018, Zolberg Institute on Migration and Mobility/Kaldor Center for International Refugee law.

[80]   www.un.org/en/conf/migration/index.shtml

[81]   www.nytimes.com/2017/12/03/world/americas/united-nations-migration-pact.html?module=inline (accessed 20 March 2020)

[82]   See www.theguardian.com/australia-news/2018/jul/25/dutton-says-australia-wont-surrender-our-sovereignty-by-signing-un-migration-deal, www.kormany.hu/en/ministry-of-foreign-affairs-and-trade/news/hungary-is-exiting-the-adoption-process-of-the-global-compact-for-migration, www.reuters.com/article/us-un-migrants-austria/austria-to-withdraw-from-u-n-mi gration-agreement-apa-idUSKCN1N50JZ, https://www.ft.com/content/49335a14-debo-11e8-9f 04-38d397e6661c, https://balkaninsight.com/2018/11/13/balkan-states-split-on-migration-ahead-of-the-un-summit-11–12-2018/, www.politico.eu/article/czech-republic-migration-refugees-latest-eu-country-to-reject-united-nations-treaty/

[83]   Most characteristically in Belgium, www.lesoir.be/191060/article/2018–11-20/theo-francken-sur -le-pacte-migratoire-de-lonu-cest-au-chef-du-gouvernement-de (accessed 20 March 2020)

[84]   See http://eumigrationlawblog.eu/too-much-unity-in-the-european-unions-external-migration-policy/ (accessed 21 March 2020)

220   *Maria Varaki*

disappointment, stating that these 'U-turns on Global Compact reflect poorly on countries concerned'.[85]

The image of a massive influx of migrants in countries already susceptible to populist rhetoric, nationalist hysteria, and xenophobic sentiment[86] haunted political leaders, diplomats, and civil society. The perceived danger of migration for state sovereignty, together with some, admittedly anaemic, references to human rights law, generated hostility and panic about an emerging 'human right to immigration'. Here one could claim that this was not a totally surprising move given the previous problematic EU-Turkey 'Pact',[87] the infamous cooperation of Italy/EU with Libya,[88] and the shameful closed Western Balkan route,[89] despite persistent allegations of human rights violations, push backs, torture, and modern forms of slavery taking place just a couple of kilometres away from the coast line of Europe. Still, the Compact was adopted, 152 states voted in favour, 5 cast a negative vote (Czech Republic, Hungary, Israel, Poland, and the United States), and 12 abstained.

8.3.2 *From Berlin to New York*

In the meantime, it was not only Trump, Orbán, or Bolsonaro who made headlines. In the fall of 2015, one leader who occupied the interest of the media was Chancellor Merkel with her decision not to close the borders to one million migrants, stuck between borders on their way from Greece.[90] Of course, one could say that the rise of the extreme right at least in some European countries can be partly attributed to those decisions of 'opening' borders. Additionally, there are some voices that argue that Merkel's policy to bypass the official European asylum system contributed to its further collapse.[91] These

---

[85] https://news.un.org/en/story/2018/11/1026791 (accessed 21 March 2020)

[86] In this regard, see the Venice Commission opinion for Hungary, www.osce.org/odihr/385932?, and the 2018 report by the UN Special Rapporteur on Contemporary Forms of Racism, Racial Discrimination, Xenophobia and other forms of Intolerance before the UN General Assembly, UNHCR' Report by the UN Special Rapporteur on Contemporary Forms of Racism, Racial Discrimination, Xenophobia and other forms of Intolerance' (2018) UN Doc A/73/305

[87] www.consilium.europa.eu/en/press/press-releases/2016/03/18/eu-turkey-statement/ (accessed 23 March 2020)

[88] http://eumigrationlawblog.eu/a-blind-spot-in-the-migration-debate-international-responsibility-of -the-eu-and-its-member-states-for-cooperating-with-the-libyan-coastguard-and-militias/ (accessed 23 March 2020)

[89] For an overview, see V. Stoyanova and E. Karageorgiou (eds.), *The New Asylum and Transit Countries in Europe During and in the Aftermath of the 2015/2016 Crisis* (Brill, 2018).

[90] www.nytimes.com/2015/09/06/world/europe/migrant-crisis-austria-hungary-germany.html (accessed 22 March 2020)

[91] Betts & Collier (eds.), *Refuge: Transforming a Broken Refugee System* (Penguin Classics, 2017) at 84.

Imaginary Leadership and Displacement

are legitimate arguments that reflect a pragmatic analysis of the current zeitgeist, although some of them have been rebutted by subsequent quantitative analysis.[92] More recently, a book appeared claiming that her motives were less humanitarian and more typical of a pragmatic approach, since she was predominantly concerned about her future legacy, rather than being remembered as the Chancellor of closed borders.[93] It could be the case; still this is not my reading of her behaviour. As I emphasized at the beginning of this chapter, the scope of the current contribution is not to adopt a theory of who is a virtuous leader and what is a virtuous behaviour. In a more modest way, my aim is to shed light on particular decisions and invite the readers to reflect on them and their significance deploying a sensibility of virtue ethics. This is a narrower invitation that acknowledges the cultural, temporal, and contextual diversity of the virtues I mentioned earlier.

Another actor who displayed his own stigma during this period was the UN Secretary-General, António Guterres, no stranger to the global developments around the phenomenon of forced displacement. For years he acted as the UN High Commissioner for Refugees and one could diagnose his particularly dynamic role in framing the agenda during the period we discuss. In December 2017, he produced a report purported to act as an input to the ongoing negotiations regarding the Global Compact for safe, orderly, and regular migration. The title of the report 'Making Migration Work For All' indicates a particular idea of migration through the Sustainable Development Framework, and provides some very intriguing references and suggestions to those who were about to participate in the consultation and negotiation process. In particular, the SG, while framing his intervention, highlighted the four 'fundamental considerations' that should guide joint state action:[94] (a) maximize the benefits of migration for

---

[92] Ludger Pries, 'We Will Manage It' – Did Chancellor Merkel's Dictum Increase or Even Cause the Refugee Movement in 2015?' (2019) *International Migration*, 18.

[93] As this chapter is finalized, a movie based on this book is about to be released, shedding light on those intense days of the 2015 fall, Robin Alexander, *The Driven Ones, Merkel and Refugee Policy*, 2017.

[94] Report of the Secretary General, 'Making Migration Work for All', (2017) UN Doc A/72/643 par.5 'In the light of these four considerations, Member States must act together to protect the human rights of migrants and expand pathways for safe, orderly and regular migration, while safeguarding their borders, laws and the interests of their societies. National authorities are responsible for defining effective responses to migration, but no State can address the issue alone. Individual Governments can set the terms for access to their territory and the treatment of migrants within their borders – subject to international legal obligations – but they cannot unilaterally override the economic, demographic, environmental and other factors that shape migration and will continue to do so, including in ways we do not yet fully anticipate. Migration, as noted in the New York Declaration for Refugees and Migrants (see resolution 71/1), demands global approaches and solutions'.

everyone instead of minimizing risks, (b) strengthen the rule of law by committing to international law and human rights, (c) promote a vision of security that reflects both state and human components, and (d) transform migration from an act of desperation to a workable choice for everyone.[95] Yet the most powerful component of the Secretary-General's message is his call for 'a respectful and realistic debate about migration'. There António Guterres stressed that

> [W]e must sadly acknowledge that xenophobic political narratives about migration are all too widespread today. . . . [P]olitical leaders must take responsibility for reframing national discourses on the issue, as well as for policy reforms.
> [W]e must also show respect for communities that fear they are 'losing out' because of migration . . . . Communities blighted by inequality and economic deprivation frequently blame migration for their troubles. While it is necessary to explain why such views are mistaken, it is essential to address the underlying vulnerabilities and fears of all citizens so that we can make migration work.
> [W]e should reinforce more realistic policy debates with better data about migration.
> [A] final way to promote more respectful discussions regarding migration is to avoid dehumanizing language. Pejorative talk of 'illegal immigrants' blocks reasoned discussions about the motives and needs of individuals . . . . We should aim to discuss migrants in terms that respect their dignity and rights, just as we must respect the needs and views of communities affected by migration.[96]

The report produced by Guterres, apart from the symbolic validation that it conferred upon the entire negotiation process of the Global Compact on Migration, can be also perceived as a fine balance exercise. On the one hand, it makes a strong argument against xenophobia and dehumanizing language, urging the usage of data and evidence. On the other hand, it acknowledges the fear of the receiving communities, indicating respect and civility. His call for taking seriously the concerns of the affected communities is a call to move beyond complacency and intransigence.

8.4 IMAGINARY LEADERSHIP AND MIGRATION GOVERNANCE

The current chapter, by focusing on the virtues of *phronesis*, courage, imagination, and moderation, purports to help build an argument in favour of an ethical re-assessment of decisions that determine the fate of ordinary people. In this regard, I concur with those who contest the magnanimity of a rule-oriented

---

[95] Ibid.
[96] *Ibid.* par.18.

Imaginary Leadership and Displacement

solution to problems, recognizing the existence of gaps that cannot be addressed solely by rules. Forced displacement dilemmas indicate the extent of this problem. My argument is that different leaders, those endowed with the virtue of *phronesis*, including imaginary deliberation, are more likely to behave differently, showing various shades of empathy and moderation according to the challenges on the ground. This can be attributed to the diagnosis that phronetic judgment takes into consideration the concerns of other people, while moving beyond intransigence and complacency. At the same time, phronetic assessment is not based on predetermined criteria and thus it accommodates the necessary flexibility.

Here, I would like to return to the diversity on state behaviour I briefly mentioned earlier. For the purposes of this piece, I focus on the decision by some states not to adopt the Compact on Migration and compare it with the decision by Chancellor Merkel to 'open' the German borders together with the report of the Secretary-General. I will not focus extensively on the EU-Turkey pact or the Italy (EU)-Libya cooperation agreement. The reason for this choice, as I already mentioned at the beginning, lies first with the significance of the GCM as the very first global response to the phenomenon of mixed forced displacement,[97] reflecting how Aleinikoff described the legal fragmentation of migration as *substance without architecture*.[98] Despite its shortcomings, in strictly legal terms, I concur with those who believe that the Global Compact is a major achievement that can be further developed, functioning as a platform for common action and shared perceptions. Secondly, I do not focus on the infamous EU-Turkey pact, because I think it deserves a separate full account analysis due to its particularities and legal, policy, and moral implications. The so-called 'one for one scheme' pact, between the EU and Turkey in March 2016, prescribed that, for the return to Turkey from the Greek islands of every irregular migrant or asylum seeker whose application had been declared inadmissible, another Syrian would be resettled to the EU from Turkey.[99] This 'statement'[100] also authorized a financial assistance of

[97] A series of scholars from various disciplines have highlighted the importance of the GCM as a centralized and multilevel attempt to understand migration; Colleen Thouez, 'Strengthening Migration Governance: The UN as "Wingman"' (2019) 45 *Journal of Ethnic and Migration Studies*, 1242.

[98] Alexander T. Aleinikoff, 'International Legal Norms on Migration: Substance Without Architecture', in Cholewinski, Perruchoud & McDonald (eds.), *International Migration Law: Developing Paradigms and Key Challenges* (TMC Asser Press, 2007), 467–479, Alexander Betts (ed.), *Global Migration Governance* (Oxford University Press, 2011).

[99] EU-Turkey Statement, 18 March 2017, www.consilium.europa.eu/en/press/press-releases/20 16/03/18-eu-turkey-sta-tement/ (accessed 23 March 2020)

[100] The EU General Court rendered it lacked jurisdiction to assess the substance of this statement, https://eur-lex.europa.eu/legal-content/en/TXT/?uri=celex:62016TO0193

Maria Varaki

six billion euros to Turkey in order to accommodate this arrangement. This pact has been extensively analysed, criticized, and mystified by a series of scholars and politicians.[101] Yet, it is not the subject of this analysis.

Contrary to that, I chose to focus on the decision by Chancellor Merkel in the fall of 2015 to defy the context of hostility and suspicion towards the *xenos* and act proactively in a moment of dystopic inaction, while thousands of people were trapped among European borders. The reason for choosing this case is related to the immense contrast between her behaviour and that of several other European leaders. Additionally, one should not overlook the domestic political environment that reflected uneasiness, not to mention hostility, towards her thoughts of not closing the borders.

From one side, several states decided to abstain from a non-legally binding document (they had actually negotiated for long time) and were informed about its symbolic significance. Some of them not only abstained or voted against but they also sabotaged it and misused its language and purpose for domestic political gains.[102] On the other hand, a 'lone' leader, contrary to the overall negative climate, decided to welcome one million strangers, while she had no time to deliberate further and no luxury to procrastinate her decision. It was a seminal action in terms of both time and place. Not only that, but two years later when she was asked about her 2015 decision she replied that she would do exactly the same because the circumstances were 'extraordinary'.[103] Via the lenses of the particular sensibility I explained earlier, the decision by Chancellor Merkel to open the German borders can be cast as a case study of empathetic, courageous, and imaginary leadership. An exemplary leadership that responded to 'extraordinary' circumstances as she said when a dire reality stigmatized the European continent. In that particular moment, she exercised phronetic judgment, and while considering the general and the particular she somehow managed to 'save' the ideal of Europe. That of solidarity, humanism,

---

[101] For a critical analysis of the EU-Turkey pact, see, characteristically, Violeta Moreno-Lax, 'The Migration Partnership Framework and the EU-Turkey Deal: Lessons for the Global Compact on Migration Process?', in Gammeltoft-Hansen, Guild, Moreno-Lax, Panizzon, Roele (eds.,) What is a Compact? (Raul Wallenberg Institute, 2017) (Raul Wallenberg Institute, 2017), but also see Vincent Chetail, 'Will the EU-Turkey migrant deal work in practice?', 29 March 2016, http://graduateinstitute.ch/home/research/research-news.html/_/news/research/2016/will-the-eu-turkey-migrant-deal; Henri Labayle and Philippe de Bruycker, 'The EU-Turkey Agreement on migration and asylum: False pretences or a fool's bargain?', 1 April 2016, http://eumigrationlawblog.eu/the-eu-turkey-agreement-on-migration-and-asylum-false-prete nces-or-a-fools-bargain/

[102] For an excellent historical overview of the two Compacts, see Ferris & Donato (eds.), *Refugees, Migration and Global Governance* (Routledge, 2020).

[103] www.politico.eu/article/angela-merkel-defends-open-border-migration-refugee-policy-germany/ (accessed 23 March 2020)

Imaginary Leadership and Displacement

and consideration of the common good, strengthening at the same time the normative foundations of the international legal order.

Yet, here I would like to clarify once more that I am not suggesting that her decision was the only 'right' action. As I have explained at the beginning of this chapter, due to the elusiveness of the content of the virtues, one could reasonably argue that an opposite decision could be equally phronetic, maybe though less empathetic. A decision not to open the borders perhaps would not have contributed towards the rise of the extreme right and it could may have avoided the accusations of the defiance of the Dublin system. Although I disagree with this position, I feel obliged to illustrate it. This can be explained from my understanding of virtues, which does not imply a causation of right action. Additionally, it is important to highlight here that I am not suggesting that she is a virtuous person while the other leaders are not. The same person can behave differently in various contexts. Particularly in her case, it is intriguing to explore, only a couple of months later, her personal role in the infamous EU-Turkey pact. In this regard, what can be argued here is that one person can display some shades of virtues in one case and different shades in another case. This example sheds light both on the contextual and on the indeterminate elements of virtues[104] and justifies a more cautious and modest sensibility in the evaluation of behaviours and actions.

Regarding the report of the Secretary-General and his recommendation, I concentrate on its main call for 'a respectful and realistic debate about migration'. I contend that his phrase reasonably reflects a phronetic judgment that entails not only empathy but also moderation. It is a call that encourages the development of a shared prospect, acknowledging at the same time the limits of this endeavour. In this sense, his intervention can be assessed as an example of imaginary leadership that illustrates wisdom and empathy, in a fine combination of realism and constructive idealism. It is a call to world leaders not to miss the opportunity for a shared effort, without being at the same time overly ambitious and thus avoiding the risk of a strong backlash. One could reasonably argue that the recommendations of the Secretary-General reflected the three Weberian qualities for a politician or in our case for a leader; passion for a cause, feeling of responsibility, and a sense of proportion.[105]

So how could this ethical standing or its lack matter? I argue here that the behaviour of individuals matters in both ways. In other words, I concur with those who support that leaders are paradigms of excellence and inspiration, as

---

[104] See Daniel Russell, 'Putting Ideals in their Place', in Snow (ed.), *The Oxford Handbook of Virtue* (Oxford University Press, 2018), exploring a path-dependent development of virtues that requires practical wisdom.

[105] See Max Weber, 'The Profession and Vocation of Politics', in Lassman & Speirs (eds.), *Max Weber, Political Writings* (Cambridge University Press, 1994).

226   *Maria Varaki*

Amalia Amaya has meticulously argued.[106] In this sense, the decision by several
political leaders to withdraw from the Compact just before its adoption reflects
the kind of controversial leadership that may produce imitators or followers. My
central proposition claims that this decision functions in a multilayered dimension of ethical judgment and semiology. The former is related to the decision
per se, its effects, utility, and wisdom. The latter reflects the message it conveys.
Both of them are linked to the responsible exercise of judgment and ultimately
authority. As I have mentioned above, leaders bear responsibility for the way
they exercise their judgment. This exercise entails thinking and judging or else
deliberation. They have to make choices and take decisions while exercising
their discretion. This is the moment where I argue that *phronesis* is of indispensable importance as part of the desired intellectual kit of a leader. This is so,
because *phronesis* functions as a liberating force that connects the general with
the particular and accommodates the kind of deliberation that purports to
promote the common good. In this exercise, the virtue of *phronesis* provides
the necessary perspective of common sense that is representative of various views
and dimensions. The GCM represents this common good. As it emphasizes:

> This Global Compact offers a 360-degree vision of international migration and
> recognizes that a comprehensive approach is needed to optimize the overall
> benefits of migration, while addressing risks and challenges for individuals and
> communities in countries of origin, transit and destination. No country can
> address the challenges and opportunities of this global phenomenon on its
> own . . .. We acknowledge our shared responsibilities to one another as States
> Members of the United Nations to address each other's needs and concerns
> over migration, and an overarching obligation to respect, protect and fulfil the
> human rights of all migrants, regardless of their migration status, while pro-
> moting the security and prosperity of all our communities.[107]

The decision by particular leaders to withdraw from the GCM reflects their
failure to undertake this shared responsibility that ethical leadership implies.
Their behaviour becomes even more problematic when compared with the fine
balanced recommendations of the Secretary-General I mentioned above.

On a second level, one could question to what extent the particular attitude by
leaders affects the normativity of a non-legally binging document such as the
Global Compact on Migration?[108] Several experts have meticulously explained

---

[106]   See, in this volume, Amalia Amaya, 'Exemplarism, Virtue, and Ethical Leadership in
        International Organizations'. Ch.4.
[107]   Global Compact par. 11.
[108]   For an overview of the legal normativity of the Compact, see Gammeltoft-Hansen, Guild,
        Moreno-Lax, Panizzon, Roele (eds.,) *What is a Compact?* (Raul Wallenberg Institute, 2017).

Imaginary Leadership and Displacement 227

that the GCM is not a legally binding document but it could work instead in various ways, including leading to the future crystallization as binding normativity.[109] In this context, the exemplarism effects of ethical leadership described earlier can also consolidate different paths of normative understandings. Yes, the GCM is not legally binding, still it reiterates fundamental principles of international law and human rights. This is not of lesser importance especially in an era where the fundamental conceptions of the international legal order are severely challenged. When leaders adhere to the normative framework of the Compact, they express their commitment to keep open the modes of communication that can trigger action and thus normative developments. Additionally, in an era of de-formalization and managerialism, the Compact operates as an alternative platform of policy making and norm creation. The endorsement of this exceptional endeavour that attempts to provide an 'architectural' framework to the fragmented migration structure[110] conveys a message of responsible leadership that understands the challenges of our interdependent world and the risks of isolation. Yes, sovereignty defines some of the parameters of migration, still responsible leaders opt for joint action that indicates shared responsibility for the common good. This type of ethical leadership expresses resilience to the phenomenon of populist sovereignism; the establishment of binaries that nihilistically reject multilateralism without providing constructive critique and solutions but endorse instead polarisation, isolation, and parochialism. Against this background, if one adds the emotions of fear[111] or *thymos* for the other, together with growing uneasiness about identity questions,[112] then one is likely to face an explosive dystopian cocktail of nativism and resentment.

8.4.1 *Laboratory of Dilemmas*

Aeschylus' play *Iketides* (Suppliant Women) mirrors a laboratory of dilemmas: to accommodate people in need while securing the safety of the local ones. This is a historical dilemma of humanity, whereas Paul Ricoeur notices practical wisdom

---

[109] Chetail, *International Migration Law* supra note 65 speaking of the perils and promises of soft law in the migration front, Anne Peters, 'The Global Compact For Migration; to sign or not to sign?', November 2018, www.ejiltalk.org/the-global-compact-for-migration-to-sign-or-not-to-sign/ (accessed 23 March 2020).

[110] Alexander T. Aleinikoff, 'International Legal Norms on Migration: Substance Without Architecture', supra note 98; Vincent Chetail, 'The Architecture of International Migration Law: A Deconstructivist Design of Complexity and Contradiction', *AJIL Unbound*, 2017.

[111] Martha Nussbaum, *The Monarchy of Fear*, (Oxford University Press, 2018).

[112] Francis Fukuyama, *Identity* (Profile Books, 2018). This chapter is beyond the discussion of identity politics.

needs to be deployed in a way *'that best responds to tragic wisdom'*.[113] Until recently, the predominant focus was on refugees, people who are persecuted and require international protection outside the territory of their own country. Yet, history has proved that life moves beyond binaries and the emergence of mixed migration movements has rendered the line between the strict definition of refugees and migrants blurry. In this context, migration dilemmas become more demanding and complicated. This piece argues that a particular kind of leadership, the one I call imaginary leadership, can shed light on the complexity of decision-making in an era where leaders and policy makers oscillate between the calls of traditional sovereignty and the demands of universal justice. The reason this particular leadership can become critical is due to its 'enlarged mentality' sensibility. Seyla Benhabib has highlighted in her recent work on the lives of prominent Jewish exiles how this concept of enlarged mentality for the 'eternally half-other' developed by Kant was further embraced by Arendt and others especially during the '30s and '40s.[114] This enlarged mentality, as Benhabib says, is a kind of culture that

> [e]nables us to take the standpoint of the other, not by eliminating the distance between us through some impossible expectations of full empathy, but rather, by helping us create that negotiable in-betweenness, through which I come to respect you as my equal, as the bearer of shared universal human dignity.[115]

For Benhabib, the cultivation of such enlarged mentality '[i]s never an act of passive contemplation but demands the unsettling encounter with the other, whose otherness compels us to turn inward and to reflect upon the stranger in ourselves'.[116] This enlarged mentality is the essence of imaginary leadership, when those who exercise their judgment and take decisions have to transcend the borders of their mind and implement what António Guterres in January 2020 asked them to do: 'My message to world leaders is simple. Put People first, their needs, their aspirations, their rights.'[117] I would also add 'show empathy, exercise imagination, and embrace a sensibility of humanity, where people are not just numbers but souls with dreams and feelings of fear and hope.'

---

[113]   Paul Ricoeur, *Oneself as Another*, (University of Chicago Press, 1991, Blamey trans.), 247.
[114]   Seyla Benhabib, *Exile, Statelessness and Migration* (Princeton University Press, 2018) at 32.
[115]   *Ibid.*
[116]   *Ibid.*
[117]   António Guterres, UN Secretary General's Press Conference at the outset of the 74th Session of the General Assembly (Sept. 18, 2019) available at https://www.un.org/sg/en/content/sg/press-encounter/2019-09-18/secretary-generals-press-conference-the-outset-of-the-74th-session-of-the-general-assembly

9

Revisiting *Rainbow Warrior*

Virtue and Understanding in International Arbitration

Jan Klabbers[*]

9.1 INTRODUCTION

In the burgeoning realm of global governance, ethics has occupied an increasingly prominent place in recent years. One of the buzzwords of the last two decades or so has been 'accountability', a term which carries overtones of proper behaviour, control and responsibility.[1] Persons in a position of leadership emphasize their concern for such things as full financial disclosure and transparency.[2] The humanitarian intervention over Kosovo may have been illegal but was nonetheless, many have claimed, ethically justifiable.[3] Codes of ethics have been devised both for the international bar and, somewhat lukewarm, for the international judiciary.[4] The infamous 'torture memos' have thrown into perspective the need for legal advisors to behave ethically;[5] writings have appeared on the ethical aspects of humanitarian missions,[6] and

---

[*] I am indebted to the editors for their incisive comments on an earlier draft, and for much, much else besides.

[1] Onora O'Neill, *A Question of Trust* (Cambridge University Press, 2002).

[2] This prominently featured on the website of the previous United Nations Secretary-General, Ban Ki-moon.

[3] The classic rendition is Bruno Simma, 'NATO, the UN, and the Use of Force: Legal Aspects', (1999) 10 *European Journal of International Law*, 1–22.

[4] See, for example, the Burgh House Principles on the Independence of the International Judiciary, adopted in 2004 and available via www.brandeis.edu/ethics/internationaljustice/ethicsintljud.html (accessed 13 December 2018); related are the Oslo Recommendations for Enhancing the Legitimacy of International Courts, adopted in 2018 and available at www.jus.uio.no/pluricourts/english/blog/geir-ulfstein/2018–08–01-biij.html (accessed 13 December 2018).

[5] For instance, David Luban, 'The Torture Lawyers of Washington', in David Luban, *Legal Ethics and Human Dignity* (Cambridge University Press, 2007), 162–205; one version of the inside story is told in Jack L. Goldsmith, *The Terror Presidency: Law and Judgment Inside the Bush Administration* (New York: Norton, 2007).

[6] Hugo Slim, *Humanitarian Ethics: A Guide to the Morality of Aid in War and Disaster* (London: Hurst & Co., 2015).

several studies have been published focusing on the ethics of the international legal order as such,[7] the ethics of international commercial arbitration,[8] or the ethics of the international bar.[9] Most of this has been Kantian in one way or another, at least nominally so, although one or two consequentialists have chipped in as well.[10]

Perhaps surprisingly, there have been very few attempts to discuss global governance or international law from a virtue ethical perspective,[11] despite the circumstance that virtue ethics has started to influence thinking about law and the judiciary in domestic settings. For several decades now, lawyers and moral philosophers have been discussing the possibilities for a virtuous law,[12] discussing such issues as whether the law should stimulate particular virtues,[13] whether the law should set a good example and not sponsor or endorse non-virtuous behaviour,[14] or discussing the relations between virtue ethics and the Rule of Law.[15] And for some ten to fifteen years now,[16] special attention has been directed at the virtues of judges, often if not exclusively[17] under the heading of virtue jurisprudence.[18]

Much of this literature, both on law and virtues generally and on virtue jurisprudence more specifically, has remained limited to the domestic legal setting. The law at issue is, typically, domestic law; the courts and judges at issue are, equally typically, domestic courts and judges. The international judiciary

---

[7] Steven R. Ratner, *The Thin Justice of International Law: A Moral Reckoning of the Law of Nations* (Oxford University Press, 2015).

[8] Catherine A. Rogers, *Ethics in International Arbitration* (Oxford University Press, 2014).

[9] Arman Sarvarian, *Professional Ethics at the International Bar* (Oxford University Press, 2013).

[10] Most well known is Peter Singer, *One World: The Ethics of Globalization*, 2nd edn. (New Haven CT: Yale University Press, 2004); Ratner, *Thin Justice*, is a rare example of an international lawyer self-identifying as a consequentialist.

[11] With the exception of Jamie Gaskarth, 'Where Would We Be Without Rules? A Virtue Ethics Approach to Foreign Policy Analysis', (2011) 37 *Review of International Studies*, 393–415, and Jamie Gaskarth, 'The Virtues in International Society', (2012) 18 *European Journal of International Relations*, 431–453.

[12] For a good general overview, see Amalia Amaya and Ho Hock Lai (eds.), *Law, Virtue and Justice* (Oxford: Hart, 2013).

[13] Robert P. George, *Making Men Moral: Civil Liberties and Public Morality* (Oxford: Clarendon Press, 1993).

[14] Kimberley Brownlee, 'What's Virtuous about the Law?', (2015) 22 *Legal Theory*, 1–17.

[15] George R. Wright, 'The Rule of Law: A Currently Incoherent Idea That Can be Redeemed through Virtue', (2015) 43 *Hofstra Law Review*, 1123–1147.

[16] An early and somewhat ambivalent forerunner is Stephen J. Burton, *Judging in Good Faith* (Cambridge University Press, 1992).

[17] H. Jefferson Powell, *Constitutional Conscience: The Moral Dimension of Judicial Decision* (Chicago, IL: University of Chicago Press, 2008).

[18] See Colin Farrelly and Lawrence B. Solum (eds.), *Virtue Jurisprudence* (New York: Palgrave MacMillan, 2008); Jonathan Soeharno, *The Integrity of the Judge* (Aldershot: Ashgate, 2009).

has been by and large neglected – indeed, to the limited extent that there have been attempts at presenting an ethics for the international judiciary, these have manifested a strongly deontological approach to ethics, and have embedded ethical principles into wider thoughts on the legal status of international judges. The Burgh House Principles, for example, the most emblematic attempt to date, aim to capture the independence of the judiciary through a number of rules about, for instance, extra-curricular activities, past links to either cases or parties, or instructions concerning conflict of interest, instructing judges not to sit in cases in the outcome of which they 'hold any material personal, professional or financial interest'.[19] The underlying premise, it seems, is to set ideal standards of more or less universal validity and applicability, suitable for an abstract universe in which one case is much the same as the next case, zooming in on particular acts that may be reproachable, and with scant attention for the sort of person who ends up on the international bench. The one exception is the reminder that persons appointed to such office should be individuals of 'high moral character, integrity and conscientiousness';[20] the other principles (and sub-principles) are all related to appointment procedures, working conditions, and objectively verifiable conduct.

And yet, the international judiciary, although being a judiciary, is working in a setting radically different from most domestic judges, even though there might be some overlap with domestic constitutional courts. To make a trite point, there is no constitution in the international legal order, no recognized hierarchy of norms; there are no prisons to lock up recalcitrant states, and no police forces to hunt them down. The international legal order is a legal order, but is both embedded in and constituted by its political environment in ways that do not quite apply to a family court in Long Island or a district court somewhere in Bavaria.

And this entails that international judges are confronted with judicial or ethical dilemmas unlikely to occur in the same way in domestic settings. One can think, for instance, of the dilemma confronting one of the judges (judge Röling) sitting on the post-war Tokyo tribunal, who once he had started his work found to his dismay that he had been lured into what was largely a show trial. How then do you find an ethically sound way of addressing your dilemma?[21] Röling did so not by resigning (as he had seriously considered a few times) but, eventually, by re-thinking the notion of crimes against peace

---

[19] See the *Burgh House Principles*, principle 11.1.
[20] *Ibid.*, principle 2.1.
[21] Jan Klabbers, 'Principled Pragmatist? Bert Röling and the Emergence of International Criminal Law', in Frédéric Mégrét and Immi Tallgren (eds.), *The Dawn of a Discipline* (Cambridge University Press, 2020), 205–229.

to underline that it was a retroactive invention in the years immediately after the Second World War. He had no problem punishing enemies, but cherished the classic *nullum crime sine lege* principle; to him, post-war action was a matter of incapacitating the enemy in the absence of a legal prohibition concerning the commencement of war, rather than pretending to apply non-existent 'law'. In the end, he resolved his personal discomfort by writing a dissenting opinion that, unlike the majority opinion, has stood the test of time.[22]

One can think of the ethical issues emerging, in particular in international criminal tribunals, due to judges having earlier been vocally discussing individuals and groups later appearing before the tribunals on which they sit. A well-known example is that of Geoffrey Robertson, sitting on the Appeals Chamber of the Special Court for Sierra Leone, having earlier expressed strong opinions on behaviour taking place in Sierra Leone. He agreed to step down as president of the Appeals Chamber and recused himself from some cases, but did not resign altogether, suggesting that doing so would endanger the independence of the judiciary. The bigger question, though, as some have observed, is why he accepted the appointment to begin with – surely, a lawyer of his calibre must have realized that his earlier writings could cast a shadow over his own judicial independence.[23]

One can also think of the example of the human rights judge who would prefer to dissent on a substantive decision, but feels that the need for a unanimous judgment outweighs his own individual opinion, given the political situation in the state against which the judgment is being rendered: should such a judge join the majority for political reasons, or stick to his individual opinion? And is there a sliding scale here: the more tangential the object of disagreement, the stronger the pull of the majority? Issues such as these are almost the bread and butter of international lawyers, but are unlikely to surface in domestic settings in quite the same ways.

In turn, virtue jurisprudence usually occupies itself with a limited set of questions, often relating to the activity of judging *stricto sensu*: is a judgment ethically justifiable or not, and if so, under what conditions? Which virtues

---

[22] Röling's dissent is conveniently reproduced in B. V. A. Röling and C. F. Rüter (eds.), *The Tokyo Judgment: The International Military Tribunal for the Far East (IMTFE) 29 April 1946–12 November 1948* (Amsterdam: University Press Amsterdam, 1977), Volume II, 1041–1148.

[23] For a useful discussion of the incident, see James Cockayne, 'Special Court for Sierra Leone: Decisions on the Recusal of Judge Robertson and Winter', (2004) 2 *Journal of International Criminal Justice*, 1154–1162; a more in-depth exploration is Frédéric Mégrét, 'International Judges and Experts' Impartiality and the Problem of Past Declarations', (2011) 10 *Law and Practice of International Courts and Tribunals*, 31–66.

does a virtuous judge display, or should a virtuous judge display? Hence, much of the literature focuses on corruption, or partiality, or laziness or some such traits – much of the literature on virtue jurisprudence, for all its merits, is preoccupied with the question of how virtue ethics can contribute to virtuous judgments. To the extent that the virtues are made to serve a goal, it is the goal of arriving at virtuous judgments, trying to flesh out what a virtuous judge would do.

Purists might claim that virtue for a purpose is not proper virtue, but that is a discussion for another day. I would like to explore a different role that virtue ethics, or virtue jurisprudence, may perform, and that is an explanatory purpose: the virtues may not only be instrumental in arriving at better judgments, but can also help us to understand aspects of judgments that, on a different analysis, remain hidden from view. Borrowing an analogy, one might say that a virtue-based analysis can act like a colouring agent, highlighting aspects that cannot otherwise be seen.[24]

Hence, this chapter aims to kill two birds with one stone. I aim to discuss some of the specific ethical issues arising in an international setting, issues that may arise in ways that are unlikely to occur before domestic courts. And I aim to point to an explanatory role for the virtues, instead of a strictly normative role. A good example of an issue bringing both elements to the fore is the classic *Rainbow Warrior* arbitration, an international award rendered in 1990, which has always contained a puzzling element, an element that somehow cannot be grasped by legal analysis alone nor, as it will transpire, by employing ethical perspectives other than the virtues.[25] Let me begin by recalling the facts of the case, and follow up by suggesting that the case neatly illustrates some pressures unlikely to be present before domestic courts, and discussing the ethical problem thus identified. In the process, I aim to shed light on this particular arbitration, and aim to illustrate how virtue ethics can be of use for understanding and evaluating manifestations of global governance. That is not particularly ambitious: I am not claiming a role for the virtues in guiding global governance – at least not here, and that owes something, in part, to the idea that international courts and tribunals have as their primary task the settlement of disputes rather than guiding action. What I am claiming though

---

[24] I borrow the analogy from Joseph H. H. Weiler, as mentioned during a discussion on global governance at New York University School of Law, in 2010: https://blogs.law.nyu.edu/maga zine/2010/roundtable-global-governance/ (accessed 12 December 2018).

[25] For general commentaries, see Michael Pugh, 'Legal Aspects of the *Rainbow Warrior* Affair', (1987) 36 *International and Comparative Law Quarterly*, 655–669; Scott Davidson, 'The *Rainbow Warrior* Arbitration Concerning the Treatment of the French Agents Mafart and Prieur', (1991) 40 *International and Comparative Law Quarterly*, 446–457.

234   *Jan Klabbers*

is that a virtue perspective can help us understand a decision that otherwise remains sketchy at best, and this explanatory or epistemological role is the result not of ascribing virtue to the tribunal, but because a virtue perspective may even help to 'open up' a decision that is not in itself particularly virtuous. Instead of trying to find virtue, then, I am using virtue here as a prism, a way of looking at an arbitral award, a microscope if you will. All this sounds hopelessly abstract and counter-intuitive, so I should share my journey. This journey started, years ago, with reading the award and not understanding a particular aspect of the decision.[26]

9.2 THE HORNS OF THE DILEMMA

In July 1985, a Greenpeace ship, the *Rainbow Warrior*, was lying in port in Auckland, New Zealand, apparently awaiting the possibility to disrupt French nuclear testing in French Polynesia. An explosion took place on board, killing a Dutch photographer and destroying the ship. It quickly transpired that this was the work of two agents of the French secret service, Major Alain Mafart and Captain Dominique Prieur, both of whom were arrested by the New Zealand authorities, tried for manslaughter, and sentenced to ten years' imprisonment. The French, horrified by the thought of French government agents in a foreign prison, thought that this was a bad idea and suggested a different settlement, involving the payment of compensation. New Zealand initially disagreed, and following a stalemate, the UN Secretary-General was asked for a binding ruling. Part of his ruling, rendered in 1986 and confirmed in a subsequent set of agreements between the two states, was that Mafart and Prieur would spend a period of three years in relative isolation on a French military base on the island of Hao. This was not incarceration strictly speaking, but obviously limited their freedom to move considerably: while their families were allowed to join them, Mafart and Prieur could not be removed from Hao, except with the consent of New Zealand.

And so it went, until Mafart fell ill and was removed from Hao in order to receive treatment in Paris for what was labelled an urgent medical condition – without the consent of New Zealand. And so it went, until Prieur was removed from the island in order to address possible complications regarding her

---

[26] *Case Concerning the Difference between New Zealand and France Concerning the Interpretation or Application of Two Agreements, Concluded on 9 July 1986 Between the Two States and which Related to the Problems Arising from the Rainbow Warrior Affair*, award of 30 April 1990, reproduced in 20 *UN Reports of International Arbitral Awards*, 215–284 (hereinafter referred to as Award, if only for brevity's sake).

pregnancy[27] and visit her dying father in France – again without the consent of New Zealand. France flagrantly violated the terms of the agreement, and New Zealand, obviously, was none too happy with this. Eventually, the matter was submitted to arbitration before a panel of three lawyers: one appointed by France, one by New Zealand, and one appointed by the parties together, a prominent international lawyer from Uruguay.

This is where matters became curious for, remember, the idea had been that Mafart and Prieur would be held on Hao for a period of three years: this was what the Secretary-General's ruling and the subsequent bilateral agreement had provided. In the words of the agreement, 'Major Mafart and Captain Prieur will be transferred to a French military facility on the island of Hao for a period of not less than three-years.' It seems that there is only one plausible reading of this clause: they shall spend at least three years on Hao, and not a day less.

Still, the arbitral tribunal decided otherwise. It decided that the three-year period mentioned in the agreement referred to the duration of the agreement, not the duration of the confinement. Instead of freezing the clock upon the departures of Mafart and Prieur, the clock continued ticking, and by the time of the award, the three-year period had passed. Hence, so the tribunal decided, there was no need to transfer the two agents back to Hao.

The reasoning seems impossible to justify on the basis of the text of the agreement, according to which the two are to be transferred to Hao 'for a period of not less than three years'.[28] It is difficult to read this in any other way than to hold that Mafart and Prieur were to spend three years on the island. Admittedly, the text leaves some ambiguities: it does not specify an exact starting date, and it does not indicate whether a leap year shall be counted as a year.[29] But still, upon any regular or ordinary reading, the text does not suggest anything other than that the two culprits shall spend three years on Hao – and possibly more.

What is more, the reasoning of the tribunal is also difficult to justify with the apparent thought behind the provision: the thought that the two agents should

---

[27] In the classroom, this usually provokes a gasp: secret service agents, especially those who blow up ships, are still widely presumed to be men.

[28] It has not been subjected to a lot of scrutiny in the literature though. Crawford, for example, in his monumental work on responsibility, merely issues a parenthetical remark that the Tribunal decided 'somewhat controversially' on this point. See James Crawford, *State Responsibility: The General Part* (Cambridge University Press, 2013), at 265. Salmon likewise merely mentions the decision on this point while questioning whether the Tribunal reached its conclusion 'rightly or not', but without analysing the matter. See Jean Salmon, 'Duration of the Breach', in James Crawford, Alain Pellet, and Simon Olleson (eds.), *The Law of International Responsibility* (Oxford University Press, 2010), 383–396, at 388.

[29] For the record, the duration would have included the year 1988, which was indeed a leap year.

receive some kind of punishment for having been involved in manslaughter. Compared to ten years in prison in New Zealand, three years on a French military facility accompanied by family and without deprivation of conjugal rights seems like a pretty good deal for them at any rate. Indeed, in a powerful opinion, the arbitrator submitting a separate opinion, Sir Kenneth Keith, reaches much the same conclusion: the majority decision is difficult to justify under any regular approach to treaty interpretation.[30] And in fact, the Tribunal itself suggested much the same when it stated that 'the essential object or purpose of the First Agreement was not fulfilled, since the two agents left the island before the expiry of the three-year period.'[31] Hence, the Tribunal's reasoning is based neither on the text of the agreement nor on the purpose behind it.

The Tribunal classified France's breach as a 'continuous breach',[32] therewith presupposing that the clock did not stop with the departure of Mafart and Prieur. This, as such, seems sensible enough, but then the Tribunal reached an awkward conclusion. It concluded (again, in itself sensible enough) that the removal of those two would no longer constitute a violation upon expiry of the agreement. However, the agreement had no explicit expiry date,[33] so the Tribunal saw fit to deduce one: since the incarceration had started on 23 July 1986, the agreement expired on 22 July 1989, and therewith expired also the obligation to incarcerate, regardless of the circumstance that for a considerable part of this time neither Mafart nor Prieur was in confinement, and despite the agreement specifying that they will be in confinement for a period of no less than three years. The result is counter-intuitive, as if someone who escapes from prison nonetheless is considered as serving time during his or her escape.

What then might explain it? One possible explanation may reside in the circumstance that the Tribunal was worried about Mafart or Prieur (or both) appealing under the law of the European Convention on Human Rights. For regular criminal lawyers, the *Rainbow Warrior* case was a highly peculiar case, and with potentially a highly peculiar outcome. It was an inter-state dispute that could possibly result in two individuals being further incarcerated on the basis of a ruling by the UN Secretary-General and a treaty between two states, without those two individuals actually having been given the chance, in this phase of proceedings, to defend themselves – as a trial then, it would be as far

---

[30] Arbitrator Keith's separate opinion is appended to the Award, 276–284.
[31] Award, para. 100.
[32] Award, para. 101.
[33] It provided that its main provisions ought to be implemented 'not later than 25 July 1986', but contained few other formal clauses.

removed from a fair trial as it could possibly be, and therewith difficult to reconcile with Article 6 of the European Convention on Human Rights. This Convention is not terribly relevant for New Zealand of course, but France is bound to abide by its provisions and bound to protect everyone within its jurisdiction – and this clearly covered Mafart and Prieur.[34]

The continued confinement of Mafart and Prieur could be equally difficult to reconcile with the *habeas corpus* provision of Article 5 of the same European Convention: everyone is entitled to liberty and security of person, unless convicted by a competent court. So here is an ethical dilemma: should the Tribunal insist on the proper 'legal' interpretation of an inter-state agreement, and as a result condemn two individuals to incarceration without giving those individuals the chance to defend themselves? Or should it honour the reach and scope of human rights law, according to which no one shall be deprived of their liberty except by a competent court and on the basis of a fair trial?

If the horns of the dilemma are clear enough, there are a few complicating factors. One is, lest it be forgotten, that Mafart and Prieur had actually been found guilty by a competent court in New Zealand,[35] and had originally been sentenced to ten years in prison. In this light, there would be something curious about a complaint that their rights to liberty and a fair trial would have been violated by the Arbitral Tribunal confirming a far lesser sentence decided upon by the UN Secretary-General and accepted by the two states concerned. And, lest we forget, their actions actually resulted in the loss of a human life.

That said, it is of course also a complicating factor precisely that the sentence was one agreed upon by two states; this is difficult to sustain in light of Rule of Law concerns. And yet another complicating factor is that it is clear that Mafart and Prieur were acting on behalf of the French government: they were government agents acting on instructions, rather than private agents acting out of private motives. And France itself, it seems, was not too concerned about human rights when it ordered that the ship be blown to pieces. Even if it never intended that anyone would die, nonetheless preventing political protest is not easy to square with freedom of expression or assembly, freedoms that also meet with strong protection under the

---

[34] If the right to a fair trial is accepted as part of customary international law, then New Zealand too could be legally implicated.

[35] And it would be difficult to invoke the sort of argument often invoked to justify the inclusion of international arbitration provisions in investment agreements, to the effect that somehow New Zealand courts would not measure up to Rule of Law standards.

European Convention. In the end, the case raises intriguing issues of 'inter-legality': how to come to terms with interlocking legal orders.[36]

Perhaps the most complicating factor, though, is that, while the award is not particularly commendable, it is not obviously wrong either. It may set the law aside for no identifiable reason, but the outcome is, curiously perhaps, not particularly outrageous – and has never been received as such. France, obviously perhaps, seems to have been reasonably pleased,[37] but New Zealand too seems to have been puzzled rather than displeased. The outcome does not really engender moral outrage; it is more a matter of intellectual bewilderment – how can the tribunal have decided the way it did? And the upshot of this is that the analysis is driven to finding an explanation, not so much to offering a critique or to suggesting alternatives. And this in turn means that much of the writings on virtue jurisprudence are not particularly helpful: they can help to pinpoint that a corrupt or lazy or biased judgment is flawed, but none of these or similar factors is the case here. Put differently, for all its puzzling aspects this still is an award that could have been rendered by virtuous arbitrators – and the same holds true for a panel that would have reached the opposite conclusion. There is, in yet other words, nothing in virtue jurisprudence that would suggest that the panel ought to have reached a different conclusion. The award is strange, but not, it seems, non-virtuous, unless one would claim that a virtuous arbitrator never departs from a written treaty provision, not even for good reasons – but that comes close to positing a categorical imperative.

9.3 ETHICALLY JUSTIFIABLE?

But first things first: is the Tribunal's approach ethically justifiable? Is it justifiable to go against the relatively clear injunction of the law that is to be applied, and set it aside for considerations that are external to the case at hand – in this case, the fear of encountering different legal issues? A deontologist would run into problems here, as is usually the case when he (let's assume our deontologist is male, for argument's sake) is confronted with normative conflicts. The deontologist would be asked to make a choice between different applicable rules, and can only do so by relying on

---

[36] See Jan Klabbers and Gianluigi Palombella (eds.), *The Challenge of Inter-legality* (Cambridge University Press, 2019).

[37] Being pleased shines through in Gilbert Guillaume's in-depth discussion of the affair: Guillaume had been involved in secret negotiations on behalf of the French government, and would later become a judge at the International Court of Judge. See Gilbert Guillaume, *Les grandes crises internationales et le droit* (Paris: Éditions du Seuil, 1994), 219–238.

Revisiting Rainbow Warrior

a different, higher, rule while remaining true to deontology. Other techniques (balancing, applying proportionality) are not available to the pure deontologist.[38] Hence, he would have to decide on the basis of a possible hierarchy of norms – and indeed, the structure of both parties' arguments mirrored a dichotomy, with New Zealand sponsoring an approach based on the law of treaties, and France endorsing an approach concentrating on the law of responsibility. The Tribunal split the difference, denying any distinction between contractual and tortuous obligations in international law.[39] Nonetheless, the distinction played out, implicitly,[40] between a faithful reading of the agreement, and an implicit insistence on extraneous factors. The bilateral agreement said one thing; other factors, however unmentioned these may have remained, pointed in the opposite direction.

International law provides arguments supporting both positions. On the assumption that the Tribunal had human rights in mind, some might say human rights are substantively superior, and should always trump other agreements. Others might counter that the right to life, itself a human rights norm, was callously treated by Mafart and Prieur and the French government – and much the same would apply to freedom of expression. The *lex posterior* argument would suggest that the two should have been sent back to Hao, as the bilateral agreement was of later date than France's commitments under the European Convention. And likewise, the *lex specialis* argument would probably have to be construed in favour of applying the bilateral agreement. Compared to the general nature of the European Convention, the bilateral agreement dealt with a rather special and narrow topic, and between fewer states at that: so unless one would feel that human rights by definition trump other manifestations of international law, the deontologist would probably have to conclude that the Tribunal erred.[41] And yet, somehow this reasoning, while defensible, strikes as too easy, or at least as difficult to generalize: there

---

[38] This suggests that pure deontology is rare indeed; instead, deontological and consequentialist arguments are structurally related, so to speak, leading to MacIntyre's observation that many ethical debates 'can find no terminus'. See Alasdair MacIntyre, *After Virtue: A Study in Moral Theory*, 2nd edn. (London: Duckworth, 1985), at 6. Some of the consequences for the law of international organizations are explored in Jan Klabbers, 'Interminable Disagreement? Reflections on the Autonomy of International Organisations', (2019) 88 *Nordic Journal of International Law*, 111–133.

[39] Award, esp. para. 74–75.

[40] France at no point expressly invoked human rights considerations or relied on the European Convention, and had it done so it would have made it far more difficult for the Tribunal to apply human rights-related logic, for, in that case, it would have had to explain why it seemingly could not accept the outcome of proceedings in New Zealand.

[41] For an overview of the international law mechanisms to address treaty conflicts, see Jan Klabbers, *Treaty Conflict and the European Union* (Cambridge University Press, 2008).

must after all be circumstances thinkable where an appeal to human rights should set aside a bilateral agreement between states, even a later and narrower agreement. One example concerns the voluntary rendition agreements states have concluded in their struggles to contain terrorism: surely, such agreements should not be allowed to depart from established human rights law. So, our deontologist has a problem, although it remains possible that the problem stems not from deontology, but from the configuration of obligations at issue.[42]

To the very limited extent that there is any reasoning to be found in the award on this point, it suggests something along vaguely consequentialist lines, perhaps paying some lip service to traditional great power sovereignty. Having established that the period of incarceration, if it commenced on 22 July 1986, would have ended on 22 July 1989, the tribunal noted without further illustration or reference that it would be 'contrary to the principles concerning treaty interpretation to reach a more extensive construction of the provisions which thus established a limited duration to the special undertakings assumed by France'.[43]

This focus on 'erring on the side of the sovereign' is, in law, an untenable proposition. To the extent that there is (or can be) a general rule of interpretation, it is a rule which favours the ordinary meaning of the terms of the treaty in their context, and in light of the treaty's object and purpose. Instead, the tribunal relied on an old and outdated maxim, to the effect that, when in doubt, one should apply the least onerous international obligations, especially perhaps when it concerns great powers – and for some reason France seemed to warrant such treatment. The reasoning followed from the conclusion, rather than the other way around. Perhaps it is useful to remember here that even Vattel, otherwise rather sensitive to the plight of the great powers, would have balked: to his mind, interpretations that result in absurdities or that would render the treaty null and void were unacceptable: the parties cannot be presumed to have intended to create an absurdity or to render a treaty nugatory.[44] And that was in the eighteenth century.

This is vaguely consequentialist in that it seems mostly concerned with the consequences for France: surely, France could not be expected to welcome its agents incarcerated on Hao for a period of three years, even if this is what the

---

[42] That said, for all its popularity, the *lex specialis* rule often ends up in this kind of trouble: it would often warrant application of a bilateral agreement so as to overrule a contrary multilateral agreement. Note also that the *lex specialis* rule does not feature in the Vienna Convention on the Law of Treaties.

[43] Award, para. 104.

[44] Emer de Vattel, *The Law of Nations* (Indianapolis IN: Liberty Fund, 2008 [1758], Nugent transl.), at 418–419.

agreement specified, and even if this is what the Secretary-General of the UN had already decided should happen. Of course, the problem then is that, while the consequences of the award might be nice for France, they were not all that happily embraced by New Zealand. This can possibly be overcome by a reliance on overall positive consequences (thus sacrificing New Zealand's desires in the name of the greater good), but it is difficult to sell an unsubstantiated conclusion undermining the sanctity of treaties as somehow overall positive – and it is probably no coincidence that there seems to be no other case adopting a similar approach, or even of the *Rainbow Warrior* point being invoked in legal proceedings as somehow a useful precedent. And here the analytical problem seems to be with consequentialism as such, not just with the materials at hand. Consequentialist reasoning, whatever its merits, seems to be always vulnerable to the critique that the consequences deemed desirable are either too broad or too narrow, and always depending on who makes the decision. There is, in other words, no standard equation: every equation is an inclusion of some factors while it excludes others, and there is no way of telling in advance (or often even afterwards) what the precise factors in the equation were. The problem might be less pronounced in rule-utilitarian approaches, but these depend on being able to identify an applicable rule (something which is not always self-evident) and still suffer from the absence of standard-equations. Rule-utilitarians have less equations to worry about than act-utilitarians, but cannot escape making calculations altogether. But at least Elizabeth Anscombe's rather scathing conclusion of consequentialism in general will apply with less force: 'you can exculpate yourself from the actual consequences of the most disgraceful [sic] actions, so long as you can make out a case for not having foreseen them.'[45]

9.4 ON COURAGE AND FOOLHARDINESS

This still leaves open the possibility of a virtue-based justification, or explanation rather. The search is not for a condemnation of the award in terms of the absence of judicial virtue: I am not looking to claim that the arbitrators were corrupted, or did not do their homework properly, or were biased in favour of France, or lacked empathy,[46] or any suchlike construction. Instead, I am

---

[45] G. E. M. Anscombe, 'Modern Moral Philosophy', reproduced in Roger Crisp and Michael Slote (eds.), *Virtue Ethics* (Oxford University Press, 1997), 26–44, at 37 (italics omitted – JK).

[46] I have explored a possible role for empathy elsewhere: see Jan Klabbers, 'Doing Justice? Bureaucracy, the Rule of Law and Virtue Ethics', (2017) 6 *Rivista di Filosofia del Diritto*, 27–50.

looking to find out whether the award can be justified on the basis of a virtue ethics approach. Many of the often-mentioned judicial virtues have little bearing on the matter. Take, for example, Van Domselaar's recent conceptualization of the judge as a 'civic friend', friendly disposed towards both parties and willing to listen to both without preconceptions: this is an appealing notion in various respects, but does not apply to the case at hand. There was little in the panel that was truly friendly towards New Zealand (this is an empirical point, and as such not fatal to Van Domselaar's concept), but, more importantly, the notion of civic friendship is better suited to private law disputes involving concrete material interests, rather than the more abstract type of political question mixed with criminal law that was at issue in *Rainbow Warrior*.[47]

Likewise, the checklist proposed by Farrelly and Solum offers little solace.[48] It lists such traits as incorruptibility, sobriety, judicial courage, temperament and impartiality, diligence and carefulness, intelligence and learnedness, and craft and skill. Yet none of these, it seems, was lacking. It is not that the panellists were corrupt, or did not know the law or how to interpret a treaty provision. What characterizes *Rainbow Warrior*, instead, is the wilful setting aside of what was the most obvious solution, possibly in order to prevent possible further legal problems. Perhaps the only judicial virtue mentioned by Farrelly and Solum that can have a bearing on the problem is the idea of judicial courage, but this seems to work in both directions.

On the one hand, the majority could be criticized for lacking courage. Surely, so the argument could go, France made its own bed, and thus had to lie in it. It is not for arbitrators to take possible negative consequences for one of the sides into account, at the expense of the other party to the dispute. Clearly, one might think, the panel bowed to great power politics, perhaps afraid that France would refuse to cooperate (which would not be unprecedented) with any award, whether in the guise of a threat of human rights litigation or not. Clearly, it seemed, France was afraid that its darker practices could be exposed in human rights litigation, and the panel lacked the courage to tell France to accept responsibility for its actions and let the chips land where they fall. Hence, one might conclude, the panel lacked judicial courage.

[47] Iris van Domselaar, *The Fragility of Rightness: Adjudication and the Primacy of Practice* (PhD thesis, University of Amsterdam, 2014). After all, some crimes might make it difficult for a judge to be friendly disposed towards the suspect, and faking a friendly disposition would not be particularly virtuous.

[48] Colin Farrelly and Lawrence B. Solum, 'An Introduction to Aretaic Theories of Law', in Farrelly and Solum (eds.), *Virtue Jurisprudence*, 1–23.

On the other hand, it takes considerable courage to wilfully devise an arbitral decision that is counter-intuitive and seems to depart from traditional expectations about the meaning of treaty provisions. It would have been easier for the panel, no doubt, to just order that Mafart and Prieur be sent back to Hao; and should France refuse to comply, then France would have a huge public relations problem, if nothing else. But at least on paper New Zealand would have been vindicated, the sanctity of treaties would have been confirmed, and most people's belief in the fairness of international law would have been strengthened. To go against all this, then, must have taken considerable courage.

This raises the obvious question then regarding how to assess judicial courage: how to distinguish courage from foolhardiness? And that question, it seems, requires an additional element: judicial virtue cannot be assessed as self-standing judicial virtue alone, but somehow needs to be embedded in something larger. One way of approaching this might be to invoke such factors as legitimacy, but this is rarely helpful: whoever invokes legitimacy wants to cheat, one might be tempted to quip, if only because legitimacy is an open-ended and slippery concept.[49]

Van Domselaar provides a clue in tying the exercise of judicial virtue to the exercise of public authority, suggesting that judicial authority is part of public authority and therewith in need of justification. A related, more specific approach is provided by Jonathan Soeharno, who points out that, generally, a distinction can be made between the virtues of the judge, and the legitimacy of the office of the judge. The former can be evaluated by enquiring into individual judicial characteristics; the latter, however, is impervious to this, and requires instead an analysis in terms of what he calls 'external accountability'. The starting point of his discussion is that people may come to accept judgments not only because they believe the judge is a decent human being but also, regardless of who the judge is, because the court in question can generally be trusted. Hence, assessments tend to depend on both factors, and both individual judges and courts can over time develop their reputations.[50]

From this angle, it would seem that the award in *Rainbow Warrior* can possibly be defended by pointing to the embeddedness of the Tribunal in the international legal order. The Tribunal's task is, first of all, to settle the dispute before it, but it cannot do so in a vacuum. It is perhaps useful to suggest here

---

[49] The seminal critique is Martti Koskenniemi, 'Legitimacy, Rights, and Ideology: Notes Towards a Critique of the New Moral Internationalism', (2003) 7 *Associations*, 349–373.

[50] Soeharno, *The Integrity of the Judge*.

that tensions between France and New Zealand had escalated, to the point that France had persuaded the EU to impose import restrictions on butter stemming from New Zealand. The award is usually credited with having helped to alleviate these tensions, and the panel's idea to establish a 'friendship fund', to be financed (at least initially) by France, has often been deemed a useful intervention as well.

On the other hand, and perhaps more to the point, Soeharno's invocation of the integrity of the office hardly applies here. Arbitration tribunals are by definition set up on an ad hoc basis: they exist to settle a dispute, and once that work is done, they stop working and are disbanded. In an important sense therewith, there is no office whose integrity could be at stake, or whose integrity or legitimacy could be relied on to strengthen the appeal of the award.

9.5 BACK TO SQUARE ONE

So this brings us back to square one: is the award in *Rainbow Warrior*, departing as it seems to do from applicable law and the obvious way of reading the applicable law, nonetheless ethically justifiable? One other avenue is immediately closed off: it is generally accepted that tribunals may go against the law (*contra legem*) if equity so demands, but it would be difficult to squeeze the *Rainbow Warrior* into this conception – if anything, equity would have demanded the opposite of what the Tribunal decided. Or, at least, it is not immediately obvious what equity would mean here, and between whom it should apply. If the matter is framed as one between France and New Zealand, then there is something to the claim that the latter was not treated very equitably. If the case is framed as one involving two individuals following superior orders, then it becomes more persuasive to think of the Tribunal as engaged in correcting the written law by means of resorting to equity. But this particular framing in itself is not all that compelling perhaps.

Still, the discussion of judicial courage points to something else: given the escalation of the conflict between the two countries, perhaps the prudent thing to do was to defuse the situation by not sending Mafart and Prieur back, but instead opening a friendship fund. This would be in line with the terms of reference of arbitration panels generally (to settle concrete disputes), even if at the expense of one of the parties. In a world of great powers, this inevitably entails that the prudent thing to do is often to let the great powers have their way, and that is a sobering conclusion. Then again, the virtue ethics tradition shares this with other ethical traditions: leading consequentialists have argued that humanitarian interventions should only be undertaken if there is a chance of success, which effectively means that the great powers are exempt.[51]

The problem with this explanation though is that it does not utilize what I thought could be the justification, and has no need for it: the fear for legal ramifications under the European Convention of Human Rights. If the Tribunal's aim was indeed to defuse the dispute between France and New Zealand (and this is highly plausible), then it could have done so by invoking just about any additional reason, whether possible human rights ramifications in France or anything else; and indeed human rights ramifications would, on balance, probably have been a fairly strong argument – not a conclusive one, as discussed above, but a fairly strong one. If so, then the question remains why the Tribunal did not make it explicit.

And perhaps then one is forced to conclude that sometimes a cigar is, well, just a cigar. The Tribunal decided the way it did without relying on a specific form of justification beyond the vague and unsustainable suggestion that it was merely interpreting the bilateral agreement between the two states concerned in a time-honoured manner. This, as we have seen, was not a particularly good argument, and arguably, better arguments would have been available. The point though is that none would have been invulnerable.

Now what to make of all this? In one way, the Tribunal should be applauded, as it did indeed manage to defuse a tense situation. Whether that was a task of Herculean proportions is doubtful, however: France and New Zealand have their differences, especially on nuclear matters, but their relations have never been so strained as to make war a probability. This was not a James Bond-type scenario with a clock ticking inexorably and the Tribunal engaging in legal-ethical heroics to defuse a time-bomb with half a second left on the clock; it was rather the equivalent of a leisurely stroll with like-minded friends who happened to have a difference of opinion but nothing a little give-and-take could not solve. The Tribunal must have also thought that, in the end, this was a relatively minor incident: it had found the unauthorized removal of Major Mafart justified in light of his health condition, and while it was convinced that removing Captain Prieur without consent on the part of New Zealand had not been a justifiable 'necessity', it nonetheless must have felt that this was a bit of a 'first world problem': it is not like genocide or crimes against humanity had been committed, and both Mafart and Prieur had spent some time on Hao, even if not the full three years. Hence, there was possibly little interest being served by returning the two for the remainder of their three years, except obviously New Zealand's rightful indignation.

---

[51] Singer, *One World*.

So, what France got out of this was that the policies of its secret service were not subjected to further scrutiny, and that in the end it did not have to suffer the indignity of seeing two of its agents confined at the behest of a friendly state – not for very long, at any rate. New Zealand did not get what it wanted (the return of Mafart and Prieur), but it got the satisfaction of the Tribunal condemning some of the French actions and the Tribunal recommending the establishment of a fund to promote close and friendly relations, bolstered with the suggestion that France make a starting contribution of two million US dollars, something that has sometimes been referred to as 'pecuniary compensation' for New Zealand.[52]

This suggests that maybe, from the perspective of the Tribunal, the prudent thing to do was to decide the way it did, and then hope that the fall-out would be limited. Prudence here should be understood as Aristotle's *phronesis*, practical wisdom: the wisdom of being able to recognize what course to follow given the circumstances – and those are always less than ideal.[53] The hope that fall-out would remain limited turns out to have been justified: the literature takes the *Rainbow Warrior* decision largely as a given. It is not particularly admiring of the construction the Tribunal chose, but not very critical either. The case is usually cited as authority for a number of finer points on responsibility, including the general proposition that, once an obligation terminates, so too does a breach of that obligation, but without much attention for the veritable absence of reasoning on the Tribunal's part.[54] Be that as it may, neither a consequentialist nor a deontologist would have easily decided the way the Tribunal did: the latter would have been troubled by the absence of a clear mandate, and the former would have included the normative fall-out (e.g. undermining the sanctity of treaties) in the equation.

9.6 TO CONCLUDE

If all this is plausible or correct, then it would seem to follow that virtue ethics can contribute to our understanding of particular decisions taken by relevant actors in the international arena, including individuals who individually or collectively exercise a judicial function – such as the arbitrators deciding the

---

[52] See Yann Kerbrat, 'Interaction between the Forms of Reparation', in Crawford, et al. (eds.), *International Responsibility*, 573–587, at 577.

[53] See generally Friedrich Kratochwil, *Praxis: On Acting and Knowing* (Cambridge University Press, 2018).

[54] See, for example, Joost Pauwelyn, 'The Concept of a 'Continuing Violation' of an International Obligation: Selected Problems', (1995) 66 *British Yearbook of International Law*, 415–450, at 443.

Rainbow Warrior. Whether that renders the award the sort of award that a virtuous person would have reached – as is sometimes deemed the decisive test[55] – is a question that must be treated carefully, for two reasons.

First, most of the regular judicial virtues are to be expected as a matter of course. We assume, and need to assume, that our judges are not corrupt, that they do their work properly, that they are not drunk when deciding cases, that they keep their temper in check, etc. Judgments or awards failing on these grounds will be rare, and as a result, these virtues have fairly little analytical traction. Judicial corruption only comes in analytically when there is a clear suspicion of corruption, but not otherwise.

Second, a virtuous panel may just as easily have reached the opposite conclusion. I may contend that the decision is explicable in terms of prudence, but I could probably make a similar case had the Tribunal decided that France should return the two agents for further confinement. This too could be labelled 'prudent', albeit for other reasons. Such a panel might have appreciated the fairness of two individuals guilty of manslaughter serving what is, in the end, a fairly minimal period of time in fairly comfortable conditions. Such a panel might have thought it prudent to hold that France, as a great power, should not tell its agents to blow up ships in faraway lands. And such a panel might have thought it prudent to honour a ruling of the Secretary-General of the United Nations and a set of bilateral agreements. Prudence, it seems, can play out in a variety of ways, and if that is so, it is difficult to predict with any certitude what a virtuous person will do, or what a virtuous panel will decide.

But perhaps that is the point. Prudence, or practical wisdom, can apply in a variety of ways, but the ways in which it applies are not unlimited. Decisions are always contextual, and what is prudent in one setting might not be prudent in the next, or might be differently prudent in the next. It is tempting no doubt, but downright impossible, to try to develop an algorithm (or even merely a general rule) telling us how to choose between competing versions of prudential action, but this only confirms what has been said about using exemplars as a virtue-related method: one should not follow someone else's example to the letter, but rather to the spirit.[56] And it seems that, all things considered, the Tribunal in *Rainbow Warrior* made a serious and prudent effort to defuse an awkward political dispute. It is unlikely to have been

---

[55] Amalia Amaya, 'The Role of Virtue in Legal Justification', in Amaya and Ho (eds.), *Law, Virtue and Justice*, 51–66.

[56] Amalia Amaya, 'Exemplarism and Judicial Virtue', (2013) 25 *Law and Literature*, 428–445. More inclined to follow the exemplar's lead is Linda Trinkaus Zagzebski, *Exemplarist Moral Theory* (Oxford University Press, 2017).

inspired too much by human rights considerations – while intriguing and not completely impossible, this strikes too much as *ex post facto* justification. But it seems perfectly plausible that the Tribunal wanted to prevent relations between the two countries from undergoing serious and possibly permanent damage – and in this it has succeeded quite well, even if legal purists might be tempted to complain that, in doing so, the Tribunal blurred the distinction between law and compromise.

The role for the virtues then, in this case, seems to be largely explanatory. It is not so much the case that the Tribunal aimed to act with particular virtue, or employed all virtues in its behaviour, but that the virtue perspective can help us understand what otherwise seems a puzzling decision: the virtue perspective can go where deontology and consequentialism cannot go. And that in itself establishes a prudent reason for not discarding the virtues in reflecting upon global governance.

10

Virtue and Leadership in the World Health Organization

Guilherme Vasconcelos Vilaça[*]

Is a man selling newspapers in a stand an expert in news and politics? I'm a newsvendor goddamnit! I'm informed on the situation. We oughtta nuke'em till they glow!

Alan More and Dave Gibbons, *Watchmen*

10.1 INTRODUCTION

10.1.1 *Uses of Virtue Ethics to Appraise Leadership*

In the public sphere, it is unequivocal that the language of virtues impregnates much of our discourse and analyses about domestic and international leaders. Dominique Strauss-Kahn, Christine Lagarde, Donald Trump, Luis Moreno Ocampo, or Silvio Berlusconi often trigger-(ed) heated reactions about their official and private behaviours deemed to be inappropriate and found wanting from a moral standpoint. On the other side of the fence, Barack Obama, António Guterres, Nelson Mandela, or Dag Hammarskjöld and Greta Thunberg are or have been praised as being virtuous and inspirational leaders capable of moving the world towards a brighter future.

In recent years, we have also witnessed a revival of virtue ethics in international law and international relations thinking across the world.[1] This recovery could be

---

[*] I thank Pablo Rapetti, Pedro Caballero, Ukri Soirila, and William Kirkland for sharp comments to earlier versions of the chapter. I also thank Jorge Baloura for the expert proofreading. All errors remain mine.

[1] See Fröhlich, Manuel (2010), *Political Ethics and the United Nations: Dag Hammarskjöld as Secretary-General* (New York: Routledge), Klabbers, Jan (2014), 'The Virtues of Expertise', in Monika Ambrus et al. (eds.), *The Role of 'Experts' in International and European Decision-Making* (Cambridge: Cambridge University Press), 82–102, and Gaskarth, Jamie (2012), 'The

interpreted as an awakening from a deep period of slumber since it is an ancient vocabulary with resonance in many disparate civilizational resources ranging from Aristotelian, Christian, and Confucian ethical conceptions to Bushido and Meso-American moral views.[2]

Intuitively, a focus on virtues allows our descriptions to transcend the law when examining a leader's behaviour, to ask new questions about the morality of our institutions and change the ethical frameworks we apply.

Classically, questions of the sort 'Should International Organizations promote human rights and global health?' or 'Ought we to promote humanitarian interventions?' led to asking whether that promotes the 'greatest welfare of the greatest number' (the utilitarian canon in Bentham's kind of consequentialism) and whether it is in accordance with human dignity and 'treating persons as ends in themselves' (deontologism)? Rather than concentrating on institutional outcomes or the rules and values they should conform to, virtues zero in on *persons* bringing to the fore the question of knowing whether a given leader is virtuous or acts virtuously. But what makes a leader a virtuous one? And by virtue of what can we make such an assessment?

On paper, virtue ethics' answer is straightforward. It prescribes that virtuous agents act with the right motivation and according to the right reasons while pursuing a humanly desirable *telos*.[3] This 'virtues discourse', often premised upon Aristotle's work,[4] recovers the importance of *character* traits put by Homiak as follows:

> When we speak of a moral virtue or an excellence of character, the emphasis is not on mere distinctiveness or individuality [as it is for character *tout court*],

---

Virtues in International Society', *European Journal of International Relations*, 18 (3), 431–53. For a game-theoretical account, see Malici, Akan (2008), *When Leaders Learn and When They Don't: Mikhail Gorbachev and Kim Il Sung at the End of the Cold War* (New York: State University New York Press). For a Chinese argument that moral leadership is key to the stability and values of the international order, see Yan, Xuetong (2011), *Ancient Chinese Thought, Modern Chinese Power*, trans. Edmund Ryden (Princeton; Oxford: Princeton University Press). At the domestic level, authors have also pushed towards the need to evaluate presidents and presidential candidates on the basis of 'constitutional character'. See Thompson, Dennis F. (2010), 'Constitutional Character: Virtues and Vices in Presidential Leadership', *Presidential Studies Quarterly*, 40 (1), 23–37 at 24.

[2] Proper references to these traditions will be made throughout the text.

[3] Audi, Robert (2001), 'Epistemic Virtue and Justified Belief', in Linda Zagzebski and Abrol Fairweather (eds.), *Virtue Epistemology: Essays on Epistemic Virtue and Responsibility* (Oxford: Oxford University Press), 82–97. See also Homiak, Marcia (2019), 'Moral Character', in Edward N. Zalta (ed.), *Stanford Encyclopedia of Philosophy*.

[4] Aristotle (2000), *Nicomachean Ethics*, trans. Roger Crisp (Cambridge: Cambridge University Press).

Virtue and Leadership in the World Health Organization 251

but on *the combination of qualities that make an individual the sort of ethically admirable person he is.*[5]

The list of virtues typically includes intellectual honesty, courage, impartiality, cordiality, empathy, and reasonability, as well as moderation, respect, deference, and the exercise of a sense of justice. From an Aristotelian perspective, there is something else to be added though, that is, prudence or phronesis, since, in addition to knowing what is required by virtues, agents must also know when and how to exercise them since virtue is always a (geometric not arithmetic) mean that is context-sensitive.[6] For this reason, virtues and the exercise of virtues cannot be fully known in abstract outside concrete situations. In Aristotle's words:

> So too anyone can get angry, or give and spend money – these are easy; *but doing them in relation to the right person, in the right amount, at the right time, with the right aim in view, and in the right way* – that is not something anyone can do, nor is it easy. This is why excellence in these things is rare, praiseworthy and noble.[7]

The same emphasis on the need for practical wisdom when acting can also be found in Confucian and Bushido's moral texts

> The Master said: 'A man may know by heart the three hundred *Songs*, but if he is given a post in government and cannot successfully carry out his duties, and if he is sent to far places and *cannot react to the circumstances as he finds them*, then even if he has learnt to recite many of them, of what use is this to him?'[8]

> A common proverb ridicules one who has only an intellectual knowledge of Confucius, as a man ever studious but ignorant of Analects. A typical samurai calls a literary savant a book-smelling sot. Another compares *learning to an illsmelling vegetable that must be boiled and boiled before it is fit for use* ... The writer meant thereby that knowledge becomes really such only when it is assimilated in the mind of the learner and *shows* in his character.[9]

While these teachings are quite clear, they also introduce a difficulty for all those who wish to deploy the virtues to describe and appraise ethical

---

[5] Homiak, Marcia (2019), 'Moral Character', in Edward N. Zalta (ed.), *Stanford Encyclopedia of Philosophy*.

[6] Aristotle (2000), *Nicomachean Ethics*, trans. Roger Crisp (Cambridge: Cambridge University Press), 1106b36–1107a3. For a detailed account, see Wood, W. Jay (2014), 'Prudence', in Kevin Timpe and Craig A. Body (eds.), *Virtues and Their Vices* (Oxford: Oxford University Press), 37–58.

[7] Aristotle (2000), *Nicomachean Ethics*, trans. Roger Crisp (Cambridge: Cambridge University Press), 1109a26–30, emphasis added.

[8] Dawson, Raymond (2008), *The Analects*, trans. Raymond Dawson (Reprint edn.; New York: Oxford University Press), Book 13(5), emphasis added.

[9] Nitobe, Inazo (1969), *Bushido: The Soul of Japan* (Singapore: Tuttle) at 11, emphasis added.

leadership. After all, if virtue is about developing a morally excellent character, but we cannot fully know in advance of practical situations what is virtue and how a virtuous person would act, how are we to cast judgments on the moral excellence of the character of our leaders?[10] In other words, how can we evaluate António Guterres', Ban Ki-Moon's, or Margaret Chan's character, moral worth, and actions without thoroughly examining their lives, commitments and decisions against the context in which those developed?

10.1.2 Assumptions: Virtuous Leaders Always Act Well and We 'Just Know' What Virtue Is!

Indeed, most uses of virtue ethics simply assume that a virtuous agent acts well, resolving by metaphysical fiat a question that is deeply practical and situated and that cannot be decided without mixing factual, conceptual, and normative materials. I surmise this happens for two reasons. First, in virtue ethics accounts, focus is placed on the development of character through self-cultivation and experience in social and political life. After an agent achieves sagehood (a life-long project),[11] the texts simply assume the agent knows how to act well and *does so*. This is clear in the Analects as moral dilemmas never appear to create serious obstacles despite the fact that attentive thinking quickly dissipates such ideas.[12] Second, there is a separation between the tasks of the ethical theorist and the ethical practitioner with the odd result that 'the task of deciding what are good and bad ethical arguments belongs to someone else, though it is never quite made clear to whom.'[13]

[10] A more radical criticism, such as that of the Daoist Zhuangzi, questions the process itself of cultivating virtues. See Watson, Burton (2013), *The Complete Works of Zhuangzi*, trans. Burton Watson (New York: Columbia University Press) at 284, footnote omitted, 'There is no greater evil than for the mind to be aware of virtue and to act as though it were a pair of eyes. For when it starts acting like a pair of eyes, it will peer out from within, and when it peers out from within, it is ruined. There are five types of dangerous virtue, of which inner virtue is the worst. What do I mean by inner virtue? He who possesses inner virtue thinks himself always in the right and denigrates those who do not do as he does.'

[11] Practically all virtue accounts, from Aristotle to Confucius list age, continuous self-cultivation, and wide social experience as necessary to reach sagehood or moral excellency.

[12] See Dawson, Raymond (2008), *The Analects*, trans. Raymond Dawson (Reprint edn.; New York: Oxford University Press), Book 13(18), in which Confucius candidly sustains that sons should not report their parents to authorities for wrongdoings and vice-versa, assuming without argument that this is what a virtuous (upright) person ought to do while neglecting the obvious conflict between duties towards one's family members and those towards the state or other authorities.

[13] Lemmon, E. J. (1987), 'Moral Dilemmas', in Christopher W. Gowans (ed.), *Moral Dilemmas* (New York: Oxford University Press), 101–14 at 111.

Virtue and Leadership in the World Health Organization   253

Either way, the point is that academic writing rarely dirties its hands in trying to discern the ethics of *actual* characters, scenarios, and choices[14] since, for one, it adopts a meta-theoretical standpoint (I won't tell you what to do or do it myself but tell you how you should speak about what you should do).[15] For instance, consider Thomas Nagel's stance when talking about the fragmentation of value and its consequences for ethical analysis.

> *Most practical issues are much messier than this, and their ethical dimensions are much more complex.* One needs a method of insuring that where relevant understanding exists, it is made available, and where there is an aspect of the problem that nobody understands very well, this is understood too. *I have not devised such a method*, but clearly it would have to provide that factors considered should include, among others, the following: economic, political, and personal liberty, equality, equity, privacy, procedural fairness, intellectual and aesthetic development.[16]

But how can Nagel exempt himself so easily from the task of pursuing his account to its full complexity? We could not be further away from staking one's life on pursuing and providing deep accounts of what we are studying as embodied in Robert A. Caro's life and work as his following remark while writing Lyndon Johnson's biography reveals

> I said to Ina, 'I'm not understanding these people and therefore I'm not understanding Lyndon Johnson. We're going to have to move to the Hill Country and live there.' . . . where we were to live for most of the next three years.[17]

---

[14] Consider the provocative comment in Alexander, Larry and Sherwin, Emily (2009), 'Law and Philosophy at Odds', in Francis J. Mootz III (ed.), *On Philosophy in American Law* (New York: Cambridge University Press), 241–48 at 247, 'But it may be just as well that few if any philosophers or philosopher-judges are capable of applying the discipline of philosophy to the choices they make in daily life.'

[15] Not even the pragmatists, that have otherwise greatly contributed to our emancipation from ideal theory, are immune to the fall on meta-theorizing. For an example, see Margolis, Joseph (1996), *Life Without Principles: Reconciling Theory and Practice* (Cambridge; Oxford: Blackwell Publishers). A few studies in international relations have analysed individual leadership, including personality traits in international organizations, but they focus on effective, not ethical, leadership. See Cox, Robert (1969), 'The Executive Head: An Essay on Leadership in International Organization', *International Organization*, 23 (2), 205–30. For a rare example studying leaders and both their ethical frameworks and mandates, see Kent J. Kille (ed.) (2007), *The UN Secretary-General And Moral Authority: Ethics And Religion In International Leadership* (Washington, DC: Georgetown University Press).

[16] Nagel, Thomas (1987), 'The Fragmentation of Value', in Christopher W. Gowans (ed.), *Moral Dilemmas* (New York; Oxford: Oxford University Press), 174–87 at 185–86, emphasis added.

[17] Caro, Robert A. (2020), *Working* (New York: Vintage Books) at 103.

254   *Guilherme Vasconcelos Vilaça*

Academic writing also embodies a strange form of mysticism as if by magic one could know whether a given leader is or was virtuous or acted well. The appropriate metaphor here is given to us by the Daoist (which, roughly put, eschewed moral virtues) character Cook Ding who embodying *wu-wei* could cut effortlessly through meat (since 'he just knew') without damaging his knife in the process.

> What I care about is the Way, which goes beyond skill. When I first began cutting up oxen, all I could see was the ox itself. After three years I no longer saw the whole ox. And now—now I go at it by spirit and don't look with my eyes. *Perception and understanding have come to a stop, and spirit moves where it wants.* I go along with the natural makeup, strike in the big hollows, guide the knife through the big openings, and follow things as they are. So I never touch the smallest ligament or tendon, much less a main joint.[18]

I find this stance in the literature deeply unsatisfactory because to marshal all the elements in each situation or factor in all the dimensions mentioned by Nagel earlier and then cast a judgment does not seem obvious or straightforward at all. Rather, it seems to require a different stance towards the kind of work that research in ethics demands.

What to make, for example, of the fact that Peter Piot, famous for his role in curbing Ebola and overall global leadership towards the eradication of deadly viruses and the improvement of the lives of millions, hid from his research team what looked like early symptoms of Ebola infection against explicit and strict instructions? Or when going against procedures he himself advocated, he pinched his hand while recapping a syringe used to draw blood that had a very high probability of being infected with AIDS? Or still that his research team handled, in 1976, in a rather negligent way – taking as sole precautions the use of latex gloves – what became the first Ebola sample (that had been shipped in a simple thermos resulting in one broken tube which contents mixed with the defrosted ice, luckily not producing a disaster when exposed)?[19]

Furthermore, the postmodern mentality is one that disapproves of essences and has made the task of overcoming moral disagreement a daunting one. In losing our ontological and epistemological innocence, we can no longer believe in Diogenes' technique to find honest persons, that is, brandishing a lamp in daylight, or in the Nahuatl commandment that one ought to face constantly a mirror to confront oneself with one's actions and never lose one's

---

[18] Watson, Burton (2013), *The Complete Works of Zhuangzi*, trans. Burton Watson (New York: Columbia University Press) at 19, emphasis added.

[19] Piot, Peter (2013), *No Time To Lose: A Life in Pursuit of Deadly Viruses* (New York: W. W. Norton & Company) at 61, 136 and 4, respectively.

Virtue and Leadership in the World Health Organization 255

face and heart (the symbols of our personal identity).[20] This state of affairs is particularly problematic for virtue ethics. Since the latter traditionally links virtue to a given *telos*, that is, human flourishing – which could be known because of a predetermined human nature and a social structure based on fixed roles known by everyone – disagreement as to what counted as flourishing and virtue could be avoided.[21] In pluralist societies in which there is no tight and apriori relationship between ethics, human nature, and social structure,[22] neither can there be a *natural* human *telos*.

Finally, when analysing ethical leadership within organizations, further complexity arises due to the fact that leaders are expected to exercise their personal virtues while contributing to the flourishing of the organization and its mission, that is, taking into account their professional *roles*.[23] Thus, personal moral excellence is not the sole, and perhaps not the primary, goal to be pursued. Leaders are expected to both fulfil their technical roles, that is, being performant and accountable, and contribute to the elevation and flourishing of the organization promoting the common good.[24]

10.1.3 *Chapter's Goals, Contributions, and Roadmap*

This chapter aims to correct the situation portrayed above by investigating *in a concrete manner* how to assess the virtue of one's character (and actions) and how the latter assessment fits in a holistic ethical evaluation of a given person, situation, and scenario. The chapter addresses these questions by scrutinizing the neglected ethical dimension of the character and actions of international

---

[20] See León-Portilla, Miguel (1974), *La Filosofía Náhuatl Estudiada en sus Fuentes* (4th edn.; Ciudad de México: Instituto de Investigaciones Históricas – UNAM) at 179, 'poner un espejo delante de la gente para hacerla cuerda y cuidadosa'.

[21] See MacIntyre, Alasdair (2007), *After Virtue: A Study in Moral Theory* (3rd edn.; London: Duckworth) for details. On the difficulty of doing ethics without an Archimedean point, see Bauman, Zygmunt (1993), *Postmodern Ethics* (Malden; Oxford; Carlton: Blackwell Publishing).

[22] For an account of this link in the Chinese Confucian society speaking of a 'differential mode of association', see Fei, Xiaotong (1992), *From the Soil, The Foundations of Chinese Society: A Translation of Fei Xiaotong's Xiangtu Zhongguo*, trans. Gary G. Hamilton and Wang Zheng (Berkeley; Los Angeles: University of California Press).

[23] Oakley, Justin and Cocking, Dean (2001), *Virtue Ethics and Professional Roles* (Cambridge: Cambridge University Press). A similar debate rages in Chinese philosophy with some authors claiming that virtues come first, whereas others claim that roles are the primary element. For a discussion, see Connolly, Tim (2016), 'Virtues and Roles in Early Confucian Ethics', *Confluence: Online Journal of World Philosophies*, 4, 272–84.

[24] Rhode, Deborah L. (2006), 'Introduction: Where is the Leadership in Moral Leadership?', in Deborah L. Rhode (ed.), *Moral Leadership: The Theory and Practice of Power, Judgment, and Policy* (San Francisco: Jossey-Bass), 1–53.

256   *Guilherme Vasconcelos Vilaça*

leaders of one specific international organization, that is, the World Health Organization's (WHO) Director-Generals.

The structure of the chapter is as follows. First, in Section 10.2, I provide an overview of the ethical mechanisms in place at the WHO as well as its mission. This is necessary to understand the institutional and normative framework that surrounds and guides the selection and mission of Director-Generals' accordingly, I devote Section 10.3 to deal with a puzzle: if (moral) character may change after a leader takes office what are we to make of the procedures adopted by many international organizations to ensure the selection of morally excellent leaders? I develop this argument by examining Brock Chisholm, the first WHO Director-General, linking his personality, actions, and vision with the specific *telos* and challenges of the latter organization. In order to strengthen the idea that a robust form of virtue ethics requires plunging into cultural, contextual, and holistic ethical arguments, I compare Chisholm with Hiroshi Nakajima, a later Director-General known for an unimpressive leadership record. While Section 10.3 focuses on character, Section 10.4 examines decisions taken by Director-Generals that went blatantly against the mandate of the WHO, its constitution, and legal rules (thus, transcending the will of the Member States) being carried out in the name of human welfare. While, on the one hand, these are decisions that seem to express courage and other virtues, once read according to different ethical traditions, their moral adequacy becomes more contentious. Section 10.5 concludes highlighting the lessons learned and discussing critically moral exemplarity and the 'skills model' of virtues that further relies on an ideal conception of virtue.

By looking into biographical details and actions of the select leaders, combining them with the broader institutional and international context, and placing them within wider ethical frameworks that value other ethical values and goals, the chapter concludes that, despite the apparent potential, use, and revival of virtue ethics, its deployment to assess the goodness and adequacy of characters and actions is loaded with problems. Perhaps the potential of virtue ethics lies in its capacity to make salient features of moral life that are often neglected and resort to storytelling as a tool to engage ethics in a morally fragmented world. After all, focusing on the character of individuals makes a common, but often forgotten, moral intuition clearer, that is, 'individuals are not inter-substitutable'[25] and they matter next to the quality of rules, practices, ideas, and organizations.

---

[25] Williams, Bernard (1981), 'Persons, Character and Morality', *Moral Luck* (Cambridge: Cambridge University Press), 1–19 at 15, blaming Kantianism, but the same could be said about classical Utilitarianism, for the persistence, within moral theory, of impartiality and abstraction from personal features and relations.

Virtue and Leadership in the World Health Organization   257

Beyond probing deeper into the application problems of virtue ethics to actual choices and scenarios, the approach deployed here adds to the literature in a number of ways. First, it overcomes the economic and managerial tone adopted by principal–agent studies of leadership in international organizations in which leaders' performance is analysed from the point of view of *how much they deviate* from their original mandate established by nation-states and what are the costs of doing it as well as the costs of inducing and restoring compliance or punishing deviations. Instead, an examination of their agency from a virtues perspective allows us to focus on the full moral implications of character and actions at large and not only on whether the actions of the agent are against the best interests of the principals (a purely internal relation).[26] Second, it goes beyond functionalist readings of the expansion of international organizations' reach that tend to assume that broad mandates to pursue and promote global health as well as the globalization of lifeforms trigger a natural and unstoppable process in which national interests give way to global functional imperatives.[27] Third, it helps to provide a richer picture necessary to put in perspective claims, such as those made by Fiona Godlee, that excessive attention has been paid to issues of individual leadership when the WHO problems concern institutional design aspects.[28] Overall, thus, this chapter corrects the lack of mention of ethics in approaches to the study of the behaviour of the WHO.[29]

10.1.4 *A Short Note on the Research Approach*

The research approach deployed in this chapter combines pragmatism, story-telling, and narrative ethics. Part of its allure lies in the power to show that

---

[26] The seminal paper on agency costs is Jensen, Michael C. and Meckling, William H. (1976), 'Theory of the Firm: Managerial Behavior, Agency Costs and Ownership Structure', *Journal of Financial Economics*, 3 (4), 305–360. For an application to leadership in the WHO, see Cortell, Andrew P. and Peterson, Susan (2006), 'Dutiful Agents, Rogue Actors, or Both? Staffing, Voting Rules, and Slack in the WHO and WTO', in Darren G. Hawkins et al. (eds.), *Delegation and Agency in International Organizations* (New York: Cambridge University Press), 255–80.

[27] Fidler, David P. (2004), *SARS, Governance and the Globalization of Disease* (Basingstoke; New York: Palgrave MacMillan).

[28] Godlee, Fiona (1994), 'The World Health Organization: WHO in Crisis', *BMJ*, 309 (6966), 1424–28.

[29] Chorev, Nitsan (2012), *The World Health Organization: Between North and South* (Ithaca; London: Cornell University Press) offers a very interesting account of the WHO's secretariat and leadership strategic reaction against environmental pressures during select periods. While Chorev establishes that the WHO exercised agency, and thus was no simple pawn of its Member States, she is concerned primarily with the strategies employed; neither with the ethical frameworks deployed nor with the ethical assessment of such strategies.

neither ontological nor epistemological realism will get us anywhere because ethics is a practical matter. The cases discussed throughout the chapter demonstrate that to theorize in order to make moral judgments is a largely hopeless enterprise, that is, to know that exemplars or ethical theories ought to be followed if we want to uphold values A and B with the consequences C and D tell us very little on *how to do it*.

Conversely, I suggest throughout the chapter that to make ethical judgements cannot be done unless we engage historical materials and in turn this makes us sensitive to values that matter to us (e.g. that person seemed to have acted virtuously) highlighting new salient moral features in a non-decisive way. Thus, the point is to build a persuasive narrative, not a true or right narrative. The chapter deals in complexity and argues that ethical thinking is not complex enough, and analytical ethical theory oversimplifies the descriptive situation of moral choice as well as the relevant landscape needed for moral decision-making.

From this angle, we do not have any other way forward but to tell stories, knowing that stories can always be opposed by other stories. They are contingent arrangements of normative and factual materials compiled and digested by a given person according to specific biases, values, and goals. Theorizing, in this sense, is another form of storytelling which, however, as identified in the text, has been invested with a power greater than storytelling and narrative-making.

10.2 THE WORLD HEALTH ORGANIZATION: MANDATE AND ETHICS

The WHO was created in 1948, after the Technical Preparatory Committee (18 March–5 April 1946), replacing the League of Nations Health Organization (and the earlier Office International d'Hygiène Publique). It is structured around the Director-General and Secretariat, the World Health Assembly, and the Executive Board. According to article 1 of the WHO Constitution, its main objective 'shall be the attainment by all peoples of the highest possible level of health'.

The WHO pursues its core objective through the creation, dissemination and monitoring of technical standards, the provision of leadership and technical support on health-related issues and knowledge production, among other activities.[30] The WHO's vectors are health systems, communicable and noncommunicable diseases, promoting health through the life-course,

---

[30] The International Health Regulations are the most visible expression of the WHO's regulatory powers. For a historical account, see Gostin, Lawrence O. and Katz, Rebecca (2016), 'The International Health Regulations: The Governing Framework for Global Health Security', *Milbank Quarterly: A Multidisciplinary Journal of Population Health and Health Policy*, 94 (2), 264–313. For an eye-opening description of the wide normative and epistemic authority of

Virtue and Leadership in the World Health Organization 259

the provision of corporate services and preparedness, surveillance, and response during emergencies. The World Health Assembly (WHA) makes decisions by simple majority save for constitutional choices requiring a two-thirds majority. It is responsible for approving the budget, formulating policies (to be implemented by the Executive Board), and appointing the Director-General (DG). Article 31 of the WHO constitution reads

> The Director-General shall be appointed by the Health Assembly on the nomination of the Board on such terms as the Health Assembly may determine. The Director-General, subject to the authority of the Board, shall be the chief technical and administrative officer of the Organization.[31]

Many international organizations include in their constitutional rules dispositions requiring a high moral character and virtues from their civil servants as well as devise a series of procedures to ensure the selection of technically competent, wise, and ethically robust leaders.[32] The WHO is no exception, affirming in its Code of Ethics and Professional Conduct (Code) that

> Responsibility for ethical behaviour and professional conduct lies with all staff members at all levels, and must be taken seriously, as it forms the basis of WHO's reputation.[33]

Point 9 of the same Code identifies five principles of ethical behaviour that must be upheld by all staff members: integrity; accountability; independence and impartiality; respect for the dignity, worth, equality, diversity, and privacy of all persons; and professional commitment. Furthermore, high-level staff members have to serve as 'models of integrity' (point 18 of the Code).

While the WHO constitution does not prescribe explicitly Director-General-specific moral standards, the organization has evolved a series of policies that pursue the concerns listed above. A survey of the election of the

---

the WHO (well beyond formal law) and its innovative network of partnerships with domestic and international institutions, see Klabbers, Jan (2019), 'The Normative Gap in International Organizations Law: The Case of the World Health Organization', *International Organizations Law Review*, 16 (2), 272–98.

[31] Available at www.who.int/governance/eb/who_constitution_en.pdf.

[32] For examples, see Klabbers, Jan (2014), 'The Virtues of Expertise', in Monika Ambrus et al. (eds.), *The Role of 'Experts' in International and European Decision-Making* (Cambridge: Cambridge University Press), 82–102 and Gaskarth, Jamie (2012), 'The Virtues in International Society', *European Journal of International Relations*, 18 (3), 431–53.

[33] See point 1(4) of the Code available at www.who.int/about/ethics/code_of_ethics_full_version.pdf. This code further subjects WHO staff to the International Civil Service Commission's Standards of Conduct which again emphasize a number of virtues that must be observed while carrying out the mission of international organizations. This last document is available at https://icsc.un.org/Reso urces/General/Publications/standardsE.pdf?r=004535276.

260 *Guilherme Vasconcelos Vilaça*

last-elected WHO Director-General, Tedros Adhanom Ghebreyesus, places us before an ethically-informed and transparency-seeking procedure displaying a panoply of mechanisms designed to overcome what is known in economics as the problem of adverse selection (due to ex ante asymmetries of information) or, in lay terms, ending up choosing the wrong candidate. Thus, a whole set of documentation exclusively election-related was (and still is) made available online: Handbook, Legal Counsel Note, Roadmap, WHA Rules of Procedure, Code of Conduct, and one Live Forum with the three final Nominees, their Curriculum vitae, and written statements detailing their vision for the institution, a webpage plus the specifics of campaign activities and funding.[34]

It is quite clear that the WHO acknowledges the virtues and general ethics discourses, and has taken action to embed them in its internal and external workings. Furthermore, the meticulous scrutiny of the candidates applying for the Director-General position also evidences that great care is put into selecting the right person, technical and character wise, for the job. This could be seen as a straightforward vindication of the thesis that virtues matter for the WHO and shape leadership selection procedures. Unfortunately, the (ethical) literature is very much silent on the effectiveness of such mechanisms. After all, if candidates reveal a solid character throughout the battery of tests they are subject to, why should we not expect them to perform well their function once they take office?

In the next section, I would like to challenge this idea by showing that it is based on two questionable assumptions: (i) that candidates do not change their character and modus operandi over time, that is, before and after being selected; and, (ii) that, if selected, apriori inadequate candidates will prove to be inadequate leaders. In other words, while selection procedures which aim to correct the problem of adverse selection focus on picking the right candidate, I shall suggest that this may not always be conducive to the fulfilment of the mission of an international organization since sometimes what looks like an undesirable character may prove to be an excellent leader. This has to do with the fact that the character of persons may change, that the exercise of the virtues *in organizational settings* is connected to the *telos* of the specific organization (and not simply to individual moral flourishment),[35] and that different contexts may require different leaders since a prudent leader (i.e. a *phronimos*) always reacts and adapts her behaviour to the circumstances at hand.

---

[34] These materials can be found at www.who.int/dg/election/en/.

[35] For the articulation and normative defence of this claim, see Oakley, Justin and Cocking, Dean (2001), *Virtue Ethics and Professional Roles* (Cambridge: Cambridge University Press).

10.3 CHARACTER & THE WORLD HEALTH ORGANIZATION

10.3.1 *The First Director-General of the WHO: Brock Chisholm*

The World Health Organization was born in a moment of awareness that more ought to be done in the field of *international* health even if within a statist conception of healthcare provision. Visionaries advocated for social medicine given that general social and economic conditions determined health. Simultaneously, the functional needs tied to commerce required the observance of a minimum set of health prescriptions as well as the prevention and containment of epidemics of different sorts.[36]

The political setting surrounding the establishment of the WHO was unstable, adding particular challenges to any first Director-General. For instance, France held dearly to the Office International d'Hygiène Publique while the Pan American Sanitary Organization (a US health organization set up in 1902 that attracted many South American countries) declined to join forces with the WHO.[37] There was the Cold War balance to be maintained between the United States and the Soviet Union and their respective satellite countries, as well as the shadow of the Catholic Church that could always turn to be a menace, for reasons we shall see, to the mission and durability of the WHO.

Against this background of colonialism, Cold War, competition with other agencies, and Catholicism, and their implications for membership and funding, the question to be asked from a virtues perspective is: *which kind of leader* would have been deemed appropriate to launch the operations of a *new* international organization while laying the foundations necessary for the organization *to flourish and last?*

Logically, one would expect that the choice would have been made according to the candidate's record of institutional capacity building and consensus generation. The challenging context apparently screamed for a first Director-General that could have displayed, beyond immaculate technical knowledge and organizational skills, virtues such as prudence, moderation, diplomacy, and humility. Such virtues would certainly have appeared, at the time, crucial for the implementation, survival, and success of the organizational mission of the WHO.

---

[36] Fidler, David P. (2004), *SARS, Governance and the Globalization of Disease* (Basingstoke; New York: Palgrave MacMillan).

[37] See Fairley, John (2008), *Brock Chisholm, the World Health Organization, and the Cold War* (Vancouver: UBC Press), chapter 1.

262   *Guilherme Vasconcelos Vilaça*

On paper, and throughout the Technical Preparatory Committee's work, Brock Chisholm,[38] the Canadian who became the first Director-General of the WHO (1948–1953) and the person who actually suggested including 'World' (or 'Universal') in the official name of the organization, had proved to be *technically* competent and prepared. He was a famous psychiatrist, war hero (having received the Military Cross twice and commendations for his leadership while serving in WWII), former Director General of Medical Services in the Canadian Army, Deputy Minister of Health in Canada (1944), and Executive Secretary of the Interim Commission of the WHO (1946), having participated in the drafting of the first constitution of the WHO and serving as rapporteur and chairman of the Technical Preparatory Meeting. Chisholm was known too for holding strong and progressive views on birth control, sterilization practices, euthanasia, and negative eugenics.[39]

Was he a right fit for the task described earlier, that is, laying the ground for a new, lasting, and well-functioning international health organization while imbuing it with an ethical spirit?[40]

Undoubtedly, beyond his technical competence, Chisholm was recognized as a gifted orator, having successfully influenced the writing of the preamble of the WHO Constitution to include his views on social medicine, broadening the mandate of the WHO by linking health to 'mental health', 'housing', 'working conditions', 'well-being of children', and similar holistic concerns.[41]

Chisholm was also a visionary and a deeply committed *cosmopolitan*, having imposed an oral oath to be performed by new WHO staff members:

> I solemnly swear to exercise in all loyalty, discretion, and conscience the functions entrusted to me as an international civil servant of the WHO, to discharge those functions and regulate my conduct with the interests of the WHO only in view, and not seek or accept instructions in regard the performance of my duties from any government or other external authority.[42]

---

[38] On Brock Chisholm, see Irving, Allan (1998), *Brock Chisholm: Doctor to the World* (Toronto: Fitzhenry and Whiteside), though my account draws essentially from the richer and more complex biography by Fairley, John (2008), *Brock Chisholm, the World Health Organization, and the Cold War* (Vancouver: UBC Press).

[39] *Ibidem*, chapter 2.

[40] I am ignoring here the political machinations that may lead an ethically sub-optimal candidate to be chosen. Indeed, in regards to technical competence, international experience, character, and reputation, Chisholm was not perceived to be the best candidate. See Fairley, John (2008), *Brock Chisholm, the World Health Organization, and the Cold War* (Vancouver: UBC Press), chapter 1.

[41] See www.who.int/dg/chisholm/chisholm/en/.

[42] Fairley, John (2008), *Brock Chisholm, the World Health Organization, and the Cold War* (Vancouver: UBC Press) at 69.

Virtue and Leadership in the World Health Organization   263

Upon the reception of the Lasker Award, Chisholm voiced the same message, that is, 'We are citizens of the world', an anti-nuclear stance and the need for a world government. It is unequivocal that such a globalist stance seems appropriate for the task of developing an international organization. His social medicine approach to health can also be framed as virtuous, imbued of an ethics of care premised upon the values of humanness and human dignity.

On the other hand, however, Chisholm was said to have *no international public experience*. More importantly, regarding the capacity to build consensus around a new organization by arbitrating between very different constituencies and interests, Chisholm was called a 'godless iconoclast'[43] and considered to be too outspoken and *unsuitable for senior civil servant positions*. This reputation, preceding the WHO tenure, was the result of a series of inflaming public statements demolishing traditional social institutions such as the press, political community, family, religion, Santa Claus (!), the moral distinction between good and evil, as well as 'softie' educational methods

> ... for many generations we have bowed our necks to the yoke of the conviction of sin. We have swallowed all manner of poisonous certainties fed us by our parents, our Sunday and day school teachers, our politicians, our priests, our newspapers and others with a vested interest in controlling us ... The results, the inevitable results, are frustration, inferiority, neurosis and inability to enjoy living, to reason clearly or to make the world fit to live in.[44]
>
> ... the thinking of children must not be crippled by teaching them the principles of supposed right and wrong.[45]
>
> Any man who tells his son that the sun goes to bed at night is contributing directly to the next war ... Any child who believes in Santa Claus has had his ability to think permanently destroyed ... Can you imagine a child of four being led to believe that a man of grown stature is able to climb down a chimney ... that Santa Claus can cover the entire world in one night distributing presents to everyone! He will become a man who has ulcers at 40, develops a sore back when there is a tough job to do, and refuses to think realistically when war threatens.[46]
>
> To this list, one could add Chisholm's declaration blaming mothers for educating their male children on 'women's values' with harmful consequences to the army life.[47]

---

[43]   *Ibidem*, at 2.
[44]   *Ibidem*, at 41.
[45]   *Ibidem*, at 43.
[46]   *Ibidem*.
[47]   *Ibidem*, at 45.

264   Guilherme Vasconcelos Vilaça

Importantly, his 'we have bowed our necks to the yoke of the conviction of sin' speech delivered during the 1945 William Alanson White Memorial Lectures in Washington was deemed inappropriate for a bureaucrat. Chisholm was described as 'temperamentally instable' and someone who 'would not like the restrictions necessarily placed on the activities and utterances of senior civil servants',[48] leading to loss of confidence in the Canadian Ministry of Health and Welfare and himself. The more Catholic audience judged it as 'sound[ing] very much like an eloquent streamlined 1945 version of the Nietzschean point of view which was the basis of the Nazi philosophy'.[49]

What then do such statements tell us about the person that proffered them as well as how his moral character fit the nature of the task ahead?

Chisholm's speeches and public declarations highlight character traits going against widely perceived virtues such as moderation and self-control, tolerance and leniency, politeness and diplomacy, but also reasonableness and wisdom given their rashness and crudeness. Proof of this was the mentioned removal of trust in Chisholm by the Canadian Ministry after his William Alanson White Memorial Lectures. Furthermore, the vocal and antagonizing nature of the statements against established social powers suggests an uncompromising personality that, at least in some respects, could hinder being accepted by the groups he attacked thus compromising institutional development and the survival of the WHO.

Indeed, Chisholm's radical stance against organized religion almost brought the WHO to an end. In 1951, he accepted Nehru's request to have the WHO help operationalizing an ambitious birth control and family planning policy adopted to curb population growth in Europe. Even though the WHO chose the 'rhythm method' in order to minimize frictions with Pius XII's position excluding 'birth control', it did not avoid a severe backlash against such intervention. Most likely, Chisholm's decision to send Abraham Stone, already well known for holding progressive birth control and family planning views, did not help, since Stone insisted upon the use of sterilization and scientific contraceptives in India. Given that many Catholic European countries threatened to withdraw from the WHO (at the Fifth WHA) in case population control became part of WHO's intervention,

---

[48] *Ibidem*, at 47 for both quotations, attributed to Brooke Claxton, then Canada's Minister of Health and Welfare.

[49] Fairley, John (2008), *Brock Chisholm, the World Health Organization, and the Cold War* (Vancouver: UBC Press) at 42 attributes the quotation to Rabi Abraham Feinberg. Still today, several webpages display similar accusations.

Virtue and Leadership in the World Health Organization 265

the latter topic was successfully removed (despite its relevance for achieving decent standards of living) from the WHO's agenda for a long time.[50]

If we go back to the current mechanisms the WHO deploys to elect its Director-General, it becomes difficult to believe that someone like Chisholm could present himself as possessing the right qualities and virtues to fulfil the task of building a new international organization. Furthermore, the short biographical sketch makes one fear that Chisholm would have proved unsuitable for the job, especially given the delicacy of the institutional setting due to the fact that a number of constituencies still had to be convinced of the desirability of the organization.

Interestingly, however, Brock Chisholm's tenure is judged as both having been successful and having laid the foundations for a modern, stable, and professional WHO. In fact, he is credited with having taken effective action against Malaria outbreaks and cholera epidemics and having developed a conception of WHO staff as apolitical medical experts that had made an oath to the world, not domestic interests, to advance the international goals of the WHO.[51] He also fostered regionalization under 'One WHO', having struck a direct blow against local interests who favoured autonomous regional chapters of the WHO, an achievement that further entrenched the organization.

Together these last two aspects seem to embody courage to create an *esprit de corps* that effectively and virtuously pushed the WHO to focus on global welfare rather than national interest, a cosmopolitan rather than a self-interest stance. As mentioned before, his focus on social medicine as opposed to vertical medicine (e.g., vaccines) and his defence of have-nots may also be framed as expressing benevolence and justice concerns in improving the welfare of the worst-off. Finally, the birth control, family planning, and sterilization-driven controversy with the Catholic Church which nearly destroyed the WHO can also be read as a tribute to *intellectual courage* advancing a commitment to make decisions based not on faith, ideology, or prejudice but on existing scientific knowledge. There is a further fact of utmost interest for the purposes of this chapter, that is, the widespread conviction that Chisholm became less outspoken and more diplomatic during his tenure at the WHO in order to build a stable and working WHO with his imprint.[52] One can think that, somehow, he succeeded even if such an outcome was far from predictable.

---

[50] *Ibidem*, chapter 11 for a detailed description of the situation.
[51] *Ibidem*, at 32.
[52] *Ibidem*.

266 Guilherme Vasconcelos Vilaça

Overall, though, what to make of Chisholm virtues and vices? Was he a courageous visionary or an imprudent polemical individual who could have jeopardized the WHO enterprise? To sensitize us further to the complexities that such a balancing act generates, let us look into the character and leadership provided by another WHO Director-General: Hiroshi Nakajima.

10.3.2 Another Kind of Director-General: Hiroshi Nakajima

Hiroshi Nakajima served as Director-General of the WHO between 1988 and 1998. He had ample experience, having acted as the WHO Western-Pacific Regional Director between 1979 and 1988. During his tenure as Director-General, he famously launched the Global Polio Eradication Initiative, promoted the fight against tuberculosis and children vaccination campaigns, having raised awareness to end female genital mutilation.[53]

Nakajima, a Japanese national, was unanimously recognized as a technically competent and *experienced leader* (differently from Chisholm as we may recall). However, he did not leave much of an impression for posterity regarding his leadership,[54] appearing to be a *most dissimilar case* to Chisholm.[55] Despite the undisputed technical expertise, he was unanimously regarded as a terrible public speaker, even failing to convey his technical competence in public speeches due to the difficulty in understanding him when he spoke and irrespective of the language used, English or Japanese. Consider the trenchant words of Fiona Godlee, the assistant editor of the *British Medical Journal*, introducing an interview she conducted with Nakajima

> I spoke to him at WHO's headquarters in Geneva in July. I have presented the interview in the form of questions and answers. It would be misleading, however, not to make clear that in doing so I have transcribed conversation which was at times extremely difficult to follow. I feel that it is important to emphasise this in the context of an interview with an international leader, one of whose primary tasks must be to communicate his views on health to people across the world. The interview gave me first hand experience of the

[53] As far as I can tell, there is no comprehensive biography about Nakajima published in English. See Takuma, Kayo (2019), 'Nakajima, Hiroshi', in Bob Reinalda, Kent J. Kille, and Jaci Eisenberg (eds.), *IO BIO, Biographical Dictionary of Secretaries-General of International Organizations*, available at www.ru.nl/fm/iobio.

[54] For many commentators, the WHO was 'inactive' during Nakajima's leadership, arguably, among other things, due to resistance he met from Western countries. Chorev, Nitsan (2012), *The World Health Organization: Between North and South* (Ithaca; London: Cornell University Press) at 39.

[55] *Ibidem.*

difficulties in communication that staff, diplomats, and others, including Japanese leaders, have consistently commented on since Dr Nakajima took office.[56]

Lack of tact was also something he was criticized for, having pointed out Africans' poor conceptual skills and capacity to write reports (a declaration that arguably cost him a third re-election).[57] Of course, it did not help that he replaced a charismatic Director-General, that is, Halfdan Mahler, telling us that where one comes in the line-up of leaders is important for how one will be judged.

Nakajima's mandate is associated with the loss of power of the central WHO to regional offices towards whom he was seen as being too conciliatory. Furthermore, it is widely held that his tenure coincided with the WHO's loss of importance in global health largely due to his perceived inability to manage donors and downgrading of the importance of AIDS. This enabled UNAIDS and the Global Fund to take the space and role of the WHO in AIDS governance.

Nakajima's leadership came under attack for other reasons. He was accused of promoting staff on the basis of personal loyalty, not meritocracy, as well as of misuse of funds and unrestrained growth of staff and budget. There were further accusations of vote-rigging regarding his re-election, and a sharp increase in the number of cases of aggrieved staff.[58]

Vote-rigging, misuse of and lack of control over funds, and a toxic working environment are recognized priorities in today's IOs' working ethics. Since most accusations against Nakajima could not be substantiated, I shall focus on other character issues. For instance, from a virtues discourse perspective, the absence of public speaking skills amounts to a vice because, according to Aristotle, rhetoric is constitutive of affirming one's knowledge practically in social and political life.[59] As Amélie Rorty has written:

---

[56] Godlee, Fiona (1995), 'The World Health Organization: Interview with the Director General', *BMJ*, 310 (6979), 583–586 at 583.

[57] See Takuma, Kayo (2019), 'Nakajima, Hiroshi', in Bob Reinalda, Kent J. Kille, and Jaci Eisenberg (eds.), *IO BIO, Biographical Dictionary of Secretaries-General of International Organizations*, available at www.ru.nl/fm/iobio.

[58] Chorev, Nitsan (2012), *The World Health Organization: Between North and South* (Ithaca; London: Cornell University Press) at 125.

[59] Aristotle (2004), *The Art of Rhetoric*, trans. H. C. Lawson-Tancred (London: Penguin). Recovering the importance of 'epideictic oratory' to complement persuasion leading the audience to act by increasing adherence to the values being communicated, see Perelman, Chaïm and Olbrechts-Tyteca, Lucie (2018), *Tratado de la Argumentación: La Nueva Retórica*, trans. Julia Sevilla Muñoz (4th edn.; Barcelona: GREDOS).

268   *Guilherme Vasconcelos Vilaça*

Speaking persuasively – rightly and reasonably saying the right things in
the right way at the right time – is a central part of acting rightly. The
phronimos – the man of practical wisdom – typically participates in public
life.[60]
The skilled Persuader must know how to present his own character in a way
that will appeal to his audience, to convey authority and a sense of trust.[61]

Nakajima's failure to maintain a strong grip on regional offices and discipline
donors (i.e. Member States) could also be conceptualized as arising due to
lack of charisma and courage to impose a clear vision for the relationship
between the central and regional bodies of the WHO.

10.3.3 *Balancing and Evaluating Virtues and Vices*

But what exactly does it mean to be *courageous*? I see two different aspects to
this question. One is definitional and conceptual, whereas the other one is
cultural.

Courage can best be understood as the display of a firm mind in the face of
challenges and evil, that is, the mastery of fear and confidence in one's deeds.[62]
Received Aristotelian, Bushido, and Confucian wisdom establishes that courage is neither rashness nor cowardice in trying to do what is right,[63] all agreeing
that the exact measure of courage can only be defined in reference to specific
circumstances. And this creates a first difficulty in trying to determine whether
Nakajima and Chisholm were courageous, because in order to find it out we
also need to establish the requirements placed upon them by context and how
they responded.

International leaders fulfil roles in changing environments and different
historical periods. This means that not all virtues or qualities will always be
deemed equally important or desirable. Different circumstances may demand
different virtues, leaders, and modes of leadership.[64] Chisholm's firmness,

---

[60]   Rorty, Amélie (2011), 'Aristotle on the Virtues of Rhetoric', *The Review of Metaphysics*, 64 (4),
       715–33 at 715, emphasis in the original.
[61]   *Ibidem*, at 721, emphasis in the original.
[62]   Pope, Stephen J. (2002), 'The Ethics of Aquinas', in Stephen J. Pope (ed.), *Overview of the
       Ethics of Aquinas* (Washington: Georgetown University Press), 30–53 at 43–44.
[63]   Nitobe, Inazo (1969), *Bushido: The Soul of Japan* (Singapore: Tuttle) at 19, rooting its message
       in *The Analects*.
[64]   This is the key lesson of Schechter, Michael G. (1987), 'Leadership in International
       Organizations: Systemic, Organizational and Personality Factors', *Review of International
       Studies*, 13 (3), 197–220, distinguishing between expansive and friendly environments to IOs,
       congenial to activist leaders, and uncertain limited-budget periods in which pragmatic leaders
       prove superior.

Virtue and Leadership in the World Health Organization 269

honesty, and directness may have served well the WHO's goal of the time, that is, establishing itself being a new IO, but could also have torn it apart as the episode with the Catholic Church suggests. Ultimately, it is supremely hard to judge whether he was courageous or rash if we let go of the comfortable position of judging with hindsight. We should not confuse two different things: it is not because we now think and judge Chisholm's tenure as successful that the latter was necessarily generated by his courageous character.

By the same token, it could be argued that the context in which Nakajima led the WHO required a less confrontational character. Arguably, regional offices had been pushed to the extreme by Halfdan Mahler, the practice of earmarked donations had been brewing, international organizations in general were facing a funding crisis, and new players such as the World Bank had started to intervene in global health matters. In this context, a stronger leader could have worsened the problem by confronting donors and national/regional interests too harshly (which could have placed their money somewhere else) thereby compromising further the WHO's mission. Nakajima's often-quoted feebleness could thus be re-read in a much more positive, virtues-wise, light.

The same could be said about his leadership over the Palestine Liberation Organization (PLO) episode. After being accepted as an observer, the PLO applied for full membership in 1989. Predictably, the US threatened to remove their funding (around 25 per cent of the annual budget of the WHO by then) which would have halted most of the WHO's yearly activities. Nakajima was criticized for both seeking to convince Arafat to withdraw the application and delaying a decision on the matter.[65] Given the dependence on American monies and his focus on improving the health of millions around the world, Nakajima prioritized the WHO mission to save lives over taking a courageous stance regarding a matter of political membership to the WHO.

All in all, to define what courage is cannot be done without analysing the shifting context surrounding the WHO and the needs of the Director-General's role and without having an idea of what institutional flourishing is, and requires, at a given point in time. Again, this makes all-too-quick judgments on the qualities of leaders based on assessments made with hindsight plainly inadequate because insufficiently complex.

The second issue when approaching virtues through concrete scenarios and lives is that virtues are cultural products and thus general definitions of

---

[65] For details, see Takuma, Kayo (2019), 'Nakajima, Hiroshi', in Bob Reinalda, Kent J. Kille, and Jaci Eisenberg (eds.), *IO BIO, Biographical Dictionary of Secretaries-General of International Organizations*, available at www.ru.nl/fm/iobio.

270   *Guilherme Vasconcelos Vilaça*

courage such as the ones mentioned earlier do not tell us much. As McInerny put it:

> One response to such a plurality of accounts is to seek a generic conception of courage, one that is neutral to all cultures. Something, presumably, such as: 'Courage is that characteristic which allows us to face up to our fears and overcome obstacles for the sake of some deeply-cherished value.' But this is not so much a definition of courage as a ghost of the virtue. *What sort of characteristics are we talking about? What fears and obstacles? What cherished value?* When answers are provided for these questions, we find ourselves right back in the thick of particular cultural frameworks.[66]

Interestingly, and resorting to McIntyre, McInerny suggests that, in heroic cultures such as that enveloping *Beowulf*, being virtuous, that is, courageous, leads to death not victory.[67] This evokes the Japanese custom, described in Shusaku Endo's *The Samurai*, according to which whoever petitioned the Emperor had to die in order to simultaneously change and preserve the stability of social order.[68]

This is important if we go back to Nakajima. Recall that he was criticized for emphasising personal loyalty over meritocracy, which could also be said to go against impartial treatment as measured by rules that are equal to everyone. Instead, Nakajima's lack of charisma, apparent feebleness, and focus on personal loyalty could well be understood as tributary of an *alternative Asian style of leadership*[69] and work ethics in which hard work, social relations, and loyalty garnered over time together with a conciliatory tone rank as qualities and virtues, not vices![70]

---

[66]   McInerny, Daniel (2014), 'Fortitude and the Conflict of Frameworks', in Kevin Timpe and Craig A. Boyd (eds.), *Virtues and Their Vices* (Oxford: Oxford University Press), 75–92 at 75.

[67]   See (2013), *Beowulf*, trans. Michael Alexander (London: Penguin Books) at 4 and 51:

> It is by glorious action
> that a man comes by honour in any people.
> … daring is the thing
> for a fighting man to be remembered by.

[68]   Endo, Shusaku (1997), *The Samurai*, trans. Van C. Gessel (New York: New Directions).

[69]   See in general Bary, Wm. Theodore de (2004), *Nobility & Civility: Asian Ideals of Leadership and the Common Good* (Cambridge; London: Harvard University Press).

[70]   It is appropriate to ponder that Nakajima, like Margaret Chan (another Asian leader of the WHO), greatly emphasized the respect that Director-Generals should display towards national governments as part of abiding by the WHO's constitution. Isn't this the expression of *humility*? See Godlee, Fiona (1995), 'The World Health Organization: Interview with the Director General', *BMJ*, 310 (6979), 583–86.

Indeed, Asian ethics tends to nurture and prescribe respect towards superiors and group-loyalty mentality, an idea that can be derived from Confucian filial piety (Confucianism travelled from China to Japan and Korea first and foremost, deeply impacting these societies and cultures).[71] Since families are the first and main source of virtue formation of individuals in Asian thinking, but at the same time are also highly hierarchical, filial piety imposes deep respect for elders, authority, and the (affective) effort made in bringing us up which ought to be repaid (justifying that we ought to look after those who nurtured and educated us).[72] The latter would influence the whole society since, according to Confucianism, social order would come from adopting filial piety in other social relations (that is, the world and the state should follow the ordering of families).[73] Consequently, social life would also be characterized by the same emphasis on *unequal hierarchical relations* that assign different rights and duties according to the roles and statuses of the parties at stake.[74] Cecilia Wee summarizes the workings of such special obligations as follows:

> Confucianism emphasizes the various special obligations that an individual must honor in virtue of the specific relationships that she has with relevant others. Thus, suppose that Mei is a daughter, sister, and citizen. Confucianism holds that, insofar as Mei is each of these, *she has specific obligations to the other with whom she stands in that particular relation.*[75]

The point here is twofold. On the one hand, even if virtues across ethical traditions can be defined abstractly in similar terms, their application to specific scenarios and situations is largely determined by local views about them.[76] Thus, whereas loyalty can be defined unproblematically as being

---

[71] For an overview of filial piety, see Sarkissian, Hagop (2010), 'Recent Approaches to Confucian Filial Morality', *Philosophy Compass*, 5 (9), 725–34, and Kim, Richard T., Mondejar, Reuben, and Chu, Chris W. L. (2017), 'Filial Piety and Business Ethics: A Confucian Reflection', in Alejo José G. Sison, Gregory R. Beabout, and Ignacio Ferrero (eds.), *Handbook of Virtue Ethics in Business and Management* (Dordrecht: Springer), 467–79.

[72] Hwang, Kwang-Kuo (1999), 'Filial Piety and Loyalty: Two Types of Social Identification in Confucianism', *Asian Journal of Social Psychology*, (2), 163–83.

[73] Plaks, Andrew (2003), *Ta Hsueh and Chung Yung (The Highest Order of Cultivation and On the Practice of the Mean)*, trans. Andrew Plaks (London: Penguin).

[74] For the importance of *guanxi*, see Bian, Yanjie and Zhang, Lei (2014), 'Corporate Social Capital in Chinese Guanxi Culture', *Research in the Sociology of Organizations*, 40, 417–39.

[75] Wee, Cecilia (2014), 'Filial Obligations: A Comparative Study', *Dao*, 13 (1), 83–97 at 83, emphasis added.

[76] Slingerland, Edward (2001), 'Virtue Ethics, The Analects, and the Problem of Commensurability', *Journal of Religious Ethics*, 29 (1), 97–125, argues that Aristotle and Confucian traditions (on 'self-cultivation') are generally commensurable but issue very different specific content. While the author argues for cross-cultural commensurability, he

faithful to an idea or person, *being* loyal in specific circumstances and organizations may mean very different things across cultures. As in the earlier example, loyalty in Asian contexts may require *deference* and trample equality, whereas, in the West, it is often subordinated to the latter justifying constructive criticism in the name of one's faith in something or someone. On the other hand, virtues are not separable from social structure; they are not simply teachings or ideas without materiality but instead impregnate and take shape in actual forms of social life. Consequently, we cannot render virtues concrete outside individualist or communitarian paradigms of social order. As such, the remarks just made on loyalty find their basis precisely in the different requirements that the latter paradigms place when one acts.

A communitarian background tends to assume that social relations are defined by roles and hierarchies in which other norms are embedded (and not the other way around), making it impossible to prescribe a social-relations-independent rule of behaviour. Accordingly, Nakajima's weaker grip on regional offices could also be seen as respectful of regional differences, tributary of a relational approach to politics that is more contextual, contractual, and subject to the specific configuration of the relations (their scope and differences in prestige and power) involved in a concrete issue rather than an apriori equal-for-all rule-based style of governance.[77]

This of course raises the cultural relativist question from a very pragmatic standpoint, that is, what if we are assuming that the virtues, values, and their backgrounds and application we deem as appropriate for international leaders are fundamentally Western? In that case, if we already expect leaders to exhibit virtues modelled according to Western conceptions, then their adoption when evaluating international leadership further reinforces the fact that our assessments are fundamentally biased and partial. Interestingly, in a recent book, psychologist David Nisbet has argued that Asians and Westerners think differently, linking Asian society's relationality or interdependence with Asian social ontology and contextual view of the world which sees objects always enmeshed in a complex network of other objects and factors.[78] In ethical thinking, it is also the preference for personal and social relations, described

---

does so only theoretically, falling prey of the theorist/practitioner divide highlighted in the first section of this chapter.

[77] Vilaça, Guilherme Vasconcelos (2018), 'China, International Responsibility and Law', in Jan Klabbers, Maria Varaki, and Guilherme Vasconcelos Vilaça (eds.), *Towards Responsible Global Governance* (Helsinki: Helsinki University Press), 53–73 at 67–68.

[78] Nisbett, Richard E. (2004), *The Geography of Thought: How Asians and Westerners Think Differently . . . and Why* (New York: Free Press).

Virtue and Leadership in the World Health Organization 273

above, over impartialism that has triggered stronger criticism against Confucianism and Asian ethics.

All this appears to me as critical because spreading the language of virtues into international leadership may lead to spreading the idea that the flourishing of international organizations requires leaders that display Western conceptions of the virtues. In such a way, we would risk contributing to colonizing further international organizations with Western thinking, this time premised upon the mistaken assumption that virtues and their application are universal.[79]

Finally, the argument about an Asian style of leadership does not pretend to be definitive and theoretical. Empirical examination of the leadership values and actions has to be carried out always. In this context, it is revealing to consider the leadership of another Asian international leader, the Burmese U Thant who served as the United Nations Secretary-General between 1951 and 1961. U Thant was revered as a living moral force and was known for his indifference to the material aspects of life and independence from political and social loyalties. As such, he transported to his mandates nothing of the Asian features described earlier, though the fact that he was a Buddhist could account for that, given Buddhism's eschewal of social structure and particular attachments. However, some of U Thant's features, such as the 'noble silence' he applied every time he was criticized or saw his views disputed, as well as his virtually undisturbed calm, were often deemed frustrating and inadequate by Western international leaders.[80]

10.3.4 *Virtue Ethics' Narrative and Changes of Character*

The last section tried to map out some troubles when deploying virtue ethics to evaluate actual characters against complex and multifactorial scenarios,

---

[79] On Western epistemological imperialism, see in general Dabashi, Hamid (2015), *Can Non-Europeans Think?* (London: Zed Books) and applied to IOs, Sinclair, Guy Fiti (2017), *To Reform the World: International Organizations and the Making of Modern States* (New York: Oxford University Press). This is compounded by the fact that Westerners are overly represented in the international civil service. Whereas in 2005 Western Europe accounted for 13% of the world's population, its share of international senior secretariat positions was 45%! See Novosad, Paul and Werker, Eric (2019), 'Who Runs the International System? Nationality and Leadership in the United Nations Secretariat', *The Review of International Organizations*, 4 (1), 1–33 at 3.

[80] For a comprehensive analysis of U Thant's personal traits and his mandates as Secretary-General, see Dorn, A. Walter (2007), 'U Thant: Buddhism in Action', in Kent J. Kille (ed.), *The UN Secretary-General and Moral Authority: Ethics and Religion in International Leadership* (Washington: Georgetown University Press), 143–86.

making it harder to say with propriety that Chisholm was virtuous, whereas Nakajima was not. But the description made above tells us that we need to consider how the virtues shape both the *internal* workings of the institution (i.e. institutional culture) as well as its *external fit* to the environmental context. As such, we may admire someone's qualities in one of these spheres that, however, may prove inadequate in the other.

The accusations that hang over Nakajima (absent regarding Chisholm) I mostly skipped over before speak to a lack of capacity to instil a culture of institutional integrity, transparency, and healthy workplace that is of paramount importance in today's organizational ethos. Intra-institution leadership may well be the best a virtue ethics narrative can offer with confidence (subject to the cultural objections provided above) since judging traits such as courage or diplomatic skills regarding the IO's vision of a leader largely depends on shifting contexts and claims difficult to establish. After all, how to answer these questions: (i) 'How did Chisholm manage to establish such a robust WHO?'; and, (ii) 'Would a stronger leader have further weakened or strengthened the WHO during those times?'

Returning to Chisholm, his example further testifies to the fact that it is very hard to make a holistic assessment of a character as virtuous given the multidimensional issues a leader has to act in and upon. While character is not the sole factor to be taken into account when selecting a leader, my purpose was to show that we should not necessarily expect an ex ante and ex post alignment of the evaluation of characters and achievements.

If *one's character changes*[81] then selection procedures aimed to filter specific characters deemed 'good' may actually exclude apriori candidates that are able to adjust and focus on what needs to be done to advance their vision of the IO, rather than to advance their own idiosyncratic features once they take office. But notice that apparent changes of character or virtues may take place the other way around.

For example, Aung San Suu Kyi, Myanmar's State Counsellor, an icon for the pacific struggle for human rights and democracy, was criticized for her silence and inaction regarding the persecution suffered (with 'genocidal intent' said UN investigators) by the Rohingya at the hands of the military. More graphically, it has been suggested that she should be stripped of her 1991 Nobel Peace Prize even though the Nobel Committee refused to do it. As its head in 2017, Berit Reiss-Andersen, declared:

---

[81] Or beliefs? See Malici, Akan (2008), *When Leaders Learn and When They Don't: Mikhail Gorbachev and Kim Il Sung at the End of the Cold War* (New York: State University New York Press) at 48ff, highlighting how the shift from a reformist to a transformative stance of Gorbachev could not be guessed from his previous leadership features and the first years of his government.

Virtue and Leadership in the World Health Organization 275

'We don't do it. It's not our task to oversee or censor what a laureate does after the prize has been won', adding that 'The prize-winners themselves have to safeguard their own reputations.'[82]

Irrespective of the Committee's position and what we may think of Aung San Suu Kyi's stance (she argued her silence had been the wisest thing to do in order to avoid even worse consequences given the context), the fact is that the requests for stripping her of the Nobel Peace Prize have largely to do with the shared belief that prizes that recognize virtuous lives are based on the assumption that these reveal a longstanding, consistent, *unchanging*, and brave commitment to a set of values.[83] As pointed out before, this is the old link between virtues, age, and experience superbly captured in Confucius' passage

> At fifteen, I set my heart on learning, at thirty I was established, at forty I had no perplexities, at fifty I understood the decrees of Heaven, at sixty my ear was in accord and at seventy I followed what my heart desired but did not transgress what was right.[84]

A betrayal of the grounds that had dictated widespread moral recognition puts into question the idea itself that a morally excellent character and life had been achieved in the first place. But this is just the other face of the same coin, that is, selection of character is a tricky business since persons can change or different contexts may make us perceive their characters and values to have changed, making the usefulness of selection procedures to document character less impressive than what one might have expected.

10.4 VIRTUES AND ACTIONS

10.4.1 *Virtue Ethics and Other Ethical Traditions*

So far, we have been focusing on virtues as if they exhausted the universe of relevant moral concerns associated to persons, situations, and choices. This is

---

[82] See Reuters, "Aung San Suu Kyi won't be stripped of Nobel Peace Prize: committee", 29 August 2018, available at https://www.reuters.com/article/us-myanmar-rohingya-nobelpeace-prize-idUSKCN1LE1X7.

[83] I have highlighted the 'peace' category within Nobel prizes because in it the connection to virtuous behaviour at large is clearer than in other categories such as medicine. Discussions on stripping Egas Moniz of the Nobel Prize in Medicine for his pioneering studies on lobotomy, a practice now deemed barbaric, forget that such a prize recognized what was believed to be state-of-the-art science, whereas the Nobel Peace Prize recognizes a commitment to human, not disciplinary, values.

[84] Dawson, Raymond (2008), *The Analects*, trans. Raymond Dawson (Reprint edn.; New York: Oxford University Press), Book 2(4).

276 Guilherme Vasconcelos Vilaça

partially explained by our goal to highlight the potential but also the limits in deploying virtue ethics. It goes without saying that the latter is but one among different ethical traditions (basically: deontologism and consequentialism)[85] and thus a virtues-based analysis does not exhaust the moral relevance of leaders' and organizations' behaviour making our ethical narrative incomplete.

For example, the functionalism and internationalism that Chisholm cherished and successfully imprinted in the WHO are the same values that critical readings of international law hold responsible for the development of a Western imperialist set of IOs.[86] This further complicates the picture because the ethos and virtues that we may admire in abstract (e.g. a courageous leader that fights against prejudice and bad science as Chisholm) or that may be appropriate to develop the organizational mission may end up creating and perpetuating an enchained world, by expanding IOs' reach and scope,[87] that reproduces an unfair and exploitative state of affairs, despite the good intentions of international leaders and staffs.

In other words, while virtue ethics focuses on traits that we deem admirable and worth of emulation, this does not guarantee that the aggregate *effects* of actions performed or pushed forward by such traits are morally good. Then, Nakajima's weaker grip on regional offices out of respect for regional differences could be read as countering, desirably, both the expansion of IOs' powers and the spread of Western mentality. But how are we supposed to add consequentialist considerations – measuring the goodness of an action based on its effects – to our virtue ethics narrative of Director-Generals' character? Can we mix and evaluate them holistically or are they to remain fundamentally incommensurable as MacIntyre famously held?[88]

---

[85] For a good overview of the different ethical traditions, see MacIntyre, Alasdair (2007), *After Virtue: A Study in Moral Theory* (3rd edn.; London: Duckworth) and Smart, J. J. C. and Williams, Bernard (1973), *Utilitarianism: For and Against* (Cambridge University Press). For an account of Chinese consequentialism (much older than the Western school), see Fraser, Chris (2016), *The Philosophy of Mozi: The First Consequentialists* (New York: Columbia University Press). The classical source is Johnston, Ian (2013), *The Book of Master Mo*, trans. Ian Johnston (London: Penguin Books).

[86] Sinclair, Guy Fiti (2017), *To Reform the World: International Organizations and the Making of Modern States* (New York: Oxford University Press).

[87] Indeed, in the seminal article Cox, Robert (1969), 'The Executive Head: An Essay on Leadership in International Organization', *International Organization*, 23 (2), 205–30 at 205, emphasis added, the author famously proposed and argued that 'The quality of executive leadership may prove to be the most critical single determinant of the *growth in scope and authority* of international organization.'

[88] MacIntyre, Alasdair (2007), *After Virtue: A Study in Moral Theory* (3rd edn.; London: Duckworth).

Linda Zagzebski has tried to offer an account of virtue ethics incorporating the language and normative concerns of other ethical traditions

> A *virtue* is a trait we admire in an admirable person. It is a trait that makes the person paradigmatically good in a certain respect.
> A *right act* in some set of circumstances C is what the admirable person would take to be most favored by the balance of reasons in circumstances C.
> A *good outcome* is a state of affairs at which admirable persons aim.
> A *good life* (a desirable life, a life of well-being) is a life desired by admirable persons.[89]

Does it do the trick? Well, not really since all propositions depend on knowing that someone is admirable. All ethical labels (virtue, right act, good outcome, and good life) follow from it, taking us back to the starting point, that is, what is an admirable person and in virtue of what can we reach such judgment?[90]

The circularity of Zagzebski's reconstruction gives priority to virtues over other ethical traditions limiting the relevance of the latter's distinctive normative concerns which are 'disarmed' of their critical potential. Indeed, to claim that '[a] *good outcome* is a state of affairs at which admirable persons aim' is very different from the consequentialist concern with studying the whole set of *actual* or *probable* effects of decisions over a given period. If we deem Chisholm an admirable person, then logically his internationalist and cosmopolitan stance would appear to us as producing good outcomes. But notice how much this would distort consequentialism's distinctive moral outlook while leaving us in a rather comical predicament. As beautifully put by W. D. Ross

> ... any particular act will in all probability in the course of time contribute to the bringing about of good or of evil for many human beings, and thus have a *prima facie* rightness or wrongness of which we know nothing.[91]
>
> ...
>
> There is therefore much truth in the description of the right act as a fortunate act. If we cannot be certain that it is right, it is our good fortune if the act we do is the right act.[92]

---

[89] Zagzebski, Linda (2013), 'Moral Exemplars in Theory and Practice', *Theory and Research in Education*, 11 (2), 193–206 at 202, emphasis in the original.

[90] I shall criticize the way Zagzebski answers this question in the final section of this chapter.

[91] Ross, William David (2003), *The Right and the Good* (Oxford: Oxford University Press) at 31, emphasis in the original.

[92] *Ibidem*.

278   *Guilherme Vasconcelos Vilaça*

Virtue ethics narratives focusing on character do indeed run into the difficulty of the complexity of the actual moral scenario and moral resources agents *descriptively* face and employ, because the nature of moral choice is never entirely captured solely by a single moral tradition. Let us try to delve deeper into this issue by moving our focus from characters onto actions.

10.4.2 *Going beyond the Call of Duty in the WHO: Marcolino Candau and the Guinea Outbreak of Cholera*

While in the previous sections I focused on leaders' *overall features*, I now turn to examine one *action*[93] that went openly against the mandate of the WHO with such deviation arguably being justified on moral grounds, that is, the need to do something even if illegal and potentially generating immense political backlash.[94] A kind of action which the frame of virtue ethics is particularly well suited to recognize and applaud. Which action was that?

In 1970, there was a severe outbreak of cholera in Guinea. Existing international health regulations prescribed that WHO outbreak reports were conditional on previous explicit notification by affected states. Guinea refused to do it despite repeated appeals from Marcolino Candau, the WHO's Director-General between 1953 and 1973. Eventually, Candau decided to make public the information of the outbreak against the WHO's law and Guinea's position

> During the present outbreak of cholera *eltor* in the Eastern Mediterranean and Africa, it has become evident that some countries are not notifying the presence of the disease. The Organization is required under Article 11 of the International Sanitary Regulations to provide daily information on a worldwide scale regarding the changing epidemiological situation in order to facilitate the planning of appropriate action by governments. This it cannot do in the absence of notifications from the countries. Furthermore, the resulting uncertainty has given rise to widespread anxiety and rumours, which is bound to adversely influence the public in general and causes the application of excessive measures to international trade and travel. To rectify this situation, the Director-General considers that, in order to fulfil the

---

[93] For a defence of the compatibility of character-based virtue ethics with the idea of right action, see Swanton, Christine (2001), 'A Virtue Ethical Account of Right Action', *Ethics*, 112, 32–52, and Annas, Julia (2014), 'Why Virtue Ethics Does Not Have a Problem with Right Action', in Mark Timmons (ed.), *Oxford Studies in Normative Ethics* (New York; Oxford: Oxford University Press), 13–33.

[94] A similar action in structure could be the NATO bombings against Yugoslavia deemed 'illegal, yet legitimate'. See The Independent International Commission on Kosovo (2000), *The Kosovo Report: Conflict, International Response, Lessons Learned* (Oxford: Oxford University Press) at 186.

Virtue and Leadership in the World Health Organization 279

Organization's obligations under Article 2 of the WHO Constitution, the presence of cholera should be disclosed in the absence of notification when reliable technical evidence is available.[95]

This remains a quite unique case in the WHO's history since never again did a Director-General issue an outbreak against states' will. On the one hand, such a decision could be justified based on art. article 2(V) of the WHO Constitution which determines its functions to be 'generally to take all necessary action to attain the objective of the Organization'. On the other hand, many of the other functions established in article 2 as well as in the international health regulations establish that the WHO needs to obtain national consent before being able to intervene.

Despite its uniqueness, however, Candau's decision did not generate a public outcry. Several aspects may help to explain such a reaction. The Director-General's decision was ratified both by the Executive Board and the WHO's Committee on Communicable Diseases who stated that 'the Director General should take similar action in future, should circumstances warrant it, in the interests of all states'.[96] It seems clear that this organ laid down the view that a functional reading of the WHO's mission was largely incompatible with its statist conception.

Guinea had a poor health system, no previous exposure to cholera the WHO's and the outbreak was severe. Before his decision to go public, Candau tried, unsuccessfully, to obtain the consent of Guinean authorities. Furthermore, the WHO had reliable and solid epidemiological data on the outbreak which made blatant the conflict between scientific expertise and apparently arbitrary national stubbornness legitimated by international health law. It could be added that Guinea was a poor country, it being rather difficult to imagine such a decision against a powerful and influential state.

Candau's stellar reputation might have pacified potential qualms about the decision.[97] Candau was Brazilian, a rather independent country in the international system. It is held that the British and worldwide participation of doctors in the WHO was 'largely due to the personality and qualities of

---

[95] See WHO, 'Cholera' the WHO's *Weekly Epidemiological Record* 45, no. 36 (1970): 377, emphasis added.

[96] Fidler, David P. (2004), *SARS, Governance and the Globalization of Disease* (Basingstoke; New York: Palgrave MacMillan) at 64.

[97] For accounts of Candau's legacy and performance while leading the WHO, see *British Medical Journal* (1973), 'Dr. M. G. Candau and W.H.O.', *BMJ*, 2 (5864), 433–34 the WHO's and Cueto, Marcos and Reinalda, Bob (2015), 'Candau, Marcolino Gomes', in Bob Reinalda, Kent Kille, and Jaci Eisenberg (eds.), *IO BIO: Biographical Dictionary Of Secretaries-General Of International Organization*, available at www.ru.nl/fm/iobio.

leadership of its director-general'.[98] Candau's tenure at the WHO came after his experience at the Pan-American Sanitary Bureau or the Regional Office of the WHO for the Americas. He is also credited with the consolidation of the WHO's position, not UNESCO, as the research focal point in medical sciences. His contribution was judged in the following terms

> The monument that Candau has left is an organization that has come to be universally recognized as an effective instrument for serving the health needs of humanity.[99]

Lancet was more moderate in its evaluation of Candau's legacy but recognized his work in granting the WHO with an effective structure and his role in the return of COMINFORM countries in 1955, the Congo emergency of 1960, smallpox eradication, and malaria programme.[100] Another appraisal of Candau reads

> In 20 years Candau, as he was universally known, brought WHO from a struggling aid agency in the UN family to a position of great influence and real achievement ... WHO is probably the most respected of all the international agencies and the least disrupted by political differences ... Candau was an urbane, unpretentious, friendly man. He could fight fiercely in defence of his staff, but utterly lacked consciousness of his own dignity. He was a charming host and a welcome and delightful guest. His intellectual quality was of the highest, but he was never the condescending expert some people of high attainments become. He was fluent and idiomatic in at least three languages with odd little quirks in pronunciation that endeared him the more to Assemblies. When he died suddenly at 71, nearly a decade after his retirement, he was mourned by the many at the ensuing Assembly who remembered him and his work, but also by uncountable numbers in the health field throughout the world.[101]

The narrative of Candau's character, competences, and reputation is certainly relevant to understand why his decision to go against the law, while trying to pursue what he believed was the right thing and the real mandate of the WHO, remained unchallenged. Life teaches us indeed that some courses of action are only available to persons of high moral stature to whom going beyond written and unwritten norms is allowed in the name of pushing human life to

---

[98] *British Medical Journal* (1973), 'Dr. M. G. Candau and W.H.O.', BMJ, 2 (5864), 433–34 at 433.

[99] *Ibidem.*

[100] *The Lancet* (1973), 'Retirement of Dr M. G. Candau', *The Lancet*, 302 (7821), at 138.

[101] 'Marcolino Gomes Candau', Lives of the Fellows Royal Colleges of Physicians, available at http://munksroll.rcplondon.ac.uk/Biography/Details/740.

a new moral level.[102] Is it this easy though to claim that Candau's action was good and virtuous?

Of course, one could settle for the morality of that action especially in virtue of the approval it was met with. Certainly, this suffices to evaluate a past action but what about thinking of the latter as a guide to action in similar situations in the future? Even if Candau's decision was warmly received, it was never repeated. This would be unintelligible if the answer to our question would be easy, that is, a leader should always act to protect the goods that are served by the mission of the organization (but given that health is central in human life what would institutional and legal constraints be for?). Yet, it did not happen again. Things get thornier once we abandon A. J. Ayer's hurrah and boo emotivism and perform a comprehensive analysis of the consequences and context of Candau's action.

The first thing to consider is that such a decision has a timeline of its own and its effects cannot be measured by treating it as a single event. On the one hand, such a decision was a courageous act that not only advanced the WHO's mission in the attempt to promote general welfare but also protected the rights and well-being of the affected populations (thus upholding beneficence or humanness), blocked seemingly by an arbitrary distinction such as nation-states' borders and sovereign powers. Considering the above and given that the WHO possessed reliable data and earlier attempts to obtain Guinea's consent were made, it may appear spurious to continue questioning the moral goodness of an action that everyone condoned.

On the other hand, however, rule-following and loyalty to one's organization are typically understood as virtues and moral values one should also uphold. Especially, because in this case there was a clear breach of his professional duties, understood in a legalistic way, as represented by WHO laws. It would be naïve to see the statist nature of the WHO as an outdated caprice since rules that protect state consent prior to being intervened or labelled in a certain way also prevent the political instrumentalization of such 'power to name'. Without such guarantees, strong leaders, serving all types of interests and factions, could easily declare epidemics with obvious impact on tourism and national and regional economies legitimating further interventions and technical guidance. Hence a decision like this carries the germ of expanding an interventionist mentality that if carried repeatedly by Director-Generals' decisions would risk imploding or threatening the impartiality of an organization like the WHO.

---

[102] This is a line of argument developed in Bergson, Henri (1977), *The Two Sources of Morality and Religion*, trans. Ashley Audra and Cloudesley Brereton (Notre Dame: University of Notre Dame Press).

282　　　*Guilherme Vasconcelos Vilaça*

Ultimately, the kind of choice Candau had to make amounts most likely to a dilemma in which there is no right answer, since each possible decision implies the sacrifice of important moral values. Deontologism, in its Kantian robes, and virtue ethics can be used to applaud Candau's decision because it upheld human dignity and contributed to the institutional flourishing of the WHO. Indeed, the first article of its constitution prescribes as its core objective the attainment of the highest possible level of health of all peoples. Nonetheless, without further specifications, such an objective would justify any action whatsoever jeopardizing institutional flourishing as well as other moral values: what would happen if Director-Generals could set aside rules whenever they pleased?

What is more, it is largely implausible that any Director-General would take such a stance against a superpower raising the issue of partiality and the exercise of moral leadership within a narrower frame defined by the actual distribution of power in the international system. Candau's action, to put it otherwise, seems to be less courageous after all. Furthermore, for some commentators and even Director-Generals, key to the WHO's survival is the maintenance of its functional orientation avoiding the over-politicization of the WHO and the WHA.[103] So Candau's kind of action could be performed only rarely but also only against not so powerful countries lacking the power to possibly disrupt the activities of the WHO when retaliating. Unfortunately, these are most likely also the countries more prone to being intervened by IOs and Western states. The international system, its asymmetries of power, and the legacy of Western domination make it simply impossible to compare doing the right thing by bending the law in our private lives against doing the right thing in an international organizational setting. Against this background, is it enough to consider prudence solely according to the virtue framework or should prudence be made to include considerations from other ethical traditions?

10.4.3 *Doing the Right Thing? The 2002 SARS Outbreak*

The unrepeatability of Candau's decision came easily to mind in 2002 apropos the SARS outbreak in China.[104] Legally speaking, China had no international

---

[103] For instance, both Brundtland and Mahler were against the over-politicization of the WHA seeing it both as a threat to reputation and functionally inadequate. See Cortell, Andrew P. and Peterson, Susan (2006), 'Dutiful Agents, Rogue Actors, or Both? Staffing, Voting Rules, and Slack in the WHO and WTO', in Darren G. Hawkins et al. (eds.), *Delegation and Agency in International Organizations* (New York: Cambridge University Press), 255–80 at 266–267.

[104] See Fidler, David P. (2004), *SARS, Governance and the Globalization of Disease* (Basingstoke; New York: Palgrave MacMillan), and Chan, Lai-Ha, Chen, Lucy, and Xu, Jin (2010), 'China's Engagement with Global Health Diplomacy: Was SARS a Watershed?', *PLoS Med*, 7 (4), 1–6.

obligation to report SARS cases to states or other international organizations. Since article 1 of the 1969 International Health Regulations did not include SARS on its list of infectious diseases, China had no obligation to utilize the WHO in dealing with SARS. As per the IHR, it was only obliged to report cholera, plague, and yellow fever, and the WHO constitution imposed no duties on controlling infectious diseases or cooperating towards its eradication.

And, as a matter of fact, China did hide the outbreak, suppressing information about an unidentified respiratory disease. Eventually, the strategy failed due to the spread of messages in different media leading to China's recognition of the outbreak while simultaneously covering up and denying its effects and scope. Finally, after five months of the initial signs of the outbreak, China admitted it and within two months the SARS was contained.

China's behaviour was not illegal even if it cost lives that could have been saved. It also endangered the world since its inability to deal with the issue and its delay in notifying international authorities enhanced the risk of spreading SARS. All other affected countries, Canada, Singapore, and Vietnam, did notify the WHO despite being under no obligation to do so.

However, and even though the WHO did not explicitly disseminate the outbreak in China, under the leadership of Gro Brundtland, it adopted a bunch of novel measures outside the delegation contract and powers of authority granted by its laws. The WHO issued its first Global Alert on 12 March 2003 so that national health authorities could heighten surveillance and response systems, its first Emergency Travel Advisory 'to what was [then] perceived to be a worldwide threat to health', and its first Geographically Specific Travel Recommendations made to travellers to postpone non-essential travel to Hong Kong, Guangdong and other Chinese territories, and Toronto, among other locations.[105] The WHO also voiced rare public criticism against a Member State, that is, China, criticizing its lack of investment in public health.[106]

David Fidler, who studied the situation in detail, argues that the WHO's bold approach was justified by its lack of confidence in China's internal doings and consequently by the risk it posed to all other countries. Fidler further claims that the WHO's unusually bold stance succeeded in triggering a change in Chinese authorities' behaviour that finally started cooperating.[107] Given the prompt and

---

[105]   Cortell, Andrew P. and Peterson, Susan (2006), 'Dutiful Agents, Rogue Actors, or Both? Staffing, Voting Rules, and Slack in the WHO and WTO', in Darren G. Hawkins et al. (eds.), *Delegation and Agency in International Organizations* (New York: Cambridge University Press), 255–80 at 270.

[106]   Fidler, David P. (2004), *SARS, Governance and the Globalization of Disease* (Basingstoke; New York: Palgrave MacMillan), at 96ff.

[107]   *Ibidem* at 97ff.

284 *Guilherme Vasconcelos Vilaça*

adequate reaction of China and other Asian countries to Covid-19, it seems that a long-term effect was also achieved.

The fundamental point here is that, in dealing with SARS, the WHO exercised a range of powers that did not exist in its constitutional mandate without the consent of Member States and affected states, as well as without legitimating WHA's decisions and recommendations.[108] Furthermore, this time it was not against a small African country but countries like Canada and China. States did not complain about the WHO's expansion of powers but rather about having it applied against them specifically. At last the WHA empowered the WHO Director-General

> to alert, when necessary and after *informing* the government concerned, the international community to the presence of a public health threat that may constitute a serious threat to neighbouring countries or to international health on the basis of criteria and procedures jointly developed with Members.[109]

These developments within the WHO could be interpreted as steps towards a WHO based on global common interests rather than state consent. And yet, the same steps do not dissipate the importance of leadership and the different styles it can adopt. When asked to provide the basis for the WHO action on the 2002 SARS outbreak, the former Director-General Jong-Wook Lee replied that 'in a sense our mandate is ... the truth'.[110] Conversely, and after the mentioned WHA's act of empowering the Director-General, Margaret Chan, the Chinese former Director-General of the WHO, adopted a deferential attitude towards states in the 2014 Ebola outbreak in West Africa, leaving the responsibility to take action to them (the crisis killed 11,000 people).[111]

Chan was known for deploying a conciliatory, humane, and patient leadership anchored in a sense of humility and propriety, as shown when she replied, 'I'm not MSF [Médecins Sans Frontières], you name and shame people, I don't'[112] to criticisms of not having denounced publicly West African

---

[108]   *Ibidem* at 139ff.

[109]   *In* Fidler, David P. (2004), *SARS, Governance and the Globalization of Disease* (Basingstoke; New York: Palgrave MacMillan) at 143.

[110]   *In* Cortell, Andrew P. and Peterson, Susan (2006), 'Dutiful Agents, Rogue Actors, or Both? Staffing, Voting Rules, and Slack in the WHO and WTO', in Darren G. Hawkins et al. (eds.), *Delegation and Agency in International Organizations* (New York: Cambridge University Press), 255–80 at 270.

[111]   Huet, Natalie (2017), 'World Looks for a Better Doctor', 01.22.2017, available at www.politico.eu/article/world-looks-for-a-better-doctor/.

[112]   *Ibidem.*

Virtue and Leadership in the World Health Organization 285

countries for their failures to tackle the Ebola outbreak. It cannot be forgotten that the activist and heroic stance of the WHO acting outside of its sphere of competences or simply acting as if impatience were a virtue can come at a high price. For instance, the same Margaret Chan is known 'as the woman who cried wolf during a flu pandemic' in 2009,[113] being accused, by some commentators, of having reacted exaggeratedly to a H1N1 swine flu pandemic influenced by big manufacturers of vaccines.

It is difficult not to think that it all boils down to, as mentioned in section 10.3, the kind of leadership we deem apriori appropriate to guide an international organization like the WHO.

> 'The next director general must have political courage: internally, to carry out a real reform, and externally, so that when there are tensions with countries, he or she has the political courage to stand up to them,' said Joanne Liu, president of medical charity Doctors Without Borders, which has blasted WHO [under Margaret Chan] for letting Ebola get out of hand.[114]

> Chris Murray, a professor of global health at the University of Washington and director of the Institute for Health Metrics and Evaluation, said of Brundtland 'She was the sort of visionary, highly-principled leader who always did what she thought was needed for the world, whether or not that was politically convenient.'[115]

10.5 CONCLUSION: AN ENGAGEMENT WITH MORAL EXEMPLARISM AND VIRTUES AS SKILLS

This chapter uncovers the contradictory aspects associated with the use of virtue ethics to examine moral behaviour in international organizations. The analytical deconstruction performed is key to be able to hold a meaningful conversation on the role virtue ethics may play.

On the one hand, it is unequivocal that the language of virtues is widely relied upon if not explicitly deployed when evaluating candidates, office holders, and the needs of international organizations' leadership roles alike. Such an assessment transcends positivist standards such as the law, performance indicators, and empirical effects, suggesting that we value something *in excess* of what there

---

[113] *Ibidem.*
[114] *Ibidem.*
[115] Kelland, Kate (2016) 'A Fighter for Global Health: Who Will Be Next to Lead the WHO?', 23.09.2016, available at www.reuters.com/investigates/special-report/health-who-leader/.

286   *Guilherme Vasconcelos Vilaça*

is and the actual rules that need to be met. Human beings value vision and character.

On the other hand, however, the chapter shows how hard it is to assess character and the moral adequacy of choices carried out by so-called exemplars especially in the context of large impersonal organizations. Moral exemplars often strike us in the form of encounters and trigger feelings of emulation and admiration[116] as if we were in the presence of sages or morally enlightened persons.

> Good persons are persons *like that*, just as gold is stuff *like that*. Picking out exemplars can fix the reference of the term 'good person' without the use of descriptive concepts. It is not necessary for ordinary people engaged in moral practice to know the nature of good persons – what makes them good."[117]

But then, how to distinguish feelings of admiration for the wrong persons if morality and good life have no foundation? Zagzebski's account of exemplars repeats the belief that somehow it is obvious to identify what is a good person worthy of emulation and that such identification is unanimous, forgetting that leaders like Trump, Lagarde, or Berlusconi are certainly exemplars to many citizens in the world. The assumption in the literature on virtues that 'one knows' becomes untenable unless we are holding undisclosed normative ideals. Since other persons may hold different normative ideals, exemplars lie in the eye of the beholder. It is thus a rather empty reference: 'Virtuous for whom?' With the disadvantage that it covers virtue ethics with a mantle of elitism and the undisclosed moral superiority of those that claim to know what good people are."[118] We also assume that actions performed by exemplars are morally good *per se*.

Against this modus operandi, in this chapter I tried to overcome black-box accounts of virtues of international leaders by means of a close analysis of their characters, actions, and the situations in which they were called to exercise judgment. So, we narrate in order to make the moral features of the situation more salient even if all narratives are faulty or partial."[119] We may well not have any

---

[116] See Zagzebski, Linda (2013), 'Moral Exemplars in Theory and Practice', *Theory and Research in Education*, 11 (2), 193–206.

[117] *Ibidem* at 199, emphasis added.

[118] I have the impression this could be a generational issue since we no longer live in times of Cold War or Nazism and fascism in which pressing moral judgments were arguably of a binary nature in stark contrast with the plurality of interests and dimensions that leaders of international organizations like the WHO need to take into account. To get a grasp of this perception, consult Judt, Tony (2013), *Thinking the Twentieth Century* (London: Penguin).

[119] Phelan, James (2014), 'Narrative Ethics', in Peter Hühn (ed.), *The Living Handbook of Narratology* (Hamburg: Hamburg University), available at www.lhn.uni-hamburg.de/article/narrative-ethics#.

other option since narrating may be an inescapable part of what it means to be human.[120]

The 2006 movie *Ten Canoes*,[121] the first to be shot fully in Australian Aboriginal languages, is useful to make us think of the potential of such an approach. In *Ten Canoes*, an unmarried young brother finds himself desiring the second wife of his older brother. Rather than proceeding by means of rational moral argument, the older brother tells the younger one a story of a time gone. There, a younger brother also desired one of his older brother's wives and in pursuing his desire brought about and upon himself grave consequences ending up having to take care of all three wives. Ultimately, the younger brother takes seriously the moral of the story and gives up pursuing his brother's wife.

The virtue ethics narratives built during the chapter highlighted certain aspects that are often neglected. Clearly, we cannot expect that a leader (or a person) is worthy of admiration as a whole or that she always acts well.[122] We learned that, because *judgment* has to be exercised in concrete instances of life, international leaders cannot and should not exhibit the same character traits and adopt identical decisions. This may go against different cultural expectations as to (i) what constitutes virtuous leadership; (ii) what do specific virtues such as courage demand when rendered concrete; and, (iii) which virtues are more important (e.g. respect for authority and humility vs. courage and assertiveness).

The chapter's narratives also highlight the importance of ethical leadership in pushing international organizations beyond their mandates as well as in contributing to their flourishing. In this regard, even if an organization does the right thing and promotes social welfare in its actions, it may do so by means of a non-virtuous internal culture (subject to corruption, lack of transparency, and so on). Thus, virtuous leadership could amount, for instance, to ensure 'lack of scandals'.

Analysing the structural effects produced by supposedly virtuous leaders of the WHO tells us, conversely, that a virtuous character does not suffice because these leaders have consciously and unconsciously pushed for

---

[120] Meretoja, Hanna (2014), 'Narrative and Human Existence: Ontology, Epistemology, and Ethics', *New Literary History*, 45 (1), 89–109.

[121] *Ten Canoes* (2006), Heer, Rolf de and Djigirr, Peter (dir.).

[122] See Wolf, Susan (1982), 'Moral Saints', *The Journal of Philosophy*, 79 (8), 419–39 highlighting our pre-theoretical idea of saints as those committed to social welfare at the expense of their own well-being and commodities. See also, for a non-Western account, Kelleher, M. Theresa (2013), *The Journal of Wu Yubi: The Path to Sagehood*, trans. M. Theresa Kelleher (Indianapolis; Cambridge: Hackett Publishing Company).

288   *Guilherme Vasconcelos Vilaça*

Western internationalism and the deepening of IOs' interventionist powers (embodying a particular Western epistemology) over states. Thus, the relationship between character and the broader effects of actions certainly questions the adequacy of the virtues *per se* as a vocabulary to praise action that goes beyond the call of duty.

However, a question remains unsettled: what makes a given ethical narrative a good, or preferable, one? And what can we learn from narrative ethics if narratives seem to expose even further the quicksand on which ethical analysis is conducted? These are questions that perhaps must remain unanswered. In any case, what the chapter tries to clarify is that we cannot expect virtue ethical accounts to dissolve the problem of assessing the morality of characters and actions when conceptualized simultaneously by different moral traditions and vocabularies. This is altogether different from claiming

> That is why different moral theories yield mostly the same moral verdicts about particular cases. When they do not, we know that one of them is defective.[123]

Unfortunately, it is never explained how we can reach this conclusion. Similarly, one of the most celebrated virtue ethicists, Rosalind Hursthouse, could candidly retain as wrong an abortion performed

> *for the worthless one* [pursuit] *of 'having a good time,'* or for the pursuit of some false vision of the ideals of freedom or self-realization. And some others who say 'I am not ready for parenthood yet' are making some sort of mistake about the extent to which one can manipulate the circumstances of one's life so as to make it fulfill some dream that one has.[124]

But again: who set up the hierarchy of values Hursthouse relies upon and why is it obviously correct? This chapter advocates against a dogmatic and mysterious use of virtue ethics and argues that, even if the latter framework can be useful to communicate neglected values across cultures, it is prone to create additional moral disagreement that cannot be decided theoretically without engaging in concrete ethical analysis.

I would like to end by claiming that the conclusions of the chapter make it hard to imagine a form of moral education appropriate to create virtuous leaders *that* act virtuously. As we have seen, characters do change and when seen in all their complexity prudent actions are largely unrepeatable, making

---

[123] Zagzebski, Linda (2013), 'Moral Exemplars in Theory and Practice', *Theory and Research in Education*, 11 (2), 193–206 at 196.

[124] Hursthouse, Rosalind (1991), 'Virtue Theory and Abortion', *Philosophy and Public Affairs*, 20 (3), 223–46 at 242, emphasis added.

Virtue and Leadership in the World Health Organization 289

it difficult to learn from the past. Furthermore, a person that is socialized into virtues through family life, schooling, and different mentors may ultimately fail to act well, not to mention that the complexity of the decisions and exercise of judgment in international organizations have little to do with daily life choices.

Virtue theorists often claim or assume that it is possible to acquire moral virtues in the same way one acquires excellence in craftsmanship, sports, or martial arts[125] as if a leader's choice regarding whether or not to go against the mandate of her international organization is of the same nature as repairing a motorcycle engine,[126] working wood (e.g. Tadao Ando's reflection on how his apprenticeship working wood led him to understand how to respect the limits and possibilities of the materials – context – one works with),[127] throwing one thousand punches in order to master a *kata*, or to use a typhoon to improve one's karate stance.[128] These are all practices that cannot be understood outside of a particular *master/disciple relationship* that is largely absent in today's secular and Westernized world. Furthermore, they all have a *material* element (the wood, the body, the engine) one must acknowledge and struggle against but also in which one can experience, visualize, and feel *directly* the authenticity of one's excellence. This is not the case of ethical action. It is revealing that we now follow Confucius' teachings when it is known he failed to live a practical life through political service which was, at the time, the ultimate goal of virtuous human beings. Indeed, ethics was not the matter of book-writing or theoretical reflection but action and judgment in the political and social world!

---

[125] See Annas, Julia (2011), 'Practical Expertise', in John Bengson and Marc A. Moffett (eds.), *Knowing How* (New York; Oxford: Oxford University Press), 101–12, and Stichter, Matt (2007), 'Ethical Expertise: The Skill Model of Virtue', *Ethics, Theory, Moral Practice*, 10, 183–94. Notice, however, that in this line of writing the focus lies on the internal mindset that one ought to develop to achieve excellence without, however, (i) providing ways in which one can train and practise moral excellence; and, (ii) articulating the self-cultivation of moral excellence and its practical deployment.

[126] Crawford, Matthew B. (2010), *Shop Class as Soulcraft: An Inquiry into the Value of Work* (New York: Penguin Books).

[127] Furuyama, Masao (2015), *Tadao Ando* (Taschen).

[128] Funakoshi, Gichin (2012), *Karate-Do: My Way of Life* (New York: Kodansha) at 46.

11

Ethical Leadership in Times of 'Crisis'[*]

Maria Varaki

11.1 THINKING OF LEADERSHIP IN TIMES OF PANDEMIC

During the second year of the Peloponnesian War (430BC) the city-state of Athens was ravaged by a plague. The great historian Thucydides, who himself survived the disease, documented the social effect of the pandemic upon the city, where almost 100,000 people died. According to his account 'the catastrophe was so overwhelming that men, not knowing what would happen to them next, became indifferent to every rule of religion or law.'[1] The ancient plague had triggered an ethical crisis, but the Athenian democracy had to survive, due to the characteristics Pericles highlighted in his famous Funeral's Oration.[2] In this speech dedicated to the dead fighters of the first year of the war, Pericles emphasized that one of the emancipatory elements of the Athenian democracy was the sensibility of measure and the combination of philosophy with action. *'Φιλοκαλοῦμέν τε γὰρ μετ' εὐτελείας κα φιλοσοφοῦμεν ἄνευ μαλακίας.'* This revival of trust in the 'glorious' uniqueness of the Athenian democracy required the intervention of a leader like Pericles who reminded Athenians of their philosophical wealth and resilience. However, as Thucydides writes, the Athenian democracy never fully recovered from the effect of the plague and Pericles died by the epidemic during the second year of the war.

While we finalize this book, the world is literally in lockdown. The coronavirus pandemic (Covid-19) has forced millions of people around the globe to

---

[*] Simon Chesterman has highlighted that in Chinese the word crisis entails both the component of danger but also of opportunity, https://simonchesterman.com/blog/2020/05/01/covid-19/

[1] www.economist.com/books-and-arts/2020/03/26/when-athenians-feared-a-disease-would-wreck-theirdemocracy?fbclid=IwAR0MhL1d48IC2n18J540fK3sk2ATN8nP1TzoJ5WJ4FPxkKDG6ZGnb1czU0 (accessed 30 March 2020)

[2] Thucydides, *The History of the Peloponnesian War* (Penguin Classics 1954, Warner trans.).

stay inside and adapt their lifestyle to the new reality of quarantine, while familiarizing themselves with Zoom meetings and other platforms of online communication.

In a daily marathon, the media are covered with emotional and apocalyptic headlines about deaths, therapies, and conspiracy theories. Numbers have replaced human lives and political leaders are forced to respond to this unprecedented challenge exercising judgment in a decisive and rapid way, with decisions that affect the lives of common people. The scientific search for an effective vaccine, but mainly the appeal of some leaders and experts to make it a global public good, is one of the issues that will legitimately dominate future journalistic and scholarly writing.[3] If one observes the overwhelming, production of information and analysis by pundits and laymen (especially in social media), one could draw some preliminary conclusions about the nature and content of the prevailing discourse. The discussion below cannot do justice to the very complicated and constantly fluid sociopolitical context we experience. Instead, this initial analysis observes some salient elements that permeate the public sphere, and operates as a bridge to the subsequent analysis on ethical leadership.

Within this framework, a mixed scholarly reaction has developed about the *demise* or resistance of the international legal order at least as we knew it. From one side, the so called 'backlash' against liberal ideas and institutions of global governance that are supposed to accommodate further cooperation in promotion of the so-called common good, has generated a vivid discussion about the phenomenon of populism, its causes and dynamics, and the future (death or survival) of multilateralism or the rise or decline of the international rule of law.[4] The 'global liberal' legal order as we thought we knew it, together with the admittedly contested 'oceanic feeling'[5] of common shared values, interests, and preferences, is severely challenged and appears to lose ground even to the surprise of those who repeatedly criticized the liberal project as a hegemonic one.[6]

---

3   www.faz.net/aktuell/wirtschaft/corona-impfstoff-griechenland-will-gemeinsamen-kauf-von-patenten-16713753.html (accessed 15 May 2020)

4   Krieger, Nolte and Zimmermann (eds.), *The International Rule of Law, Rise or Decline?* (Oxford University Press, 2019).

5   Martti Koskenniemi, 'Projects of World Community', in Cassese (ed.), *Realizing Utopia, The Future of International Law* (Oxford University Press, 2012) 3.

6   James Crawford, 'The Current Political Discourse Concerning International Law' (2018) 81 *Modern Law Review*, 1, where he questions the 'susceptibility' of international law, in the current context of defiance by political practice, Alain Pellet, 'Values and Power Relations – The Disillusionment of International Law?' KFG Working Paper Series, No. 34, Berlin Potsdam Research Group 'The International Rule of Law- Rise or Decline?' Berlin.

Several surveys and commentators have stressed the loss of trust in domestic and international institutions and the rise of mistrust among states.[7] Especially as we experience the unfolding of this pandemic, one can observe a strong return to nativism and isolationism, contrary to a highly anticipated spirit of further coordination and shared responsibility against an 'unknown' enemy.[8]

However, there is another view that proposes a less dramatic and more nuanced position regarding the *death* of the legal global order as we knew it, shedding light on a selective position towards international organizations that can provide an alternative reading of the so-called backlash.[9] Similarly, against this background of return to nativism at least from some big powers, it should not go unnoticed that other smaller states expressed their intention to fill the gap in the global arena. Notwithstanding this observation, that proves the grey dimension of global governance, compared to the simplified binary of white and black, I still contend that an overall trend of nativism should not be perceived solely as a sign of scholarly exaggeration but instead as an additional analytical tool that should be properly assessed and wisely used.

This becomes even more relevant in a political context where the usage of the word *war* by several political leaders is indicative of the overall polemic mind-set combined with the instrumental *carte blanche* it may facilitate for every authority. A series of human rights experts have raised the alarm of a dangerous trend of consolidating authoritarianism in the name of public health emergency, with official and de facto states of emergency, accompanied by derogations from human rights treaties,[10] while openly some leaders (such as Orbán in Hungary) embrace a Schmittian theory of exception.[11] Characteristically enough, Israel has applied counter-terrorism technology to track potential covid cases in order to curb the spread, with full access to the phone of every citizen, while other states appear keen to adopt various

---

[7] www.project-syndicate.org/onpoint/covid-19-and-the-trust-deficit-by-david-w-brady-and-michael-spence-2020–04 (accessed 15 May 2020)

[8] See the recent comment by Chesterman, https://simonchesterman.com/blog/2020/05/01/covid-19/?fbclid=IwAR2b6JVyI6wM_-5sA-XZaOMyYdM7c9QPv71jSLMMnOLmBeH5aoKLUiI Aodo. It was not only the US, Russia, China and UK, but also within the European Union several states did not show the expected solidarity, a pandemic would trigger.

[9] See characteristically Jan Klabbers and his fine observations about the WHO in corona times in 'The Second Most Difficult Job in the World: Reflections on Covid-19' (2020) 11 *Journal of International Humanitarian Legal Studies*, 1.

[10] In this regard see https://verfassungsblog.de/introduction-list-of-country-reports/

[11] www.coe.int/en/web/portal/-/secretary-general-writes-to-victor-orban-regarding-covid-19-state-of-emergency-in-hungary (accessed 15 May 2020)

Ethical Leadership in Times of 'Crisis' 293

surveillance tools in the *war* against the pandemic.[12] It has been argued, though, that the South East Asia combination of civic collective responsibility, together with extending application of contact-tracing technologies, would turn contentious if applied in Western societies with a different value system.[13] Again, only the future will show to what extent this kind of approach will be further spread or contained, rejected or tailored into new realities.

Against this background, one could observe an emerging call for a global wake-up reaction and a reappraisal of the importance of leadership, which once more appears to be structured in a binary way; either 'we', political leaders, international institutions, and global citizens, forge forces for a common effort or we will be witnesses to a destructive future. The options on the table seem to be framed in the following way: multilateralism, solidarity, and shared responsibility v. isolation/nativism.[14] Re-trust in the so much defamed expert knowledge, science, and institutions v. conspiracy theories and populist demagogues who defy *orthon logo* and stir instead the sentiments of fear and hostility via oversimplification between *us* and *them*.

Thus the current epidemic has reopened the discourse about the power, limits, role, and responsibility of scientific knowledge, while the divergent position adopted by various states – this time not the usual suspects but Sweden for instance – indicate a more complicated picture than the one prescribed in binary terms. The Swedish example also highlights the need to add complexity to the picture because its rather unconventional approach to deal with covid cannot be interpreted in isolation from the population's trust in medical and political authorities, as well as its capacity to respond to the warnings made and advice prescribed. Thus, expertise, communication, leadership features, social trust, and cultural and contextual features have to be included, as this book has made clear, in our frameworks of analysis.[15]

In a more particular mode, one cannot avoid mentioning that the overall handling of the pandemic by the WHO has also instigated an intense debate about the normative and political limits of its design, and

---

[12] www.bbc.com/news/technology-52401763 (accessed 15 May 2020)

[13] https://hbr.org/2020/04/how-digital-contact-tracing-slowed-covid-19-in-east-asia (accessed 15 May 2020)

[14] But see the very interesting initiative by the UN for its 75 years which was released in September 2020, https://news.un.org/en/story/2020/04/1062122 (accessed 15 May 2020)

[15] See David Kennedy, *A World of Struggle: How Power, Law, and Expertise Shape Global Political Economy* (Princeton University Press, 2016).

the responsibility, if any, of its Director-General about the way he addressed the Chinese reaction at the beginning of the pandemic.[16] Some scholars opt for an international commission of inquiry[17] or even a request for an advisory opinion from the International Court of Justice (ICJ),[18] while others propose a more nuanced reading of the WHO's reaction, taking into consideration the particularities of its institutional framework, and the complex dilemmas behind decision-making as vividly illustrated in this book.[19]

Yet this first discursive trend underscores the quest for the kind of leadership Kratochwil has highlighted in times of 'crisis', when actors have to make choices within a turmoil. In particular what kind of leadership and account of action can respond to the new global threats or identify what is the common good as Kratochwil concludes? How can leaders exercise discretion and make practical choices that reflect prudence and perspective while operating within organizational limitations and narrow professional roles? Admittedly, this is a thick brush depiction that does not do justice to the various nuanced propositions for a more humane multilateralism or a more transparent and accountable expert knowledge. This is not the place for such a discussion. Instead, this sweeping narrative aims to situate the importance of this edited volume as a timely and very relevant contribution to the broader on-going public debate about the future of global governance via the angle of ethical leadership.

On this note, I would like to pause and draw the attention of the readers to some thought-provoking interventions. In March 2020, while we started grasping the extent of the tremendous effects of the pandemic, the famous Israeli historian Yuval Harari argued first in a pessimist note that 'In the battle against coronavirus, Humanity lacks leadership ... due to the lack of leaders that can inspire, organize and finance a coordinated global response.'[20] To warn further that:

---

[16] See characteristically www.theguardian.com/news/2020/apr/10/world-health-organization-who-v-coronavirus-why-it-cant-handle-pandemic (accessed 15 May 2020)

[17] Michael A Becker, 'Do we need an International Commission of Inquiry for Covid-19, Part I? May18, 2020, https://www.ejiltalk.org/do-we-need-an-international-commission-of-inquiry-for-covid-19-part-i/

[18] Sandrine De Herdt, 'A reference to the ICJ for an Advisory Opinion over Covid -19 Pandemic', May 20, 2020, www.ejiltalk.org/a-reference-to-the-icj-for-an-advisory-opinion-over-covid-19-pandemic/?utm_source=mailpoet&utm_medium=email&utm_campaign=ejil-talk-newsletter-post-title_2

[19] Klabbers supra note 9.

[20] https://time.com/5803225/yuval-noah-harari-coronavirus-humanity-leadership/?utm_source=facebook&utm_medium=social&utm_campaign=editorial&utm_term=ideas_&linkId=85262154&fbclid=IwAR2p8zHcnmbZOBzDF3WCYEz3XuaPbCyoxqysQxiWiEAN8FSXyWAqObFiv9o (accessed 20 April 2020)

Ethical Leadership in Times of 'Crisis'

Humankind is now facing a global crisis. Perhaps the biggest crisis of our generation. The decisions people and governments take in the next few weeks will probably shape the world for years to come. They will shape not just our healthcare systems but also our economy, politics and culture. We must act quickly and decisively. We should also take into account the long-term consequences of our actions. When choosing between alternatives, we should ask ourselves not only how to overcome the immediate threat, but also what kind of world we will inhabit once the storm passes. Yes, the storm will pass, humankind will survive, most of us will still be alive – but we will inhabit a different world.[21]

The same day, another commentator Martin Wolf supported that:

Unlike the virus, humans make choices. This pandemic will pass into history. But the way in which it passes will shape the world it leaves behind ... Fortunately, the disease we now confront is nothing like as bad as the plagues that repeatedly devastated the lives of our ancestors. Yet it is still something virtually no living person has experienced. It is a practical challenge that must be met with well-informed decisions. But it is also an ethical challenge. We should recognise both aspects of the decisions we must make.[22]

The focus upon those statements lies primarily in the importance both writers cast on judgment as a core element of leadership in times of great or unprecedented challenges. Whether one takes inspiration from Kant, Arendt, or others,[23] exercising judgment is a constitutive component of leadership that reflects its potential and limits, or as it has been argued 'Judgment is the core, the nucleus of leadership. With Good judgment, little else matters. Without it, nothing else matters.'[24] On a second level, both commentators emphasize the ethical dimension of leadership. Yuval Harari makes a call for a rehabilitation of trust. As he explains:

People need to trust science, to trust public authorities, and to trust the media. Over the past few years, irresponsible politicians have deliberately undermined trust in science, in public authorities and in the media. Now

---

[21] www.ft.com/content/19d90308-6858-11ea-a3c9-1fe6fedcca75 (accessed 10 May 2020)
[22] www.ft.com/content/de7796b6-6cef-11ea-9bca-bf503995cd6f (accessed 15 May 2020)
[23] Immanuel Kant, *Critique of Judgment* (Oxford University Press, 2007 Meredith trans.), Hannah Arendt, Lectures on Kant's Political Philosophy, ed. Beiner (The University of Chicago Press, 1982), Hannah Arendt, 'The Crisis in Culture', in *Between Past and Future* (Penguin Classics, 2006).
[24] Noel Tichy & Warren G. Bennis, *Judgment: How Winning Leaders Make Great Calls* (Portfolio, 2007).

296 *Maria Varaki*

these same irresponsible politicians might be tempted to take the high road to authoritarianism, arguing that you just cannot trust the public to do the right thing.[25]

Whereas Wolf, while acknowledging the daunting dilemmas between economic survival and human cost, argues in support of global solidarity and cooperation before a massive financial meltdown that is going to affect disproportionately the most vulnerable. As he says:

> Making the right decisions requires that we understand the options and their moral implications. We now confront two fundamental sets of choices: within our countries and across borders. In high-income countries, the biggest choice is how aggressively to halt transmission of the virus. But we also need to decide who will bear the costs of that choice and how.[26]

In this sense both interventions do not only highlight the need for strong leadership but they also use the language of ethics in the broader framework of shared responsibility for the common good while addressing moral dilemmas, policy choices, and trade-offs that will decisively shape the future of many generations to come. This position seems to reflect a description of Isaiah Berlin's thesis about political judgment. As one commentator noticed,

> ... judgment for Berlin represents a mode of engaging with the world which brings together questions of efficacy and of desirability or rightness – thus bridging politics and ethics, and avoiding both an amoralism which ignores values, and an idealism which ignores realities.[27]

However, the above-mentioned calls for some kind of ethical leadership, either explicitly or implicitly, are not coupled with ideas of how this idea could be envisioned and substantiated. They are calls for good, strong, and ethical leadership in an abstract and thus easily contested way. This is an intriguing observation if one considers also the proliferation of recent writings on this front, since the nihilist dismissal of ethical considerations with regard to global governance both from critical and realist voices, apart from a very narrow academic circle, does not appeal with the same old fascination to the broader scholarly community. It becomes

[25] www.ft.com/content/19d90308-6858-11ea-a3c9-1fe6fedcca75 (accessed 20 April 2020)
[26] www.ft.com/content/de7796b6-6cef-11ea-9bca-bf503995cd6f (accessed 10 May 2020)
[27] Joshua L. Cherniss, '"The Sense of Reality": Berlin on Political Judgment, Political Ethics, and Leadership', in Cherniss & Smith (eds.), *Cambridge Companion to Isaiah Berlin* (Cambridge University Press, 2018) 55.

more obvious that a pure technocratic managerial language or an arrogant superior complacency, distant from ethical dilemmas type of governance, sounds problematic and not satisfactory.[28] Still the question that remains more pertinent than ever is what kind of ethical leadership could provide this alternative narrative and vision?

This pandemic could not be timelier for the conclusion of this book. I assert that it operates as a magnifying glass, that sheds more light into the salient question(s) of this volume, the way they have been elegantly described by the various contributors. Is there a unified understanding of ethical leadership, how can it be substantiated, what are the means of assessment, and to what extent can the virtues, those personal traits of individual leaders and staffs, make a difference? Again, what do we mean by virtues and how can they be examined in the divergent areas the contributors have covered? Is there an umbrella theory, a blueprint that can be applied for a future crisis like the one we experience today? Or is it all idiosyncratic and thus of no normative significance and concrete guidance? What is the added value of a virtue-inspired ethical leadership with regard to broader paradigms of exemplars and vision?

11.2 VIRTUES AND ETHICAL LEADERSHIP

While finalizing the conclusion, I was positively surprised to read the following lines in an article by the editorial team of *The New York Times*, while comparing the diverse kinds of leadership that emerged during the corona crisis:

> Leadership may be hard to define, but in times of crisis it is easy to identify. As the pandemic has spread fear, disease and death, national leaders across the globe have been severely tested. Some have fallen short, sometimes dismally, but there are also those leaders who have risen to the moment, demonstrating resolve, courage, empathy, respect for science and elemental decency, and thereby dulling the impact of the disease on their people.
>
> Beyond politics, economics and science lie qualities of character that can't be faked, chiefly compassion, which may be the most important in reassuring a frightened, insecure and stricken population. Ms.

---

[28] See the latest book by Kathryn Sikkink, *The Hidden Face of Rights: Towards a Politics of Responsibility* (Yale University Press, 2020), developing a theory of shared responsibility before global challenges, drawing on the work of Arendt, Weber, Iris Young and O'Neill. See also Joseph Nye, *Do Morals Matter? Presidents and Foreign Policy from FDR to Trump* (Oxford University Press, 2020).

Maria Varaki

Merkel is arguably among the least flashy, charismatic or eloquent of Europe's leaders, but nobody would ever question her decency. When she addressed her nation on television, something she does rarely and with evident reluctance, there was nothing pompous or bombastic in her parting words 'Take good care of yourselves and your loved ones.'[29]

Another article published some hours later, following the same spirit of analysis, concluded that Prime Minister Johnson, contrary to what was anticipated, eluded severe criticism in his own country, because, when compared with President Trump, the former showed at least a 'modicum' of empathetic leadership.[30] In other words, the leadership of Trump with its lack of empathy, the defiance of credible science, and its systematic distrust of the media has established a very high line of comparison for any other leader. However, what it is recognized in both media pieces is the importance of leadership highlighting certain qualities we can comfortably call virtues.

Journalists on both sides of the Atlantic refer to those leadership traits that inspire confidence and trust but also some kind of compassion in times of massive insecurity and anxiety. Other journalists have supported that female leaders can demonstrate better leadership in times of emergency because they can easily develop the sentiments of empathy and care, convey clear messages to the public, and thus generate trust in institutional decision making.[31] The examples of New Zealand, Denmark, Finland, Taiwan, or Germany[32] are frequently mentioned as indicative cases of transformative leadership as opposed to transactional leadership, which is preferred by men.[33]

I would add here also the reverse side of the coin, where the lack of those traits can produce other kinds of mimesis like the ones we witnessed in Michigan after the support President Trump provided to anti-lockdown measures[34] or when Prime Minister Johnson publicly claimed

---

[29] www.nytimes.com/2020/04/30/opinion/coronavirus-leadership.html?smid=fb-share&fbclid=I wAR1Vfx_DaEdwrg9FB2MnOTttcTHPUUCoopDOVCgUeKO8FMpLwsHPJpJQMvs (accessed 15 May 2020)

[30] www.theguardian.com/commentisfree/2020/may/01/donald-trump-coronavirus-boris-johnson -failures-president?CMP=share_btn_fb&fbclid=IwAR0BpAiToze64AQOWktIejmw38ivmd HyKNoMgOW_ZzPYyAHkVdA_po6ZytM (accessed 15 May 2020)

[31] www.theguardian.com/world/2020/apr/25/why-do-female-leaders-seem-to-be-more-successful-at-managing-the-coronavirus-crisis

[32] Several commentators have also attributed Merkel's attitude to her professional role as a scientist.

[33] https://edition.cnn.com/2020/05/05/perspectives/women-leaders-coronavirus/index.html (accessed 15 May 2020)

[34] https://edition.cnn.com/2020/05/05/opinions/michigan-militia-coronavirus-protests-soifer/ind ex.html (accessed 15 May 2020)

that he takes no precautions when greeting covid patients, despite the clear warning to the government his scientific committee had issued the exact same day.[35]

In those countries, one can also observe a conflict between the different ways in which leaders assess scientific knowledge. It is hard to ignore the debate between President Trump and New York Governor Cuomo, or the conflict of views between Prime Minister Johnson and London mayor Khan. Each of these leaders deployed different traits that arguably contributed towards the strengthening of trust or mistrust in social groups, political factions, public institutions, and fora of knowledge.

To this extent, the argument here follows the work of Amalia Amaya, who claims that leaders are paradigms of excellence and inspiration.[36] In this sense the behaviour of the various leaders mentioned earlier reflects the kind of ethical leadership that may produce imitators or followers. This is the type of leadership that either conveys clear messages of information and thus safe(r) guidance or confusing messages of ambiguity and disorientation.[37] Either way, it is a framework that allows us to learn from good and bad examples of leadership. In this sense, this model of leadership carries an enhanced significance, since it addresses public health emergencies that affect the lives of common people.

Overall, it can be legitimately argued that this pandemic somehow paved the way to reconsider the importance of ethical leadership via a virtue ethics perspective. Our endeavour had already opened this path and for this reason this volume carries a further symbolic validation, apart from its scholarly contribution to the debate on the various *shades* of ethical leadership.

The introductory chapter of this volume by my co-editor has provided a very fine and sophisticated analysis of the place of ethical leadership through a virtue ethics perspective, together with the *philosophy* of this academic endeavour; via an inter-disciplinary approach that combined in-depth theoretical analysis, applied specific narratives, and triggered questions of assessment.

---

[35] www.theguardian.com/politics/2020/may/05/boris-johnson-boasted-of-shaking-hands-on-day-sage-warned-not-to (accessed 15 May 2020)

[36] See, in this volume, Amalia Amaya, 'Exemplarism, Virtue, and Ethical Leadership in International Organizations', Ch.4.

[37] As we put the final points on this conclusion, the latest message of Prime Minister Boris Johnson for the partial lifting of lockdown has been received in a caricature way due to his lack of clarity and profound failure to guide the public.

300 *Maria Varaki*

From the beginning, this book was not an academic journey devoted to developing a grand unified ideal theory. Rather, it was an exploration of the potential and limits of virtues theory(ies), discovering at the same time elements of strength but also of vulnerability. In a subtle and intriguing way, this exercise *itself* mirrored some of the elements of virtues that our writers mentioned in their work, such as phronesis, moderation, imagination, courage, but also self-doubt, self-assessment, and compromise. Yet, having said this, I feel compelled to emphasize that this volume was not a purely theoretical and abstract exercise. Quite the contrary. While applying a narrative technique, it tried to shed light on concrete cases of exemplary or frequently mentioned leadership. In this way, this volume appears to invite readers to think in a tangible way, those previous calls I mentioned for ethical leadership when discussing responses to the current pandemic. Thus, it is not limited to a descriptive mode. Instead, it carries elements that can shed light on how an ethical leadership might be conceived, structured, and operationalized in an intelligible and feasible way, responding at the same time to the critique of being an overly illusionary or idealistically utopian proposition of no practical merit.

Additionally, this exercise is neither done in an overly idealistic heroic way nor with cynical nihilism. Contrary to such oversimplification, the spirit of this book is developed around an understanding of an imperfect concept of virtue and an equally imperfect *tragic* leadership, the way it was envisioned by Isaiah Berlin in his writings on political judgment.[38] For Berlin, great leaders combined traits of strength but also weaknesses, reflecting the absurdity of human nature. As it has been highlighted

> by acknowledging crucial limitations of both men, and using each as a foil to highlight the virtues and weaknesses of the other, he suggests not only that no politician is perfect – and that success depends in large part on the (fortuitous) 'fit' between a leader' s personal qualities and the circumstances – but also that the very virtues which make a given politician capable of doing great things are inseparable from limitations, faults, even vices.[39]

Inspired by this realistic sensibility of the limits of human and also organizational capacity, together with an equally realistic feasibility of ethical leadership,

---

[38] Hardy & Snyder (eds.), *Isaiah Berlin, The Sense of Reality: Studies in Ideas and Their History* (Princeton University Press, 2019).

[39] Joshua L. Cherniss, '"The Sense of Reality": Berlin on Political Judgment, Political Ethics, and Leadership' in Cherniss & Smith (eds.) *Cambridge Companion to Isaiah Berlin* (Cambridge University Press, 2018) 65.

this volume operates on a threefold front. Thus, this dual sense of complexity, imperfection, but also actual possibility can be further traced in the work of Friedrich Kratochwil and the emphasis he places on the difficulty to extract certain evaluative conclusions, due to the uniqueness and volatility of the contextual organizational framework and the mystery and open-endedness of individual and collective human action. In the same cautious but in a more optimistic way, Amalia Amaya builds an exemplarist ethical leadership account from a virtue ethics approach, carefully recognising the context sensitivity and inherent limits of human action. Her position supports a further link between exemplar and organization legitimacy that in a domino effect can trigger further normative developments. This initial component of the volume is completed by Sanne Taekema's work on the importance of a virtue rule of law understanding that it becomes an organizational ideal, beyond the narrow definition of legality, focusing instead on an internal reduction of arbitrariness. These three chapters, while addressing divergent phenomena, emphasize in an innovative way the versatility of the language of virtue ethics that can, first, provide a renewed conceptual organizational framework and, second, facilitate a sharper and multilayered understanding of ethical leadership, which is more conducive to capture properly complex social challenges, a need the current covid pandemic has manifestly stressed.

The contributions of Part II shed light on the different ways in which the virtues and ethical thinking can infuse actual regulation of challenging new phenomena such as algorithmic governance, so as to expand our (ethically informed) regulatory options and capacities (René Urueña), constitute fields of action, such as sports by providing a unifying sense that informs the whole institutional practice (Lorenzo Casini), as well as guide actors' concrete action within organizational settings in a parrhesiastic sensibility exercised by states' representatives, as Jane Cowan observed in her research on the practice of the Universal Periodic Review before the Human Rights Council. All contributions follow the same cautious and nuanced approach between the desirable and the feasible, mirroring the initial sensibility that oscillates between the tragicity of imperfection and the actual potential of a better leadership.

Part III of the volume depicts different stories of individuals who were faced with challenges in hard cases and they decided one way or another. Individuals who exercised reflective judgment and moderation in a compromising tone, acknowledging the space and convictions of the others, away from dogmatic ideas. Individuals who changed their mind and developed their identities reflecting what is called *leadership at edge*, a constant self-exploration and navigation between oneself and the other, without absolute

302   *Maria Varaki*

convictions and exclusionary beliefs,[40] like the example of Chancellor Merkel and her reaction to the 2015 refugee emergency compared to her subsequent role in the EU-Turkey Pact. Finally, in a similar mode of reflective scholarly prudence, Jan Klabbers offers an alternative reading of virtues as an exemplanatory lens of judicial behaviour in a decision that could not be understood ethically either from a deontological or consequentialist approach. This *other* virtue-oriented perspective provides another point of view that can accommodate a more nuanced and diverse context than is usually the case in the international legal arena. The final chapter by Guilherme Vasconcelos Vilaça elucidates in the most characteristic way this same joint sensibility of imperfection and feasibility, highlighting the limits of evaluative judgments based on virtues, made without acknowledging the entire surrounding context. At the same time, narrative analysis offers concrete lenses to assess particular behaviours and decisions, facilitating the path for a non-abstract normative discussion of what an ethical leadership could be.

Altogether, the book helps us to grasp the position and action of individuals and organizations who, in the sensibility of Dag Hammarskjöld, tried to exercise the '*art of leadership*' via an ethic of dialogue following in the steps of Camus and Buber.[41] Individuals whose actions evoked traits such as courage, integrity, compassion, responsibility, moral imagination, moderation, humility, and self-doubt that reflect shades of virtues but also vices when examined moer closely.

Returning to the pandemic and the articles devoted to the comparative portraits of the various leaders, one could also identify a thread of common traits that laymen are inclined to appreciate more and search for in times of crisis and absurdity. Because, in those times, the particular traits trigger a sensibility of togetherness and commonality, beyond the abstract and legitimately contested language of cosmopolitanism. The concrete consideration for the other, the attempt to put oneself into the shoes of the other and thus reflect upon one's own self in the spirit of Buber's *I and Thou* provides an alternative path of human connection and comprehension. Imagined this way, it could be argued that this thread of commonality outside the framework of universality in the name of humanity (either in deontological or consequentialist accounts), but instead as a *human to human* interaction embodying the virtue of mindfulness, can act as a cathartic response both to cynical realism and to nihilistic dogmatism. In those times of crisis, people also need

---

[40]   See Marc Jacquand, 'Leadership and Identity' in *The Art of Leadership in the United Nations, Framing What's Blue* (Dag Hammarskjöld Foundation, 2020), drawing upon the work of Tony Judt, 'Edge People', New York Review of Books, 23 February 2010.

[41]   See Roger Lipsey, *Politics and Conscience, Dag Hammarskjöld on the Art of Ethical Leadership* (Penguin Random House, 2020), 34–36.

Ethical Leadership in Times of 'Crisis'

comfort and kindness and a sense that they do not fight alone. They need someone to tell them 'take good care of yourself and your loved ones', 'be safe', 'we are all together in this', 'I understand how you feel'. Those leaders who have deployed the traits mentioned earlier may be able to instill higher levels of trust when conveying their messages, and thus operate as exemplars who are followed by the people.

This kind of leadership can be deployed via a contextualized and situation-alist sensibility that can offer an equilibrium between empathy, phronesis, and moderation. A leadership ready to adapt to new challenges, keen to evolve, and courageous enough to change. That kind of leadership demonstrates both power and responsibility since it lies in persuasiveness and togetherness. It is a leadership of moderation without being weak and of compassion and *enlarged mentality* without losing *the sense of reality*, the way the former was understood by Arendt, and the latter developed by Berlin. This is why *we* assert that virtue ethics might enlighten an additional dimension of ethical leadership, not based on rules or results but founded on traits that reflect a sensibility of concrete togetherness in a more authentic manner that avoids the legitimate critique of universality, without annulling the particular in the universal and vice versa.

11.3 A COMMON CALL FOR DECENT LEADERSHIP IN TIMES OF 'CRISIS'

The most usual question when someone submits a proposal for a paper or a book concerns its added value. I feel compelled once more to share my strong thoughts about the significance of this edited volume, mainly from the perspective of an international lawyer, in a self-confessing mode. This endeavour that started some years ago in Helsinki (in a moment of personal *crisis*) introduced me to the world of virtues in a way I had never imagined. Although in my previous work I had explored the idea of μέτρο (measure) within a different normative framework, this was the first time I delved with curiosity and enthusiasm into the work of Aristotle, since my last time in high school. Being Greek myself, I felt an additional burden about '*my heritage*' together with a fear not to become the cliche caricature, who suggests that everything originates from her country. In this course, I admit that self-sarcasm helped a lot.

Yet, in this journey I found myself constantly self-challenged and in doubt. What are the virtues, what do we mean by empathy (in Greek the word has the exact opposite meaning), who is virtuous, what is a virtuous judgment, how can we assess it, what kind of certainty does this approach provide, how can we respond to the critique that virtue ethics is no different from other theories,

304 *Maria Varaki*

and finally how can we avoid the risk of turning into a preaching moralist that dictates to others how to live and what to do?

These dilemmas and challenges appeared in a recurring mode every time I presented my work mainly in legal fora and tried to explain virtue ethics in different sub-fields of international law. There was a suspicious, even hostile and sometimes ironic attitude towards the ideas I put on the table. I don't know if it is related to a traditional dismissal of ethical considerations or the linkage of virtues with darkness,[42] but there were many times I felt that I had to explain every single word I used and referred to. Maybe as my co-editor and friend suggested to me, this has to do with a conservative aspect of the virtues that presupposed a common fixed social structure, typical of Ancient societies or the Victorian era, that is no longer shared in our modern world. Or maybe it was the result of the inherited prejudice we all bring to the act of reading and thinking when we encounter a concept. As I mentioned before, the word 'virtue', at least in the international law arena, is mainly associated with hegemony and liberal interventionism and thus it instinctively triggers a reaction.

Whereas then I grew angry and discouraged, I realize now how much I have benefited from this exercise. First, it challenged my own 'identity' as an international lawyer. I do not like labels, yet, if I were further asked, I would reply that my own *cosmotheory* is fundamentally inspired and constantly influenced by the wisdom of Tom Franck and, in particular, the way his cosmopolitanism was masterfully painted by Koskenniemi as '[a] baffling combination of critique and celebration of international law, a combination that is optimistic without being naive and politically engaged without being dogmatic',[43] highlighting further that '[i]n Tom's cosmopolitanism, normativity is central. But normativity is neither positivist obedience .... nor naturalist principle, but rather pragmatic good sense, deliberation, and fairness.'[44] In this spirit, the centrality of good sense, deliberation and fairness in the sense of measure pervade my own understanding of international law.

Second, the constant criticism I encountered led me into exploring further the interdisciplinary dimension of the virtue ethics approach. This is not an easy exercise especially for a lawyer who is embedded in

---

[42] For example, David Kennedy, *The Dark Sides of Virtue: Reassessing International Humanitarianism* (Princeton University Press, 2004).

[43] Martti Koskenniemi, 'The Messianic Cosmopolitanism of Thomas Franck' (2002) 35 N.Y.U. *Journal of International Law and Politics*, 478.

[44] *Ibid*, at 483.

Ethical Leadership in Times of 'Crisis' 305

a particular legal mentality. Yet, I belong to those lawyers who have accepted the limits of rules and an exclusive rule-oriented solution to problems. Virtue ethics, I contest, operates as a valuable tool either to analyse, explain or assess issues of concern that cannot be addressed in a robotic *objective* rule-application manner, the way Jan Klabbers' chapter has so vividly depicted.

This is quite evident in the current corona epidemic where several scholars present very detailed and fine papers, listing a series of legal obligations of states followed by a full stop. I am not suggesting that legal normativity is not important. I emphasize instead that it is not enough and sometimes it is of no assistance. Yes, it is important to identify the potential actors who carry potential legal responsibility for their action or inaction in the spread and handling of the pandemic. Still, by simply enumerating in a mechanical way this alleged multi-layered responsibility does not take us too far. In this sense, this type of legal discourse focuses on *ex post* accountability which is of course crucial, although debatable, but for a later stage. However, our academic journey here emphasizes the element of *ex ante* judgment and responsibility as it is embedded within our concept of ethical leadership. In other words, the question here appears to be framed in a manner that takes some inspiration from the way Iris Young spoke of responsibility v. accountability.[45]

In international law, traditionally, we speak of states and abstract entities but it is a common secret that individual human agents exercise discretion and make judgments. Shedding more light on this element of human judgment (the way also René Urueña has highlighted in his own chapter) can provide an alternative vision about the limits and prospects of international law that transcends a sterilized discourse of objective rule application, irrespective of its context. Human agency does matter and it can make a difference in the field of international law, especially in an era where not only laymen but also legal experts express their doubts or criticism about the viability of the so-called liberal legal project, at least the way it was depicted in the post-Second World War era. In this sense, the way different leaders exercise their judgment and act before new challenges not only re-boosts trust in institutions but it can also play a decisive role in the acceleration of normative developments.

---

[45]   Iris Young, *Responsibility for Justice* (Oxford University Press, 2011), where she develops her social connection model to address structural injustices.

This interdisciplinary exercise was both rewarding and challenging. Overall, though, it accommodated an enhancement of an academic *'enlarged mentality'*, and opened my eyes to other disciplines and schools of thought. Even if I am not sure to what extent I fully grasp their depth and particularities, they definitely made me think in different ways, without my own academic *bannisters*.

Third, this academic endeavour demanded a more nuanced and fine approach that acknowledged both the potential and the limits of virtue ethics. Even now, while I conclude this effort, it might appear to some readers that I over-idealize the value of virtue ethics. Responding to this likely observation, I would highlight what I have tried to convey in my own chapter. The elusiveness of their content, the importance of context, the necessity of a path-dependent comprehension, the acceptance of no exclusivity, and the avoidance of a causation claim of purist nature about who is a virtuous person. Instead, the position adopted here invites readers to explore virtues in a piecemeal approach, without abandoning a legitimate expectation that leaders and those in policy-making positions should carry traits that can be identified or perceived as elements of an ethical leadership.

Finally, I would like to devote the last part of this conclusion to a common thread that all chapters share. My co-editor provided already a very meticulous and extremely fine analysis of each chapter, while linking them to the overall theoretical discussion about the necessity and contribution of this book. Repeating his observations would be a useless duplication without making any real difference. This book is an edited volume of various scholars from different disciplines with divergent interests, representing a plurality of methodological approaches and writing style. I would add that the overall book mirrors this plurality of understandings, style, and expectations. Some of us are more positively inclined, whereas others are more sceptical and cautious. The introduction and conclusion of this book are also proof of this plurality and diversity that tries to facilitate the uniqueness of perception, comprehension, and assessment.

Still, here I would like to draw attention to one common element that I think all chapters share, despite their different departure and arrival points. My reading of all chapters is that they appear to reflect a thread of sensibility that entails a fundamental element of decency. Whether is it the importance of 'practical reason', the significance of exemplarism, the ideal of the rule of law by men in an institutional setting, the parrhesiastic reaction in the human rights arena, the sports ethics of ancient Olympism, the necessity of internal ethical configuration of algorithmic governance, the explanatory phronetic

Ethical Leadership in Times of 'Crisis' 307

judicial judgment, the imaginary leadership in times of forced displacement, or the plurality of leadership that demands a broader contextual understanding in times of health emergency, I argue that there is an underlying call for *decent* leadership. Maybe this call is more modest than the one anticipated in moments of crisis and demanding dilemmas. Certainly, it is no less thought provoking. Even if decency is understood the way Margalit developed it, as the avoidance of humiliation,[46] all chapters of this edited volume appear to be linked to each other via this invisible thread. The understanding, role, and operation of various virtues in the areas and perspectives they address can be read as an invitation to stand out in decency.

This is not a grandiose theory of ethics but, if decency is substantiated in concrete acts of empathetic, imaginary, exemplary, courageous, or phronetic leadership or when fashioning regulation to capture elusive phenomena, then this sensibility of decency can be conceived as an umbrella idea(l) for a better world. In other words, decency in times of *crisis* could operate as the thread between the feeling of danger and the sensibility of opportunity, if we follow the Chinese definition of the word. Maybe the way Camus perceived the potential of decency in *The Plague* is the epitome of ethical calls in times of crisis. As he wrote, 'It may seem a ridiculous idea, but the only way to fight the plague is with decency.'[47]

Returning once more to Isaiah Berlin, it has been argued that his understanding of political judgment and subsequent activity should entail both the element of decency but also one of humanity. As it was observed by one of his commentators:

> Those who enter politics, Berlin suggests, should be politicians, with all the pragmatism and readiness to compromise and to forego the satisfactions of personal purity that being a politician entails; but, amidst all their political activity, they should not cease to be both human and humane.[48]

I would like to pause here and ask readers to imagine this invisible thread that connects all contributions that can be translated as a call for decency and humanity. I do understand that this final appeal may sound problematic, triggering the same feeling of suspicion or irony like the word virtue. Still, I will take this risk and invite readers to display a kind of '*enlarged mentality*',

---

[46] Avishai Margalit, *The Decent Society* (Harvard University Press, 1996, Goldblum trans.).

[47] Albert Camus, *The Plague* (Penguin Classics, 2003, Buss trans.).

[48] Joshua L. Cherniss, '"The Sense of Reality": Berlin on Political Judgment, Political Ethics, and Leadership' in Cherniss & Smith (eds.) *Cambridge Companion to Isaiah Berlin* (Cambridge University Press, 2018) 77.

308   Maria Varaki

where the call for humanity can be viewed not as a reference to an abstract Kantian value, but instead as a sensibility of *being humane*.

It is well known that the language of humanity on the one hand has been linked to the so-called liberal cosmopolitan project of shared values and universal goals, which represents the 'international community as a whole' in various fields of legal normativity. A series of scholars have supported this idea in their writings and work, speaking of *humanity's law*,[49] the *humanization* of international law,[50] and even the *constitutionalization* of international law via *jus cogens* norms and *erga omnes* obligations.[51] On the other hand, this same language of humanity has been criticized by other scholars as a tool of hegemonic instrumentalization, operating in darkness and hypocrisy. In the name of humanity, military and judicial interventions take place, while the drive behind international 'crisis' such as structural biases and social inequality remain under-addressed. The Schmittian reference on humanity is almost always invoked.

Taking into consideration this background, the *telos* of this invitation is to reconsider the concept of humanity by separating its historical usage from its potential content, focusing instead on a 'pluralistic' individualism that the idea of humanity may carry. Imagined this way, this approach explores the innocence *in* humanity of individuals as a recognizable element of ethical leadership that can instigate exemplar and this shared feeling of commonality, which is not framed in abstract words but in concrete paradigms. The same call for decency and humanity that permeates this kind of ethical leadership can operate with catalytic effect, not only regarding social developments but also in the arena of legal normativity. Disregarding ethics and human sentiments as relevant variants of human judgment has been a trend for a long time now. The common thread of the book for a decent and humane ethical leadership calls for a re-assessment of the premises of social and legal thought. Yet, it should not be misunderstood as a call for a new theory, but rather perceived as a moderate, cautious, and realistically visionary invitation that

---

[49]   Ruti Teitel, *Humanity's Law* (Oxford University Press, 2011).
[50]   Anne Peters, 'Humanity as the A and Ω of Sovereignty' (2009) 20 *European Journal of International Law*, 51, 3.
[51]   Erika De Wet, 'The Emergence of International and Regional Value Systems as a Manifestation of the Emerging Constitutional Order' (2006) 19 *Leiden Journal of International Law* 3, Jan Klabbers, Anne Peters, & Geir Ulfstein (eds.), *The Constitutionalization of International Law* (Oxford University Press, 2009), Nico Krisch, *Beyond Constitutionalism, The Pluralist Structure of Postnational Law* (Oxford University Press, 2010), Jeffrey L. Dunoff and Joel P. Trachtman, 'A Functional Approach to International Constitutionalization' in Dunoff & Trachtman (eds.) *Ruling the World? Constitutionalism, International Law and Global Governance* (Cambridge University Press, 2009).

Ethical Leadership in Times of 'Crisis'

acknowledges this Berlinian sensibility of imperfection, combined with the art of the possible for a better world.

This conclusion opened up with a pandemic that took place centuries ago and tested the ethics of a prosperous city-state, built up on sentiments of measure, philosophy, and action. Pericles, as a leader, stood out in a moment of moral panic and reminded the Athenians of their democratic (for the particular era) credentials in order to survive the plague. As I write the last lines of this final chapter, humanity experiences another pandemic, that not only reminds us of the absurdity of human nature but also casts even more seminally the necessity for some kind of ethical leadership. As we propose in this book, virtue ethics provides one powerful narrative for exploring this daunting demand. The book does not offer a magic formula or a blueprint, because this is not the rationale of virtue ethics. Instead, this edited volume is an invitation for a perpetual reassessment and imaginary deliberation in context-specific frameworks. In this sense, it could be of no satisfaction to those who ask for definite answers. Instead, it might be seen as an inspirational reading in moments of high complexity, intense fluidity, and massive insecurity. Ethical leadership is not a fictional scenario. Ethical leadership exists. This book unequivocally reflects the complexity of the virtue ethics approach and provides a nuanced understanding of its role, prospects and limits. In this sense, ethical leadership can be understood as an intelligible human project, where different decisions by different people in different times and places can cast a different action. Our proposal for a virtue ethics approach offers the tool for this acknowledgment, which may sound simple but surprisingly it has not been fully understood.

Index

abortion, moral conflict and, 16
accountability, 9, 176. *See also* algorithmic
    accountability
Achilles, 167
ACM (Association for Computer Machinery),
    157–58
action
    collective action, 69–71
    as involving moral risk, 22
    knowledge versus, 22
    rational action model, 55
    virtues and, 81–82, 279–82
admiration, 117, 120
adverse selection problem, 263
Aeschylus, 214, 234
agent/principal, 60–61, 62
algorithmic accountability
    fiduciary duties and, 160–62
    human accountability and, 150–52
    human rights/human dignity framework for,
        138, 142–44, 145–46, 149, 150, 154
    law and, 142–45
    organizational compliance procedures and,
        158–60
    overview, 137–39, 162–63
    transparency mindset for, 138, 145, 146–49,
        150, 154
    virtue ethics and, 152–62
algorithms, defined, 140
Alphabet, 159
Anscombe, Elizabeth, 14, 246
answers, impossibility of single, 40
anthropology, 30–31
anti-corruption legislation, 159
anxiety, as part of human condition, 79

appraisal of leadership. *See* assessment of
    leadership
arbitration. *See Rainbow Warrior* arbitration
argumentation, 41
Aristotle. *See also* phronesis (prudence)
    context and, 255–56
    history of virtue ethics and, 20–22
    imaginary leadership and, 217–20
    virtues and, 80, 82, 115
artificial neural networks, 140–41
Asian ethics, 275–76
assessment of leadership. *See also* World
        Health Organization (WHO)
    assumptions and, 258–60
    character as changing over time, 264, 277–78
    context and, 255–56, 274–75, 290–91
    culture and, 275–77
    ethical traditions other than virtue ethics
        and, 279–83
    narrative and, 262
    overview, 254–58, 261
    predecessor impacting, 271
    research approach and, 262
    virtue ethics and, 254–58, 290
Association for Computer Machinery (ACM),
    157–58
Athens, ii, 296
atonement, 68–69
audit rituals, 185, 189
austerity as a virtue, 112
austerity measures, impacts of, 198, 200
authority, exemplarist virtue theory and,
    123–27, 132
automated decision systems, 139–41. *See also*
    algorithmic accountability

Index

Bakhtin, Mikhail M., 31
Balkin, Jack M., 160, 162
Behrakis, Yannis, 216
Benhabib, Seyla, 216, 234
Beowulf, 275
Berlin, Isaiah, ii
bias in legal system, 238
big data, 137, 138, 139. *See also* algorithmic
    accountability
biographical research, 31, 261. *See also* World
    Health Organization (WHO)
birth control issues, 268, 269
black box of algorithms, 145
Bokova, Irina, 28
Bolkovac, Kathryn, 183
Booth, Wayne C., 42
bribery, 159
Brundtland, Gro, 287, 290
Burgh House Principles, 237
Bushido, 256, 257
Butler, Judith, 193

Cambridge Analytica, 137
Cameron, Kim, 32–34
Camus, Albert, ii, 220
Candau, Marcolino, 283–86
cannabis use, 174
cardinal virtues, 80
Caro, Robert A., 258
Carpenter v. United States, 137
CAS (Court of Arbitration for Sports), 174, 176
Casas, Fray Bartolomé de las, 40
casuistry, 30
cause, efforts and, 75
Chan, Margaret, 288
character. *See also* assessment of leadership;
    virtues
    changing over time of, 264, 277–78
    class and capital and, 31
    deontologism and utilitarianism and, 16
    education for, 22
    importance of, 23
    situationist critique against ethical
        approaches based on, 25
    virtue ethics and, 22, 23
characters, 31
charismatic leadership, 35
charismatic legitimacy, 175–76
charter-based versus treaty-based
    mechanisms, 190
Chetail, Vincent, 222–24

China, 287–90
Chisholm, Brock, 265–70, 274, 277, 279, 281
choice. *See* practical versus rational choice
cholera outbreak in Guinea, 283–86
circles, moderation and, 220
De Cive (Hobbes), 71
civic friendship, 247
civil society, 84–85
Cocking, Dean, 27, 28
code, defined, 140
Code of Conduct (FIFA), 172–73
Code of Ethics (FIFA), 171–72
Code of Ethics (International Sports
    Federation), 174
Code of Ethics (IOC), 170–71
Code of Ethics (World Athletics), 173
Code of Ethics and Professional Conduct
    (ACM), 157
Code of Ethics and Professional Conduct
    (WHO), 263
codes of conduct, 7, 131, 156–58. *See also*
    specific codes
collective action, 69–71
Commission on Human Rights, 184–85, 188.
    See also Universal Periodic Review (UPR)
communication virtues, 115
Compact for Migration. *See* Global Compact
    for Migration (GCM)
compassion as a virtue, 114
COMPAS tool, 142–43, 146, 148
completeness, 76
complete versus partial exempla, 118
computational capacity, 137, 140
computer ethics. *See* algorithmic
    accountability
Confucianism, 256–57, 275–76, 278, 295
consequentialism/utilitarianism
    assessment of leadership and, 279–82
    overview, 14–19
    virtue jurisprudence and, 246, 249, 250
    virtue theory compared, 22, 23, 108–9
corruption, 159, 177–80, 251
cosmopolitanism, ii, 12–14
courage as a virtue
    Chisholm at WHO, 269
    importance of, 183–84
    judges, 247–49
    overview, 111
    phronesis and, 219
    understanding of depending on context,
        274–75

Index

Court of Arbitration for Sports (CAS), 174, 176
Covid-19 pandemic, 296
creation of the universe, 67–68
critical cosmopolitanism, 13
culture, impacts of, 187, 276–77, 292

damages, legal, 61–62
Daqneesh, Omran, 215
Dauvergne, Catherine, 222
decent leadership, ii
decision-making. *See also* algorithmic
  accountability
  automated decision systems, 139–41
  big data and, 138
  examination of, 65
  morality and authority and, 124
  social ordering and, 83
  virtuous behaviour, institutional design
    and, 131
declaration by recognized authorities, 69–70
deep learning, 140–41, 146, 148, 149
Delphi Method, 131
Dembour, Marie-Bénédicte, 187
deontologism
  algorithmic accountability and, 155–56
  cholera outbreak in Guinea and, 286
  international judiciary and, 237
  overview, 14–19
  virtue jurisprudence and, 245, 250
  virtue theory compared, 22, 23, 108–9
Descartes, Rene, 71
Dewey, John, 16, 17
dialectical virtues, 115
dignity, 143–44, 146
disasters, 83
discrimination, algorithmic, 142–43, 146–48
doping, 171, 173, 174, 176, 178, 180

Ebola, 259, 288–89
education and training
  algorithmic accountability and, 158
  character and, 22
  exemplarist virtue theory and, 131
  morality and, 22, 295
empathy as a virtue, 216, 219, 304
ends
  best practices and, 76
  cause and, 75
  choice of, 55, 57
  ordering of priorities for, 55
  virtuous character traits and, 110

endurance as a virtue, 113
enlarged mentality concept, ii, 234
equilibrium, 56, 64
equity versus law, 249
Erasmus, 120
ethical leadership. *See also* virtue ethics;
  virtues
  benefits of, 37
  context and, 36
  importance of, 7, 8
  personality features and, 8
  virtues and, 303
ethical vacuum, 154
ethics. *See also* international ethics; sports
  ethics; virtue ethics
  character and, 22
  increasing prominence of, 236
  in postmodern times, 39–43
  practicality and, 19
  training programs for, 131
  virtues and complexity in analysis of, 19–26
Ethics (Spinoza), 71
ethnography, 30
European Convention on Human Rights,
  243–44, 249
EU-Turkey pact (one for one scheme), 230, 232
exemplarist virtue theory
  authority and, 123–27, 132
  following spirit rather than letter, 251
  fostering of virtuous leadership, 131, 133
  identification of virtuous character traits in,
    110–17
  overview, 105–7, 131–34
  role of leaders in, 120–23, 131
  skepticism about, 129
  varieties of exempla in, 117–19
  virtue ethics and, 105–6, 107–9
exemplarity, 36–37, 105–6, 231, 290–91
experience, 74, 76–77, 78
expertise, professionalization of social life
  and, 124
externalities, 61
external versus internal leadership, 110

fair by design, 157
fallacy of the homunculus, 152
Farrelly, Colin, 247
fearless speech (parrhesia), 195, 198–202
feelings, radical individualization of, 80
fetishism of commodities, 152
Fidler, David, 288

Index

fiduciary duties, 78, 160–62
FIFA (Fédération Internationale de Football Association), 171–73, 180
filial piety, 275–76
Floridi, Luciano, 154
forced displacement. *See* refugee crisis
Foucault, Michel, 167
fragmentation, 62, 258–59
France. *See Rainbow Warrior* arbitration
Franck, Tom, ii
freedom, politics of, 84
friendship, 80
friendship fund for New Zealand, 249, 250
From Apology to Utopia (Koskenniemi), 202
frugality as a virtue, 112
Funeral's Oration (Pericles), 296

GCM. *See* Global Compact for Migration (GCM)
General Data Protection Regulation (GDPR), 145
Genesis, book of, 67–68
Germany, 32
global civil society, 84–85
Global Compact for Migration (GCM)
Guterres report and, 229
hostility towards, 231
importance of, 217, 230
overview, 225–26
phronesis and, 232–34
Godlee, Fiona, 270–71
good lives, defined, 281
good outcomes, defined, 280, 281
good sense ethics. *See* virtue ethics
Google, 146–48, 159
Grandi, Filippo, 224
Greece, 198–202
Grodzinsky, Frances, 154
Guinea, cholera outbreak in, 283–86
Guterres, António, 228–29, 234

Hammarskjöld, Dag, 118, 122
Harari, Yuval, 299, 300
heroes, 118
Hesiod, 167
history, 56
Hobbes, Thomas, 70, 71
Homiak, Marcia, 255
homunculus fallacy, 152
hospitality, 14
human dignity, 143–44, 146

humanity, language of, ii
human rights. *See also* Global Compact for Migration (GCM)
algorithmic accountability and, 138, 142–44, 145–46, 149, 150, 154
European Convention on Human Rights, 243–44, 249
limits of standards for, 7
public health emergencies and authoritarianism, 297
Rainbow Warrior arbitration and, 245
schools of, 187
United Nations Commission on Human Rights, 184–85, 188
Universal Periodic Review and, 190–92
Human Rights Council, 192, 194
human value, 13
Hume, David
anti-Cartesian project, 71
praxis and, 55, 71
rationality and, 76
unlearning and, 57
humility as a virtue, 114
Hursthouse, Rosalind, 294–95

IAAF (International Association of Athletics Federations), 173
Iceland, 201–2
ideal theory, 13. *See also* practical versus rational choice
IFs (International Federations), 165, 169
Iketides (Aeschylus), 214, 234
Iliad (Homer), 167
images, power of, 214–16
imaginary leadership
Aristotle and, 217–20
displacement dilemmas and, 220–24
enlarged mentality concept and, 234
laboratory of dilemmas and, 234
migration governance and, 230–34
overview, 216
imagination, 31, 42, 76, 219
imitation, 120, 121, 131
immunity, 62
impartiality in legal system, 238
independent learning/machine learning, 140–41
inference, 76
information processing speed, 137
institutional design, 131
institutional plurality, 176

integrity, 126, 183–84, 249
intellectual virtues, 115, 218, 269
interdisciplinary approach to ethics, 9
internal versus external leadership, 110
International Association of Athletics
  Federations (IAAF), 173
international ethics
  cosmopolitanism and, 12–14
  deontologism and, 14–19
  interdisciplinary approach to, 9
  neutralization of non-Western ethical
    theories, 15
  universalism and, 13
  utilitarianism/consequentialism and, 14–19
International Federations (IFs), 165, 169
international law, ii
International Olympic Committee (IOC)
  accountability and, 176
  constitutional dimension of ethics and, 173
  fair play and, 174
  global organizational structure and, 169
  mission of, 168
  publicness of, 165
  rules and, 165, 180
international organizations (IOs)
  big data and, 138
  efforts to control, 5–8
  as hierarchical, 26
  questioning of, 4
  as untrustworthy, 4–5
international politics, overview of ethics in,
    12–14
International Sports Federation, 174
IOC. See International Olympic
    Committee (IOC)
isolationism, 297

Johnson, Boris, 304, 305
Jones, D., 122
judges
  as civic friends, 247
  corruption of, 251
  courage and, 247–49
  integrity and, 249
  international versus domestic, 237–39
judgment, ii, 76–77, 299–300. See also
    leadership; phronesis (prudence)
judicial system, 18–19, 238. See also judges; law;
    legal reasoning
jurisprudence, 237–40. See also law
justice, 80, 113

kairos. See virtues
Kandinsky, Wassily, 220
Kant, Immanuel, 63, 72, 76–77, 83
Keith, Kenneth, 243
Klabbers, Jan, 146, 152–54
knowledge, 18–19, 22, 56, 76. See also action
Koskenniemi, Martti, ii, 202, 220
Kurdi, Alan, 214

Laboratory of Dilemmas exhibition, 214
language, feelings and, 80
law. See also Rainbow Warrior arbitration
  algorithmic accountability and, 142–45
  big data and, 138
  demise of international legal order, 296–97
  equity versus, 249
  exemplarist virtue theory and, 106, 120–21
  immunity, 62
  limits of, 65
  principal/agent and, 60–61, 62
  respect for, 78
  responsibility and, 62, 64–65
  sports law, 165
  virtue ethics and, ii
leaders. See also assessment of leadership;
    ethical leadership
  comparison of views of, 38
  defined, 35
  expectations of, 27–28
  focus on, 8
  importance of, 183
  as key to values, 26–28, 38
  limits of, 307
  networks of, 31
  roles of, 260
leadership. See also assessment of leadership;
    ethical leadership; imaginary leadership;
    virtuous leadership
  alienated passive members created by, 37
  crisis to help identify, 303–4
  decent leadership, ii
  gender and, 305
  global pandemic and, 298–303
  impacts of, 36
  internal versus external, 110, 277
  skepticism against, 37–38
  as social hoax, 37
  visionary leadership, 35
Lee, Jong-Wook, 288
legal reasoning, 138, 158. See also law; Rainbow
    Warrior arbitration

Index

legitimacy of institutions, 126–27, 175–76, 249
lethal weapons systems, 143–44
Leviathan (Hobbes), 71
Lewis, Wilmarth, 27–28
lex specialis argument, 245
liability, 61
literary theory, 31
Liu, Joanne, 289
logical model of inference, 76
Loomis, Eric, 148
love of humanity, 114
loyalty as a virtue, 111, 276

machine learning/independent learning,
    140–41
Maduro, Miguel, 180
Mafart, Alain. *See Rainbow Warrior* arbitration
'Making Migration work for all' report, 228, 232
Malloch-Brown, Mark, 4–5
Man, Paul de, 40
marijuana use, 174
Marks, Susan, 202
McInerny, Daniel, 275
McMahon, Edward, 196
Merkel, Angela, 227, 231–32, 304
migrants. *See* refugee crisis
moderation as a virtue, 112, 216, 220
money, as instrumental, 28
Moor, James H., 153, 154
Moore's law, 137
moral conflict, paradox of, 16
moral education, 295
moral imagination, 31, 42
moral intuition, virtue ethics and, 22–23
morality, knowledge and, 18–19
moral knowledge, 18–19
moral reasoning, 18, 124–26
moral standards, 23
Murray, Chris, 290

Nagel, Thomas, 258–59
Nakajima, Hiroshi, 270–73, 274–77, 279
narrative
    assessment of leadership and, 262, 291–95
    discursive power of, 40
    organizations making, 24
    virtue ethics and, 24–26, 29–31
    virtues and, 38
National Federations (NFs), 169
National Olympic Committees (NOCs), 169
nativism, 297

negative versus positive exempla, 118
Nelson, Hilde Lindemann, 18
neural networks, 140–41
New York Declaration for Refugees and
    Migrants, 224–25
New York Times articles, 303–4
New Zealand. *See Rainbow Warrior* arbitration
NFs (National Federations), 169
Nicomachean Ethics (Aristotle), 218
Nobel Peace Prize, 277–78
NOCs (National Olympic Committees), 169
normative pluralism, 176
norms
    exemplarist virtue theory and, 122, 126, 131
    legal norms as not enough, ii
    rule-based approaches and, 35
    sports ethics and, 174, 176
Northpointe company, 142, 148
Nussbaum, Martha, 19

Oakley, Justin, 27, 28
obligations, 60, 78, 160–62
Olbrechts-Tyteca, Lucie, 41
Olympic Charter, 165, 168–69, 170–71, 176
Olympic Solidarity Programme, 168, 173
online service providers, as fiduciaries, 160–62
organizational leadership, defined, 35
organizations, 24, 26, 32–34. *See also* inter-
    national organizations (IOs); *specific*
    organizations

Palestine, membership in UNESCO, 28
Palestine Liberation Organization (PLO)
    attempt to join WHO, 275
pandemics, 296–303, 309
Papaioannou, Kostis, 200
Papandreou, Georgios, 198
paradox in moral conflict, 16
parrhesia (fearless speech), 195, 198–202
partial versus complete exempla, 118
pattern recognition, 76, 140
peace-making operations, 73
Perelman, Chaïm, 41
Pericles, ii, 296
perseverance as a virtue, 113
phronesis (prudence). *See also* action;
        knowledge; virtue ethics
    Global Compact for Migration and, 232–34
    imaginary leadership and, 216, 218–19, 230
    importance of, 115, 232, 255
    Rainbow Warrior arbitration and, 250, 251

316 *Index*

phronimos, 20–22
piety as a virtue, 111
Piot, Peter, 259
Platini, Michel, 167, 175–76
Plato, choosing/steering analogy, 75
politics, 84, 106, 120–21
polyphony, 31
population control issues, 268, 269
populist sovereignism, 222, 234, 296
positive defiance, 32
positive psychology, 32
positive versus negative exempla, 118
power, 40, 150–52, 214–16, 286
practical reasoning, 76
practical versus rational choice. *See also* responsibility
  acting as making practical choices, 75–79
  overview, 54–58
  production model and, 75
  reasons to examine, 56–57
  systems and plans and, 63–66
  theoretical reason and, 57
  vocabulary and, 59–63
pragmatism, 17
Pragmatists, 72
praxis. *See also* action
  distinguishing features of acting in, 76–79
  Hume on, 55, 71
  knowledge required by, 56
  rational action model and, 55
prevention, importance of, 35
Prieur, Dominique. *See Rainbow Warrior* arbitration
principal/agent, 60–61, 62
privacy, 137, 146, 155. *See also* algorithmic accountability
problem identification, 76
production model, 73, 74, 75
product liability, 61
professional codes of conduct, 7, 131, 156–58. *See also specific codes*
professional duties, 60
professional roles, virtue ethics and, 26–28
prudence. *See* phronesis (prudence); *Rainbow Warrior* arbitration
psychology, 32
public audit rituals, 185, 189
public figures, as role models, 120
public speaking, 270–71, 272
public trust, 126

racism, 222–23. *See also* refugee crisis
Rainbow Warrior arbitration
  complicating factors, 243–45
  ethical justification for, 245–46, 249–50
  facts of, 241–42
  friendship fund for New Zealand, 249, 250
  overview, 236–40
  ruling in, 242–43
  virtue-based justification for, 247–49
  virtue ethics and, 240, 251
ratchet effect, 121
rational choice. *See* practical versus rational choice
The Rebel (Camus), 220
recidivism, 142–43, 146, 149
Rees, Madeleine, 183
refugee crisis
  common responsibility for, 217
  displacement dilemmas and, 220–24
  EU-Turkey pact (one for one scheme), 230, 232
  Germany's response to, 227, 231–32
  Global Compact for Migration and, 217, 225–26, 229
  Greece and, 198–202
  overview of issues, 14
  state sovereignty and ideal of humanity, 216
  UN New York Declaration for Refugees and Migrants, 224–25
Reiss-Andersen, Berit, 277–78
respondeat superior, 83
responsibility
  accountability versus, 9
  archaeology of, 66–74
  fragmentation of, 62
  law and, 62, 64–65
  politics of, 84
  systemic order and, 63
  universal responsibility, 62–63
  virtuous people and, 82
rhetorical virtues, 115
Ricupero, Rubens, 183
right acts, defined, 280
rituals, 68–69
Robertson, Geoffrey, 238
Robinson, Mary, 183
role models, 120, 131, 185, 202. *See also* exemplarist virtue theory; exemplarity
roles, virtue ethics and, 26–28
Röling (judge), 238
Rorty, Amélie, 272–73

Index

317

Ross, W. D., 22, 281–82
rule-based approaches. *See also* deontologism
  human application of, 9
  limits of, ii
  norms lacking for, 35
  in sports, 167
  third party rule, 137
  virtue ethics and, 108

Sanders, Jeff W., 154
SARS outbreak, 287–90
Scheler, Max, 37
scientific knowledge, 298, 305
self-control as a virtue, 112
semiology, 232
settlement of fundamental social issues, 71
sexual orientation, deep learning and, 149
Shapin, S., 126
Sinclair, G. F., 122
social life, bureaucratization of, 124
social ordering
  disaster and fragility of, 83
  ordo ordinans versus ordo ordinatus, 56,
    63–64, 67
  organizational decision making and, 83
  rituals and atonement to restore, 68–69
  systems and plans and, 63–66
  universal order, 63
social systems, purposes of, 56
Soeharno, Jonathan, 249
Software Engineering Code of Ethics, 157
Solum, Lawrence B., 247
Sontag, Susan, 216
Spinoza, Baruch, 71
sports ethics
  constitutional dimension of, 168–69
  future of, 177–80
  international sporting institutions and, 167
  legal instruments and, 170–73
  legitimacy and accountability and, 175–77
  multiple dimensions of, 173–74
  premises for, 164–66
sports law, 165
Stamellos Giannis, 154
standards of care, algorithmic accountability
  and, 158
Stone, Abraham, 268
Stored Communications Act, 137
storytelling, 262
strategy, experience versus, 74
substitution effect, 152

Suu Kyi, Aung San, 277–78
Sweden, 298
Syria, war in, 214. *See also* refugee crisis

temperance as a virtue, 112
Ten Canoes, 292
theory, limits of single, 16
third party rule, 137
thoughts, radical individualization of, 80
Thucydides, 83, 296
Tokyo tribunal, 238
torts, 61
training programs. *See* education and training
transferability of practices, 73
transformative change, equilibrium versus,
  56
treaty-based versus charter-based
  mechanisms, 190
treaty bodies, 191–92
Trump, Donald, 222, 226, 304, 305
trust in institutions, 126, 297, 298, 300, 309
Truth, 71
Turing, Alan, 140
Turkey, 230, 232

UNESCO, US withdrawal from, 28
United Nations. *See also* Universal Periodic
  Review (UPR)
  charter-based versus treaty-based
    mechanisms, 190
  Global Compact for Migration, 217, 225–26,
    229, 230, 231, 232–34
  Malloch-Brown on, 4–5
  New York Declaration for Refugees and
    Migrants, 224–25
  professional perils for leaders acting
    ethically in, 183–84
United States (USA), 183–84, 196, 226. *See also*
  Trump, Donald
unity of science position, 67
universalism, 13
universal order, 63
Universal Periodic Review (UPR)
  constructive criticism, 194, 196
  cooperative learning in, 185
  examination of virtue in, 186–88
  fearless speech mode and, 195, 198–202
  liberal mode and, 195–97, 202
  origins of, 184–85
  overview, 183–85, 202
  phases of, 188–90

Index

Universal Periodic Review (UPR) (cont.)
in relation to UN human rights system,
190–92
repetition and, 193
role of diplomats in, 186–87
subaltern mode and, 195–97, 202
treaty bodies compared, 191–92
universal responsibility, 62–63
universe, creation of, 67–68
U Thant, 277
utilitarianism. *See* consequentialism/
utilitarianism
utility maximization, 14

value, fragmentation of, 258–59
van der Sloot, Bart, 155
van Domselaar, Iris, 247, 249
Vattel, Emer de, 246
Veitch, Scott, 64–65
virtue ethics
algorithmic accountability and, 152–62
assessment of leadership and, 254–58, 290
character and, 22, 23
competence acquisition, 83
context and, 23, 42
deontologism and utilitarianism, 22, 23
education of moral character and, 22, 295
exemplarist virtue theory and, 105–6, 107–9
history of, 20
internal versus external leadership, 277
jurisprudence and, 236–37
law and, ii
moral intuition and, 22–23
narrative and, 24–26, 29–31
need for, 8
nudging of, 160, 163
overview, 19–24, 255–58
pandemics and, 306
positive defiance and, 32
professional roles and, 26–28
questions asked by, 22
Rainbow Warrior arbitration and, 240, 251
revival of, 254
as socializing ethics, 24
virtue jurisprudence, 237–40, 244, 249, 250
virtues
actions versus, 279–82
business ethics and, 34
cardinal virtues, 80
character trait combination, 255
context and, 274

defined, 20, 280
Eastern versus Western view of,
275–77
going beyond expectations, 32
interdisciplinary approach to, 11
leadership historically and, 107–9
moral imagination and, 31, 42
narrative and, 38
organizational culture and, 32–34
potential of, 9
as skills, 290–95
as thick concepts, 108
virtuous actions, 81–82
virtuous leadership
cascading effect of, 120
compared with other types, 35
defined, 35
exemplarity and, 36–37
exemplary leaders and, 121, 133
visionary leadership, 35

WADA (World Anti-Doping Agency), 164, 167,
171, 176
WADC (World Anti-Doping Code), 164,
165, 171
Weber, Max, 35–36
Wee, Cecilia, 275–76
Weiler, Joseph H. H., 180
Western and Others Group (WEOG), 196
WHA (World Health Assembly), 263, 288
WHO. *See* World Health
Organization (WHO)
wisdom as a virtue, 115
Wolf, Martin, 299, 300–1
Works and Days (Hesiod), 167
World Anti-Doping Agency (WADA), 164, 167,
171, 176
World Anti-Doping Code (WADC), 164,
165, 171
World Anti-Doping Programme, 180
World Athletics, 173
World Cup, 167
World Health Assembly (WHA), 263, 288
World Health Organization (WHO)
Brock Chisholm as Director-General,
265–70, 274, 277, 279, 281
cholera outbreak in Guinea and, 283–86
Code of Ethics and Professional
Conduct, 263
Covid-19 pandemic and, 298
establishment of, 265

Hiroshi Nakajima as Director-General, 270–73, 274–77, 279
mandate, 262–64
Marcolino Candau's handling of cholera outbreak in Guinea, 283–86
Margaret Chan as Director-General, 288
SARS outbreak in China, 288
selection of staff, 263–64, 269, 277, 278
structure of, 262

xenophobia, 222–23, 228, 229. *See also* refugee crisis

Yale University leadership, 27–28
Yarmouk refugee camp, 215

Zagzebski, Linda, 280–81, 290–91

CPSIA information can be obtained
at www.ICGtesting.com
Printed in the USA
LVHW011611030821
694430LV00003B/283